THE BOOK OF LOVE

THE BOOK

A TOM DOHERTY ASSOCIATES BOOK

OF LOVE

*A Treasury Inspired by the
Greatest of Virtues*

. . .

ANDREW M. GREELEY
MARY G. DURKIN

THE BOOK OF LOVE

This book is printed on acid-free paper.

Book design by Judith Stagnitto Abbate

A Forge Book
Published by Tom Doherty Associates, LLC
175 Fifth Avenue
New York, NY 10010

www.tor.com

Forge® is a registered trademark of
Tom Doherty Associates, LLC.

ISBN: 0-312-87183-X

First Edition: November 2002

Printed in the United States of America

0 9 8 7 6 5 4 3 2 1

In Loving Memory
of
JACK DURKIN

CONTENTS

...

FOREWORD

...

Love Before Love

t is odd that God has chosen the name of Love.

Maybe it's only a human name that we ascribe to God. Maybe we've imposed it on God without His permission. Or Her permission. Christianity is more explicit about the name. St. John says flatly that God *is* love. Other religions, as the selections in this *Book of Love* will illustrate, say pretty much the same thing, though perhaps more cautiously. Even the saints and the mystics, who may have had more contact with God than the rest of us, claim that they encounter overwhelming love.

If God didn't like the name, He could have easily rebuked those who use it, one way or another. If one is a Christian, one has to say that St. John's naming of God is inspired, that in some fashion God and St. John conspired to call Her Love.

Odd.

All right, our efforts at naming God are pale metaphors that reveal to us a little about God, a lot less than they don't reveal. God is like human love but also unlike it. Less passionate, less forceful, less determined, less enraptured? We can hardly say that because if we do the metaphor collapses. Love in its very nature is passionate, forceful, determined, enraptured. So if the metaphor has any validity at all it must mean that God is like human love only more so, more passionate, more forceful, more determined, more enraptured.

Scary.

Persistently passionate human lovers can be very scary. However, we can cool them off in various ways. A God who is infinitely more passionate? A God whom we can't cool off? A God from whom we can't escape? Very scary indeed.

And very odd.

Love is not just hearts and flowers and St. Valentine's Day lace—though it is that too. Love is essentially a raging torrent rushing inexorably toward union. A river tumbling irresistibly toward the ocean, the ocean sweeping up into the river mouth in its high tide. Love is usually very messy, very troublesome, very dangerous, very consuming. It is, as Father Martin Darcy S.J. wrote in his classic *The Mind and Heart of Love*, finally not so much the desire to possess as the desire to be possessed. God is like that?

Most odd.

We are tempted to say that God doesn't really mean that. She conspired with St. John to say she was something sweet and nice, not something turbulent and demanding and fearsome. The word doesn't mean the same thing at all when it is used of human love as when it is used as God. Certainly Love is not love, right?

Wrong! Unless you want to argue that God plays word games as well as dice.

Love emerged in humankind not as a result of our being human but as a precondition of our becoming human. In our hominid ancestors the bonding between male and female, already passionate enough, had to extend to the female's children for humanity as we know it to emerge. The bond of love produced a family and, by so doing, produced humankind. Moreover, to really bond the family together humans had to develop in such a way that the male and female were capable of sex not merely episodically (once a month, once a year) but all the time. Now that is really messy!

Did God really want to compare Himself to the hunger of man and woman for one another, a hunger which in its pervasiveness is unique among the species about which we know? A hunger which causes all kinds of trouble in the human condition? A hunger which has developed out of the bonding propensities that we share with other less passionate species? A propensity to bond rooted in the earth and in bodies? Did God want us to think that He's really like that?

If He did, that is outrageously odd. However, one learns, like Job, not to argue with God. If God wants to be Love, then that's His business. One can understand, however, why many people try to pretend that God doesn't really mean it or to pretty the name over with a sentimental veneer. The implications of the notion that there is something in the messy joy of human passion that is very like God are too disturbing to have to take seriously.

Not only, then, do we pretend that the passion between man and woman is totally different from God's passion for us, we also try to pretend that all the other varieties of love that are part of human life are totally different from sexual passion. The word obviously means three totally different things—God, human sexual attraction, and all the other loves in our life. There is love[1], love[2], and love[3]. The first is God, the second is sexual attraction, the third is the way we feel about our friends and relatives. All are different. They merely happen to have the same name.

Stated that baldly, our attempt to eliminate the body from our friendships and from God may seem hilarious to some. Nonetheless, it is the implied conventional wisdom of those who want to escape from the scary implications of love as passion.

In fact, we know of no other species that have as many different kinds of love as we do. Clearly all our other loves are possible only because we are a species endowed with a very unique kind of sexuality, one oriented not merely, and not even principally, toward reproduction but toward bonding. Humans can have a wide variety of loves because they have such a powerful capacity to bond. The other loves are not the same as passion between man and woman, but the ability to engage in passionate sexual bonding makes possible all the other loves. They are not watered-down versions of sexual love but rather the result of our vast, amorphous, and desperate need to bond. Close friendship is not the same as sexual love, but it's not completely different either and is possible because we are creatures who can bond.

That leaves unanswered the question of why God wants to identify herself with human bonding, why She wants to create the impression that it is in her nature to bond with us. We often wish God would go away with that metaphor, but clearly there is no escaping it though we pretend to try.

Perhaps that is the reason that in so many of the current spate of books about virtues (*Books of Virtue*, etc.) love is absent. In these books one encounters much about various stoic virtues as honesty, reliability, industry, and suchlike—all doubtless admirable virtues. However, one reads nothing in these inestimable anthologies about love.

One wonders why. Did St. Paul not say the greatest virtue was love? Have the anthologists dismissed him because love has somehow come to be identified with nineteen sixties' hedonism (as in "make love not war"), drugs, and rock music? Might it be that love is perceived as a soft, mushy, self-indulgent, undisciplined quality that hardly deserves the name of a virtue? How could one who writes editorials for the *Wall Street Journal* and cries for more outrage from Americans possibly sing the praises of something like love, for which there is, anyhow, little room in a free market economy? Why, of all things, should parents want to put in the hands of their children a book about love? Given the very conservative orientation of the anthologists, that may well be the case. Too bad for St. Paul. And for St. John too.

If love is a torrential force toward a union that bonds, it will bring sustained happiness only when it is focused, disciplined, intent, experienced, mature, patient, kind, and all those other nice things St. Paul says about it. The ability to love wisely and well is the most important trait parents can pass on to their children. It is not, however, sentimental mush.

Thus it seemed to us that the omission of Love from those anthologies is passing strange. So we decided to prepare a book that might be a supplement or a corrective or even a challenge to such books of virtue, minimally a polite reminder from St. Paul that without love the stoic virtues are sounding brass and tinkling cymbals.

Therefore we commit this book to two fundamental propositions:

God is Love.

The greatest of all virtues is love.

THE BOOK OF LOVE

INTRODUCTION

...

The Greatest Virtue

Meanwhile these three remain: faith, hope, and love; and the greatest of these is love.
SAINT PAUL

A songwriter plaintively asks, "What is this thing called love?" His question is the question of everyone who seeks to make sense out of the ever-present desire to love and be loved. The disciple Paul, while not giving a direct answer to the songwriter's question, asserts that the human desire to understand what love is all about is a virtuous, and necessary, quest—an affair of the soul.

Affairs of the soul, of that center of the human spirit, are resistant to quick, easy, simple analysis. Neither the acquisition of more knowledge about love, nor even the will to love, automatically assures people that they will succeed at giving and receiving love. The human ego sets up barriers to love with the threat that love somehow will destroy our fragile sense of self.

Throughout human history, storytellers, poets, composers, preachers, and ordinary people have reflected on the wonder, mystery, and challenge of love. This collection of stories, poems, and reflections grows out of the belief that the human spirit, nourished by meditations on love, can penetrate the defenses of the ego. Only then will the human heart be free to cultivate the virtue of love. Certain assumptions underlie this belief, which in turn influence the direction and format of the collection.

Love is humankind's origin and destiny. The human desire for love is intimately linked with what philosophers identify as the constant human search for the good, the true, and the beautiful. Some thinkers link this quest with the search for the divine. Everyone who spends any time considering this thing called love agrees that love is necessary for both individual and community survival. Everyone also agrees there is more to this business of love than anyone ever imagines at first or second or even their hundredth glance.

The enigma of the present age is the dichotomy between its enormous store of information about love and the ever-present signs that more knowledge does not necessarily make this era any better at the business of love than preceding ages. Love's wrongs face us every day and everywhere: wars, infidelities, family discords, distrust, prejudices, and ethnic and religious conflicts, all of which destroy love, continue to abound.

Why, we wonder, is love so difficult? Why do we undermine our own and others' efforts to love and be loved? What must we know, read, do, etc., to be better at this business of love?

A quest of the spirit needs more than analysis of what love is all about and more than programs designed to identify psychological barriers to being a loving person. The storytellers and poets of the past and present know that our hunger for love is never fully satisfied. Just as we feed our bodies in order to survive, we need to feed our spiritual hunger if we wish to uncover the resources necessary to foster an ongoing feast of love.

Love comes in a variety of guises. We love persons. We love places. We love things. Though there are many loves, there is a common factor in every experience of love. Every love leads us to embrace a good outside of ourselves. We willingly open ourselves to the risk of loss of ego. We take a long stride.

We began this collection with the intention of gathering works that would nourish an appreciation of the possibilities and challenges of this greatest of virtues. The authors of the works included here invite us to enter their imaginations and allow their images of love to bypass our fears and weave their way through our imaginations to our spirits. Our spirits, nourished by this meditation, will in turn feed us new images of how we might participate in the feast of love.

As examples of the many works available to those who want to partake of the feast of love, we include poetry, folklore, sayings, music, children's stories, autobiographical reflections, classic stories, stories from religious traditions, our own published and unpublished works, as well as other unpublished material.

Some selections appear to give obvious answers to the question of love's meaning. Others are more obscure. Some are old favorites, perhaps seen in a new light. None, standing alone, supplies the exact road map for the soul-size exploration unto a deeper appreciation of the greatest of virtues. All invite meditation as a way of opening the spirit to fuller awareness of this wonder that is both our origin and destiny.

This kitchen table book of love—a hands-on, there-every-morning-and-evening collection of reflections on love—offers food for the spirit of those who stride. Not unlike a menu planner, it presents a strategy for a celebration of the feast of human love. The chapters represent what we consider essential components of that strategy.

We hope this exploration into love will encourage readers to recall their own favorite love stories and share them—and any new images they uncover—with those they love.

CHAPTER ONE

Generic Love:
A Many-Splendored Thing

To love deeply in one direction makes us more loving in all directions.
MADAME SWITCHINE

I do love I know not what;
Sometimes this and sometimes that.
ROBERT HERRICK

There is only one kind of love, but there are a thousand different ver-
sions.
FRANÇOIS DE LA ROCHEFOUCAULD

L ove, it is said, is a many-splendored thing. The various
experiences of love, as well as the effects of each experience
and the interplay between them, give love its claim to
splendor.
    There are a variety of loves, but they all have the same
spirit. The selections in this chapter suggest that this spirit is the generic
ingredient in every type of love. Love's splendor is most obvious in its
effects, in the way it moves us out of our narrowness to another level
of existence.

Love, like the stories, poetry, and songs that proclaim its joy and its sorrows, does not lend itself to rational, scientific analysis. Why do two people fall in love? Why is it that a beautiful sunset can dispel the frustration of a rush-hour driver headed home after a busy day? Why does a teenage boy, given to monosyllabic answers and careless dress, suddenly become concerned about his appearance and sound a bit more civilized after a certain young woman smiles at him? Why is it that the birth of a grandchild turns staid, mature adults into euphoric grand-parents? Why is it that when we are loved we begin to open ourselves to heretofore-undreamed-of adventures? Why do memories of certain places stir glad feelings? Why does the concern of a friend during a time of trial lighten our burden? Why do all these things happen if not because just even a hint of love arms us against our need always to be on guard, fearful of a loss of self.

True love, no matter what its focus, entices our spirits to move out of the constricted confines of self. It impels us to sing a song that encompasses not only our own souls but also the soul of the other, be it a spouse, a child, a neighbor, our community, our neighborhood, the stranger, all humanity, the universe, and beyond. The narrow circle widens each time we feel we are loved as well as each time we allow ourselves to love something or someone.

At times the term love is misapplied. People are said to love every-thing from fame, fortune, power, and prestige to the latest fashion, movie, television show, rock star, or novel. These are false loves when they are based in a compulsion or a sense of greed. Compulsion and greed focus our energies on the acquisition of things as a means of satisfying the ego. We are shaped by what we love, even when these are false loves. The circle narrows. The spirit withers.

The dichotomy between our expressed desire to love and be loved and our actions to protect us from what we imagine to be a loss of self sets up obstacles to our participation in the feast of love. Yet, when properly nourished, our ability to love grows. We work our way up to participation in the feast of love when we explore the various love challenges and love opportunities available to us. The spirit thrives.

When the spirit thrives, both individuals and communities are open to the splendor of the varieties of loves. When we are mindful of love's possibilities, good things happen. We have a hint of what it means to be real.

We seek to understand what it means to love, thinking that once we have the wisdom we will conquer all life's obstacles. Unfortunately, like the he-mouse, we want things our way. Our self-centered desires often make it difficult, if not impossible, to recognize love when it is waiting for us to embrace it.

Love took up the glass of Time, and turn'd it in his
  glowing hands;
Every moment, lightly shaken, ran itself in golden sands.

Love took up the harp of Life, and smote on all the
  chords with might;
Smote the chord of Self, that, trembling, pass'd in
  music out of sight.

ALFRED, LORD TENNYSON,
from *Locksley Hall*

THE HE-MOUSE AND THE SHE-MOUSE

This tale appears in Indian, classical, midrashic, and medieval fable literatures, as well as in modern oral tradition.

Thus said a mouse: "What good is a male without the female who is his wife? I have seen every kind of thing that is alive, yet among all these I have found none that is fit to be my wife." And he did greatly desire to seek for himself a wife most fair, and he could find none to suit his thought and aim except the sun, who was fair beyond all compare. So he said: "If all who dwell on earth are in darkness when she is not there, the good sun brings healing with her when she comes." And when the sun began shining again, she found much favor in his eyes, and he said to her: "I love you with an everlasting love, therefore I beg you to come down from above and I shall pay your bridal price and wed you in a trice." And the sun answered with guile and deceit: "Surely it would not be meet to take the light which grew dark yesterday and shines again today, and then sets in the evening. As soon as you look at it, it will pass away and clouds can conceal it anyway, and so I am but a servant to the cloud for whenever it desires I am clad in darkness. But if you should offer your pleas to the cloud, I am sure that it will not turn you away."

The mouse thought it over and hastened away to seek the cloud and said to her: "Indeed, I have toiled and found, O cloud most fair and fine, and by counsel of the sun I wish to make you mine, and I shall never forsake you." But the cloud answered and said: "He who is high above the high has placed me in the hands of the wind which bears me wherever it finds to be best, whether north or south or east or west. With might and main it carries me away. Now if a wife like me you desire, you will be wandering to and fro on earth until you tire. Forsake the maid and the lady take, for the wind can make me or she can break. Go to the wind and dwell with her, entice her if you can."

So the mouse went away to the wind and found her in a desolate land and to her he did say: "Have no fear. But haste away to the hills with me for of all the females I did see in these times and our present age you are the best and most fit for me, so you be mine and I shall be yours." But the wind answered: "Why do you come to take me? You do not know how abject I be for I have no strength or power to blow down a wall at any hour, whether of stone or earth it be. I am not strong at all, you see, when a wall is stronger than me. So if it should seem fit to you and you can persuade her to be faithful and true, let her be your citadel and stay."

So he went to the wall and this did say: "Listen to me, for I would have you know the counsel of the sun and the cloud and the wind and they advise that I should ask you to be sweet and kind to me, so that we may wed, you see." But the wall answered in rage and wrath: "They sent you to me to display my shame and reproach. You have come to remind me that they are all of them free to rise up and go down while my stone and wall cannot move at all, and I have neither strength nor power and any mouse or worm can make me bare and dig into my base and make themselves a ladder and a stair. Though I may be an upthrust wall, they injure me with their mouths and feet as though I had no strength at all, and the mice come here with all of their kin and dwell in me, the mothers and their litters. And they have many a hundred nests, and I cannot stand against them at the best. And do you desire a wife like me?"

So when the mouse saw that his hopes were in vain, he took a wife of his own kith and kin who had been born not far away, and she became his helpmate on that day.

DANIEL BEN-AMOR,
from *Mimekor Yisrael: Selected Classical Jewish Folktales*

If we are willing to risk love, to let love arm us, we will eventually find the answer to the ultimate questions.

OUR HEARTS

To love "very much" is to love poorly: one loves—that is all—it cannot be modified or completed without being nullified. It is a short word, but it contains all: it means the body, the soul, the life, the entire being. We feel it as we feel the warmth of the blood, we breathe it as we breathe the air, we carry it in ourselves as we carry our thoughts. Nothing more exists for us. It is not a word; it is an inexpressible state indicated by four letters.

GUY DE MAUPASSANT

LONELINESS

From the soul's proper loneliness love and affection seem
part substance and part dream
held in the mouth in the same way the snake carries its eggs
if gripped too hard they break,
leaving a few grains of dust
and a heart crippled by its weight of lust.

ALASDAIR GRAY

Even though love often disappoints us from every direction, in the end love will triumph.

OUTWITTED

He drew a circle that shut me out—
Heretic, rebel, a thing to flout.
But Love and I had the wit to win:
We drew a circle that took him in!

EDWIN MARKHAM

THE HOSPITAL

A year ago I fell in love with the functional ward
Of a chest hospital: square cubicles in a row
Plain concrete, wash basins—an art lover's woe,
Not counting how the fellow in the next bed snored.
But nothing whatever is by love debarred,
The common and banal her heat can know.
The corridor led to a stairway below
Was the inexhaustible adventure of a gravelled yard.

This is what love does to things: the Rialto Bridge,
The main gate that was bent by a heavy lorry,
The seat at the back of a shed that was a suntrap.
Naming these things is the love-act and its pledge;
For we must record love's mystery without claptrap,
Snatch out of time the passionate transitory.

PATRICK KAVANAUGH

Love is one of the great mysteries of human experience. Religious traditions from every time and culture offer insights into the meaning of love. Though they sometimes look at love from different perspectives, they all acknowledge the essential role of love in our lives. As we consider the various experiences of human love, we will turn to the wisdom of these traditions for their insights.

LOVE OF ENEMIES

But I tell you who hear me: Love your enemies, do good to those who hate you, bless those who curse you, and pray for those who mistreat you. If anyone hits you on one cheek, let him hit the other one too; if someone takes your coat, let him have your shirt as well. Give to everyone who asks you for something, and when someone takes what is yours, do not ask for it back. Do for others just what you want them to do for you.

If you love only the people who love you, why should you receive a blessing? Even sinners love those who love them! And if you do good only to those who do good to you, why should you receive a blessing? Even sinners do that! And if you lend only to those from whom you hope to get it back, why should you receive a blessing? Even sinners lend to sinners, to get back the same amount! No! Love your enemies and do good to them; lend and expect nothing back. You will then have a great reward, and you will be children of the Most High God. For he is good to the ungrateful and the wicked. Be merciful just as your Father is merciful.

LUKE *6:27–36*

You are the people of God; he loved you and chose you for his own. So then, you must clothe yourselves with compassion, kindness, humility, gentleness, and patience. Be tolerant with one another and forgive one another whenever any of you has a complaint against someone else. You must forgive one another just as the Lord has forgiven you.

And to all these qualities add love, which binds all things together in perfect unity.

COLOSSIANS *3:12–14*

Dear friends, let us love one another, because love comes from God. Whoever loves is a child of God and knows God. Whoever does not love does not know God, for God is love. And God showed his love for us by sending his only Son into the world, so that we might have life through him. This is what love is: it is not that we have loved God, but that he loved us and sent his Son to be the means by which our sins are forgiven.

Dear friends, if this is how God loved us, then we should love one another. No one has ever seen God, but if we love one another, God lives in union with us, and his love is made perfect in us.

1 JOHN *4:7–11*

THE PROPHET

Then said Almitra, Speak to us of *Love*.
And he raised his head and looked upon
the people, and there fell stillness upon them.
And with a great voice he said:
   When love beckons to you follow him,
Though his ways are *hard* and *steep*.
   And when his wings enfold you yield to him,

Though the sword hidden among his pinions
may wound you.

And when he speaks to you believe in him,

Though his voice may shatter your dreams as
the north wind lays waste the garden.

For even as love *crowns* you so shall he
crucify you.

Even as he is for your growth so is he
for your pruning.

Even as he ascends to your height and
caresses your tenderest branches that quiver in
the sun,

So shall he descend to your roots and shake
them in their clinging to the earth.

Like sheaves of corn he gathers you unto
himself.

He threshes you to make you naked.

He sifts you to free you from your husks.

He grinds you to whiteness.

He kneads you until you are pliant;

And then he assigns you to his sacred fire,
that you may become sacred bread for God's sacred feast.

All these things shall love do unto you that
you may know the secrets of your heart, and in
that knowledge become a fragment of Life's
heart.

But if in your fear you would seek only love's
peace and love's pleasure,

Then it is better for you that you cover your
nakedness and pass out of love's threshing-
floor,

Into the seasonless world where you shall
laugh, but not all of your laughter, and weep,
but not all of your tears.

Love gives naught but itself and takes naught
but from itself.

Love possesses not nor would it be possessed;

For love is sufficient unto love.

When you love you should not say, "God is

in my heart," but rather, "I am in the heart of God."

And think not you can direct the course of love, for love, if it finds you worthy, directs your course.

Love has no other desire but to fulfill itself.

But if you love and must needs have desires, let these be *your desires* of love:

To melt and be like a running brook that sings its melody to the night.

To know the pain of too much tenderness.

To be wounded by your own understanding of love;

And to bleed willingly and joyfully.

To wake at dawn with a winged heart and give thanks for another day of loving;

To rest at the noon hour and meditate love's ecstasy;

To return home at eventide with gratitude;

And then to sleep with a prayer for the beloved in your heart and a song of praise upon your lips.

KAHLIL GIBRAN,
from *The Prophet*

PRAYER OF ST. FRANCIS

Lord, make me an instrument of your peace:
where there is hatred, let me sow love
where there is injury, pardon;
where there is doubt, faith;
where there is despair, hope;
where there is darkness, light
and where there is sadness, joy;

O Divine Master, grant that I might not so much seek
to be consoled as to console,
to be understood as to understand,
to be loved as to love.
For it is in giving that we receive,
it is in pardoning that we are pardoned,
and it is in dying that we are born
to eternal life.

There is one who *sings the song* of his soul, discovering in his soul everything—utter *spiritual fulfillment*.

There is one who sings the song of his people. Emerging from the private circle of his soul—not expansive enough, not yet tranquil—he strives for fierce heights, clinging to the entire community of Israel in tender love. Together with her, he sings her song, feels her anguish, delights in her hopes. He conceives profound insights into her past and her future, deftly probing the inwardness of her spirit with the wisdom of love.

Then there is one whose soul expands until it extends beyond the border of Israel, singing the song of humanity. In the glory of the entire human race, in the glory of the human form, his spirit spreads, aspiring to the goal of humankind, envisioning its consummation. From this spring of life, he draws all his deepest reflections, his searching, striving, and vision.

Then there is one who expands even further until he unites with all of existence, with all creatures, with all worlds, singing a song with them all.

There is one who ascends with all these songs in unison—*the song of the soul, the song of the nation, the song of humanity, the song of the cosmos*—resounding together, blending in harmony, circulating the sap of life, the sound of holy joy.

ABRAHAM ISAAC KOOK

Jesus answered, " 'Love the Lord your God with all your heart, with all your soul, and with all your mind.' This is the greatest and the most important commandment. The second most important commandment is like it: 'Love your neighbor as you love yourself.' The whole Law of Moses and the teachings of the prophets depend on those two commandments."

MATTHEW *22:37–40*

Set your hearts, then, on the more important gifts.

Best of all, however, is the following way.

I may be able to speak the languages of human beings and even of angels, but if I have no love, my speech is no more than a noisy gong or a clanging bell. I may have the gift of inspired preaching; I may have all knowledge and understand all secrets; I may have all the faith needed to move mountains—but if I have no love, I am nothing. I may give away everything I have, and even give up my body to be burned—but if I have no love, this does me no good.

Love is patient and kind; it is not jealous or conceited or proud; love is not ill-mannered or selfish or irritable; love does not keep a record of wrongs; love is not happy with evil, but is happy with the truth. Love never gives up; and its faith, hope, and patience never fail.

Love is eternal. There are inspired messages, but they are temporary; there are gifts of speaking in strange tongues, but they will cease; there is knowledge, but it will pass. For our gifts of knowledge and of inspired messages are only partial; but when what is perfect comes, then what is partial will disappear.

When I was a child, my speech, feelings, and thinking were all those of a child; now that I am an adult, I have no more use for childish ways. What we see now is like a dim image in a mirror; then we shall see face-to-face. What I know now is only partial; then it will be complete—as complete as God's knowledge of me.

Meanwhile these three remain: faith, hope, and love; and the greatest of these is love.

1 CORINTHIANS *12:31–13:13*

CHAPTER TWO

Falling in Love/Young Love

Some say that the most beautiful thing on this dark earth is a cavalry regiment, some a battalion of infantry on the march, and some a fleet of long oars. But to me the fairest thing is when one is in love with someone else.

SAPPHO

One of life's great mysteries is: How is it that two people fall in love? What is it that makes the stranger across the crowded room set a person's heart aflutter? What happens to move two people, who have been in the ring's opposite corners, suddenly to embrace rather than begin the fight? How do two young people remain staunch in their commitment despite strong familial and societal opposition? What happens to make the carefree, "I want no commitments," person start thinking about being true to a love?

We humans are genetically programmed to mate. The survival of the species depends on a commitment from a male to care both for the mother and the child. For most of human history, and even today in some cultures, decisions on marriage and continuing the family line are based on concerns of the family and the culture. Love is not a priority, though it may be hoped that it will develop between the partners. Much of the romantic poetry from these cultures refers to someone other than a spouse.

Falling in love, at whatever age and no matter how many times, is a powerful example of how love moves us out of ourselves into a hoped-for union with another. Despite all the obstacles, falling in love is wonderful. It's also a roller-coaster ride of ups and downs, moments of certainty assailed by periodic concerns, putting yourself on the line with the hope, often with little evidence, that the other feels the same about you.

Sometimes our own insecurities short-circuit a romance. Though we have a glimpse of the possibilities of a lifetime of love with another, we can't bring ourselves to move that far out of our own ego's needs. We betray love.

Other times, we discover that the object of our affection while seeming to love us cannot, or will not, make a commitment. Our love is betrayed.

The happy ending to our romantic encounter seems to come when we agree to grow together in love. Of course, it's not a real ending. It's the beginning of the possibility of discovering what true love is all about and how it enriches our lives. Our love is real.

Some of the great literary classics are stories of the lengths a lover will go in order to win the heart, and hopefully the hand, of a beloved. Romances are bestsellers. The poetry, sayings, and stories in this chapter capture the highs and the lows of romantic love and the optimism of the human spirit in our pursuit of love.

The splendor works its magic.

*M*emories *of childhood crushes remind us that love is possible at an early age. Someone outside of us and outside of our family assumed a critical role in our lives. Preschool, kindergarten, and grade school crushes are initial skirmishes in the game of love.*

BROWN PENNY

I whispered, "I am too young,"
And then, "I am old enough";
Wherefore I threw a penny
To find out if I might love.
"Go and love, go and love, young man,
If the lady be young and fair."
Ah, penny, brown penny, brown penny,
I am looped in the loops of her hair.

O love is the crooked thing,
There is nobody wise enough
To find out all that is in it,
For he would be thinking of love
Till the stars had run away
And the shadows eaten the moon.
Ah, penny, brown penny, brown penny,
One cannot begin it too soon.

W. B. YEATS

"Obsolescent," said Sister Alphonse Mary, a young nun with the serene loveliness of an ivory statue. The year was 1942.

"Obsolescent, O-B-S-O-L-E-S-C-E-N-T, obsolescent," volunteered the boy. "It means out of date, as in the P-thirty-eight fighter plane is obsolescent."

The class groaned as if someone on the other team had made a free throw. They were weary of Mike Casey's preoccupation with the war.

But none of them had a father in the jungles of Guadalcanal.

"Or," he added brightly, "as in spelling bees are obsolescent."

The class laughed. Mike Casey could always get a quick laugh from them, even if they did not like him.

"That will do," S'ter said sternly. Much of S'ter's energy was devoted to restraining her impulses to laugh at the seventh grade several times every hour.

"We'll let you try *enervate*, Anne Marie." She turned to the other side of the crowded classroom, where Mike's last opponent was standing.

Loud cheers for the other side. First and goal.

"That is if your noisy supporters will give you a chance to spell it."

It was an old battle. For the last two years Anne Marie O'Brien and Michael Casey had been the finalists in every contest in the class—and education in St. Ursula's was mostly a contest.

Mike always won.

And Anne Marie despised him.

"It means wear out or tire," said the little girl with the long, black hair and blazing gray eyes and the first hints of a woman's body, "as in contests with Michael Casey enervate me."

The class howled, as they did at every joke at Mike's expense. He was too smart, he worked too hard, and his family was reputed to be rich.

Anne Marie they worshiped. They had little choice. The alternative, doing battle with her strong will and wild anger, was terrifying. "That little O'Brien girl is going to grow up to be a black Irish beauty," Mike's aunt Katie had said, "and she'll have the temper to go with it."

"No personalities, Anne Marie." S'ter did not even try to hide her own laughter. "Stop stalling."

Sister Alphonse Mary was the only one who dared to challenge Anne Marie and hope to get away with it.

"Yes, S'ter, stop stalling, S-T-O-P, one word, S-T . . ."

More merriment from the seventh grade. But not this time from S'ter.

"I'll disqualify you, young woman," she warned stiffly, a referee giving a last warning before throwing a player out of the game.

"Sorry, S'ter." Anne Marie was contrite. Only S'ter received apologies from the reigning monarch of the seventh grade. "Enervate," she said smiling appealingly. "E-N-N-E-R-V-A-T-E, enervate?"

She was uncertain. Mike knew he'd won. When Anne Marie lost her confidence she was finished, like the Japs would be once they began to lose the war.

"One more chance." Sister Alphonse Mary was as solemn as King Solomon preparing to cut the baby in two. She liked Anne Marie and found Mike a trial. But unlike many of the other nuns at St. Ursula, she played no favorites.

"E-N-N-A-R-V-A-T-E?"

S'ter pounded the hand bell, a nun's badge of office and the gong of defeat for Anne Marie. "If you spell it right, Michael, you win."

His heart beat rapidly with the thrill of victory, as though he were fighting Japs at the edge of Henderson Field. He loved victory over Anne Marie, who was the Monstress of Mongo from the Flash Gordon comic strip.

"I believe that Anne had it right the first time except for two n's," he said.

"I'm the teacher, Michael," S'ter said impatiently, "just spell it for us."

"E-N-E-R-V-A-T-E." He trailed out the letters, savoring his triumph and the frustrated rage on his opponent's pretty, elfin face.

"Michael Casey wins again." S'ter pounded her bell three times.

The class booed.

"That will be quite enough, class, unless you want to spend your Christmas vacation doing homework."

The class settled down promptly, like soldiers when a top sergeant came into the barracks. S'ter Alphonse Mary was pure poison when you made her mad.

They had many reasons for not liking Mike. Because his uncle, Monsignor Quinlan, was the Cardinal's secretary, the priests made a fuss over him. His mother and father were separated—"divorced," many parents said in hushed whispers. His father was rumored to be a "Communist and an alcoholic." His mother was running her family's manufacturing business, making parts for B-17s; most people in St. Ursula's did not think it was right for a woman to preside over a factory, despite the fact that she did so for "the war effort." She rode in a chauffeur-driven LaSalle with a "C" gasoline ration sticker. Even if Mike had not earned himself the reputation of being a "walking encyclopedia" in his first week in school after he and his mother had moved into St. Ursula's, the other things would have caught up anyway.

He pretended it did not matter, that he did not need friends, that he did not mind the envy of his classmates, that their taunts did not hurt him. But they did hurt. His mother often said, as though discussing a physical handicap, "Michael is so sensitive, just like his father."

He retreated into a dreamworld of books, radio programs, and war reports and looked forward eagerly to escaping from St. Ursula's to the seminary, where he could begin his studies for the priesthood.

Anne Marie walked back to her seat, her mouth a razor-thin line. She whispered a very vulgar word as she walked by his desk. The girls around her giggled.

"What's going on back there?" S'ter thundered.

"He called me a name, S'ter." Anne Marie was outraged innocence.

The daughter of Judge Larry O'Brien, Anne Marie came from a family whose Catholicism and political clout—which were virtually the same thing—were unquestioned on the West Side of Chicago. She was pretty, she was fun, she was popular.

And she received special sympathy from the nuns because her two sisters had died in a school fire.

"Did you, Michael?"

Sister Alphonse Mary was familiar with Anne Marie's tricks. Yet she would show no preference either for the daughter of a politically powerful judge or the son of a rich divorcée with her own war plant.

"No, S'ter, I'm going to be a priest. I don't use vulgar language."

The class groaned.

"We are well aware of *that*," said the nun. "It's not necessary to remind us. We will talk about this after school. Both of you will remain when class is dismissed. I do not want to hear another word out of either of you. Do you understand?"

"Yes, S'ter," they responded in a meek duet.

The nun was not eager to begin the conversation after school. She busied herself with record keeping while the two of them sat anxiously at their desks, Mike in the second seat of the third row, near the chart with the stars after the names of those who went to Mass every day, and Anne Marie at the back of the second row, under the pictures of the Holy Land that S'ter used for her Advent lessons.

Mike opened his geography book and began to read about copper mining in Chile. Copper was essential to the war effort. He had heard his mother say on the phone one Saturday that she didn't care how much it cost or where they bought it, she had to have more copper.

No one in St. Ursula's ever mentioned his father's dispatches, which appeared almost every night on the front page of the *Chicago Daily News* with the dateline "Henderson Field, Guadalcanal." The Japs were closing in. Some experts felt that Henderson Field would fall soon. The Marines were virtually cut off.

Yet his father's stories were lighthearted and cheerful, much like the handsome reporter himself, though Mike could hardly remember what "Patrick M. Casey" looked like. His mother never mentioned him, not even when he won the Pulitzer Prize for his stories about the war in New Guinea.

She did read his dispatches every night, however. Even when his uncle, a dapper little man in clerical vest and French cuffs, would visit them and assure her that the "annulment" was "coming along."

Michael tried to explain at first to his classmates the difference between an "annulment" and a "divorce." They were not interested.

He looked nervously at his watch. If S'ter kept them too long, his mother would be home before he was and would worry about him. Whenever he seemed to do something wrong, she worried that "Casey blood" might turn him into an alcoholic.

He would also miss *Don Winslow of the Navy; Jack Armstrong, the All-American Boy;* and maybe *Little Orphan Annie*. And if his mother was angry at him, she might forbid him to listen to *The Lone Ranger* after supper. She often said that he read too much and that, instead of being glued to the radio, he should become friends "with the other boys your age."

From the corner of his eye he watched Anne Marie; she was fidgeting like a tiger in a circus cage. With loud sighs and noisy pen scratching, she pretended to be busy at work on an arithmetic problem.

An hour passed. S'ter worked implacably at her records. The seat of his desk was as uncomfortable as a concrete slab. The minute hand dragged itself slowly around the clock.

Anne Marie caught him looking at her. She made an ugly face and turned away in disgust.

"Daydreaming again, miss?" S'ter demanded. "Making up those silly romantic stories of yours?"

"No, S'ter," she said.

"Yes, S'ter, is what you mean. Leave your dreamworld and return to your arithmetic, if you please."

"Yes, S'ter."

Anne made up stories too. Wasn't that strange? He thought he was the only one in class who lived in a dreamworld.

The Monstress of Mongo. Mike hated her with single-minded fury. She was everything he wanted to be, popular, brave, athletic, a leader.

Even though he was tall, he was clumsy and useless at sports. And his mother wouldn't let him play football for fear he would hurt himself. His health was "delicate," just as his disposition was "sensitive." He broke his finger playing softball and missed a week of school.

Anne Marie had fractured a collarbone during a game against the eighth-grade volleyball team from Tower of Ivory parish and had not shed a tear. Two days later she was back on the team, playing with a cast.

"Just sitting there?" S'ter looked up at them in mock surprise. "Make yourselves useful. Erase the blackboard and clean the erasers. Get on with it."

Under other circumstances it would be a sign of favor to help Sister Alphonse Mary after class. Now it compounded their disgrace. It was also a sign that they were in very serious trouble. A long wait and then the erasers were invariably a prelude to a severe tongue-lashing.

It might be easier, Mike thought, to be fighting Japs at Henderson Field.

Quietly they erased the boards and gathered armfuls of erasers to take outside.

Anne Marie stuck out her tongue at him.

Monstress.

"Going out without your wraps? Too busy with your sinful fighting to notice that it's December? We had the spelling bee because it's the last day of school before Christmas, don't you remember that?"

"Yes, S'ter, no, S'ter," they said in unison again. Mike was afraid that they had the words in the wrong order and that would infuriate Sister Alphonse Mary even more.

"Do you want both your mothers to complain about my ruining your health? Put on your coats this minute."

"No, S'ter, yes, S'ter." This time they had said it right.

Suddenly Mike felt very angry. He had done nothing wrong. His only offense was to win a spelling bee. It would be unmanly, a Casey-like weakness, to lose to placate Anne Marie. She had caused all the trouble and he was being punished for it.

Worse than Ming's daughter.

Outside the wind was bitter. Mike shivered as he pounded the erasers against one another, sending clouds of chalk dust floating like frozen mist over the snow piles at the edge of the school yard.

"If you tell her it was me, sissy, I'll make you pay. . . ."

Mike wanted to smash her nasty little head between the erasers.

Of course he wouldn't tell. To do anything to hurt a woman was unmanly.

The threat of a winter storm was still on S'ter's face when they returned to the classroom.

"Take off your coats and come up here to the front of the room. Now, then," she began when the two of the them were standing side by side in front of her desk, heads bowed before the solemn bar of justice. "I think everyone knows that Michael does not use vulgar language. He is invariably courteous to women."

"I-N-V-A-R-I-A-B-L-Y," said Anne Marie, a hint of her most winning smile flashing across her piquant face.

"That will do, miss. You lost the spelling bee, as I remember?"

"Yes, S'ter," she said contritely, but her tiny hands were clutched in fury.

"Do you like Michael?"

The girl was thrown off-balance. And Michael wished the floor would disappear beneath him.

"What . . . what do you mean, S'ter?"

"You know very well what I mean, miss."

"Well"—she hesitated—"Mickey would be kind of cute if he wasn't such an overgrown sissy and a stuck-up mama's boy."

"Indeed," Sister Alphonse Mary sniffed indignantly.

The Casey in him took charge. "Annie would be the prettiest girl in the class, S'ter, if she didn't have a mouth like a Marine."

The nun didn't even bother to try to hide her laughter. But Anne Marie flushed in embarrassed anger.

"That will do," said S'ter, more to herself than to them. She sighed and then tried again. "Eventually this terrible war is going to be over and our country and our Church are going to change. We will need bright and attractive young people like you. But you will have to give up your apparently incorrigible Irish propensity to fight with your own. Do you understand?"

"Yes, S'ter," they said politely, though they did not.

The young nun sighed again. "Can't you understand, Anne, that Michael's father is in a place where his life is in danger every moment? Can't you have some sympathy for that?"

"He ran away because he was a drunk." Anne Marie's voice raced like the Burlington Zephyr rushing by a crossing gate. "And his grandmother killed his grandfather and his aunt Kate is a Communist."

Sister Alphonse Mary tapped her pencil on the spotlessly clean blotter of her desk. She stared at Anne Marie as though she were watching a spider crawl across a wall. Mike noticed the look S'ter gave her and thought, *You know she's a Monstress too.*

In the silence, Mike heard the ticking clock, the voices of some boys in the school yard (a world far away), and his own breathing.

"You may be the most vicious human being I have ever known," S'ter said quietly. "Apologize to Michael."

"I apologize, Michael," she said crisply, "for being the most vicious human being S'ter has ever known."

"She doesn't mean it," he flared back.

"So you are capable of anger?" The nun considered him curiously. "Accept her apology anyway."

"Yes, S'ter. I accept your apology, Anne Marie . . ."

"Fine," said Sister Alphonse Mary.

". . . the same way you made it," he finished.

"You are both impossible." The nun pushed her pencil away impatiently. "You will suffer greatly for your stubbornness. Very well, I give up on you. You may go home now. And I hope you will find time to reflect on Christmas Day about what the Christ Child must think of both of you."

"Yes, S'ter," they said.

They left the school by separate doors. Mike glanced at his watch. His mother would be home now.

But at least he would not miss *Jack Armstrong, the All-American Boy.*

He hummed the program's theme song, "Wave the flag for Hudson High boy," as he sloshed through the snow in the fading light on the long and lonely walk to his family's house on the Oak Park side of the parish, one more thing about which he was teased.

Mike took it for granted that he would always be lonely. He was the kind of person no one seemed to like—too smart, too clumsy, too sensitive.

Since he was a little boy, adults had warned him that he would not amount to much unless he changed. And as long as he could remember, children his own age had reacted to him the way the seventh-graders at St. Ursula's had. He would have been astonished if his classmates had welcomed him when his mother moved into the parish, to be near the plant and to flee from the bitter memories of the old house in Lake Forest. A few laughs at his quips and then the same old dislike.

It would stop when he was dead.

As he crossed Mayfield Avenue the first snowball banged into the back of his head. Surprised and unprepared, he turned around and was hit in the face. His attackers had been hiding behind bushes and trees. They came at him from all directions, pelting him with snowballs, some of them rock hard. Instinctively he threw up his hands to protect his face. Someone tackled him. He crashed into a bank of freshly shoveled snow. They formed a tight ring around him and continued to throw snowballs, like Indians attacking covered wagons. Then two of them held him in the snowbank while another, Joe Kelly, repeatedly shoved globs of snow against his face, into his mouth, up his nose. He did not fight back. His mother told him that fighting was unmanly.

"Wash his face clean," shouted Anne Marie, who was lurking behind the boys in the darkness. "Priests ought to have nice clean faces."

The snow burned his skin. Tears of humiliation and rage poured down his face.

"Cry baby, cry," Anne Marie taunted him. "Go home to Momma and cry for her."

They circled around him for a final barrage of snowballs, then slipped away into the winter night.

Mike lay in the snowbank, panting. Then, slowly, he struggled to a sitting position, wiping the melting snow from his face and coughing to clear his throat. He would miss *Jack Armstrong* now, a world in which good people won instead of lost. Someday he would show them all. He might even be a monsignor like his uncle. Then they would respect him.

But for now there would be loneliness, misery, pain.

Why couldn't he be on Guadalcanal with his father?

"Enervated?" Anne Marie was standing under the streetlight at the corner of Mayfield and Potomac, savoring her triumph.

"One *n*," he muttered.

"And your father's a drunk," she spit at him.

Deep inside Mike Casey something churned and then tore loose. He sprang from his sitting position and tackled her, dragging her into the snowbank with him. They rolled over in the snow. She slipped away like a squirming goldfish and tried to run. He grabbed her again. She fought back, kicking, clawing, biting. They tumbled into the bank, struggling like two wounded animals in the pale glow of the streetlight. She clawed his face with her fingernails.

"Explain that to your bitch of a mother," she said, trying to shove her knee into his groin.

All the anger of Mike's life fused inside him and became a white fire like that of an acetylene torch.

He hit her in the stomach, once and then again. She folded up like a summer deck chair in a windstorm and collapsed into the snow. He pinned her against the ground with one hand and raised a massive handful of snow above her head.

Then in the faint light of the streetlamp, he looked into her flaming gray eyes and saw himself.

His pain and loneliness and misery in her eyes. How could that be? What was she doing with his feelings? Why would she feel that no one liked her either? Such terrible pain, much worse than his. Why?

She was not afraid of the wet snow, she didn't care about that. Yet, she was afraid.

Just as he had always been afraid.

She must see herself in his eyes just as he saw himself in hers. They shared even the surprise of discovering their own reflections.

Their pains merged, one loneliness, one fear, one despair over worthlessness.

Mike lowered the hand that held the lump of snow.

And time ground to a halt, like a streetcar lurching to a stop for a red light. The rest of the world drifted lazily away. There was only Anne Marie and Michael. And the snowbank and the pale illumination of the streetlight.

They were no longer two persons but one, united by their agony and then by something that went far beyond agony. Michael/Anne Marie or Anne Marie/Michael . . . wrapped up together like two infants in a thick winter blanket, a warm protective envelope of peace and then joy.

He wanted to kiss her and knew that she wanted to be kissed. He was afraid to touch her lips, as he would be afraid to profane the chalice a priest used at Mass. She was wonderful, beautiful, and terrifying. So he touched her face with a wet glove. She smiled gratefully.

When, later in life, he tried to analyze what happened on that shortest day of the year in 1942, he often asked whether it was merely blossoming sexuality. His intellect, trained to probe and suspect all human emotion, could never explain the merging of the two persons at the foot of the old-fashioned streetlight. But, whatever it was, it was not just sex, not as sex is normally understood.

Something much less.

Or much more.

Slowly the warmth disappeared, like a spectacular summer sunset at the end of a day when vanilla-ice-cream clouds had chased one another across the sky above a lake, leaving only two seventh-graders who would never be quite the same.

Mike helped Anne Marie up and brushed the snow off her coat.

"I really deserved to have my face washed," she said.

There seemed to be nothing for him to say.

"It isn't a very deep scratch." She touched his face and caused a lingering trace of the joy to flicker briefly inside him. "Wash it off as soon as you get home so it doesn't get infected. Your mother won't even notice."

And no need to say anything.

He picked up her briefcase, dusted off the snow, and gave it to her.

"If you hurry, you won't be late for supper. . . ." Her need to talk was as strong as his need not to talk.

Anne Marie sounded like a mother, not his mother, not her mother, but someone's mother.

She turned to walk down Mayfield toward the O'Brien house, halfway along the block to Division Street.

Then she faced him again, buried her chin on her chest, and murmured, "Sorry . . ."

She ran away rapidly, as though someone were chasing her.

Mike found his voice. "Don't fall, it will enervate you. . . ."

He strode home briskly with cheerful music playing in his head, Christmas music. It did not matter that he had missed *Jack Armstrong, the All-American Boy.*

As long as there was one other person in the world who hurt as badly as he hurt, he was not alone. Life was filled with promise and possibility.

ANDREW M. GREELEY,
from *Angels of September*

All love is sweet
Given or returned. Common as light is love,
And its familiar voice wearies not ever . . .
They who inspire it most are fortunate,
As I am now; but those who feel it most
Are happier still.

PERCY BYSSHE SHELLEY,
from *Prometheus Unbound*

NOW THAT YOU HAVE COME

Now that you have come,
dancing into
my life
a guest in a closed room—
to welcome you, love longed for so long,
I lack the words, the voice,
and I am happy just in silence by your side.

The chirping that deafens the woods
at dawn, stills
when the sun leaps to the horizon.

But my unrest sought you,
when, as a boy,
on summer nights I came
stifled to the window:
for I didn't know, and it worried my heart.
And yours are all the words
that came, like water brimming over,
unbidden to my lips,
the desert hours, when childishly
my adult lips rose
alone, longing for a kiss . . .

CANILLO STARBARO

SHE REMEMBERS, DOES HE?

It was never much of a romance. He was Prince Charming in the first-grade elocution recital. He was very cute. Did she like him then? She's not sure. Her most vivid memory was being Jill and wishing she could be Cinderella. The boy who was Jack kissed her during dress rehearsal. She was not pleased.

They were in the same room for eight years. When she was in fourth grade, her mother went to a Ladies' Society meeting. His mother told someone, "This is my future daughter-in-law's mother." The daughter blushed at that. She liked him then. She wondered what made his mother say that.

In sixth grade they had their first boy-girl party. He walked her there and back home. A first date for both. No kissing games at that party or at any they had over the next three years. By the end of seventh grade she had a wandering eye for some of the other boys in their grade. Many of the other girls had eyes for him. What were his feelings? She never knew.

You could go to the eighth-grade dance with a date or alone. She went on a date. He went alone although there were several girls wishing he would ask them. One even suggested to her that if he should ask her she should say no. A few weeks later he asked her if he could walk her home from the party the Mother's Club was giving for the class next week. She said yes. They went for ice cream after the party. She never told anyone about the invite.

They went to single-sex high schools but saw each other at parish teen functions. In freshman year, he invited her to a party for their friend's parents' anniversary. At her school, sophomores finally got a chance to go to the big fall dance. The acceptable time to ask a date was three weeks before the event. On that day, she asked him. He gave her a funny look and said someone else had asked him a week before. She was surprised. She hadn't known during those early years that this girl had any interest in him.

Only then did she learn from some other girls in their grade-school class about the party during the summer after graduation. A friend of this girl, who sometimes came to their parties though she did not go to their school, had a party. All the others in their group were invited. No one even told her about it. That hurt. She suspected that the party was meant to ensure the girl's chances to pique his interest. Did it? Only he knew if it did.

A few weeks after the dance, he took her to a movie. On Valentine's Day, she got a card signed with his name. She was never sure if he sent it or if some of the girls had done it, waiting for her to say something so they could laugh at her. She never told them nor did she thank him. What if he hadn't sent it? They both would be embarrassed.

And that was the end of the not much of a romance. She dated different people, went to proms, and had crushes. He dated others and went to proms. Did guys have crushes? She didn't know. They were still part of the neighborhood group and somewhat friendly but a bit ill at ease with each other.

They went to different commuter colleges. After graduation, she married the man she met in senior year of high school. He and some of the others from the grammar school crowd were at the wedding. He married a woman from another neighborhood some years after that. They moved to a different city. She thinks she probably saw them at their fifteen- or twenty-year class reunion. Again, she's not sure.

She didn't make their next reunion, the forty-fifth. Her husband was dying. A few years later she and her daughter attended a conference in the city where he lived. His wife, whom she had never met and who probably never knew about this "not much of a romance," was at the conference. Since they had mutual friends and his wife would know that she was in her husband's class, she introduced herself and her daughter. She liked his wife. As they talked about their families and lifestyles, she was pleasantly surprised at how similar their values were.

He came to the dinner on the last night of the conference. If his wife hadn't been there to introduce them, they probably would have passed each other by without a second glance. Neither one recognized the other. She hadn't realized she had changed that much.

They had a pleasant dinner conversation. He didn't remember many of the incidents she recalled about their class. She suspects he probably doesn't remember that time when they didn't have much of a romance.

When she does think of it, she smiles. All the angst of preteen and teenage romance makes a wonderful story to tell her children and grandchildren.

MARY G. DURKIN

THE SPINNING-WHEEL SONG

Mellow the moonlight to shine is beginning;
Close by the window young Eileen is spinning;
Bent o'er the fire, her blind grandmother, sitting,
Is croaning, and moaning, and drowsily knitting,—
"Eileen, *a chora*, I hear someone tapping."
" 'Tis the ivy, dear mother, against the glass flapping."
"Eileen, I surely hear somebody sighing."
" 'Tis the sound, mother dear, of the summer wind dying."

Merrily, cheerily, noisily whirring,
Swings the wheel, spins the wheel while the foot's stirring;
Sprightly, and lightly, and airily ringing,
Thrills the sweet voice of the young maiden singing.

"What's that noise I hear at the window, I wonder?"
" 'Tis the little birds chirping the holly-bush under."
"What makes you be shoving and moving your stool on,
And singing all wrong that old song of '*The Coolun*'?"
There's a form at the casement, the form of her true-love;
And he whispers, with face bent, "I'm waiting for you, love;
Get up on the stool, through the lattice step lightly,
We'll rove in the grove while the moon's shining brightly."

Merrily, cheerily, noisily whirring,
Swings the wheel, spins the wheel while the foot's stirring;
Sprightly, and lightly, and airily ringing,
Thrills the sweet voice of the young maiden singing.
The maid shakes her head, on her lip lays her fingers,
Steals up from her seat,—longs to go, and yet lingers;
A frightened glance turns to her drowsy grandmother,
Puts one foot on the stool, spins the wheel with the other.

Lazily, easily swings now the wheel round;
Slowly and lowly is heard now the reel's sound;
Noiseless and light to the lattice above her
The maid steps,—then leaps to the arms of her lover.

Slower—and slower—and slower the wheel swings;
Lower—and lower—and lower the reel rings;
Ere the reel and the wheel stop their ringing and moving,
Through the grove the young lovers by moonlight are roving.

JOHN FRANCIS WALLER,
from *Irish Love Poems: Danta Gra*

LOVE'S YOUNG DREAM

The days are gone, when beauty bright
    My heart's chain wove;
When my dream of life, from morn till night
    Was love still love.

    New hope may bloom,
    And days may come,
    Of milder, calmer beam;
But there's nothing half so sweet in life
    As love's young dream.

THOMAS MOORE,
from *Irish Love Poems: Danta Gra*

We are never prepared for either the ecstasy or agony of falling in love. Questions about ourselves and about the one we love quickly bring us down from the initial walking-on-air feeling of falling in love. The desire to be with our beloved all of the time and the reality of our individual lives cause us to rile at the unfairness of life. Uncertainty about the beloved's true feelings surface. Concerns arise about our ability to make a commitment to follow our avowed desire to be with the other all of the time. No one ever said falling in love is easy. However, they do say that it is wonderful!

LOVE'S PHILOSOPHY

The fountains mingle with the river,
   And the rivers with the ocean,
The winds of heaven mix for ever
   With a sweet emotion;
Nothing in the world is single,
   All things by a law divine
In one another's being mingle—
   Why not I with thine?

See the mountains kiss high heaven,
   And the waves clasp one another;
No sister-flower would be forgiven
   If it disdain'd its brother;
And the sunlight clasps the earth,
   And the moonbeams kiss the sea—
What are all these kissings worth,
   If thou kiss not me?

PERCY BYSSHE SHELLEY

GO FROM ME

Go from me. Yet I feel that I shall stand
Henceforward in thy shadow. Nevermore
Alone upon the threshold of my door
Of individual life, I shall command
The uses of my soul, nor lift my hand
Serenely in the sunshine as before,
Without the sense of that which I forebore—
Thy touch upon the palm. The widest land
Doom takes to part us, leaves thy heart in mine
With pulses that beat double. What I do
And what I dream include thee, as the wine
Must taste of its own grapes. And when I sue
God for myself, He hears that name of thine,
And sees within my eyes the tears of two.

ELIZABETH BARRETT BROWNING,
No. VI of *Sonnets from the Portuguese*

Absence diminishes weak passions and increases great ones, as the wind
blows out candles and fans fires.

FRANÇOIS DE LA ROCHEFOUCAULD

MEETING AT NIGHT

The gray sea and the long black land;
And the yellow half-moon large and low;
And the startled little waves that leap
In fiery ringlets from their sleep,
As I gain the cove with a pushing prow,
And quench it speed in the slushy sand.

Then a mile of warm sea-scented beach;
Three fields to cross till a farm appears;
A tap at the pane, the quick sharp scratch
And a blue spurt of a lighted match,
And a voice less loud, through its joys and fears,
Than the two hearts beating each to each.

ROBERT BROWNING

Go heart, hurt with adversity,
And let my lady thy wounds see!
And tell her this, as I tell thee:
    Farewell my joy, and welcome pain,
    Until I see my lady again.

ANONYMOUS

To cheat oneself out of love is the most terrible deception; it is an eternal loss for which there is no reparation, either in time or in eternity.

SÖREN KIERKEGAARD

THE WIFE OF BATH'S TALE

When good King Arthur ruled in ancient days
(A king that every Briton loves to praise)
This was a land brim-full of fairy folk.
The Elf-Queen and her courtiers joined and broke
Their elfin dance on many a green mead,
Or so was the opinion once, I read,
Hundreds of years ago, in days of yore.
But no one now sees fairies any more.
For now the saintly charity and prayer
Of holy friars seem to have purged the air;
They search the countryside through field and stream
As thick as motes that speckle a sun-beam,
Blessing the halls, the chambers, kitchens, bowers,
Cities and boroughs, castles, courts and towers,
Thorpes, barns and stables, outhouses and dairies,
And that's the reason why there are no fairies.
Wherever there was wont to walk an elf
To-day there walks the holy friar himself
As evening falls or when the daylight springs,
Saying his matins and his holy things,
Walking his limit round from town to town.
Women can now go safely up and down

By every bush or under every tree;
There is no other incubus but he,
So there is really no one else to hurt you
And he will do no more than take your virtue.

Now it so happened, I began to say,
Long, long ago in good King Arthur's day,
There was a knight who was a lusty liver.
One day as he came riding from the river
He saw a maiden walking all forlorn
Ahead of him, alone as she was born.
And of that maiden, spite of all she said,
By very force he took her maidenhead.

This act of violence made such a stir,
So much petitioning to the king for her,
That he condemned the knight to lose his head
By course of law. He was as good as dead
(It seems that then the statutes took that view)
But that the queen, and other ladies too,
Implored the king to exercise his grace
So ceaselessly, he gave the queen the case
And granted her his life, and she could choose
Whether to show him mercy or refuse.

The queen returned him thanks with all her might,
And then she sent a summons to the knight
At her convenience, and expressed her will:
"You stand, for such is the position still,
In no way certain of your life," said she,
"Yet you shall live if you can answer me:
What is the thing that women most desire?
Beware the axe and say as I require.

"If you can't answer on the moment, though,
I will concede you this: you are to go
A twelvemonth and a day to seek and learn
Sufficient answer, then you shall return.
I shall take gages from you to extort
Surrender of your body to the court."

Sad was the knight and sorrowfully sighed,
But there! All other choices were denied,
And in the end he chose to go away
And to return after a year and day

Armed with such answer as there might be sent
To him by God. He took his leave and went.

He knocked at every house, searched every place,
Yes, anywhere that offered hope of grace.
What could it be that women wanted most?
But all the same he never touched a coast,
Country or town in which there seemed to be
Any two people willing to agree.

Some said that women wanted wealth and treasure,
"Honour," said some, some "Jollity and pleasure,"
Some "Gorgeous clothes" and others "Fun in bed,"
"To be oft widowed and remarried," said
Others again, and some that what most mattered
Was that we should be cosseted and flattered.
That's very near the truth, it seems to me;
A man can win us best with flattery.
To dance attendance on us, make a fuss,
Ensnares us all, the best and worst of us.

Some say the things we most desire are these:
Freedom to do exactly as we please,

With no one to reprove our faults and lies,
Rather to have one call us good and wise,
Truly there's not a woman in ten score
Who has a fault, and someone rubs the sore,
But she will kick if what he says is true;
You try it out and you will find so too.
However vicious we may be within
We like to be thought wise and void of sin.

Others assert we women find it sweet
When we are thought dependable, discreet
And secret, firm of purpose and controlled,
Never betraying things that we are told.
But that's not worth the handle of a rake;
Women conceal a thing? For Heaven's sake!
Remember Midas? Will you hear the tale?

Among some other little things, now stale,
Ovid relates that under his long hair
The unhappy Midas grew a splendid pair

Of ass's ears; as subtly as he might,
He kept his foul deformity from sight;
Save for his wife, there was not one that knew.
He loved her best, and trusted in her too.
He begged her not to tell a living creature
That he possessed so horrible a feature.
And she—she swore, were all the world to win,
She would not do such villainy and sin
As saddle her husband with so foul a name;
Besides to speak would be to share the shame.
Nevertheless she thought she would have died
Keeping this secret bottled up inside;
It seemed to swell her heart and she, no doubt,
Thought it was on the point of bursting out.
    Fearing to speak of it to woman or man,
Down to a reedy marsh she quickly ran
And reached the sedge. Her heart was all on fire
And, as a bittern bumbles in the mire,
She whispered to the water, near the ground,
"Betray me not, O water, with thy sound!
To thee alone I tell it: it appears
My husband has a pair of ass's ears!
Ah! My heart's well again the secret's out!
I could no longer keep it, not a doubt."
And so you see, although we may hold fast
A little while, it must come out at last,
We can't keep secrets; as for Midas, well,
Read Ovid for his story; he will tell.
    This knight that I am telling you about
Perceived at last he never would find out
What it could be that women loved the best.
Faint was the soul within his sorrowful breast,
As home he went, he dared no longer stay;
His year was up and now it was the day.
    As he rode home in a dejected mood
Suddenly, at the margin of a wood,
He saw a dance upon the leafy floor
Of four and twenty ladies, nay, and more.
Eagerly he approached, in hope to learn
Some words of wisdom ere he should return;

But lo! Before he came to where they were,
Dancers and dance all vanished into air!
There wasn't a living creature to be seen
Save one old woman crouched upon the green.
A fouler-looking creature I suppose
Could scarcely be imagined. She arose
And said, "Sir knight, there's no way on from here.
Tell me what you are looking for, my dear,
For peradventure that were best for you;
We old, old women know a thing or two.

    "Dear Mother," said the knight, "alack the day!
I am as good as dead if I can't say
What thing it is that women most desire;
If you could tell me I would pay your hire."
"Give me your hand," she said, "and swear to do
Whatever I shall next require of you
If so to do should lie within your might—
And you shall know the answer before night."
"Upon my honour," he answered, "I agree."
"Then," said the crone, "I dare to guarantee
Your life is safe; I shall make good my claim.
Upon my life the queen will say the same.
Show me the very proudest of them all
In costly coverchief or jewelled caul
That dare say no to what I have to teach.
Let us go forward without further speech."
And then she crooned her gospel in his ear
And told him to be glad and not to fear.

    They came to court. This knight, in full array,
Stood forth and said "O Queen, I've kept my day
And kept my word and have an answer ready."

    There sat the noble matrons and the heady
Young girls, and widows too, that have the grace
Of wisdom, all assembled in that place,
And there the queen herself was throned to hear
And judge his answer. Then the knight drew near
And silence was commanded through the hall.

    The queen gave order he should tell them all
What thing it was that women wanted most.
He stood not silent like a beast or post,

But gave his answers with the ringing word
Of a man's voice and the assembly heard:
    "My liege and lady, in general," said he,
"A woman wants the self-same sovereignty
Over her husband as over her lover,
And master him; he must not be above her.
This is your greatest wish, whether you kill
Or spare me; please yourself. I wait your will."
    In all the court not one that shook her head
Or contradicted what the knight had said;
Maid, wife and widow cried, "He's saved his life!"
    And on the word up started the old wife,
The one the knight saw sitting on the green,
And cried, "Your mercy, sovereign lady queen!
Before the court disperses, do me right!
'Twas I who taught this answer to the knight,
For which he swore and pledged his honour to it,
That the first thing I asked of him he'd do it,
So far as it should lie within his might.
Before this court I ask you then, sir knight,
To keep your word and take me for your wife;
For well you know that I have saved your life.
If this be false, deny it on your sword!"
    "Alas!" he said, "Old lady, by the Lord
I know indeed that such was my behest,
But for God's love think of a new request,
Take all my goods, but leave my body free."
"A curse on us," she said "if I agree!
I may be foul, I may be poor and old,
Yet will not choose to be, for all the gold
That's bedded in the earth or lies above,
Less than your wife nay, than your very love!"
    "My love?" said he. "By heaven, my damnation!
Alas that any of my race and station
Should ever make so foul a misalliance!"
Yet in the end his pleading and defiance
All went for nothing, he was forced to wed.
He takes his ancient wife and goes to bed.
    Now peradventure some may well suspect

A lack of care in me since I neglect
To tell of the rejoicing and display
Made at the feast upon their wedding-day.
I have but a short answer to let fall;
I say there was no joy or feast at all,
Nothing but heaviness of heart and sorrow.
He married her in private on the morrow
And all day long stayed hidden like an owl,
It was such torture that his wife looked foul.

    Great as the anguish churning in his head
When he and she were piloted to bed;
He wallowed back and forth in desperate style.
His ancient wife lay smiling all the while;
At last she said, "Bless us! Is this, my dear,
How knights and wives get on together here?
Are these the laws of good King Arthur's house?
Are knights of his all so contemptuous?
I am your own beloved and your wife,
And I am she, indeed that saved your life;
And certainly I never did you wrong.
Then why, this first of nights, so sad a song?
You're carrying on as if you were half-witted.
Say, for God's love, what sin have I committed?
I'll put things right if you will tell me how."

    "Put right?" he cried. "That never can be now!
Nothing can ever be put right again!
You're old, and so abominably plain,
So poor to start with, so low-bred to follow;
It's little wonder if I twist and wallow!
God, that my heart would burst within my breast!"

    "Is that," said she, "the cause of your unrest?"

    "Yes, certainly," he said, "and can you wonder?"

    "I could set right what you suppose a blunder,
That's if I cared to, in a day or two,
If I were shown more courtesy by you.
Just now," she said, "you spoke of gentle birth,
Such as descends from ancient wealth and worth.
If that's the claim you make for gentlemen
Such arrogance is hardly worth a hen.

Whoever loves to work for virtuous ends,
Public and private, and who most intends
To do what deeds of gentleness he can,
Take him to be the greatest gentleman.
Christ wills we take our gentleness from Him,
Not from a wealth of ancestry long dim,
Though they bequeath their whole establishment
By which we claim to be of high descent.
Our fathers cannot make us a bequest
Of all those virtues that became them best
And earned for them the name of gentlemen,
But bade us follow them as best we can."

    Thus the wise poet of the Florentines,
Dante by name, has written in these lines,
For such is the opinion Dante launches:
"Seldom arises by these slender branches
Prowess of men, for it is God, no less,
Wills us to claim of Him our gentleness."
For of our parents nothing can we claim
Save temporal things, and these may hurt and maim.

    "But everyone knows this as well as I;
For if gentility were implanted by
The natural course of lineage down the line,
Public or private, could it cease to shine
In doing the fair work of gentle deed?
No vice or villainy could then bear seed.

    "Take fire and carry it to the darkest house
Between this kingdom and the Caucasus,
And shut the doors on it and leave it there,
It will burn on, and it will burn as fair
As if ten thousand men were there to see,
For fire will keep its nature and degree,
I can assure you, sir, until it dies.

    "But gentleness, as you will recognize,
Is not annexed in nature to possessions.
Men fail in living up to their professions;
But fire never ceases to be fire.
God knows you'll often find, if you enquire,
Some lording full of villainy and shame.

If you would be esteemed for the mere name
Of having been by birth a gentleman
And stemming from some virtuous noble clan,
And do not live yourself by gentle deed
Or take your father's noble code and creed,
You are no gentleman, though duke or earl.
Vice and bad manners are what make a churl.
    "Gentility is only the renown
For bounty that your fathers handed down,
Quite foreign to your person, not your own;
Gentility must come from God alone.
That we are gentle comes to us by grace
And by no means is it bequeathed with place.
    "Reflect how noble (says Valerius)
Was Tullius surnamed Hostilius,
Who rose from poverty to nobleness.
And read Boethius, Seneca no less,
Thus they express themselves and are agreed:
"Gentle is he that does a gentle deed."
And therefore, my dear husband, I conclude
that even if my ancestors were rude,
Yet God on high—and so I hope He will—
Can grant me grace to live in virtue still,
A gentlewoman only when beginning
To live in virtue and to shrink from sinning.
    "As for my poverty which you reprove,
Almighty God Himself in whom we move,
Believe and have our being, chose a life
Of poverty, and every man or wife
Nay, every child can see our Heavenly King
Would never stoop to choose a shameful thing.
No shame in poverty if the heart is gay,
As Seneca and all the learned say.
He who accepts his poverty unhurt
I'd say is rich although he lacked a shirt.
But truly poor are they who whine and fret
And covet what they cannot hope to get.
And he that, having nothing, covets not,
Is rich though you may think he is a sot.

"True poverty can find a song to sing.
Juvenal says a pleasant little thing:
"The poor can dance and sing in the relief
Of having nothing that will tempt a thief."
Though it be hateful, poverty is good,
A great incentive to a livelihood,
And a great help to our capacity
For wisdom, if accepted patiently.
Poverty is, though wanting in estate,
A kind of wealth that none calumniate.
Poverty often, when the heart is lowly,
Brings one to God and teaches what is holy,
Gives knowledge of oneself and even lends
A glass by which to see one's truest friends.
And since it's no offence, let me be plain;
Do not rebuke my poverty again.

"Lastly you taxed me, sir, with being old.
Yet even if you never had been told
By ancient books you gentlemen engage,
Yourselves in honour to respect old age.
To call an old man 'father' shows good breeding,
And this could be supported from my reading.

"You say I'm old and fouler than a fen.
You need not fear to be a cuckold then.
Filth and old age, I'm sure you will agree,
Are powerful wardens over chastity.
Nevertheless, well knowing your delights,
I shall fulfil your worldly appetites.

"You have two choices; which one will you try?
To have me old and ugly till I die,
But still a loyal, true and humble wife
That never will displease you all her life,
Or would you rather I were young and pretty
And chance your arm what happens in a city
Where friends will visit you because of me,
Yes and in other places too maybe.
Which would you have? The choice is all your own."

The knight thought long, and with a piteous groan
At last he said, with all the care in life,

"My lady and my love, my dearest wife,
I leave the matter to your wise decision.
You make the choice yourself, for the provision
Of what may be agreeable and rich
In honour to us both, I don't care which;
Whatever pleases you suffices me."

   "And have I won the mastery?" said she,
"Since I'm to choose and rule as I think fit?"
"Certainly, wife," he answered her, "that's it."
"Kiss me," she cried. "No quarrels! On my oath
And word of honour, you shall find me both,
That is, both fair and faithful as a wife;
May I go howling mad and take my life
Unless I prove to be as good and true
As ever wife was since the world was new!
And if to-morrow when the sun's above
I seem less fair than any lady-love.
Than any queen or empress east or west,
Do with my life and death as you think best.
Cast up the curtain, husband. Look at me!"

   And when indeed the knight had looked to see,
Lo, she was young and lovely, rich in charms.
In ecstasy he caught her in his arms.
His heart went bathing in a bath of blisses
And melted in a hundred thousand kisses,
And she responded in the fullest measure
With all that could delight or give him pleasure.

   So they lived ever after to the end
In perfect bliss; and may Christ Jesus send
Us husbands meek and young and fresh in bed,
And grace to overbid them when we wed.
And—Jesus hear my prayer!—cut short the lives
Of those who won't be governed by their wives;
And all old angry niggards of their pence,
God send them soon a very pestilence!

CHAUCER,
from *The Canterbury Tales*

WHEN LOVE IS KIND

When Love is kind,
    Cheerful and free,
Love's sure to find
    Welcome from me.
But when love brings
    Heartache or pang,
Tears, and such things—
    Love may go hang!

If Love can sigh
    For one alone,
Well pleased am I
    To be that one.

But should I see
    Love given to rove
To two or three,
    Then—good-by, Love!

Love must in short,
    Keep fond and true,
Through good report,
    And evil too.

Else, here I swear,
    Young Love may go,
For aught I care—
    To Jericho.

THOMAS MOORE

overs moved to poetry often turn to nature's delights to speak of what cannot be conveyed in prose. Flowers—especially roses—the seasons of the year, and mysterious landscapes conjure up images of how a lover would like to while away the hours with his or her beloved.

A WHITE ROSE

The red rose whispers of passion,
    And the white rose breathes of love;
O, the red rose is a falcon,
    And the white rose is a dove.

But I send you a cream-white rosebud
    with a flush upon its petal tips;
For the love that is purest and sweetest
    Has a kiss of desire on the lips.

JOHN BOYLE O'REILLY,
from *Irish Love Poems: Danta Gra*

A RED, RED ROSE

O my Luve's like a red, red rose
    That's newly sprung in June:
O my Luve's like the melodie
    That's sweetly play'd in tune—

As fair art thou, my bonnie lass,
    So deep in luve am I:
And I will luve thee still, my Dear,
    Till a' the seas gang dry—

Till a' the seas gang dry, my Dear,
    And the rocks melt wi' the sun;
I will luve thee still, my Dear,
    while the sands o' life shall run—

And fare thee weel, my only Luve!
    And fare thee weel a while!
And I will come again, my Luve,
    Tho' it were ten thousand mile!

ROBERT BURNS,
from *A Selection of Scots Songs*

TO CELIA

Drink to me only with thine eyes,
    And I will pledge with mine;
Or leave a kiss but in the cup,
    And I'll not look for wine.
The thirst that from the soul doth rise
    Doth ask a drink divine:
But might I of Jove's nectar sup,
    I would not change for thine.

I sent thee late a rosy wreath,
　　Not so much honoring thee,
As giving it a hope, that there
　　It could not withered be.
But thou thereon didst only breathe,
　　And sent'st it back to me:
Since when it grows, and smells, I swear,
　　Not of itself, but thee.

BEN JONSON

MAYTIME

The aged winter fled away
Before the bugles of the May,—
　　And love, dear love, arose.
　　But when spring's glory goes
　　The lilacs of our love shall stay,
For ever Maytime sweet and gay,—
　　Until the lilacs close
　　Beneath the deathly snows.

from *In Praise of Japanese Love Poems*

TO HIS LOVE

Shall I compare thee to a summer's day?
　　Thou art more lovely and more temperate;
Rough winds do shake the darling buds of May,
　　And summer's lease hath all too short a date:

Sometime too hot the eye of heaven shines,
    And often in his gold complexion dimmed:
And every fair from fair sometime declines,
    By chance, or nature's changing course, untrimmed.
But thy eternal summer shall not fade
    Nor lose possession of that fair thou owest;
Nor shall death brag thou wanderest in his shade,
    When in eternal lines to time thou growest.
        So long as men can breathe or eyes can see,
        So long lives this, and this gives life to thee.

WILLIAM SHAKESPEARE

THE PASSIONATE SHEPHERD
TO HIS LOVE

Come live with me and be my love,
And we will all the pleasures prove
That hills and valleys dale and field,
And all the craggy mountains yield.

There will we sit upon the rocks
And see the shepherds feed their flocks,
By shallow rivers, to whose falls
Melodious birds sing madrigals.

There will I make thee beds of roses
And a thousand fragrant posies;
A cap of flowers, and a kirtle
Embroidered all with leaves of myrtle.

A gown made of the finest wool,
Which from our pretty lambs we pull,

Fair lined slippers for the cold,
With buckles of the purest gold.

A belt of straw and ivy buds
With coral clasps and amber studs;
And if these pleasures may thee move,
Come live with me and be my love.

The shepherd swains shall dance and sing
For thy delight each May-morning;
If these delights thy mind may move,
Then live with me and be my love.

CHRISTOPHER MARLOWE

Little privations are easily endured when the heart is better treated than
the body.

ROUSSEAU

*At times external obstacles interfere with the course of true love.
Lovers want to shout, "It's not fair." Their ecstasy is muted by the need to face
certain realities. They experience the first challenge to the strength of their love.
When they overcome the obstacle, they discover their love has deepened.*

SAVITRI

{ *India* }

In ancient India there was a beautiful, pious, and uncommonly wise princess named Savitri. As she grew into a woman, her father, King Ashvapati, despaired that she would never marry and produce an heir. For Savitri was more interested in philosophical questions than in any of the young princes who visited her as suitors. Her interest was not in wealth, jewels, or power, but in spiritual things. At that time kings usually chose husbands for their daughters, but Savitri was so wise that the king decided to allow her to choose her own husband.

To her father's surprise Savitri asked to choose her husband from among the holy men, not the wealthy princes. Her father was at first very shocked. But then Savitri explained that her choice would be a holy man of princely rank. Ashvapati was so relieved that his daughter at last was interested in a husband that he readily gave his consent.

Savitri donned the costume of a holy hermit, a sadhu, and traveled throughout the land. Everywhere that she went people were moved by her beauty of face and soul, her charity, piety, and great wisdom. Indeed, she was absent so long that her father was growing worried about her. But the reports of Savitri's good deeds poured in from throughout the realm. Even the holy hermits were impressed by her wisdom for one so young.

When Savitri finally returned to her father's palace, she gave alms to the poor gathered at the gate. There was much excitement in the palace as Ashvapati and his adviser, the sage Narada, went to greet her at the gate. This was contrary to custom; the king never met any visitor at the gate.

Savitri announced that she had chosen a husband. There was a king who was completely blind and who had lost his kingdom, having been deposed by an evil usurper who took advantage of the king's blindness. This king had a son named Satyavant ("Truth-seeker") who had gone to live among the sadhus until the throne was restored. Savitri explained that only Satyavant, who had lived as a holy hermit, could rule wisely and understand the plight of the poor. Having lived a life of poverty, Satyavant alone could see through the illusions and judge the people fairly. But even as she spoke of Satyavant, Narada grew sad. The sage turned to her and said, "My child, all that you say is true, but you cannot marry him. It is ordained that Satyavant will die within a year of your wedding."

King Ashvapati, hitherto thrilled that Savitri was about to marry, was distraught. Satyavant certainly sounded like a perfect son-in-law, but he could not bear to see his beloved daughter widowed so young. Moreover, Satyavant might die before Savitri could produce an heir. With a deep sigh Ashvapati told Savitri that she must not marry her chosen prince.

But Savitri was wise and persuaded her father to give his blessing; it was better to be married for love even if just for one year. Whether or not Satyavant was to die, she was in love with him and no other. Savitri said that she was prepared for whatever the gods had ordained. Ashvapati granted her wish.

Ashvapati had just begun to plan a royal wedding with great feasts, but Savitri insisted that she marry in the style of the holy hermits, not of wealthy rulers. Luxury, she pointed out, was only an illusion. Again, Ashvapati granted her request.

Savitri went out into the forest among the sadhus and there she and Satyavant were married, clad in the robes of simple hermits. She shared her husband's contemplative life on the edge of the great forest, the deepest, darkest forest in the world. She never told Satyavant of his foretold death. As she gave alms to the poor, people would say, "May you never know widowhood," and the tears would stream down Savitri's face. As the first year of their marriage drew to a close, Savitri prayed to the gods to give her the strength to protect her husband.

On the very eve of their first anniversary, Satyavant asked Savitri to accompany him into the deep forest to cut wood. As they walked into the ever-thickening woods, the animals knew of Satyavant's imminent death, and fled. The little birds sang their best songs, thinking that this might be the last sound Satyavant heard. They proceeded farther and farther into the forest, where it was so thick that one could not see the sunlight. They walked on, Satyavant with his ax over his shoulder and Savitri at his side.

Then Satyavant began to chop down a great tree. Suddenly he dropped his ax and turned white. He was in horrible pain and he told Savitri that it felt as if his head were being pierced by a thousand needles [a cerebral hemorrhage?]. Darkness clouded his eyes and he fell to the ground barely breathing.

At that moment Savitri heard the footsteps of a stranger approaching. This stranger had dark blue skin and red eyes—he was no stranger; it was Yama, the lord of the dead. Nonetheless Savitri asked the "stranger" to identify himself. "You know who I am," said Yama. "You also know why I am here." Yama took his cord and wrenched the soul of Satyavant from the body. As Yama turned around to take the soul to his kingdom, Savitri fell on the ground in his path.

Yama told her that it was useless; Satyavant's time had come as the gods had ordained. But Savitri pleaded with him, and Yama asked her politely to get out of his way. Then Savitri rose to her feet and began to follow Yama to the Underworld.

Yama told her to turn back; this was the land of the dead, not the living. It was now Savitri's duty to be a good wife and see to it that the funeral rites were properly performed, not to detain Yama from his mission. Yama, who is often thought of as heartless and cruel, can be compassionate. Often he will take the souls of very sick people to free them from their suffering. The lord of the dead was touched by Savitri's insistence.

Yama said, "Your love for your husband is very great and so is your courage; I will grant you one wish." Savitri replied, "Restore the kingdom to Satyavant's father." Yama told her, "It is done. Now return to the living, Savitri."

But Savitri would not turn back. She was so close to the gates of Yama's kingdom that the sky was not black and she could hear the snarling of the four-headed dog that guards the gate to the dead.* No mortal had ever come this close to the land of Yama.

"Please turn back now!" ordered Yama. "No living mortal can ever enter my kingdom!" Savitri told Yama that she would not leave her husband for any reason. Yama begged her once more to turn back, but she refused. Yama then said that no man had ever entered his kingdom; Savitri, always wise, responded that she was no man, but a woman. Yama was now impressed by her wisdom as by her courage, and he offered her a second wish. "Restore the life of my husband." Yama granted this wish, saying, "It is already done—now go back and you will find Satyavant, not dead but sleeping."

Before Savitri turned back, Yama told her, "Just one more thing— my blessing goes with you always. You have learned the wisdom of

---

*In Hindu mythology a four-headed dog guards the gateway to the Underworld. The three-headed dog Cerberus performs the same function in Greek mythology.

the gods. No woman could ever have followed me alive to the very door of my kingdom if the gods were not on her side. Your wish and more will be granted you, for you know that love is stronger than death; love is the power that Yama cannot defy. Return to where you left Satyavant and live well."

She walked back to the glade where Satyavant lay, not dead, but sleeping as Yama had promised. She kissed him and his eyes opened. He told Savitri that he had a strange dream wherein Yama had carried his soul away, but Savitri's love had rescued it. Savitri laughed and told him to forget this silly dream. It was not until many years later that she told him that this story was no dream; it had actually happened.

As they left the deep forest, messengers came to Satyavant with wonderful news: His father was restored to the throne. In fact, the old king had regained his sight as soon as he sat on his rightful throne! The young couple ran to the palace and Satyavant's father was delighted to see his son for the first time in years, and to lay eyes on his beautiful daughter-in-law. Something inside the heart of the old king told him that Savitri had brought this reversal of fortune to pass.

from Parallel Myths

Where love is concerned, too much is not even enough.

PIERRE-AUGUSTIN CARON DE BEAUMARCHAIS

OLLANTAY AND CUSICOLLUR

(**Note:** This love story became the basis of a famous sixteenth-century Peruvian play that is still performed.)

Ollantay was an honest, just, and brave warrior, faithful to the emperor, or Inca. However, he broke one of the most important laws of Tahuantisuyo (the Inca Empire) by falling in love with the beautiful Cusicollur, the Inca's daughter. Cusicollur loved Ollantay as well and the two went secretly to a kindly old priest to be married.

The old priest listened to them sympathetically, but sadly replied that a commoner could never marry a daughter of the Inca, a descendant of Inti or Viracocha the sun-god. In fact, were he to marry them, the old priest himself could lose his life. Cusicollur told the priest that it was not a sin for her to marry Ollantay; rather it was a greater sin to keep them apart.

Sometime later, Cusicollur learned that she was pregnant. She told her father and he sent her away to live with the priestesses of the sun, where no man may ever go, not even the Inca himself. There she gave birth to a beautiful little daughter named Yma Sumac, which means "very beautiful." The child was taken from her to be raised in a separate part of the temple. Meanwhile, the great Inca pronounced a death sentence on Ollantay.

The Inca's troops pursued Ollantay and his men into a valley, where Ollantay's men soundly defeated the pursuers. However, the Inca's general, Rumanahui waited for Ollantay's warriors to fall asleep. Then Rumanahui opened the gates and his warriors took Ollantay and all his men prisoner. Ollantay himself was bound with ropes to be taken to Cuzco, capital of the empire, for execution.

On the journey to Cuzco a messenger ran to Rumanahui with the news that the old Inca had died and his son Tupac Yupanqui,[*] Cusicollur's brother, was now ruler of Tahuantisuyo. Ollantay was a boyhood friend of the new emperor; perhaps there was still hope.

At Cuzco, Tupac Yupanqui awaited Ollantay and looked very sad. "My father, dear friend the great Inca Pachacutec, ordered your exe-

---

[*]Tupac Yupanqui, and probably Ollantay, were historical characters who lived roughly during the twelfth or thirteenth century A.D., some three or four centuries before the arrival of the Spanish conquistadores.

cution and there is nothing I can do but carry it out. But, since you are my friend I will allow you to speak."

Ollantay told the emperor that he understood the law and his friend's duty to carry it out. But he was not a traitor to the emperor; the law was a traitor to love. This law had kept apart two people who loved each other and even had a child together. He could never love anyone but Cusicollur. Then he told the emperor, "The gods, not men, decide who falls in love with whom." Thus, it was the will of the gods that he and Cusicollur marry. Even though the new Inca was a god himself, he could not stop the power of love.

Tupac Yupanqui was deeply moved by these words. Today he is still remembered as one of the wisest and most compassionate of all the Incas. He revoked the death sentence on Ollantay, convinced that this was the will of the gods. Tupac Yupanqui then ordered Cusicollur and Yma Sumac brought to the palace. Ollantay and Cusicollur were married, and Ollantay became the Inca's chief general and adviser.

from Parallel Myths

Few people dare now to say that two beings have fallen in love because they looked at each other. Yet it is this way that love begins, and in this way only. The rest is only the rest, and comes afterwards.

VICTOR HUGO,
from Les Misérables

THE RAINBOW BRIDGE

In a certain part of the Southwest there is a deep, wide canyon, so big that you could put a city into it and no one would ever notice. One village lies on the south rim of this canyon, another village on the north. Because the canyon is so wide, it takes many days of riding a good horse to get from one side to the other. You have to go up and down the cliffs, over rocks, across a big river, and through many miles of forest.

A beautiful girl once lived along the south rim. She'd fallen in love with a boy from the north rim whom she'd met at a fair. She knew he loved her, too, so she decided to visit him, but her parents said no. She dreamed of his handsome face, his merry eyes, and the way he rode a horse. I want to marry that boy, she said to herself. I will be miserable if I don't.

Over in his village, the boy was thinking about the girl every moment of the day. He wanted to visit her, but his parents said it was too far. All he could do was dream of her beautiful dark eyes and hair and how she dressed in a calico skirt and moccasins. He remembered the way she laughed and how stars twinkled in her eyes. She was the only girl he ever truly thought about.

So the girl and boy only saw each other in their *sueños*, their dreams. They talked to each other on the wind, which carried messages back and forth, from his village to hers. Finally the girl decided to find the boy, no matter what her parents said. She called to him on *el viento*, telling him she was coming. It was a long way across, and she wondered what route to take. She couldn't climb down the steep, rocky walls of the canyon and pick her way through the wilderness. It was too dangerous. She got on her fine old *caballo*, who had been her friend since she was a little girl, and started riding along the rim, not sure of the way. She'd never traveled very far from home, and she was frightened. Through cactus and forest she went, over slick rock and sagebrush. *Hacía mucho calor*. She rode on. When she got to the edge of the canyon, where it levels off, she looked ahead. There were still miles and miles to go. She was very tired and she had eaten all her food. In her canteen, she had only a few drops of water left. Far away, on the north rim of the canyon, she heard the boy calling to her on the wind. He said he was waiting. What was she to do?

All at once it started raining, hard enough that the girl got off her horse and sat under an *árbol* and waited for the storm to pass. When it did, she looked up and saw a rainbow stretching all the way from her side of the canyon to his! She clapped her hands with joy and mounted her horse. The rainbow looked like a bridge! She galloped toward it, the horse's hooves barely touching the ground. She wasn't even tired anymore.

The rainbow waited for the girl to come, trying to keep its colors as solid as it could. The rainbow became strong enough for the girl and the horse to ride across without falling through. When she slid off the rainbow at the other end, the boy was waiting, He took the girl in his arms and kissed her. She kissed him back.

"*Yo te quiero*," he said. "And I love the rainbow, too, for bringing you to me." They went to his village together, and there they were married. They were happy together, watching rainbows form.

Now, whenever young people see a rainbow in the sky, they wonder if it might be solid enough to ride a horse across. Then again, it might not hold them up at all. Maybe all a person needs is to believe that rainbows can turn into bridges whenever someone really needs them to.

NANCY WOOD,
from *The Girl Who Loved Coyotes:
Stories of the Southwest*

Love comforteth like sunshine after rain.

WILLIAM SHAKESPEARE

At a certain point, new lovers know their love is real and will survive. The initial anxieties lessen and they are free to enjoy the wonder of their love. The walking on air no longer seems dangerous. They hold each other up with their pledge of love.

THE NEW ENGLAND SHORE

At the foot of those mountings
Where the fountings does flow,
No amusement intended,
Where the pleasant winds blow.
There I spied a fair damsel,
She's the girl I adore,
And it's you I will marry
On this New England shore.

So that her old parents
Came this far to hear.
They said they would part her
From her darling so dear.
They gathered an army
Of twenty or more,
To fight this young soldier
On the New England shore.

He drew out his broadsword
And he waved it around,
'Til seven out of twenty
Lay dead on the ground.
Three more he wounded,
And he wounded quite sore.
He gained this fair lady
On the New England shore.

She wrote her love a letter,
And she wrote it quite sad.
No amusement intended,
To make his heart glad.
She cries, "Come back, my dear Dewill,
It is you I adore."

OKEFENOKEE SWAMP YARNS,
from *Storytellers:*
Folktales & Legends from the South

MY MISTRESS' EYES

My mistress' eyes are nothing like the sun;
Coral is far more red than her lips' red:
If snow be white, why then her breasts are dun;
If hairs be wires, black wires grow on her head.
I have seen roses damasked, red and white,
But no such roses see I in her cheeks;
And in some perfumes is there more delight
Than in the breath that from my mistress reeks.
I love to hear her speak, yet well I know
That music hath a far more pleasing sound:
I grant I never saw a goddess go,—
My mistress, when she walks, treads on the ground.
And yet, by heaven, I think my love as rare
As any she belied with false compare.

WILLIAM SHAKESPEARE

SIMPLY LOVE

... Tentative sticking of heads out windows pushed up only to be pulled down. It is *not* warm yet, even if the sun is shining and the streets are dry. City sanitation trucks sprinkling pavements. Kids at stick ball competing with traffic. Marbles and tops, penny whistles, chalk on sidewalks, jumping ropes. Passers-by duck and dodge handballs against stoops. Children think it's warmer than it is, running like they do.

Joyce is not the only one to brew sassafras tea, but it's hard to find sassafras bark in Harlem. You might have to have somebody mail you a bundle from home. Earliest breath of spring, when the sunrise is bright, landladies open their front doors first things in the morning to air out the house, bright and early in the day, first thing. Joyce's big old fat landlady, still in her kimono, is sweeping out the vestibule and sweeping off the front stoop before breakfast when she almost drops her broom in a amazement as she turns to see a man come running down the steps inside. Mr. Simple!

"What are you doing, coming out of *my* house at seven-eight o'clock A.M.?"

"Coming out is all," I says.

"Mr. Simple, this is a decent house." She pauses. "Was you in there *all* night?"

"I were."

"This is the first time! . . . Or is it? . . . I am surprised at you! And doubly surprised at Joyce Lane."

"She is Joyce Lane no longer, madam."

"What?"

"She is Mrs. Simple now. March has turned to June—we got married yesterday."

"Ooh-ooo-oo-o!" she strangles.

"You could have knocked that old landlady down with a feather. She looked more surprised than you do."

"You can knock *me* down with a feather, too," I exclaimed. "Do you mean to tell me you jumped the gun and got married *before* the wedding—in March instead of June?"

"We did. Joyce and I did. And it feels like something I never done before."

"But I thought you were going to have a church wedding?"

"We were. But the feeling just overcome us early. So we went down to City Hall and rushed the season. We can get married again in a church any time we want to, when we get the dough."

"But what about the engraved invitations? What about the bridal gown she's having made? What about the relatives coming from down South for the ceremony? And what about the cake?"

"Man, that is where I was going this morning, to Cushman's to buy a cake when that big old fat landlady stopped me. Old landlady was so surprised she invited me right back in the house to call Joyce to come down and have hot cakes with her. She said, 'I'll make you your first cakes.'

"So the landlady fixed our wedding breakfast. It were *fine*. But she asked to see my license first just to be sure I were not there under false pretenses. Then she said it was O.K. that I had stayed upstairs last night."

"Well, friend, I still want to know, what about my dark-blue suit I was buying especially for the wedding, since you said I was going to be your best man?"

"You can wear it to our house to dinner. The invitations, the relatives, the cake, your suit, Joyce with a veil on—I asked her this morning, Baby will you miss all them things? Are you mad or glad?"

"Joyce says, 'Glad, Jess, glad.' "

"What happened was I took my first week's salary that I received back on the job and bought the license. I were not taking no chances of being laid off again before the wedding happened. Only thing is, buddy, I did not know where to find you yesterday morning to stand up with me, it being Saturday. We just picked out a couple of strangers who was down at City Hall getting married, too. They was our best people. And we was theirs. They were white. But we did not care, and they did not care. They stood up with us and we stood up with them. That white man were my best man, and I was his.

"We was all so happy when it was over that that white couple hauled off and kissed *my* bride, and I hauled off and kissed his. I did not think anything like that would ever happen—kissing white folks, and they kissing me. But it did—in New York—which is why I like this town where everybody is free, white, and twenty-one, including me."

"What about the wedding rings?"

"Me and Joyce is going to pick out the rings Monday."

"What about F.D. and Gloria, who were going to get married with you?"

"F.D. is grown. He can get married by his self. Joyce and me will stand up with him if he wants us to. But I will write that boy and tell him I could not wait. F.D. is young and got plenty of time. His memory don't go back no further than Sarah Vaughan—never heard of Ma Rainey. Besides he's on the baseball team, which will keep him busy pitching till June."

"Well, I did not have a chance to give that bachelor's party for you, which I regret."

"It would be no use to give it now because I have ceased from this day on to be a drinking man," said Simple, "so you'll save your money. Not that Joyce cares too much about me drinking, but I plans to respect what little objections she do have. She will never see me high again. And Zarita will never see me at all. Zarita has done cried, and wished me well, and is thinking about getting married herself—which is one more reason not to drink—with her off my mind."

"But can't I even buy you a beer in celebration of the occasion?"

"*One*—providing you got a stick of chlorophyll chewing gum about you."

"Hypocrite."

"Just kidding," said Simple. "But all kidding aside—and thanks for the beer—I *am* a new man. I intends to act like a new man, and therefore *be* a new man. I will only drink in moderation—which means small glasses—from now on. And this spring I will down as much sassafras tea as I will beer, if not more. What Joyce likes, I like. What she do, I do. Same as in the Bible—'Whither she goeth, I goeth'— even to concerts and teas."

"You are indeed a changed man," I said. "It's simply amazing."

"Simply heavenly," said Simple. "Love is as near heaven as a man gets on this earth."

LANGSTON HUGHES,
from *The Best of Simple*

In our time the destiny of man presents its meaning in political terms.

THOMAS MANN

POLITICS

How can I, that girl standing there,
My attention fix
On Roman or on Russian
Or on Spanish politics?
Yet here's a travelled man that knows
What he talks about

And there's a politician
That has read and thought,
And maybe what they say is true
Of war and war's alarms,
But O that I were young again
And held her in my arms!

W. B. YEATS

A DRINKING SONG

Wine comes in at the mouth
And love comes in at the eye;
That's all we shall know for truth
Before we grow old and die.
I lift the glass to my mouth,
I look at you, and I sigh.

W. B. YEATS

My true love hath my heart, and I have his,
By just exchange, one for the other given.
I hold his dear, and mine he cannot miss:
There never was a better bargain driven.
    My true love hath my heart, and I have his.

His heart in me, keeps me and him in one,
My heart in him, his thoughts and senses guides:
He loves my heart, for once it was his own:
I cherish his, because in me it bides . . .
My true love hath my heart, and I have his.

SIR PHILIP SIDNEY,
from *The Countess of Pembroke's Arcadia*

Chapter Three

Married Love

*Happy are those held by an unbroken bond of love
that will not be separated before death.*
Horace

Marriage offers lovers a chance to nurture their love, expanding it beyond the "walking-on-air, can't-keep-my-hands-off-you" stage of falling in love. Marital partners are in a position to foster mutual growth in a love deeper and more rewarding than any they had previously experienced. This growth is not an automatic ingredient of married life. However, the opportunity is there for those who want it.

Falling in love might be, as the songwriter claims, wonderful. Some people even see its effects as bordering on the miraculous. This is especially true when friends, who, prior to falling in love were uneasy about anything even beginning to resemble lifelong commitment, announce marriage plans. Even the most cynical find that love—romantic love, passionate love—longs for permanent commitment.

Marriage, however, is risky. Everyone knows that. Still, the intensity of passion and romance impels some couples to take the risk—though at the time forgetting they ever thought it a risk—of making a lifelong commitment. No obstacle seems insurmountable to those caught in the thrill of a passionate romance. Love will conquer all, even any doubts one or both of the partners might experience leading up to the wedding day.

Marriage does not, as cynics claim, kill the fire of love. Love dies only when the partners fail to realize that the wedding rings do not automatically produce the longed-for intimacy. Marital intimacy is a lifelong psychosocial-erotic journey that goes through cycles.

Sometime, usually in the first year of marriage, as the partners settle down into the routine of married life, the intensity of passionate romantic love lessens. Though lovers in romantic novels might be on constant highs, the reality is that love has to share center stage with other demands of daily living. There is a stability and comfort in this settling down stage of marriage. Unfortunately, at a certain point, there also is the danger of taking each other for granted.

Sooner or later this taking for granted and its related inconsiderate behavior become frustrating for at least one of the partners. The Big Fight is born. The marriage experiences its first bottoming out. The partners wonder whatever happened to their love.

Bottoming out is both a threat to a marriage and an incentive to begin anew. The bad feelings that led to the fight and the animosity expressed during this time could do irreparable harm to the relationship. However, a fight also can lead the partners to examine what went wrong, how they might repair the rupture to their love, and what they must do to avoid further damage to their marriage.

The decision to risk renewing their love ends the bottoming out experience as the partners pledge to begin again in their search for marital intimacy. The partners have completed the first of many cycles in their marriage. If the cycles are always stretching upward spirals into expanding possibilities for growth in love, the marriage will be a sign of the possibility of a life of romantic married love.

The selections in this chapter trace the cycle of marital intimacy. Storytellers, songwriters, poets, letter writers, and religious thinkers speak to our imaginations about the possibilities of a good marriage.

*n many religious traditions, marital love is seen as representative of divine-human love. These selections from the Song of Songs inspire reflection on the ups and downs of marital love.*

SONG OF SONGS 1:1–1:6

The most beautiful of songs, by Solomon

The Woman

Your lips cover me with kisses;
    your love is better than wine.
There is fragrance about you;
    the sound of your name
    recalls it.
    No woman could keep from
    loving you.
Take me with you, and we'll run
    away;
    be my king and take me to your
    room.
We will be happy together,
    drink deep, and lose ourselves in
    love.
    No wonder all women love
    you!
Women of Jerusalem, I am dark
    but beautiful,
    dark as the desert tents of

Kadar,
but beautiful as the draperies in
Solomon's palace.
Don't look down on me because of
my color,
because the sun has tanned me.
My brothers were angry with me
and made me work in the
vineyard.
I had no time to care for myself.

MEDITATION ON KISSES

We kiss, my love and I
At break and end of day, in greeting and farewell, in celebration,
For consolation,
With hostility and sadness,
With remorse and hope,
From habit—distracted,
And most important, with rapture—prolonged,
creating as we kiss our own sweet nectar.

We used to sip on water and mere wine, thirsty all the while. Now we drink deep, our desire quenched by kiss-fermented love. Our lips touch, setting off a chain reaction, exploding in love more delightful than wine. The touching of our lips becomes the touch of God, turning us ordinary mortals into royal people who are rightly loved.

How is it that a kiss can work such magic? When did God share the secret ingredient for Divine Love?

Perhaps it was in a faraway, long-ago garden, where the first mortals lay sleeping. The man exhausted from naming all that he could see, yet lonely and unnamed himself, slept, longing for a name that would link him to God. The woman, unseen and so unnamed, hid her loveliness, and loneliness, and could not tend the garden. Yahweh-God, wanting love to flourish in the masterpiece of divine creation, saw that humans needed help to be the caretakers of creation's garden.

So the creatures were awakened and presented to each other while Yahweh-God whispered, "Be like Me. Kiss. Embrace. Cling together. Become one flesh. Be lovers." Into that first kiss, Divine Love poured a love beyond wine, melding the lovers' bodies in a passionate embrace, making them the image of a passionate, loving God.

Clinging together in love's embrace, they heard their names and knew that love was the nectar they must create from the fruit of the garden. Naked and not ashamed, they delighted in each other's beauty, grateful for Yahweh's secret shared with them in that first kiss. Each subsequent kiss was a reminder that they could "Be like Me."

We, too, the toads and sleeping beauties, the ugly ducklings and the Cinderellas, the lowly shepherds and dark and swarthy maidens, the Orpheuses and the Eurydices, the Arthurs and the Gueniveres, the Dantes and the Beatrices, the Priscillas and John Aldens, have slept, unaware of life's great possibilities until we heard the whisper, "Be like Me. Kiss. Embrace. Cling together. Become one flesh. Be lovers."

Following the explosion of love's embrace, our shattered pieces reassembled, we emerged—princes and queens, royal beauties and swans, poets and leaders—with the memory of the power of a lover's kiss.

Sometimes we lose the magic touch. Our perfunctory kisses are insipid, flatter than bitter wine, and our ears are deaf to divine whispers. We don't bother to tend our gardens. We seem unable to win the battle against the weeds that threaten to rob us of the secret of Divine Love. Each kiss becomes a reminder of a joy lost forever. We mourn because we have no sweet nectar.

Perhaps it's then that Mary goes to her son and says, "They are out of wine." And he replies, "Of what concern is this to me? I gave them the formula for love and they refuse to follow it." And she responds with a glance that moves her son to shout so we can't help but hear, "Be like Me. Kiss. Embrace. Cling together. Become one flesh. Be lovers."

How else can we explain the kiss that again brings us to the king's chambers rejoicing and exulting, our cup once more filled with delightful love, our bodies responding to the sight, the sound, the feel, the taste of each other? Because a kiss restores the wonder of love, we know we have been touched by God.

And so when we kiss, my love and I, each kiss becomes a prayer. God talks to us, touching us with Divine Love as we learn the secret of becoming one flesh. As we cling together, the spreading perfume of Divine Love flows through us, sweetening our lives and renewing the promise that we can "Be like Me." We praise God for kisses.

How marvelous are you, our God, to share Love with us through the wonder of a kiss. Fill our cups, oh Lord, with delightful love. Open our ears so we will never miss your whisper. Sharpen our senses so we feel your touch in the meeting of our lips. Awaken our bodies to your sweet perfume flowing through us as we embrace. Remind us that each kiss contains your promise that we can be true lovers as you are a Lover.

Thank you, Lord, for kisses.

MARY G. DURKIN

SONG OF SONGS 1:7–2:7

The Man

Tell me, my love
Where will you lead your flock
    to graze?
Where will they rest from the
    noonday sun?
Why should I need to look for you
    among the flocks of the other
    shepherds?

Don't you know the place,
    loveliest of women?
Go and follow the flock;
    find pasture for your goats
    near the tents of the shepherds.

You, my love, excite men
    as a mare excites the stallions of
    Pharaoh's chariots.
Your hair is beautiful upon your
    cheeks
    and falls along your neck like
    jewels.
But we will make for you a chain
    of gold
    with ornaments of silver.

The Woman

My king was lying on his couch,
    and my perfume filled the air
    with fragrance.
My lover has the scent of myrrh
    as he lies upon my breasts.
My lover is like the wild flowers
    that bloom in the vineyards at
    Engedi.

The Man

How beautiful you are, my love;
    how your eyes shine with love!

The Woman

How handsome you are, my
    dearest;
    how you delight me!
The green grass will be our bed;
    the cedars will be the beams of
    our house.
    And the cypress trees the ceiling.
I am only a wild flower in the Sharon,
    a lily in a mountain valley.

The Man

Like a lily among the thorns
    is my darling among women.

The Woman

Like an apple tree among the trees
    of the forest
        so is my dearest compared to
        other men.
I love to sit in its shadow,
    and its fruit is sweet to my taste.
He brought me to his banquet hall
    and raised the banner of love
    over me.
Restore my strength with raisins
    and refresh me with apples!
    I am weak from passion.
His left hand is under my head,
    and his right hand caresses me.
Promise me, women of Jerusalem;
    swear by the swift deer and the
    gazelles
    that you will not interrupt our
    love.

MEDITATION ON THE GAME OF LOVE

He said, "Come live with me and be my love."
    I said, "I am faint with love!"
    His father said, "Can she cook?"
    He said, "Who cares? Who needs food? I have found the most
beautiful among women!"

My mother said, "Does he have a good job?"

I said, "Who cares? He and I will sleep upon a bed of roses and dine in banquet halls!"

Our aunts and uncles said, "Life is not a bed of roses. Love doesn't pay the bills. Look how hard we work. There is no time for play."

We said, "How could they let that happen? When we are together the whole world sings and dances. We live in love's own time and will play with each other forever."

Our friends said, "Getting married kills love. Passion gets robbed of its fire. He'll work overtime, she'll get headaches."

We said, "It won't happen to us. We can't keep our hands off each other. We'll guard the treasure of our passion. It is a delight worth protecting."

The movie hero told his wife that she could never leave him. She couldn't fall asleep at night unless his arms were around her.

We said, "That's for us," imagining a lifetime of nightly embraces.

The marriage-preparation priest said, "Always kiss before you go to sleep; never end the day in a quarrel."

We said, "How can we quarrel when we are going to sleep upon a verdant couch under beams of cedars and rafters of cypresses?"

Sophisticated moderns, we knew all about psychological differences, family background differences, man and woman differences, but a shepherd whom love had made a king and a swarthy maiden who was the world's most beautiful woman knew that love would conquer all. The racing of my heart at just the thought of him whose touch could change a dark winter day into the summer solstice assured me that I would always delight to rest in his shadow. He, who dreamed of his left hand under my head and his right arm embracing me, knew that he would always want to make pendants of silver and gold to delight me, his beloved. We were going to spend a lifetime getting to know each other, sharing our bodies, hearts, and minds. We would play the game of love forever.

So we sang and danced and planned our moves, convinced that we would always be playmates.

And the Lord of the Dance smiled because we had responded to the gift of our bodies. Grace would come into the world through us.

No one stole our treasure from us. Instead, like the man who buried his talent, we didn't realize that passion needs nurturing. We failed to heed the challenge of our bodily desires pushing us to explore each other's bodies, minds, and hearts ever more deeply. We wouldn't risk that we might become better players if we would be open to new possibilities. The tried and true grew boring and the game lost its appeal.

We discovered that our sleeping habits ruled out falling asleep in an embrace. I no longer grew faint with love. He thought that pendants of silver and gold were all I needed. He worked overtime. I wondered what had happened to the king in the banquet hall plying me with raisin cakes and apples. I got headaches. He found the thorns destroying the lily as I rested in his shadow. Our senses no longer delighted in the wonders of love's own time.

And the Lord of the Dance wept because there was much less singing and dancing in the world.

But then one weekend we rediscovered love's own time in the leisure of an escape to the king's banquet hall. There the Lord activated the power of our senses and called us to explore the game of love anew. The fragrance of my body and the taste of raisin cakes and apples worked its spell and restored the roses to our bed and the cedars and cypresses to our house. We learned that players of the game must be aware of each other's moves. Our dancing and singing had lacked the harmony of people who are listening to both what the other is saying and what the other is not saying but is feeling.

Now he says, "Come play with me and be my love"; and I say, "I am faint from love's dance"; and the Lord of the Dance smiles because the Dance goes on.

We thank you Lord for helping us improve as playmates. Continue to remind us of the banquet of raisin cakes and apples which you prepared for us. Keep tantalizing us with the fragrance of love. Give us the courage to dance and sing, even though at times it seems pointless. Remind us of the joys of love's own time. Let us sing the praises of the Lord of the Dance as we partake of the king's banquet.

MARY G. DURKIN

SONG OF SONGS 2:8—2:17

The Woman

I hear my lover's voice.
He comes running over
    the mountains,
      racing across the hills to me.
My lover is like a gazelle,
    like a young stag.
There he stands beside the wall.
He looks in through the window
    and glances through the lattice.
My lover speaks to me.

The Man

Come then, my love;
    my darling, come to me.
The winter is over;
    the rains have stopped;
    in the countryside the flowers
    are in bloom.
This is the time for singing;
    the song of doves is heard in the
    fields.
Figs are beginning to ripen;
    the air is fragrant with
    blossoming vines.
Come then, my love;
    my darling come with me.

You are like a dove that hides
    in the crevice of a rock.
Let me see your lovely face
    and hear your enchanting voice.

Catch the foxes, the little foxes,
before they ruin our vineyard in
bloom.

The Woman

My lover is mine, and I am his.
He feeds his flock among the lilies.
Until the morning breezes blow
And the darkness disappears.

Return, my darling, like a gazelle.
like a stag on the mountains of
Bether.

MEDITATION ON REMINISCENCE

The day had been hectic. The week had been a disaster. Everything that could go wrong at work went wrong. There had been an obligatory parent-teacher conference one night and our daughter's dance recital another. My head ached; my feet hurt. Saturday and Sunday were days that needed forty-eight hours each if we were to accomplish everything that had to be done. And the last place in the world I wanted to be that night was at a neighbor's TGIF cocktail party. I was hungry and the appetizers were planned for people on diets. I wasn't interested in talking about sports, foreign policy, the local sewer bond issue, the church benefit, teenagers, or potty training, which seemed to be the topics of major interest to the other partygoers. My mood was glum.

Then the front door opened and over the heads of the crowd, I saw you, my silver-haired lover, a slight frown on your face as your eyes scanned the crowd. When you found the object of your search, your frown disappeared. I became the recipient of a wink and a lopsided grin that immediately plunged me into an ocean of memories.

Our first date: on that blind date when you started to introduce me to a friend, you forgot my name. The wink and the grin covered up the embarrassing moment and promised, "Stick with me and your world will be filled with surprises."

The night before you left for basic training: We clung to each other until at last you had to go. Through the tears I saw you turn, wave, wink, and give me the lopsided grin. Just a kid going off, perhaps to war; but you wanted me to know that you and our love would survive.

The Christmas Eve when I opened the box with the black turtleneck sweater, I looked up to see that special grin and knew I had missed something. Buried under the sweater was a diamond ring. You were offering me a life of continual surprises.

Our wedding morning: both of us pale and nervous, but as we stumbled a bit on the altar steps, you winked and grinned and suddenly the anxieties disappeared. We could conquer the world!

The maid at our honeymoon hotel: I was embarrassed when she met us in the hall in the late afternoon and said she had "remade" our bed. But your wink and lopsided grin reminded me that our life of surprises also was going to be filled with many laughs.

A long labor with our first child: a worried look mingled with a wink whenever the nurses made some ludicrous remark. But the lopsided grin was from ear to ear when you finally saw our firstborn and gave me the news, "She's beautiful!"

The fight to end all fights. Or so we both felt when we had exploded at each other with all the pent-up frustration of lovers who have forgotten how to express our love; but then, after a few days of unbearable silence, you arrived home from work with flowers, a wink, and a grin. "Isn't it time we stop hurting each other?"

The many hectic dinners with spilled milks, sibling quarrels, tales of teachers' injustices, and three different simultaneous conversations: halfway through the meal I would look up and see a wink and lopsided grin, promising me that there were better things to come once we tucked our offspring away in bed.

Winters aplenty flashed across my memory screen, but the wink and lopsided grin always signaled, "The winter is past. Arise my beloved and come. Let us together enjoy the wonders of a world of springtime, a world of love." Your wink and grin were a shorthand message confirming that we belonged to each other. Winter, dull parties, everyday obstacles, and even tragedies couldn't overshadow our delight in each other.

I resurfaced from my sea of memories, washed clean of gloom, refreshed by the promise your wink and grin had come to mean. You had come to shake me out of my depression. How could I be glum? I could hear the spring birds' song of joy above the din of the party noises. I wanted to shout for all to hear, "See, my lover belongs to me and I to him." But they would never know that you and I were twined together in their midst.

You worked your way through the crowd to my side, brushed my cheek with your lips, and whispered, "Let's blow this place as soon as possible. You look tired. The kids don't expect us home. We can sneak off for a quiet dinner for two. That's just what the doctor ordered for tired husbands and wives on a Friday night; not all this crazy noise. I want to sit across the table from you, hold your hand, look into your eyes, and listen to your voice."

And you and I, my love, walked through the fiery mist knowing that our night would end with us folded into each other. Let us praise the Lord for a love so alive that none can slacken it.

How wonderful are you, oh Lord, to give us memories of love's delights! We thank you for the sea of memories in which my life is my beloved's and his is mine. Never let us forget the wealth of love you have helped us store up, making it impossible to forget each other. Open our ears and our eyes to your presence in the springtime of a love both pure and fine. Be with us, Lord, as we lie down together and rise up together. And in the midst of winter's darkness, thank you for the springtime brightness of a wink and a lopsided grin!

MARY G. DURKIN

The intensity of love in the early stages of marriage convinces lovers that this love will help them survive any obstacle they might encounter. They know their love will never die.

Choose in marriage only a woman who you would choose as a friend if she were a man.

JOSEPH JOUBERT

MARWE IN THE UNDERWORLD

{ *Kenya* }

There was once a girl named Marwe. She and her brother were responsible for keeping the monkeys from raiding the family bean fields. One day they had faithfully done their duty when both of them became very thirsty. They turned their backs on the fields and went to a pool to take a drink. When they returned to the fields, the monkeys had eaten all the beans. Marwe so feared the wrath of her parents that she drowned herself; her brother rushed home with the terrible news. Her parents were so shocked and grieved that they forgot about the bean field.

Marwe sank to the bottom of the pool until she entered the land of the dead. She first came to a house where an old woman lived with her children. The old woman identified herself as Marwe's guide in the land of the dead. For many years Marwe lived with the old woman and helped with the chores. After a time Marwe became very homesick and began to think of her parents and brother. The old woman was able to read the girl's heart, and she knew that Marwe wished to rejoin the living. So one day the old woman asked Marwe if she preferred the hot or the cold. Marwe didn't understand and the woman repeated the question. Finally Marwe answered that she preferred the cold, not knowing what this meant.

The old woman had Marwe dip her hands into a clay jar of cold water, and when she pulled her hands out, they were covered with jewels. She put her feet and legs into the jar, pulled them out, and they too were covered with jewels. Smiling, the old woman dressed Marwe in the finest robes and sent her home. The old woman also had the gift of prophecy, and told Marwe that she would soon marry the finest man in the world, a man named Sawoye.

When Marwe arrived home in her fine robes and jewels, her family was overjoyed. They had given her up for dead long before. They marveled at her fine clothing and their newfound wealth. Word spread quickly through the countryside that there was a rich, eligible young woman in the territory, and Marwe's home was visited by hundreds of suitors. Marwe ignored all of the men, including the most handsome, except for a man named Sawoye, who suffered from a terrible skin disease that made him look ugly. But, having been to the land of the dead, Marwe was able to read the hearts of men and knew that Sawoye was best.

Sawoye and Marwe were married with great feasting, and after their wedding night, when the marriage was consummated, Sawoye's skin disease disappeared, showing his face to be the most handsome of all. As Marwe had plenty of fine jewels to spare, they bought a herd of cattle. Soon Marwe and Sawoye were the wealthiest people in the land.

One might expect that they would now live in happiness, but the many suitors of Marwe were envious of Sawoye. All of their friends and neighbors changed, resenting the wealthy young couple. The hostility grew more bitter with each day until a group of neighbors attacked Sawoye and killed him.

But Marwe had herself already died, and knew the secrets of the Underworld, including how to revive the dead. She took her husband's body inside their home and recited magic incantations that she had learned from the old woman in the land of the dead. Sawoye revived, stronger than ever. When their enemies returned to divide up the wealth, Sawoye slew them all. Marwe and Sawoye lived in prosperity and happiness for the rest of their lives, and since both had died, they met their ends without fear.

from *Parallel Myths*

By mutual love I grow.

PROVERB

RUTH

Don't ask me to
leave you! Let me go with you. Wherever
you go, I will go; wherever you live, I will
live. Your people will be my people, and
your God will be my God. Wherever
you die, I will die, and that is where I will
be buried. May the Lord's worst punishment
come upon me if I let anything but death
separate me from you!

RUTH *1:16–17*

I swear to you were we not married I would beg you on my knees to
be my wife, which I could not do did I not esteem you as well as I
love you.

JOHN CHURCHILL,
DUKE OF MARLBOROUGH

HOW DO I LOVE THEE?

How do I love thee? Let me count the ways.
I love thee to the depth and breadth and height
My soul can reach, when feeling out of sight
For the ends of Being and ideal Grace.
I love thee to the level of every day's
Most quiet need, by sun and candle light.
I love thee freely, as men strive for Right;
I love thee purely, as they turn from Praise.
I love thee with the passion put to use
In my old griefs, and with my childhood's faith.
I love thee with a love I seemed to lose
With my lost saints—I love thee with the breath,
Smiles, tears, of all my life! And if God choose,
I shall but love thee better after death.

ELIZABETH BARRETT BROWNING,
from *Sonnets from the Portuguese*

As a couple settles down in a marriage, big things and little things
mean a lot. Faithfulness, generosity, kindness, concern, forgiveness, and love all
combine to make marriage an adventure.

VERTUMNUS AND POMONA

{ *Greco-Roman* }

The wood nymphs are beautiful creatures that love the forests and avoid the open fields as a rule. However, there was one wood nymph, Pomona, who loved the orchards best of all. Nothing gave her greater pleasure than playing among the grapevines and apple trees. She was so beautiful that many suitors came to see her, including even kings, but she was more interested in dressing vines than in loving.

Among the most ardent of her suitors was Vertumnus, who was partly immortal. It is believed that either his father or his mother was a god or goddess. He was very persistent, but Pomona ignored him. He brought her gifts of flowers and fruit, which she accepted without thanks.

Vertumnus took on the guise of a rude shepherd, and Pomona was even more scornful than before. She treated this country bumpkin with great scorn.

Then one day Vertumnus disguised himself as an old woman out picking fruit. When Pomona encountered this "old woman," she was friendly, even gracious. The "old woman" told Pomona that she was the most beautiful fruit in the orchard and the most lovely flower of the field. Pomona was flattered. Then the "old woman" kissed Pomona in a manner that no old woman would ever kiss a young girl. Pomona was aghast and disgusted.

To make his point, Vertumnus then pointed to grapes growing on a trellis, saying how lovely they were. Without the trellis, he pointed out, the grapes would be trod underfoot; without the grapes growing on it, the trellis would be useless. The two needed each other. Pomona knew exactly what point Vertumnus was trying to make and she prepared to flee.

Just then, Venus, the goddess of love, appeared and told Pomona, "This is your true husband; it is ordained that you marry him." Certainly Pomona had no choice after that; the two were married. And it so happened that she fell in love with him over time and they tended the orchards together.

from *Parallel Myths*

Whether or not it (marriage) is the last or only adventure left for the middle class, we very much doubt. But adventure it is. Few of us do great things and have the thrill of fame and adulation. We live in the shadows of the great and the famous. But many of us experience the high adventure of loving someone and being loved in return. The thrill of being thrilling to someone else is a peak in our lives. Someone has freely and knowingly chosen us out of the crowd and given us his love. Someone has been ready literally to spend her life on me. What is more ego boosting! What is more enhancing of our self-concepts! To have another human being's heart quicken at the sound of my voice or the touch of my hand! What a satisfying sensation! The only problem is that we damned mortals cannot fly forever. We cannot maintain the peak.

from *Marital Intimacy:*
A Catholic Perspective

GIFT OF THE MAGI

One dollar and eighty-seven cents. That was all. And 60 cents of it was in pennies. Pennies saved one and two at a time by bulldozing the grocer and the vegetable man and the butcher until one's cheeks burned with the silent imputation of parsimony that such close dealing implied. Three times Della counted it. One dollar and eighty-seven cents. And the next day would be Christmas.

There was clearly nothing to do but flop down on the shabby little couch and howl. So Della did it. Which instigates the moral reflection that life is made up of sobs, sniffles, and smiles, with sniffles predominating.

While the mistress of the home is gradually subsiding from the first stage to the second take a look at the home. A furnished flat at $8 per week. It did not exactly beggar description, but it certainly had that word on the lookout for the mendicancy squad.

In the vestibule below belonged to this flat a letter-box into which no letter would go, and an electric button from which no mortal finger could coax a ring. Also appertaining thereunto was a card bearing the name "Mr. James Dillingham Young."

The "Dillingham" had been flung to the breeze during a former period of prosperity when its possessor was being paid $30 per week. Now, when the income was shrunk to $20, the letters of "Dillingham" looked blurred, as though they were thinking seriously of contracting to a modest and unassuming D. But whenever Mr. James Dillingham Young came home and reached his flat above he was called "Jim" and greatly hugged by Mrs. James Dillingham Young, already introduced to you as Della. Which is all very good.

Della finished her cry and attended to her cheeks with the powder rag. She stood by the window and looked out dully at a gray cat walking a gray fence in a gray backyard. Tomorrow would be Christmas Day, and she had only $1.87 with which to buy Jim a present. She had been saving every penny she could for months, with this result. Twenty dollars a week doesn't go far. Expenses had been greater than she had calculated. They always are. Only $1.87 to buy a present for Jim. Her Jim. Many a happy hour she had spent planning for something nice for him. Something fine and rare and sterling—something just a little bit near to being worthy of the honor of being owned by Jim.

There was a pier-glass between the windows of the room. Perhaps you have seen a pier-glass in an $8 flat. A very thin and agile person may, by observing his reflection in a rapid sequence of longitudinal strips, obtain a fairly accurate conception of his looks. Della, being slender, had mastered the art.

Suddenly she whirled from the window and stood before the glass. Her eyes were shining brilliantly, but her face had lost its color within twenty seconds. Rapidly she pulled down her hair and let it fall to its full length.

Now, there were two possessions of the James Dillingham Youngs in which they both took a mighty pride. One was Jim's gold watch that had been his father's and his grandfather's. The other was Della's hair. Had the Queen of Sheba lived in the flat across the airshaft Della would have let her hair hang out the window some day to dry and mocked at Her Majesty's jewels and gifts. Had King Solomon been the janitor, with all his treasures piled up in the basement, Jim would have pulled out his watch everytime he passed, just to see him pluck at his beard from envy.

So now Della's beautiful hair fell about her, rippling and shining like a cascade of brown waters. It reached below her knee and made itself almost a garment for her. And then she did it up again nervously and quickly. Once she faltered for a minute and stood still while a tear or two splashed on the worn red carpet.

On went her old brown jacket; on went her old brown hat. With a whirl of skirts and with the brilliant sparkle still in her eyes, she fluttered out the door and down the stairs to the street.

Where she stopped the sign read: "Mme. Sofronie. Hair Goods of All Kinds." One flight up Della ran, and collected herself, panting, before Madame, large, too white, chilly, and hardly looking the "Sofronie."

"Will you buy my hair?" asked Della.

"I buy hair," said Madame. "Take yer hat off and let's have a sight at the looks of it."

Down rippled the brown cascade.

"Twenty dollars," said Madame, lifting the mass with a practiced hand.

"Give it to me quick," said Della.

Oh, and the next two hours tripped by on rosy wings. Forget the hashed metaphor. She was ransacking the stores for Jim's present.

She found it at last. It surely had been made for Jim and no one else. There was none other like it in any of the stores, and she had turned all of them inside out. It was a platinum fob chain simple and chaste in design, properly proclaiming its value by substance alone and not by meretricious ornamentation—as all good things should do. It was even worthy of The Watch. As soon as she saw it she knew that it must be Jim's. It was like him. Quietness and value—the description applied to both. Twenty-one dollars they took from her for it, and she hurried home with the 87 cents. With that chain on his watch Jim might be properly anxious about the time in any company. Grand as the watch was, he sometimes looked at it on the sly on account of the old leather strap that he used in place of a chain.

When Della reached home her intoxication gave way a little to prudence and reason. She got out her curling irons and lighted the gas and went to work repairing the ravages made by generosity added to love. Which is always a tremendous task, dear friends—a mammoth task.

Within forty minutes her head was covered with tiny, close-lying curls that made her look wonderfully like a truant schoolboy. She looked at her reflection in the mirror long, carefully and critically.

"If Jim doesn't kill me," she said to herself, "before he takes a second look at me, he'll say I look like a Coney Island chorus girl. But what could I do—oh, what could I do with a dollar and eighty-seven cents!"

At 7 o'clock the coffee was made and the frying pan was on the back of the stove hot and ready to cook the chops.

Jim was never late. Della doubled the fob chain in her hand and sat on the corner of the table near the door that he always entered. Then she heard his step on the stair away down on the first flight, and she turned white for just a moment. She had a habit of saying little silent prayers about the simplest everyday things, and now she whispered: "Please, God, make him think I am still pretty."

The door opened and Jim stepped in and closed it. He looked thin and very serious. Poor fellow, he was only twenty-two—and to be burdened with a family! He needed a new overcoat and he was without gloves.

Jim stopped inside the door, as immovable as a setter at the scent of quail. His eyes were fixed upon Della, and there was an expression in them that she could not read, and it terrified her. It was not anger, nor surprise, nor disapproval, nor horror, nor any of the sentiments that she had been prepared for. He simply stared at her fixedly with that peculiar expression on his face.

Della wriggled off the table and went for him.

"Jim, darling," she cried, "don't look at me that way. I had my hair cut off and sold it because I couldn't have lived through Christmas without giving you a present. It'll grow again—you won't mind, will you? I just had to do it. My hair grows awfully fast. Say 'Merry Christmas!' Jim, and let's be happy. You don't know what a nice—what a beautiful, nice gift I've got for you."

"You've cut off your hair?" asked Jim, laboriously, as if he had not arrived at that patent fact yet even after the hardest mental labor.

"Cut it off and sold it," said Della. "Don't you like me just as well, anyhow? I'm me without my hair, ain't I?"

Jim looked about the room curiously.

"You say your hair is gone?" he said, with an air almost of idiocy.

"You needn't look for it," said Della. "It's sold, I tell you—sold and gone too. It's Christmas Eve, boy. Be good to me, for it went for you. Maybe the hairs of my head were numbered," she went on with a sudden serious sweetness, "but nobody could ever count my love for you. Shall I put the chops on, Jim?"

Out of his trance Jim seemed to quickly wake. He enfolded his Della. For ten seconds let us regard with discreet scrutiny some inconsequential object in the other direction. Eight dollars a week or a million a year—what is the difference? A mathematician or a wit would give you the wrong answer. The magi brought valuable gifts, but that was not among them. This dark assertion will be illuminated later on.

Jim drew a package from his overcoat pocket and threw it upon the table.

"Don't make any mistake, Dell," he said, "about me. I don't think there's anything in the way of a haircut or a shave or a shampoo that could make me like my girl any less. But if you'll unwrap that package you may see why you had me going awhile at first."

White fingers and nimble tore at the string and paper. And then an ecstatic scream of joy; and then alas! A quick feminine change to hysterical tears and wails, necessitating the immediate employment of all the comforting powers of the lord of the flat.

For there lay The Combs—the set of combs, side and back, that Della had worshipped for long in a Broadway window. Beautiful combs, pure tortoise shell, with jewelled rims—just the shade to wear in the beautiful vanished hair. They were expensive combs, she knew, and her heart had simply craved and yearned over them without the least hope of possession. And now, they were hers, but the tresses that should have adorned the coveted adornments were gone.

But she hugged them to her bosom, and at length she was able to look up with dim eyes and a smile and say: "My hair grows so fast, Jim!"

And then Della leaped up like a little singed cat and cried, "Oh, oh!"

Jim had not yet seen his beautiful present. She held it out to him eagerly upon her open palm. The dull, precious metal seemed to flash with a reflection of her bright and ardent spirit.

"Isn't it a dandy, Jim? I hunted all over town to find it. You'll have to look at the time a hundred times a day now. Give me your watch. I want to see how it looks on it."

Instead of obeying, Jim tumbled down on the couch and put his hands under the back of his head and smiled.

"Dell," said he, "let's put our Christmas presents away and keep 'em a while. They're too nice to use just at present. I sold the watch to get the money to buy your combs. And now suppose you put the chops on."

The magi, as you know, were wise men—wonderfully wise men—who brought gifts to the Babe in the manger. They invented the art of giving Christmas gifts. Being wise, their gifts were no doubt wise ones, possibly bearing the privilege of exchange in case of duplication. And here I have lamely related to you the uneventful chronicle of two foolish children in a flat who most unwisely sacrificed for each other the greatest treasures of their house. But in a last word to the wise of these days let it be said that of all who give gifts these two are of the wisest. Of all who give and receive gifts, such as they are wisest. Everywhere they are wisest. They are the magi.

O. HENRY

THE PERFECT LOVERS

Once upon a time, there was a young man who was looking for the perfect young woman to be his wife. One day he encountered a young woman who was looking for the perfect young man. They both turned on the charm and won each other over. They fell hopelessly in love.

The couple told their families and friends that they had each found the perfect spouse. The families and friends were skeptical. They knew that the man and woman were both nice young people, but they were far from perfect!

Nor did the couple listen to the priest who married them when he told them that God was the only perfect lover.

"You don't understand," they told him in a condescending tone of voice.

The couple got married, and by the time they returned home from their honeymoon they were sadly disillusioned. It turned out that neither of them was perfect, far from it. They knew then that the priest was right. Only God can satisfy the human heart completely. So they went to see the priest once again, to ask what they should do.

"If you try to become more gentle and patient and loving like God is, then you'll be more like God and therefore happier than you are now," he explained.

"That's hard to do," they replied.

"Who ever said love was easy?" asked the priest.

ANDREW M. GREELEY,
from *An Epidemic of Joy*

MOZART TO HIS WIFE, CONSTANZE

Mainz
October 17, 1790

PS.—While I was writing the last page, tear after tear fell on the paper. But I must cheer up—catch!—An astonishing number of kisses are flying about—The deuce!—I see a whole crowd of them! Ha! Ha! . . . I have just caught three—They are delicious!—You can still answer this letter, but you must address your reply to Linz, Poste Restante— That is the safest course. As I do not yet know for certain whether I shall go to Regensburg. I can't tell you anything definite. Just write on the cover that the letter is to be kept until called for. Adieu—Dearest, most beloved little wife—Take care of your health—and don't think of walking into town. Do write and tell me how you like our new quarters—Adieu. I kiss you millions of times.

CZAR NICHOLAS II TO THE CZARINA ALEXANDRA

[1915]

My Precious Darling,

My warm and loving thanks for your dear letter, full of tender words and for both telegrams. I too have you in my thoughts on this our 21st anniversary! I wish you health and all that a deeply loving heart can desire, and thank you on my knees for all your love, affection, friendship and patience, which you have shown me during these long years of our married life!

Today's weather reminds me of that day in Coburg—*how sad it is that we are not together!* Nobody knew that it was the day of our betrothal—it is strange how soon people forget—besides, it means nothing to them . . .

Before the evening I drove along the old road to the town of Slonin in the province of Grodno. It was extraordinarily warm and pleasant; and the smell of the pine forest—one feels enervated and softened!

Always your hubby,

Nicky

PLINY THE YOUNGER TO HIS WIFE, CALPURNIA

c. A.D. 100

You say that you are feeling my absence very much, and your only comfort when I am not there is to hold my writings in your hand and often put them in my place by your side. I like to think that you miss me and find relief in this sort of consolation. I, too, am always reading your letters, and returning to them again and again as if they were new to me—but this only fans the fire of my longing for you. If your letters are so dear to me, you can imagine how I delight in your company; do write as often as you can, although you give me pleasure mingled with pain.

ETERNAL ECHOES

To live in such a hospitable way brings many challenges. In marriage or with a life's partner, it demands trust and flexibility in the commitment. Many relationships die quietly soon after the initial commitment. They lose their passion and adventure. The relationship becomes an arrangement. This often happens because the couple renege on a plurality of other friendships as central to their lives. Even though you have one *anam cara*, one to whom you are committed, one who reaches you where no one else can or will, this person cannot become the absolute mirror for your life. To expect any one individual to satisfy your life-longing is a completely unjust demand. No one could live up to that expectation. The self is not singular. There are many selves within the one individual. Different gifts and different challenges come through your different friendships. To hold the borders of your commitment open allows you to give and receive from others without necessarily endangering the sacredness of your *anam-cara* bond. In fact it can enrich and deepen the primordial and permanent intimacy between you. To live with this porousness can at times lead to ambivalence but with discernment and integrity that need not become destructive.

JOHN O'DONOHUE

hen one or both marriage partners grow weary of the challenge to reach for a new plateau in their life together, reasons to fight or just withdraw abound. This bottoming out is a time of great sadness in a relationship. Other hurts, often never addressed, surface. Beds and hearts are empty.

THE FIGHT

Once upon a time, a husband and a wife had a big, big fight. None of their family or friends were quite sure what the fight was about since each time one or the other told the story it changed.

After a while, the couple began fighting about what the fight had been about and what the other person had said about the fight. Technically they were not talking to each other, but they talked enough to keep the fight going.

"Maybe I should get a divorce, if you're so fed up with me," the man said.

"Fine," said his wife, "only you take the kids!"

The couple's guardian angels had a summit conference and decided that something had to be done. They arranged for the husband's car to be bumped by a hit-and-run driver. The car was not badly damaged, but the husband had to spend two days in the hospital under observation.

Suddenly, the quarrel was quickly forgotten. "Sometimes I think

I'd be better off without you," the wife said, "but this has made me face the real prospect of being without you, and I realize I would not be better off."

"Me, too," agreed the husband.

So the couple fell in love all over again.

ANDREW M. GREELEY

Love does not dominate, it cultivates.

GOETHE

THE TWO PRINCESSES

In the city of Shawakis lived a prince, and he was loved by everyone, men and women and children. Even the animals of the field came unto him in greeting.

But all the people said that his wife, the princess, loved him not; nay, that she even hated him.

And upon a day the princess of a neighboring city came to visit the princess of Shawakis. And they sat and talked together, and their words led to their husbands.

And the princess of Shawakis said with passion, "I envy you your happiness with the prince, your husband, though you have been married these many years. I hate my husband. He belongs not to me alone, and I am indeed a woman most unhappy."

Then the visiting princess gazed at her and said, "My friend, the truth is that you love your husband. Aye, and you still have for him a passion unspent, and that is life in woman like unto Spring in a garden.

But pity me, and my husband, for we do but endure one another in silent patience. And yet you and others deem this happiness."

KAHLIL GIBRAN,
from *The Prophet*

The great tragedy of life is not that men perish, but that they cease to love.

W. SOMERSET MAUGHAM

MY BED IS EMPTY

My bed is empty
   My heart is empty
Return. Return.

from *In Praise of Japanese Love Poems*

Can there be a love that does not make demands on its object?

CONFUCIUS

*B*eginning *again is an upward turn in the spiral cycle of married love. Often the movement is slow. Hurts and misunderstandings may need time to be worked out. A spirit of cooperation, memories of good times, open and honest conversations, celebration of growth in love, a return to initial promises, and prayer all help to dissipate any lingering anger or hurt.*

Love grows cold without food and wine.

PROVERB

LATE OCTOBER

Carefully
the leaves of autumn
sprinkle down the tinny
sound of little dyings
and skies sated
of ruddy sunsets
of roseate dawns
roil ceaselessly in
cobweb greys and turn
to black
for comfort.

Only lovers
See the fall

a signal end to endings
a gruffish gesture alerting
those who will not be alarmed
that we begin to stop
in order simply to begin
again.

MAYA ANGELOU

Our hearts of stone are replaced with hearts of flesh.

EZEKIEL

STAVR GODINOVICH AND HIS CLEVER WIFE

{ *Russian* }

At the palace of the gentle Prince Vladimir in the capital city of Kiev a great banquet was in progress and all the princes, boyars, and bogatyrs were gathered together. As the day turned to evening and all had eaten and drunk their fill, the merriment of the feast increased and the guests began to make their boasts. Some boasted of their fame or their sturdy youth, others of their riches or their trusty steeds, but the brave warrior Stavr Godinovich sat at the oaken table and boasted of nothing.

"Well now, Stavr Godinovich," cried Prince Vladimir, perceiving his silence. "Why do you sit so woebegone and sad at my merry feast? Why do you hang your head? Have they given you a place unworthy of your rank, or have they passed you the cup out of turn?"

"Great Prince," replied Stavr Godinovich, "I am well content with my place at your table, and am in no way offended. But alas! I have nothing to boast about. I have no family and no father or mother, for I am an orphan. I have no great riches and have no trusty steed. I have only a fair young wife, who is as brave and skilful as an Amazon. How well does she wield the bow, for when she fits the arrow to the silken string and shoots, she never misses! Place a steel knife behind a golden ring and she will shoot her arrow through the ring and split it in two against the knife. And so enchantingly does my young wife play on the maplewood psaltery, and so cunningly does she play at chess, that all good people are amazed. In one hour she could confound all the Russian knights, and in one day she would defeat the great Sun, Prince Vladimir, himself."

This talk did not please the Prince of Kiev, and his face grew pale with anger.

"Ho there, my trusty servants!" he cried. "Seize this youth by his white hands, throw him into the deep dungeons, and give him but oats and water for food, that he may boast no more such idle boasts!"

The soldiers ran up and dragged Stavr Godinovich off to the deep dungeons, shut him behind great oaken doors, and closed them with great iron locks, and Stavr sat in the darkness engrossed in melancholy thoughts, and sorrowed greatly that he had offended the Prince with a careless boast. As he looked out of the tiny window of his cell, however, the fair sun shone in and melted his fears, and he began to sing a happy song. Just at this moment there chanced to pass by his window the beautiful maiden Zabava Putyatichna, the beloved niece of Prince Vladimir, and hearing the sound of singing, she approached the tiny window of the dungeon.

"Greetings brave and goodly youth," she said, thinking him to be a pagan prisoner. "From what country do you come, from what horde? Who are your father and mother?"

"Alas! Fair maiden," replied Stavr Godinovich, "I serve the great Prince Vladimir, and have done so truly and faithfully for nine whole years. And my wages are this dark dungeon, and oats and water my food."

"What is your name, brave youth?" asked Zabava Putyatichna.

"Stavr Godinovich is my name," he replied.

Hereupon the maiden left him, but when the golden sun had set and the white light of day turned to shadows, Zabava crept up to the narrow window and lowered food down on a rope that Stavr Godinovich might eat his fill.

In the meantime, Stavr's young wife, Katrina Ivanovna, sat alone in her marble chamber in her palace of white stone and ate and drank and was happy, for she knew nothing of her husband's sorry plight. As she opened her casement window, however, a large bird flew into the room, a black raven, and perched itself upon the sill.

"Why do you sit thus, young wife?" asked the bird in a human voice. "You eat and drink and make merry as though no misfortune had fallen upon you, and yet your husband, brave Stavr Godinovich, has been thrown in the dungeons of the palace of gentle Prince Vladimir of Kiev."

Katrina felt neither fear nor despair, but leaping to her sturdy legs, she said:

"Thank you, black raven, wise bird. I have now no time to stop and speak with you. If you have spoken true, you shall be my guest; but if you have spoken false, I shall cut off your head!"

And going down into the wide courtyard, she summoned her brave druzhina of thirty archers, thirty chess-masters, and thirty minstrels, and addressed them thus:

"Prepare yourselves for the road, my trusty druzhina, true and faithful servants, for we are going to Kiev, to the palace of gentle Prince Vladimir, to rescue my husband, Stavr Godinovich, from the dungeons."

And going to her stables, she led out her black steed, and harnessed it for the road. She placed upon its back the fine Circassian saddle with the silken girths and golden stirrups—not for the sake of beauty, but for strength—and tying the horse to the golden ring in the wooden post in the courtyard, she returned to her chamber, dressed herself in her husband's clothes, took leave of her old mother, and donned the armour of the Russian bogatyr. She took the strong bow and the well-tempered arrows; she took the club of steel and the long sharp lance. She carried a falcon on her left hand and a dove on her right hand, and mounting her trusty steed, she rode out into the open plain to join her druzhina, and all set out for Kiev.

When Katrina Ivanovna and her men came within three furlongs of the walls of Kiev, she bade her druzhina rest from the long journey, and riding herself into the city, she announced her presence to the great Prince Vladimir. Katrina walked into the great banqueting hall, and the rafters shook and the floorboards trembled, and all marvelled to see such a mighty warrior, for they took her by her manner and dress to be a man. She crossed herself, bowed low on all sides and to Prince Vladimir, and addressed the great prince thus:

"Prince of Kiev," she said, "I am the Ambassador from the land of Greece, from its King, the dog Kalina. I have been sent to you to exact tribute for my King, and if you refuse to pay, we will wage a wicked war against you, for not far off in the open plain stands my army of forty thousand men!"

The sturdy legs of Prince Vladimir shook, his bright eyes clouded over, his sweet lips trembled, and he could not find words to answer.

"Prince Vladimir," said the Ambassador, "I can wait no longer. Give me your answer!"

"Give me time, terrible Ambassador," pleaded the Prince. "Grant me three days and three nights to reflect."

"We have travelled far and are weary," answered the Ambassador. "Time is precious. If you cannot pay the tribute, give me your beloved niece Zabava Putyatichna to be my wife!"

"My niece Zabava is of marriageable age," replied Prince Vladimir, "but I cannot give her to be your bride without her consent. Grant me at least one day and one night to reflect!"

"So be it!" said the Ambassador, and promising to return on the morrow, she bowed, took her leave of the Prince and returned to her brave druzhina in the open plain.

Prince Vladimir went sadly to his beloved niece Zabava with the Princess Apraksia and found her sitting at her window gazing across the open plain at the retreating Ambassador. She watched him as he walked happily back to his camp, throwing his long spear up to the clouds and catching it as it fell.

"Beloved niece Zabava," said Prince Vladimir, "save us from our dilemma. A terrible Ambassador has come from the King of Greece, the dog Kalina, and exacts much tribute from our land. If I cannot pay it quickly—and I fear I cannot pay it at all—the Ambassador has resolved to take you to be his wife, and we shall never feast or make merry again!"

"Dear uncle," said Zabava Putyatichna, "I am obedient to you in all things, and I do not refuse to take a husband. But I beg you not to make yourself the laughing-stock of all Kiev and all Chernigov too. Do not give me a woman for my husband, for your terrible Ambassador of Greece is not a man but a woman!"

"Zabava Putyatichna," said Prince Vladimir, "look out of your window and watch the Greek Ambassador as he returns to his army of forty thousand men. He shoots arrows from his stout bow, tosses his spear high in the air, and catches the swift falcon in its flight. Is *that* a woman?"

"Dear uncle, Prince Vladimir!" replied Zabava. "Can you not see that the Ambassador purrs and lisps with a woman's voice, sidles along with a woman's mincing gait, and has the white and dainty fingers of a woman that still bear the marks of golden rings? Are these signs not enough? The Ambassador of Greece is a woman!"

"You may be right," said the Prince. "But what am I to do to see if he be male or female?"

"The Ambassador is a woman and full of woman's wiles," replied Zabava. "Ask the Ambassador for yet another day to reflect and then test his skill at all the manly arts. Then you shall soon see whether he be man or woman."

But when Prince Vladimir asked the Ambassador for more time, the latter grew very angry.

"Tell me here and now whether we shall receive the tribute money," she cried, "for that is the reason we came to Kiev. If you cannot pay it, give me your fair niece Zabava to be my bride!"

"Do not be angry, Ambassador," said Vladimir, who had no hope of paying the tribute and no wish to give his niece to a Greek. "Sit at the oaken table with me and we will play the maplewood gusly together."

"I have my minstrels with me in my white tents," said Katrina Ivanovna, "but they are weary of the journey and rest in the open plain. In my childhood, however, I played the gusly myself."

And taking her maplewood gusly, Katrina plucked softly at the strings and began to sing. And she sang a song of Kiev and a song of Jerusalem, and Prince Vladimir was amazed at her skill.

"Zabava Putyatichna," said the Prince to his niece, "not only is the Ambassador a man, but we have none better in the whole of Holy Russia. My minstrels are the best in the land, but none can play the gusly as well as he."

"The Ambassador *is* a woman," cried Zabava. "Do not marry me to a woman! Find out more about the terrible Ambassador of Greece."

"Welcome guest, terrible Ambassador," said Prince Vladimir, "let us play a game of chess."

"I have my chess-masters in my white tent," replied Katrina, "but they are weary from the long journey. In my childhood, however, I used to play chess myself."

And Vladimir and the Ambassador sat at the oaken table to play a game of chess. The Prince made one move, and was checked. He made another and was checked again, and Katrina easily outplayed the great Prince Vladimir.

"Zabava Putyatichna," said Vladimir, "marry this man. I can no longer put the Ambassador to the test."

"Take the guest into the open plains, uncle," said Zabava, now in despair, "and invite him to show his skill at archery. Then you shall surely see that he is a woman."

"Let us go into the open fields and try our skill at archery, Ambassador," said Vladimir.

"I have my archers," replied Katrina Ivanovna, "but they are weary from their long journey. But I myself used in my childhood to wield the bow."

And going into the open fields they set up a golden ring in the ground and placed a steel knife behind it. Then Vladimir shot one arrow and missed; he shot a second arrow and missed again; and he shot a third time, but still he could not hit the target. Then Katrina bent her stout bow, drew taut the silken string, and shot her well-tempered arrow at the ring. The arrow hissed like a snake, and flying through the golden ring it cut itself in two equal halves against the edge of the knife.

"Well, Fair Sun Vladimir, Prince of Kiev," said the Ambassador. "Are we longer to waste our time thus? Is it not time to settle our business? Pay me the tribute you owe my King, the dog Kalina, and we will depart in peace or give me your fair niece Zabava to be my bride."

"Alas, terrible Ambassador," replied Vladimir, "I cannot pay the tribute."

"Then give me Zabava Putyatichna to be my bride," said the Ambassador, "for we can wait no longer."

Prince Vladimir went sadly to his beloved niece.

"Alas, Zabava," he said. "If you will not marry willingly, I must marry you against your will."

"If I live, I shall not marry a woman!" cried Zabava. "We should be the laughing-stock of all Russia. The Ambassador plays the gusly, plays chess, and wields the bow like any man, but he talks, walks, and sits like what he is, a woman!"

"Ho there, servants!" cried Vladimir in a loud voice. "Dress my niece in flowery dresses, put a golden crown upon her head and golden rings upon her fingers, and take her to the cathedral, for she shall marry the terrible Ambassador of Greece! The whole town of Kiev shall not suffer for the sake of one maiden!"

And to the Ambassador, he said:

"Your bride is prepared and waits for you at the church."

"Wait, Fair Sun Prince Vladimir of Kiev," said Katrina Ivanovna. "Before they place the marriage crowns upon our heads, let us ride out together and pit our manly strength one against the other."

"Dear guest, terrible Ambassador!" Cried Prince Vladimir. "Neither I nor any of my bogatyrs is any match for you!"

"Are there none in your dungeons you could spare?" asked the Ambassador, and Vladimir remembered Stavr Godinovich.

"If I release Stavr Godinovich," he thought, "I need not see him, but if I do not, I shall anger the Ambassador."

And aloud he cried:

"Ho there, servants! Take these golden keys and open up the deep dungeons, and let out all the strong young men!"

His servants obeyed the Prince's command and led Stavr out in the wide courtyard, took off his convict's garb, dressed him in knight's armour, set him on a good horse, and sent him to do battle with the terrible Ambassador of Greece. And galloping together into the open plain until the dust hid their horses from view, Katrina and Stavr sported together, leapt from horse to horse, threw their steel clubs into the air and caught them as they fell. Then, returning with Stavr Godinovich, the terrible "Ambassador of Greece," bowed low before the great Prince Vladimir, and casting off her knight's armour, revealed her woman's dress beneath and let down her long hair.

"Great Prince Vladimir, Fair Sun," laughed Katrina Ivanovna, "bring my bride, Zabava Putyatichna, back from the cathedral and return her to the women's quarters for I would not make a mockery of the girl. Never yet has it been seen or heard that a girl was married off to a woman as you, great Prince, would have done. I have rescued my beloved husband from your deep dungeons, Prince Vladimir, and now, farewell!"

And laughing and sporting together, Stavr Godinovich and his clever wife Katrina Ivanovna rode away, and Prince Vladimir saw to his sorrow and confusion that his trusty knight had made no empty boast.

from *Russian Tales and Legends*

HOLY COMMUNION

Once upon a time, a husband and a wife were having a lot of conflict with each other. They fought over money, they fought over the time they spent with their family, they fought over where they would go on their vacations, they fought over their children, and, of course, they fought over what the fights were about.

Of course, at one time the man and woman had been deeply in love. In fact, they thought that they were still in love. It's just that the conflicts had filled up the time that used to be devoted to love.

One night, however, the man suggested that they get a baby-sitter and go out for dinner. The woman said they didn't have time for that anymore, but the man insisted. The meal turned out to be wonderful, and the couple relaxed and had a good time and great conversation and began to realize how silly their quarrels had become and how easy it would be to avoid them.

"You know," the wife said on the way home, "it was almost as though God were with us while we were eating, guiding us to see how foolish we've been."

"Maybe God was," her husband replied.

Maybe it's not just in church that Jesus is present among us.

ANDREW M. GREELEY

WHY GOD MADE STRAWBERRIES

(A Seanachie's tale told at a wedding dinner)

Once upon a time, long, long ago, so long, to tell the truth, that it was the beginning of everything, First Man and First Woman lived in a snug little cottage in a neat little green field at the edge of a silver lake and they raised their own food and made their own Guinness and they were very happy together. Earth Maker was very happy with them because She thought they were a very successful experiment. She visited them occasionally and praised them for their hard work and their affection for one another.

You see, they did love one another a lot. They almost never had even a minor quarrel and when they did have a little spat didn't they get over it right away?

But finally one day, they had a huge fight, though I'm not sure what it was about. Then they fought about who started the fight and what the fight was about and they grew more and more angry.

Finally, First Woman storms out of the cottage. "You're nothing but a crude, flannel-mouth braggart," says she. "I don't know why I put up with all your talk for so long, but I don't want to hear another word out of you ever again."

So out she goes, across the green field and by the silver lake and over the hill and out beyond.

"Well," says First Man, "at last she's gone and thank heaven for that. We'll finally have some peace and quiet around here. And that'll be a good thing altogether. I won't miss her, at all, at all."

So he lights his pipe and sits back in his chair and begins to rock back and forth. Then he realizes that the fire has gone out. Try as he might he can't get it going because the woman was so much better at starting the fire, if you take me meaning.

So finally he gives up and shouts, "I want me tea."

Only First Woman isn't there, so he has to make himself his own tea. Now I hate to admit it in public like this but your man was a terrible male chauvinist. He couldn't even boil water. It took him awhile to realize that without a fire you couldn't boil water and without boiling water you couldn't make tea.

So he ate a half of a cold praty, the only food left in the cottage. It wasn't much and he was terrible hungry all together.

"Well," says he, "I'd better go to bed early and get a good, quiet night's sleep. I'll dig up some more praties tomorrow."

But it took him a long time to fall asleep, he was shivering so bad. "Well," says he, "the woman at least kept the bed warm at night."

Doesn't he wake up the next morning, groggy, cold, and unhappy. "I want me tea," he says, but not with much hope because he remembers what happened yesterday. Sure, how can he forget, himself still shaking with the cold.

So he eats the other half of the cold praty and sits in his rocking chair, chewing on his cold pipe, and thinking that life was pretty much not worth living.

Then who do you think comes into the cottage? No, not the woman, she's still furious. 'Tis Earth Maker Herself.

"Now let me see," She says, "this is the blue planet, didn't I create yuz male and female here? How come ther's only one of yuz here? Let me see, sure, you're the man all right. Where's herself?"

"Gone, your rivirince," says First Man. "Gone altogether."

"She never left you!!" says Earth Maker.

"She did, your rivirince. She said she'd never come back."

"She never did!! . . . Don't tell me you had a fight?"

"We did."

"About what?"

"We couldn't remember. So we fought about that too."

"You never did!"

"We did."

"Do you miss her?"

"Something terrible," says First Man, the tears flowing down his cheeks. "I love her more than anything else in world."

"Well up and after her, eejid! What are you waiting for?"

"It will do no good, she's had such a long head start I'll never catch up to her."

"Hmm . . . this will take some improvising, but I'm the Great Improviser, aren't I? I tell you what, you get out of this cottage and go after her and I'll go ahead of you with the speed of thought and slow her down."

So First Man jumps out of his chair and rushes out the door, across the green field and by the silver lake and over the hill and out beyond.

"Well," says Earth Maker to Herself, "he really loves her all right, the poor amadon."

So Earth Maker catches up with First Woman. She's still going down the road like a bat out of Purgatory.

"Still mad," says Earth Maker. "Let's see if I can slow her down."

So Earth Maker goes "Zap" and creates a huge forest to slow her down. Doesn't herself go through it like a knife through soft butter?

Then She goes "Zap" again and creates a broad and swift river.

Doesn't herself dive into that river, clothes and all, and swim across it, Australian crawl at that.

"Maybe I made a mistake in deciding that the woman ought to be an athlete, but what's done is done. She must be hungry now. I'll slow her down with fruit trees."

So She goes "Zap" again and lines the road with peach trees and plum trees and pear trees and apricot trees (no apple trees because that is from a different creation story).

What does the woman do? Doesn't she pick the fruit on the fly and keep right on putting more distance between herself and the cottage back in the green field by the silver lake?

"Well now," says Herself. "It looks like I'll have to use me ultimate weapon. I'll have to create strawberries, like I've been planning to do all along."

So this time She makes a very loud ZAP!

A bunch of bushes with lovely white flowers spring up, and across the road itself this time.

Who built the road you want to know? Maybe the little fellas in the flying saucers and don't distract me with your foolish questions.

"Aren't they lovely flowers now?" says First Woman.

As she's watching the flowers turn into beautiful red fruit.

"Sure, aren't they shaped just like the human heart."

She feels one of the strawberries.

"And don't they feel just like the human heart, soft and yet firm!"

So she picks one of the strawberries and bites into it.

"Glory be, are they the sweetest things in all the world, save for the sweetness of human love."

Earth Maker knows She's won.

"Speaking of love, I suppose I should wait here for the poor amadon who's out on the road trying to catch up with me. I'll pick him some of these strawberry things and feed him when he comes along, so he'll know how much I missed him."

So she picks a whole lot of strawberries and fills her apron with them. Then doesn't she sit at the side of the road, arrange her hair, and wait for himself to catch up.

How does she know the fruit was called a strawberry? Don't distract me with your silly questions.

So eventually, exhausted and sweating, doesn't First Man finally appear on the road.

"Tis yourself," says she.

"Tis," says he.

"Look at what I've found. They're called strawberries."

"Sure, aren't they shaped just like the human heart."

He feels one of the strawberries.

"And don't they feel just like the human heart, soft and yet firm!"

So she puts one of the strawberries into his mouth, just like a priest giving out Holy Communion.

Naturally he bites into it.

"Glory be, aren't they the sweetest things in all the world, save for the sweetness of human love."

So they ate a lot of strawberries and picked more of them. Then with their arms around one another they walk home together.

So much in love is herself that she doesn't notice that the river and the forest are gone.

And 'tis said that they lived happily ever after. Not that they didn't fight anymore but that they learned how much fun it is to reconcile after a fight.

Now I want the bride and the groom here today and all the rest of yuz to remember this story every time from now on when you taste the sweetness of strawberries. And when you remember the story, ask yourselves whether you should be waiting for someone or trying to catch up with someone.

And never forget that the only thing in God's creation sweeter than the taste of strawberries is the taste of human love.

I've told you me story and I'll tell you no more.

(This is an adaptation of a Cherokee
story told by Gail Ross,
herself a Cherokee princess!)
ADAPTED BY ANDREW M. GREELEY

There is but one genuine love-potion—consideration.

MENANDER

OUR LOVE HATH NO DECAY

All other things, to their destruction draw,
Only our love hath no decay;
This, no to-morrow hath, nor yesterday,
Running it never runs from us away,
But truly keeps his first, last, everlasting day.

JOHN DONNE,
from "The Anniversary"

THE OTTER

When you plunged
The light of Tuscany wavered
And swung through the pool
From top to bottom.

I loved your wet head and smashing crawl,
Your fine swimmer's back and shoulders
Surfacing and surfacing again
This year and every year since.

I sat dry-throated on the warm stones.
You were beyond me.
The mellowed clarities, the grape-deep air
Thinned and disappointed.

Thank God for the slow loadening
When I hold you now
We are close and deep
As the atmosphere on water.

My two hands are plumbed water.
You are my palpable, lithe
Otter of memory
In the pool of the moment,

Turning to swim on your back,
Each silent, thigh shaking kick
Retilting the light,
Heaving the cool at your neck.

SEAMUS HEANEY

Father, all-powerful and ever-living God,
we do well always and everywhere to give you thanks.
You created humans in love to share your divine life.
We see humankind's high destiny in the love of husband and wife,
which bears the imprint of your own divine love.
Love is our origin,
love is our constant calling,
love is our fulfillment in heaven.
The love of man and woman
is made holy in the sacrament of marriage,
and becomes the mirror of your everlasting love.

from the Preface of the Nuptial Mass

CHAPTER FOUR

Family Love

In a certain sense we become our fathers when, through a good disposition of soul, we shall have formed and engendered ourselves and have brought ourselves to light.
GREGORY OF NYSSA

Perfect love sometimes does not come until the first grandchild.
WELSH PROVERB

When I stopped seeing my mother with the eyes of a child, I saw the woman who had helped me give birth to myself.
ANONYMOUS

The first time it happens, we are surprised. Usually it's when we're in our early young adult years. We look around, wondering, "Was it I that said that?" Followed very quickly by, "I sound just like my mother (or my father)!" This is often our first realization of the immense influence our family of origin has on our adult life. Nowhere is this influence more apparent than in our experiences of love, both giving love and receiving it.

Our surprise reaction is not necessarily a sign of disrespect for a parent. During these young adult years we have little reason to pay attention to how family affects our behavior. Later, when we find ourselves repeatedly doing things our parents did, we more readily admit some similarities between our behavior and theirs.

Not until much later will we begin to notice that not only do we sound like our parents, but we also tend to repeat their pattern of relationships. The saying, "We marry our mother or our father," is not as far-fetched as it might seem. The experience of an adult child of an alcoholic marrying an alcoholic is an example of how family behavior passes from one generation to the next.

Family is the birthplace and nurturing place of love. We are born into a family. From the moment of birth, if not even before, we are emotionally influenced by our family situation. We first experience love or the lack thereof from our parents. Even though the word "love" might never be used, or at times used but accompanied by behavior that belies its presence, we pick up intimations of love at a very early age. Some of these experiences of love encourage us to risk love ourselves. Other experiences, not as pleasant from our view, make us leery of love.

Maturity comes when we are able to let go of a childish desire for perfect parents. When we give up our longing for this nonachievable goal, we are free to understand what makes them who they are. We come to appreciate whatever degree of love they have achieved. We have the opportunity to examine how we repeat patterns from their lives that hinder good relationships. We are free to love.

Perhaps one of the greatest shocks to our fragile psyches occurs at an early age when we realize we have to share love with others. We are not the complete focus of our parents' attention. Not only must we share them with each other, in many cases we must share them with siblings. Sibling rivalry begins early on and can create problems even into old age. Some of us take our sibling problems with us into other peer relationships to the detriment of friendships and career.

At the same time, sibling support often surprises us. Like a rush of grace, it changes our perceptions. We see each other through new eyes. We look for new ways to understand each other, for ways to express our delight in this special relationship. We begin to love.

Armed with love, we are open to diverse ways of passing this love on to the next generation. Love multiplies.

The selections in this chapter look at the spirit of love through the eyes of three generations—children, parents, and grandparents. The images in the stories and poems from various cultures and over many millennia remind us of the universal importance of family relationships for those who want to have love.

*H*uman children need an extended period of adult care so they may acquire the knowledge and skills that will allow them to survive on their own. Among the most essential skills a child must learn is how to give and receive love. Children learn to love when they are loved, when they grow up in an environment of love.

1950s ADVICE TO A NEW FATHER

The best gift you can give to your child is to love his mother.

MILLENNIUM ADVICE TO NEW PARENTS

The best gift you can give to your child is to love each other.

THE STRAWBERRY GARDEN

(Inspired by "Why God Made Strawberries")

Once about a time, First Man and First Woman took some strawberry plants from that magic strawberry patch where they learned that "the only thing . . . sweeter than the taste of strawberries is the taste of human love." They wanted a garden to remind them that if it had not been for the strawberries, they might have forgotten how wonderful love is. They put a stone wall around the garden to keep the animals that roamed freely in the area from eating the plants. This Strawberry Garden was their very special place.

Earthmaker was pleased that First Man and First Woman now understood how fragile love could be. Still, the more Earthmaker thought about it, the more She wondered if She were partially at fault for that first quarrel. Since they were less than gods, maybe Earth People always would have trouble knowing that love, like a strawberry garden, must be cultivated and grow or it will die.

Perhaps, Earthmaker thought, these people I created need other people to help them learn about love. So in due time, after First Man and First Woman knew each other in their Strawberry Garden, First Woman gave birth to twins, First Boy and First Girl.

Until this time, First Man and First Woman had only seen blurry images of themselves in lakes and ponds and rivers. Now when the First Woman looked at First Daughter, she saw a face that was the image of the First Man and she immediately fell in love with her daughter. When First Man saw his wife's image in First Son, he too was moved with love. Each said to the other, "See, what we have created, this baby looks just like you." Now they had a sense of their own image.

Time passed and more children were born, all the "spitting images" of their parents. Sometimes a son would resemble his father and a daughter her mother and other times the reverse would be true. From time to time, after the children were bedded down for the night, Earthmaker would drop in for a spot of tea with First Man and First Woman. She was pleased with what She saw. As time went on, Her visits were less frequent. Finally, they stopped altogether. Earthmaker thought they had no more need for Her intervention.

On many warm evenings, First Man and First Woman would visit the Strawberry Garden and remember why strawberries had helped renew their love. Unfortunately, as the children grew, First Man and First Woman were so busy they had little time to visit their garden. At the same time, the children wondered among themselves about this mysterious place behind the stone wall that was off-limits to them.

One evening, the First Parents discovered their children quarreling. The children were fighting over which one was the favorite of each of their parents and which one would be the first to visit the Strawberry Garden. The First Parents were dismayed. How could this happen? What should they do? Where was Earthmaker when they needed Her?

Earthmaker saw their dismay and longed to help them teach their children about love. She also knew that this was not the time to step in. If these Earth Children were to know the story of love, those who have experienced the story must tell it to them.

For over a week, First Man and First Woman fretted over this problem, each secretly thinking that the other was at fault for what was happening. Earthmaker worried even more. She loved these people and wanted to help them; but She knew She couldn't intervene directly.

Finally, Earthmaker had a brilliant idea. That night when First Man and First Woman went to sleep, She had them dream about their discovery of strawberries. She hoped the reminder of that time might spark an idea of how to end the family crisis.

The next morning both First Man and First Woman woke up with a vague memory of their dream. After breakfast, at which the First Children pouted and fretted over the littlest difficulty, First Man and First Woman went their separate ways. They headed for the garden, unaware of the other's destination. When they met, each reached for a strawberry to give to the other.

First Woman said, "I think we need to have a special dessert at our evening meal tonight and tell our children the Strawberry Story." First Man and First Woman harvested a feast's worth of strawberries and headed home. At dinner that evening, they gave each child two strawberries. They told them to eat one strawberry and look at the other.

The children loved the sweet taste of the strawberries. They asked why they had not tasted these before. First Man asked the children to hold up the other strawberry and say what it looked like. First Girl and First Boy said it looked like the hearts they had seen in some of the animals that gave them food. The other children agreed.

Then First Woman told their children about the times when Earthmaker visited them and how She used strawberries to tell them about the wonder of human love. The children, now sheepish about their quarreling, thought it was a wonderful story. Then everybody had a big bowl of strawberries and cream.

Later that evening, and for the last time, Earthmaker paid a brief visit to First Man and First Woman and their children. She congratulated them on how well they had handled the crisis. She then told them that the strawberry was Her sign that there would always be enough love for everyone. However, She could not force people to love. Now that they had the Strawberry Story, it was up to them to pass it on.

The next day, Earth Man and Earth Woman and Earth Children worked together to dismantle the wall hiding the strawberry garden.

MARY G. DURKIN

CHILDREN

And a woman who held a babe against her
bosom said, Speak to us of Children.
And he said:
Your children are not your children.
They are the sons and daughters of Life's longing for itself.
They come through you but not from you,
And though they are with you, yet they belong not to you.
You may give them your love but not your thoughts.
For they have their own thoughts.
You may house their bodies but not their souls,
For their souls dwell in the house of tomorrow,
which you cannot visit, not even in your dreams.
You may strive to be like them,
but seek not to make them like you.

For life goes not backward nor tarries with yesterday.
You are the bows from which your children as living arrows are sent forth.
The archer sees the mark upon the path of the infinite,
and He bends you with His might that His
arrows may go swift and far.
Let your bending in the archer's hand be for gladness;
For even as He loves the arrow that flies,
so He loves also the bow that is stable.

KHALIL GIBRAN,
The Prophet

JESUS AND THE LITTLE CHILDREN

So Jesus called a child to come and stand in front of them, and said, "I assure you that unless you change and become like children, you will never enter the Kingdom of heaven. The greatest in the Kingdom of heaven is the one who humbles himself and becomes like this child. And whoever welcomes in my name one such child as this, welcomes me.

"If anyone should cause one of these little ones to lose his faith in me, it would be better for that person to have a large millstone tied around his neck and be drowned in the deep sea . . .

"See that you don't despise any of these little ones, their angels in heaven, I tell you, are always in the presence of my Father in heaven."

MATTHEW *18:2–6; 10*

An Irish song speaks of a mother's love as a blessing. The way a mother gives her love and what she expects in return profoundly influences the child. Never underestimate the effect a mother's love has on a child, even when that child becomes an adult.

TO HAVE OR NOT TO HAVE

Once there was a young woman who was eager to have a baby. One of her friends (to test her) asked, "Why are you and your husband so set on having children? You know that their lives will be filled with suffering and disappointment. You know that they will cause you heartache and pain. You know there will be times when they will hate you and other times that you will be very angry at them. You know there will be terrible pain often in their lives. You know that someday you will die and they will suffer your loss. You know that they will die too, perhaps horribly, perhaps even before you. It doesn't make any sense at all to have children, does it?"

The future mother replied, "Even if everything goes badly eventually, it is better to have a chance to live, to love, to give, to receive, to believe. When our children come, I will tell them how precious life is and how much they should take from it—which means how much they must also give to it. Above all, I will tell them that it is necessary to hope for their children, just as I hoped for them."

"Hope that they will not suffer and die?" the friend asked.

"No, hope that they will live with enthusiasm and love," the woman replied. "If they live that way, love never ends."

"You have spoken well," her friend said.

ANDREW M. GREELEY,
from *An Epidemic of Joy*

You study not only that you become a mother when your child is born, but also that you become a child.

DOGEN

GOLD AND LOVE FOR DEARIE

Out on the mountain over the town,
    All night long, all night long,
The trolls go up and the trolls go down,
    Bearing their packs and singing a song
And this is the song the hill-folk croon,
As they trudge in the light of the misty moon—
This is ever their dolorous tune:
"Gold, gold! ever more gold—
Bright red gold for dearie!"

Deep in the hill a father delves
    All night long, all night long;
None but the peering, furtive elves
    Sees his toil and hears his song
Merrily ever the cavern rings
As merrily as ever his pick he swings,
And merrily ever this song he sings:
"Gold, gold! ever more gold—
    Bright red gold for dearie!"

Mother is rocking thy lowly bed
    All night long, all night long,
Happy to smooth thy curly head,
    To hold thy hand and to sing *her* song:
'Tis not of the hill-folk dwarfed and old,
Nor the song of thy father, stanch and bold,
And the burthen it beareth is not of gold:
But it's "Love, love! nothing but love—
Mother's love for dearie!"

EUGENE FIELD

THE ANGELS WHISPER

    A baby was sleeping,
      Its mother was weeping,
For her husband was far on the wild raging sea;
    And the tempest was swelling
      Round the fisherman's dwelling,
And she cried, "Dermot, darling, oh! come back to me."

    Her beads while she number'd,
      The baby still slumber'd,
And smiled in her face as she bended her knee;
    "Oh blest be that warning,
      My child's sleep adorning,
For I know that the angels are whispering with thee.

    "And while they are keeping
Bright watch o'er thy sleeping,
Oh, pray to them softly, my baby, with me
    And say thou wouldst rather
      They'd watch o'er thy father!
For I know that the angels are whispering with thee."

The dawn of the morning
    Saw Dermot returning.
And the wife wept with joy her babe's father to see;
    And closely caressing
    Her child, with a blessing,
Said, "I knew that the angels. were whispering with thee."

SAMUEL LOVER

WHEN MOTHER READS ALOUD

"When mother reads aloud the past
Seems real as every day;
I hear the tramp of armies vast,
I see the spears and lances cast,
I join the thrilling fray;
Brave knights and ladies fair and proud
I meet when mother reads aloud.

"When mother reads aloud, far lands
Seem very near and true;
I cross the desert's gleaming sands,
Or hunt the jungle's prowling bands,
Or sail the ocean blue;
Far heights, whose peaks the cold mists shroud,
I scale, when mother reads aloud.

"When mother reads aloud I long
For noble deeds to do—
To help the right, redress the wrong,
It seems so easy to be strong, so simple to be true,
O, thick and fast the visions crowd
When mother reads aloud."

ANONYMOUS

Give a little love to a child and you get a great deal back.

R. JOHN RUSKIN

THE TERRIBLE TWINS

Once upon a time, there was a mother who had twins when her next oldest was a senior in high school. The woman was surprised but happy for she loved all her children.

The twins were so cute and so lively that she figured they'd keep her young. Alas for her, as they grew up the twins were monsters! They fought with each other; they fought with other children. They lied; they stole; they broke things deliberately. Whenever the two of them outnumbered another child, they beat up on that child and then told their mother that the other kid had started the fight. They never studied in school. They tormented all their teachers. They were mean and nasty to their parents and to every other adult they encountered, including their older brothers and sisters. The twins started drinking in sixth grade and were smoking pot in eighth grade.

The mother did her best, but she simply could not control her two adorable but vicious little hellions. Neither could anyone else.

The summer they were fourteen, they stole their mother's car and totaled it. They ended up in the hospital where they made life miserable for the nurses and the doctors. The parish priest even suggested to the mother that she send them off to boarding school. (He thought they should go to a place that had barbed wire and cut glass on the tops of the walls.)

"No," the mother said, "I would miss them too much if they weren't home with the rest of us. I'm their mother, and I love them." And that's exactly the way it is with God and us.

ANDREW M. GREELEY,
from *An Epidemic of Joy*

THE BLIND CHILD

They tell me, Father, that tonight
You wed another bride,
That you will clasp her in your arms
Where my dear mother died.

They say her name is Mary, too,
The name my mother bore,
But Father, is she kind and true
Like the one you loved before?

And is her step so soft and light,
Her voice so meek and mild;
And Father, do you think she'll love
Your blind and helpless child?

Please, Father, do not bid me come
To meet your newly wed bride,
For I could not meet her in the room
Where my dear mother died.

Her picture's hanging on the wall,
Her books are lying near,
And there's the harp her fingers touched,
And there's her vacant chair.

The chair where by her side I knelt
To say my evening prayer.

from *Storytellers:*
Folktales & Legends from the South

Children begin by loving their parents;
As they grow older they judge them;
Sometimes they forgive them.

OSCAR WILDE

I'M TASTING ROMANO . . .

I'm tasting a bite of this Pecorino Romano that I bought at Sam's Wine and Cheese warehouse.

It's waxy, hard and a little peppery. Salty too. It's so pungent, it's carving holes in my tongue—small sandy pellets of residue. It's the first time I've tasted real Romano cheese, not the dry, gritty, Kraft-green-shaker-parmesan-romano-in-the-can variety. No, this is real cheese—to be served with real tomatoes. August tomatoes from my garden, not the tomatoes you buy in February that are gassed with some ethylene in a railroad car riding through South Dakota somewhere so they turn pink, but they're hard and woody when you cut them for your salad.

But the waxy and peppery part of the cheese is reminding me of the first time I saw someone die. Maybe everything from now on will remind me of dying. Even cheese.

But, all I can remember is the waxy face of my mother, lying in a simple bed, dying at home, like she wanted, not in some anonymous hospital room. She wore some awful flowered T-shirt, it was August 20th. Plenty hot. The family was there, all six of us standing around her bed, the window air conditioner that lacked freon blew out warm humid air.

My mother was breathing like a baby with a bad cold. I wanted to syringe out her lungs. I wanted to take her and cradle her in my arms, daughter as mother. I sat there helpless, watching the rise and fall of her chest and heard the sound of her lungs—the death rattle.

My four sisters sat around the bed and talked about everything else in the world, denying the obvious—as if she wasn't dying, as if she was a baby lying there and would soon wake up from her nap.

Their talking was the pepper. Too much pepper.

I was watching her. Gently touching the cool, waxy skin of my mother whose soul had already begun to leave her body, I was breathing, breathing double time, breathing for her, breathing for me. I knew I would not see the blue of my mother's eyes ever again. I knew the breathing would stop sometime.

About 10 minutes before she died, she opened her eyes briefly, scanned the room from left to right, as if to notice who was there and to say a wordless good bye. I remember her eyes were cloudy blue, like an overcast day. And then she closed them for the last time.

The life force is a powerful thing. She continued to take her last breath even though most of the liveliness was gone from her. Her last breath was a big sigh. A little inhale, a long exhale. My father announced softly, "That's it."

All I know is there is a sacred mystery to witnessing a death, especially my mother's. It is a historic moment in her life and in mine. I will never be the same.

LYNN STAUDACHER,
Written one week after her mother died.
Her date of death was August 20, 1998,
at 10:23 P.M.

FATHER'S LETTER

I'm going to write a letter to our oldest boy who went
Out West last spring to practice law and run for president;
I'll tell him all the gossip I guess he'd like to hear,
For he hasn't seen the home-folks for going on a year!
Most generally it's Marthy does the writing, but as she
Is suffering with a felon, why, the job devolves on me—
So, when the supper things are done and put away to-night,
I'll draw my boots and shed my coat and settle down to write.

I'll tell him crops are looking up, with prospects big for corn,
That, fooling with the barnyard gate, the off-ox hurt his horn;
That the Templar lodge is doing well—Tim Bennett joined last week
When the prohibition candidate for Congress came to speak;
That the old gray woodchuck's living still down in the pasture-lot,
A-wondering what's become of little William, like as not!
Oh, yes, there's lots of pleasant things and no bad news to tell,
Except that old Bill Graves was sick, but now he's up and well.

Cy Cooper says—(but I'll not pass my word that it is so,
For Cy he is some punkins on spinning yarns, you know)—
He says that, since the freshet, the pickerel are so thick
In Baker's pond you can wade in and kill 'em with a stick!
The Hubbard girls are teaching school, and Widow Cutler's Bill
Has taken Eli Baxter's place in Luther Eastman's mill;
Old Deacon Skinner's dog licked Deacon Howard's dog last week,
And now there are two lambkins in one flock that will not speak.

The yellow rooster froze his feet, a-wadin' through the snow,
And now he leans agin the fence when he starts in to crow;
The chestnut colt that was so skittish when *he* went away—
I've broke him to the sulky and I drive him every day!
We've got pink window curtains for the front spare-room up-stairs,
And Lizzie's made new covers for the parlor lounge and chairs;
We've roofed the barn and braced the elm that has the hangbird's
nest—
Oh, there's been lots of changes since our William went out West!

Old Uncle Enos Packard is getting mighty gay—
He gave Miss Susan Birchard a peach the other day!
His late lamented Sarah hain't been buried quite a year,
So his purring 'round Miss Susan causes criticism here.

At the last donation party, the minister opined
That, if he'd half suspicioned what was coming, he'd resigned;
For, though they brought him slippers like he was a centipede,
His pantry was depleted by the consequential feed!
These are the things I'll write him—our boy that's in the West;
And I'll tell him how we miss him—his mother and the rest,
Why, we never have an apple-pie that mother doesn't say:
"He liked it so—I wish that he could have a piece to-day!"
I'll tell him we are prospering, and hope he is the same—
That we hope he'll have no trouble getting on to wealth and fame;
And just before I write "good-by from father and the rest,"
I'll say that "mother sends her love," and that will please him best.

For when *I* went away from home, the weekly news I heard
Was nothing to the tenderness I found in that one word—
The sacred name of mother—why, even now as then,
The thought brings back the saintly face, the gracious love again;
And in my bosom seems to come a peace that is divine,
As if an angel spirit communed a while with mine;
And one man's heart is strengthened by the message from above,
And earth seems nearer heaven when "mother sends her love."

EUGENE FIELD

OLD MOTHER GOOSE

When Thamré consented to sing for the citizens of Havermash, last year, nobody was more surprised than the citizens of Havermash themselves.

It was characteristic of Havermash to have attempted it. Nothing is too good for Havermashers. Were St. Cecilia prima donna for a season, it would appear to them quite natural to seek her services. Have they not a brownstone post office and a senator, a street railway and a county jail, a local newspaper, an author (the public scarcely be reminded of the "Havermash Hand-Organ: A Tale of Love and Poverty"), and a shoe and leather trade? Transcending all, is not their city charter two years old?

When the Happy Home Handel Association, headed by little Joe Havermash (grandson of the original shoe and leather man, whose wooden cobbler's shop occupied the site of the present post office in 1793), took upon itself the performance of an "oratorio" last Christmas Eve, "We will have Thamré," said Joe, serenely.

Still when Joe came home from Boston, breathless and radiant, one night early in the season, with Thamré's tiny contract (she wrote it on a card, he said, with her glove on, just in going out, and the card was as sweet now—see!—as the glove, and the glove had just the smell of one English violet, no more) to sing in the stone post office at eight o'clock on Christmas Eve, on such and such conditions (simple enough), and for such and such remuneration—*that* was the astonishing part of it,—even Havermash was off its guard enough to be surprised.

"She'll come," said Joe. "I supposed she would. I meant she should. But the terms are *astounding*. I was prepared to offer her twice that. I'd pay a big slice of it out of my own pocket to get her here. There's no trouble about terms. Did you see what Max offered her? Do you know what she's getting a night in New York? Do you know what she asked us? Five hundred dollars, sir! Only five hundred dollars. Think of it, sir! But the conditions are the most curious thing. She scorns to take so little, maybe. I don't know. All I know is, every dollar of it is to go to old women who haven't lived as they'd ought to in this town. 'For the relief of the aged women of Havermash, who, having in their youth led questionable lives, are left friendless, needy, and perhaps repentant in their declining years.' That's the wording of the agreement. I signed it myself in her little red morocco notebook. Most curious thing all round! It's my opinion, sir, it *takes* a woman to get up an uncommon piece of work like that."

. . .

Last Christmas Eve fell in Havermash wild and windy. The gust fought furiously with each other at corners, and under fences, and over the bleak spaces in which the new little city abounded, and through which it straggled painfully away into the open country. Where the snow lay, it lay in tints of dead, sharp blue, cold as steel beneath the chilly light; where it was blown away, the dust flew fine and hard like powder. Overhead, too, there hung only shades of steel. One long, low line of corrosive red, however, had eaten its way through against the western hill-country, and looked like rust or blood upon a mighty coal of mail.

So, at least, Miss Thamré fancied, shivering a little in her folded furs, as she watched from the car window the swooping of the night upon the bleak, outlying lands and approaching twinkle of the town.

It was a cheerless night for the prima donna to be in Havermash. Joe had been saying so all day. She thought so, it would seem, when he handed her from the cars. She scarcely spoke to him, nodding only, looking hither and thither about here, through the shriek and smoke, with that keen, baffling glance of hers, which all the world so well remembers. Joe felt rather proud of this. *He* knew what the eccentricities of genius were; was glad of a chance to show himself at ease with them. Had she bidden him stand on his head while she found her trunk, or sit on a barrel in the draught and wait for her to compose an aria, he would have obeyed her sweetly, thinking all the while how it would sound, told to his grandchildren on winter nights.

Half Havermash was at the station. All Havermash remembers that. It was the difficulty that Joe could get her to her carriage quietly, as befitted, to his fancy, the conduct of a lady's welcome.

"I did not expect to see so *many* people," said Miss Thamré, in her pretty, accented, appealing way. "What are they here for?"

"I'm sure I don't know," said Joe, with a puzzled air, "unless they're here to see me."

This amused the lady, and she laughed,—a little genial laugh, which bubbled over to the ears of the people pressing nearest to her in the crowd.

"She laughs as well as she sings," said a member of the Happy Home Handel Association.

"She has the eye of a gazelle and the smile of a sphinx," said the Author, and took out his notebook to "do" her for a religious weekly.

"She travels alone," said a mother of four daughters. (She had, indeed, come to Havermash quite alone, with neither chaperone nor maid.)

"She can wear silver seal and not look green," said a brunette, in black and garnet.

"She sees everything within a mile of her," said Joe to himself, as he held the hem of her dress back reverently from the carriage-wheels.

It would seem that she saw far and distinctly, for half within her carriage door she paused and said abruptly:—

"What is that? Let me see what that is!"

An old woman was pushing her way through the reluctant crowd; a very miserable old woman, splashed with mud. She had a blanket shawl over her head, and her unhealthy yellow-gray hair blew out from under it, over her face before the wind.

A crowd of villainous urchins followed, pelting her with slush and snow, and volleys of that shrill, coarse boys' cry (one of the most pitiful sounds on earth) by which the presence of a sacred mystery or a sorrowful sin is indicated, not alone in Havermash.

"Old Mother Goose! Old Mother Goose! Hi, yi! There! Mother Goosey's out buyin' Christmas stockin's for her dar-ter! Old Mother Goo-oo-ose!"

Everybody knew how Old Mother Goose hated the boys (and with good reason, poor soul!); but nobody had ever seen her offer them violence before that night.

In a minute she had grown suddenly livid and awful to see, rearing her lank figure to its full height against the steel and blood-colored background of the sky, where a sudden gap in the crowd had left her alone.

"You stop *that!*" she fiercely cried, and dealt a few bad blows to right and left before she was interfered with.

Annoyed beyond measure, Joe entreated Miss Thamré to let him take her from the scene. She hesitated, lingered, turned after a moment's thought, and sank upon the carriage seat.

"You did not tell me who it was," she said imperiously; "I asked you. I like to be answered when I ask a question. I never *saw* such a miserable old woman!"

"One of your prospective beneficiaries, madam," said Joe, humbly. "A wretched old creature. The boys call her Old Mother Goose. Do not distress yourself about her. It is no sight for you."

"You say the boys call her—I never *heard* such a poor, sad name! Has she no other name, Mr. Havermash? Oh! *There* she is again."

A sudden turn of the carriage had brought them sharply upon the miserable sight once more. Old Mother Goose was sitting stupidly in the slush beside the hack-stands. Her shawl was off, and her gray hair had fallen raggedly upon her shoulders; her teeth chattered with chill and rage; there were drops of blood about her on the snow; a few of the more undaunted spirits among the boys still hovered near her, avenging themselves for their recent defeat by furtive attempts to purloin her drabbled shawl; and a savage expression of his country's intention to preserve virtuous order, in the garb of the police, stood threatening poor Old Mother Goose with the terrors of the law.

It was a sorry sight. A sorry sight Miss Thamré seemed to find it. She leaned forward to the window. Joe could not prevent her; she would see it all. The silver shine of her fur wrappings glittered through the dusk, as she moved; one tiny gloved and fur-bound hand hung over the window's edge; a faint sweetness, like the soul of an English violet, stirred as she stirred, and stole out upon the frost air.

"There!" cried the old woman, mouthing a hideous oath, "there's the lady! I'll see her yet, in spite of ye!"

Old Mother Goose staggered up from the mud, staring dully; but the silver-gray picture framed in the carriage window flashed by her in an instant. For an instant only the two women looked each other in the eye.

Miss Thamré turned white about the chin. Her hand rose to her eyes instinctively, covered them, and fell. It must have been such a miserable contrasting of life's chances to her young and happy fancy!

"I've seen enough," she said. "Never mind!"

"Her name," said Joe, thinking to divert her from the immediate disturbance of the sight, "is Peg, I believe,—Peg Mathers. You see the boys got it Old Mathers, then Old Mother, so Old Mother Goose, I suppose; and quite ingenious, too, I think, poor creature!"

Miss Thamré made no reply. Quite weary of the subject, she wrapped herself back into the carriage corner, and, asking only how long a ride it was, drew a little silver veil she wore across her face and said no more. Quite weary still she seemed when Joe gave her his arm at the hotel steps (she had refused to accept his or any other private hospitality in the place); and very wearily she gave him to understand that she preferred to be alone till the hour of her appearance before the Havermash public should arrive.

Joe stumbled upon Old Mother Goose again, in running briskly down the hotel steps.

She was wandering in a maudlin, aimless way up and down the sidewalk at the building's front. Her shawl was gone, and her gray head was bare to the wind, which was now as sharp as high.

"What! *You* again?" said Joe. "What are you doing here, Peg? I was ashamed of you tonight, Peg! The people had come out to see a famous lady, and you must get to fighting with the boys and frighten her. You disgraced the town. Better go home, or you'll be in more mischief. Come!"

"I'm out hunting for my shawl, Mr. Havermash," said the old woman, after a moment's sly hesitation. "I've lost my shawl. Them boys took it, curse on 'em! I'd go to see the famous lady, if I had my shawl."

"Better go home; better go home!" repeated Joe. "*She* doesn't want to see *you,* Peg."

"Don't she, Mr. Havermash?"

Old Mother Goose laughed (or did she cry? She was always doing one or the other. What did it matter which?), nodding upward at the windows of the prima donna's parlors, where against the drawn shades a slight, tall shadow passed and repassed now and then, faintly, like a figure in a dream.

"Don't she? Well, I don't know as she does. How warm she looks! She must be warm in them fur tippets that she wears; don't you think she must? I like to see a famous lady well as other folks, when I have my shawl. Mr. Havermash!"

"Well, well, well!" Joe stopped impatiently in hurrying away.

"Would you rather I'd go home and say my prayers than fight the boys? I hate the boys!"

"Prayers, Peg? Do you say your prayers? What prayers do you say, Peg? Come!"

Mr. Havermash lingered, entertained in his own despite—thinking he would tell Miss Thamré this; it might amuse her.

"I say my prayers," said Old Mother Goose, beating her white hair back from her face at a blow, as if she could give it pain. "I've said 'em this many years. I say: 'When the Devil forgets the world, may God remind him of the boys!' I don't feel so about girls, Mr. Havermash. Maybe, if I hadn't had one once myself, I should. My girl ran away from me. She ran away on a Christmas Eve, thirteen years ago. Did ye ever see my girl? Mr. Havermash!"

But Joe was gone. He looked back once in running up the street (he was late to supper now; his wife waited to know if Miss Thamré would receive a call from her, and would scold a bit,—women will, it can't be helped),—he looked back across his shoulder, and saw that Old Mother Goose was still hunting for her shawl beneath the glittering, curtained windows, where a shadow passed and repassed, high above her head, like the shadow of a figure in a dream.

Thamré took no supper. It was six o'clock when she entered into her parlors and shut her doors about her. It was five minutes before eight when Mr. Havermash called to conduct her to the concert hall in the second story of the brownstone post office. It is quite evident, I think, that in all the passage of the somewhat remarkable drama into which her appearance in Havermash resolved itself, no act can have equaled in intensity that comprised within those two solitary hours. Yet positively all that is known of it, even at this distant day, is that Miss Thamré took no supper. Every boarder in the hotel knew that in half an hour. Loiterers and lion-hunters beneath the windows where the nervous shadow passed, picked it up, as loiterers and lion-hunters will. Even Old Mother Goose knew it—coming in to ask the hotel clerk if he had seen her shawl, and being for her trouble roughly shown the door.

Miss Thamré, curtained and locked in Havermash's grand suite of rooms (of which the town is not unjustly proud, it may be said; in which the senator is always accommodated on election days; in which a Harvard professor and a Boston alderman have been known to spend a night; in which the president himself once took a private lunch, in traveling to the mountains), spent, we say, two hours alone. In all her life, perhaps, the lady never spent two hours less alone. For a year the public fancy has been a self-invited guest at the threshold of those hours. It is with reluctance that one's most reverent imagination follows the general curiosity across their sacred edge; and yet it is with something of the same inner propulsion which forces a dreamer on the seashore to keep the eyes upon the struggles of a little gala-boat wrecked by a mortal leak in calm waters on a sunny day.

One sees, in spite of oneself, the lady's soft small hands close violently on the turning key; the silver furs shine under the chandeliers as they fall, tossed hither and hither, to the floor; the little veil torn from the fine, refined, sweet face; the setness of the features and that pallor of hers about the chin.

One knows that she will pace just so across the long, unhomelike splendor of the gaudy rooms; that she will fold her hands behind her, one into the other knotted fast; that she will lift them now and then, and rub them fiercely, as if she found them in a deathly chill; that her hair will fall, perhaps, in her sharp, regardless motions, and hang about her face; that her head is bent; and that her eyes will follow that great green tulip on the Brussels carpet, from pattern to pattern, patiently, seeing only that, as the shadow of her on the curtain passes and repasses, telling only what a shadow can.

One listens, as she listens to the voices of people passing on the pavement far below; one wonders, as she wonders what they say; if they speak of her, if they would speak of her tomorrow; and what it would happen they would say, should tomorrow bring forth what tomorrow might.

One hears, for she must hear, a Christmas carol chanted flatly by some young people in the street; the bustle of a hundred Christmas seekers coming homeward, with laden arms and empty pockets, from the little shops; one notices that she draws the shade, to see if holly is hanging in the windows, as it used to hang in Havermash, all up and down the street, by five o'clock,—and if she remembers how many times she has stolen out away in her clean hood, with some care that no one else need follow, shaming her, to see the holly herself and hear the carols sung, like happier little girls—how can one but seem to remember too? And when the church bells ring out for Christmas prayers, melting through the obdurate mail of the welded clouds, till they seem to melt a star through, as still and clear as God's voice melting through a wrung, defiant heart,—if her set face quivers a little, can one prevent one's own from quivering as well?

Perhaps the church bells ring in a vision with them, to the barred and curtained glitter of Miss Thamré's rooms. Perhaps, by sheer contrast, her fancy finds the wretched creature whom she saw today, seated with the mud and blood about her, shut in from all the world with her, they two alone together in the dreadful, shining place.

Perhaps she seems to herself to escape it, fleeing with her eyes to the dimmest corner of the room. Perhaps she forces herself to face it, turning sharply back, and lifting her head superbly, as Thamré can (the shadow on the curtain lifts its head just so, as a passer in the street can see). Perhaps she reasons with it, hotly, on this wise, as she walks:—

"I did not think, in coming to Havermash, you would strike across my way like this!"

"Heaven knows what restless fancy forced me here. Would to Heaven I had never come!"

"For thirteen years I have wondered what it would be like to look upon your face again. How *could* I know it would be like what it is,—so miserable, so neglected, so alone!"

Perhaps she argues sternly, now and then:—

"I have never left you to suffer, at the worst. You can not starve. The first ten-dollar bill I ever earned I sent to you. If you are too imbecile to watch the post, am I to blame? If you will have opium or rum for it, am I to blame? I've done my duty by your shameful mother-hood, if ever a wretched daughter did! What would you have, what will you have besides?"

Perhaps she droops and pleads at moments like a little child:—

"I have fought so hard, mother, for my name and fame! You gave me such a load of shame and ignorance and squalor to shake off! It has been such a long and bitter work! Let me be for a *little* while now, mother, do! Sometime before you die, I'll search you out; but not just yet—*just* yet!"

Perhaps she falls to sobbing, as women will. Perhaps she flings her beautiful arms out, and slides with her face upon the stifling scarlet cushions of a little sofa, where she tossed her veil. Perhaps, in kneeling there, the bleeding, gray-haired figure stalks her by, and the quieter companionship of a troop of passive and exhausted thoughts will occupy her place.

It may be that she will think about a certain Christmas Eve, windy and wild like this, and with a sky of steel and red almost like this. She thought of it in seeing the sunset from the window of the cars, remembering how a streak of red light crept into the attic corner, to help her while she packed a little bundle of her ragged clothes, thirteen years ago tonight.

It may be that she remembers counting the holly wreaths to keep her wits together as she fled, guiltily and sobbing for terror at the thing that she was doing, through the happy little town; that she saw crosses of myrtle and tuberoses in Mr. Havermash's drawing-room windows as she went by, and how grand they looked; and that a butcher's wife she knew was hanging blue tissue-paper roses in her sitting room as she climbed the depot steps. She can even recall the butcher's name,—Jack Hash,—Mrs. Jack Hash; as well as a hot and hungry wonder that filled the soul of the desolate child that night, whether she should ever live to be as safe and clean and respectable as Mrs. Jack Hash, and how she would garland her sitting room with blue tissue-roses on Christmas, if she did!

It may be that her fancy, being wearied, dwells more minutely upon the half-comical, wholly pathetic irrelevance of these things than upon the swift and feverish history of the crowded interval between their occurrence and the fact that Helene Thamré is kneeling in the Havermash hotel parlor, tonight, fighting all the devils that can haunt a beautiful and gifted woman's poor soul for her poor, old, shameful mother's sake.

Her battles for bread in factories and workshops, when first she cast herself, a little girl of fifteen bitter winters, upon the perilous chances of the world; worse contests, such as the outcast child of old Peg Mathers might not escape, being unfriended and despairing as the child had been; her desperate taxation of her only power, at last,—the voice which Heaven gave her, pure and sweet as its own summer morning; the song which she sang at street corners before the twilight fell; the windows of happy people under which she chanted mournfully; the first solo which they gave her at a mission school into which she chanced; the friends who heard it, and into whose hearts God put it to stretch down their hands and draw her straightway into Paradise; her studies and struggles since in foreign lands; the death of the master who had trained her, and the falling of his great mantle upon her bewildered name—these details, perhaps, float but mistily before her mind.

Sharp, distinct, pursuing, cruel, a single question begins to imprison her tortured thoughts. It took shapes as vague as smoke, clouds, fogs, dreams, at first; it looms as clear-cut and gigantic as a pyramid before her now.

If all the world should know next year, next week, tomorrow, at once and forever, what she knows?

If Havermash should learn, suppose, tonight, that little Nell Mathers, the unfathered and forgotten child of the creature at whose gray hairs the boys hoot on the streets, is all there is of Helene Thamré (the very letters of the shameful name transposed to make the beautiful, false image), what would Havermash, falling at her feet this instant, do the next?

Perhaps to the woman's inner sense neither Havermash nor the world may matter much, indeed. She has kept, through deadly peril, soul and body pure as light. Not a sheltered wife, singing "Greenville" to her babies, vacant of ambitions and innocent of noisier powers, can show a hand or heart or name more spotless than her own. And not to dye them deep in the old, old hateful shame! One must have *been* little Nell Mathers and have become Thamré, I fancy, to measure this recoil.

Perhaps it seems to her more monstrous and impossible as the thought grows more familiar to her. Perhaps a certain hardness begins to creep across the pallor of her face; or it may be only that she has wound her fallen hair back from it and exposed the carved exactness and composure of her features. It may be that she will argue to herself again, forgetting that the gray-haired vision left her long ago:—

"I could never make you happy, if I did. It was always, always a curse to both of us. What have you ever done for me, that you should demand a right so cruel? You have no right, I say; you have no right!"

"And if you speak, indeed, why, who believes you? What can your ravings do against Thamré's denial, poor old mother!"

Perhaps she muses, half-aloud: "You need a shawl, I see. You shall have a bright, warm shawl on Christmas Day. It is better for you than a daughter. Oh! A thousand times!"

Perhaps she laughs—as Thamré does not often laugh—most bitterly; and that Joe Havermash, knocking at her door, hears, or thinks he hears, the sound, before she flashes on him, tall, serene, resplendent, in full dress and full spirit for the evening.

The Happy Home Handel Association was satisfied with the reception given by Havermash to their rendering of the oratorio *Messiah* last Christmas Eve. On settees, in the aisles, on the windowsills, in the corridors, on the stairs, Havermash overflowed the brownstone post office.

Since the incorporation of the city (which is the Christian era of Havermash, and from which everything dates accordingly) nothing approaching such an audience had been collected for the most popular of purposes. Even Signor Blitz could not have eaten swords or played baseball with uncracked eggs before a quarter of the spectators; and the New England philosopher, it is well-known, reads his lectures in Havermash to three hundred people. In this triumph the Happy Home Handel Association felt compelled to own that Thamré had her share, which for the HHHA was owning a great deal. When little Joe bowed the prima donna upon the somewhat uncertain (green cambric) stage, the East Havermash "orchestra" led off in a burst of applause, which threatened to shake the post office to its foundation stone, and which fired even the leader's dignity of Joe's rotund person to ill-concealed enthusiasm. Even Mrs. Joe, gorgeous upon the front settee, in the opera dress that (it was well-known) she wore in Boston, despite the ache of a secret chagrin that Miss Thamré had received no callers, reflected the general pride and pleasure to the very links of her great gold necklace and the tiniest wrinkle of her rose-colored gloves. Even Mrs. Jack Hash, on her campstool, by the second left, though disposed by nature and training to be critical of anything headed by a Havermash, applauded softly with the feathered tip of her silver-paper fan upon the frill of her brown poplin upper skirt. Never had there been anything like it known in Havermash.

Like a bird, like a snowflake, like a moonbeam, like a fancy, like nothing that the brownstone post office was accustomed to, Thamré stole upon the stage. She stood for an instant poised, fluttering, as if half her mind were made to fly, then fell into her unapproachable repose, and at her leisure looked the great audience over, shooting it here and there with her nervous glance.

The packed house drew and held its breath. Women thought swiftly: Silver-gray satin, up to the throat and down to the hands. No jewelry, and a live white lily on her wrist! Young men saw her through a mist, and half turned their eyes away, as if they had seen a Madonna folded in a morning cloud. Reporters pondered, twirling a moustache end, pencil held suspended: Such severity is the superbest affectation, my lady! But it tells, as straight as a carrier-dove. Before she had opened her lips, Thamré had conquered Havermash.

Conscious of this in an instant's flash, Thamré grew unconscious of it in another. For an instant every detail in her house was in her grasp, even to Mrs. Jack Hash on the campstool and the critical attitude of the silver-paper fan; even to old Mother Goose, half-fading into the shadow of the distance, quarreling with a doorkeeper about her ticket. The next she cast her audience from her like a racer casting his cloak to the wind. Her face settled; her wonderful eyes dilated; the hand with the lily on it closed over the other like a seal; the soul of the music entered into her, incorporate. She grew as sacred as her theme.

"That little country house," said a critic present, who had heard her before her best houses in the great world, "was on the knees of its heart that night. She never sang like that before, nor ever will again; nor any other artist, it is my belief. She minded the jerks of that orchestra and the flats of the Havermash *prima donna* no more than she did the whistling of the wind about the post-office windows. She rendered the text like an angel sent from Heaven for the purpose. When she lifted that hand with the flower on it (she did it only in the chorus, 'Surely, he hath borne our griefs,' and in the tenor, 'Behold, and see,' and at one other time) I could think of nothing but

> *In the beauty of the lilies*
> *Christ was born across the sea.*

Couldn't get it out of my head. I meant she should have been *encored*, when it was all over, to give us that itself; but for what happened, you know."

Did I say she grew as sacred as her theme? It might almost be said that its holy Personality environed and enveloped her. Reverent souls that listened to her that well-remembered night felt as if the Man of Sorrows confided to her the burden of his heart, as if he stooped to acquaint her with his grief, as if the travail of his soul fell upon her, and that with his satisfaction she was satisfied.

The sacred drama was unfolding to its solemn close, the wildness of the wind without was hushed, the Christmas stars were out, when Thamré glided into her last solo,—that palpitating, proud, triumphant thing, in which the soul of Divine Love avenges itself against the ingenuity of human despair:—

> *If God be for us, who can be against us?*
> *Who can be against us?*

Who shall lay anything to the charge
Of God's elect?
It is God that justifieth.
Who is he that condemneth?
It is Christ that died.

It was at this point that the interruption came.

Shrill and sharp into the thrill of the singer's liquid, clinging notes a quick cry out—

"Let me see her! Let me touch her! I can't abear it any longer! Let me see my girl!" and, forcing her way like a stream of lava through the packed and startled aisles, hot, wild, pallid, and horrible, Old Mother Goose leaped, before a hand could stay her, on the stage.

"I can't stand it any longer, Nell! It seems to craze my head! I knew you from the time I heard you laughing to the depot. I didn't mean to shame ye before so many folks, and I tried to find my shawl. They said you wouldn't want to see your poor old mother, Nelly dear. But I can't abear to hear you sing. Nell, why, Nell, you stand up like the Almighty Dead to do it!"

The shock of the shrill words and their cessation brought the house to it feet. Then came the uproar.

"Shame!" "Police!" "Order!" "Take her out!" "Arrest the hag!" "Protect the lady!" And after that the astonishment and silence of death.

High above the wavering, peering mass, clear to the apprehension of every eye in the house, appeared a lily-bound, authoritative hand. It motioned once and dropped—as the snow drops over a grave.

By those who sat nearest her it was said that the flower trembled on the lady's wrist a little; for the rest, she stood sculptured like a statue, towering about the piteous figure at her feet. Her voice when she spoke—for she spoke in the passing of a thought,—rang out to the remotest corner of the galleries, slipping even then, however, into Thamré's girlish, uneven tones.

"If you *please*, do not disturb the woman at this moment. She is a very *old* woman. Let us hear what she has to say. Her hair is gray. Let us not be *rough* or *hasty* till we have *thought* of what she says."

Old Mother Goose rose from the floor, where she had fallen, half-abashed, perhaps half-dazed at which she had done.

"I've got nothing more to say." She fumbled foolishly in the air to wrap the shawl which she had lost about her lean and tattered shoulders. "I've said as this famous lady is my daughter, that was Nell Mathers, and remembered by many folks in Havermash thirteen years ago. I wouldn't have shamed her quite so much if I'd only found my shawl. It's cold, too, without a shawl. I'll go out now, and you can sing your piece through, Nelly, without the plague of me. I wouldn't have told on you, I think, but for the music and the crazy feeling that I had. It's most too bad, Nelly, to spoil the piece. I'll go right out."

She turned, stepped off, and staggered feebly, turning her bleared eyes back to feast upon the silent, shining figure, on whose wrist the lily glittered cruelly, as only lilies can.

"What a pretty satin gown you've got, my dear!" she said.

Mr. Havermash could bear it no longer. He took Old Mother Goose by the sleeve, hurrying up, saying: "Come, come!

"The woman is drunk, Miss Thamré. She shall not be allowed to insult you anymore like this. In the kindness of your heart, you make a mistake, I think, if you will pardon me. See! She is quite beside herself. Something due to the audience. This disturbance should not continue. Come, Peg, come!"

But Thamré shook her head. She had grown now deadly pale—at least so Joe thought, letting go of the woman's arm, his own face changing color sharply, the baton in his fat, white-gloved hand beginning to shake.

"If you please, Mr. Havermash, I should like to know—the people will *pardon* me a moment, I am sure—I should like to know if this poor old creature has anything *more* to say."

"Nothing more," said Old Mother Goose, shaking her gray head, "but this, maybe, Nelly dear. I says to myself, when I sits and hears you singing,—I says, when you sang them words: 'If God be for me, my girl won't be against me! My girl can't be against me!' over and over with the music, Nelly, so I did! If God be for me, how *can* my girl be against me?"

It was said that, when Helene Thamré stretched down her lily-guarded hand, and lifting the lean, unclean fingers of Old Mother Goose, pressed them, after a moment's thought, gently and slowly to her heart, she heard the sudden break of sobs in the breathless house; and pausing to listen to the sound, flushed fitfully like a child surprised, and smiled.

"Ladies and gentlemen"—her great eyes stabbed the audience

through and through; she lifted the old woman's hand that all might see—"I am *sorry* that your entertainment should be disturbed. If you will *excuse* me, I will leave you now, and take my mother home."

Home? What home was there for Old Mother Goose and her outcast child in Thamré's hotel parlors, on that or any other night? What home was there for Thamré in the godforsaken cellar whence the woman of the town had crawled? Apparently, the lady had not thought of this. Joe found her standing serenely as an angel when he came into the stifling little green room. She was still smiling. She had buttoned her silver furs about the old woman's shrunken throat.

"This will be warmer than your shawl, mother, don't you see?" he heard her say. "The boys shall never bother you in this, poor old mother! There!"

Mrs. Havermash came with her husband. The Boston opera-cloak was in disorder; her rose-colored gloves were wet and spotted.

"Miss Thamré," said Joe, "may I make you acquainted with my wife? We would not urge upon you again the acceptance of a hospitality which has been already so decidedly refused; but perhaps considering the state of your mother's health, we can make you more comfortable now at our home than you can be elsewhere. If you will do Mrs. Havermash and myself the favor to return with us—and her—in our own carriage tonight—"

Joe's grandfather, as has been said, cobbled shoes in a wooden shop; and even Mrs. Joe today will drink with her spoon in her teacup, you will notice, if you chance to sit beside her at a supper. But show me bluer blood, if it please you, than shall flow in the veins of him and his, to preserve the existence of this most cultivated instinct and the memory of this most knightly deed.

All the world knows how Thamré suddenly and mysteriously disappeared a year ago from the public and professional life. All the world has mourned, wondered, gossiped, caught at the wings of rumors, lost them, and so mourned again at this event.

All the world does not know with what a curious development of pride in and loyalty to the personality of little Nell Mathers, Havermash has struggled, till struggle has become useless, to enforce a reticence upon the subject of Thamré's movements and their motives.

To a few friends, familiar with her private history for the past years, its results have seemed to crown its cost, I think. At least, she herself, having proved them so, has contrived to radiate upon us the light of her own content.

"You do not know the life," she said, at the outset, shaking her beautiful, determined head, "if you would ask me to return to it while my mother lives. Even my name will not bear the scorch of hers. The world is so hard on women! Do not urge me. Let me take my way. Perhaps God and I together can make her poor old hands as white as yours or mine before she dies."

Perhaps they did. It is known that when Old Mother Goose lay dying in her daughter's quiet house in Havermash, one frosty night, not many weeks ago, and after she had fallen, as they thought, past speech or recognition, she raised herself upon her pillow, and, stretching her hands, said slowly:—

"Nell! Why, Nell! It is Christ that died! If my girl was for me, Nell, *could* He be against me, do you think?"

And further it is only known that Thamré will sing this season in the oratorio of the Messiah on Christmas Eve.

ELIZABETH STUART PHELPS,
from *May Your Days Be Merry and Bright
and Other Christmas Stories by Women*

MEASURE FOR MEASURE

Once upon a time, not so very long ago, there was a mother who was a master at manipulating her children—with serious negative consequences for all of them as they grew to adulthood.

Even after her children were grown, this mom continued to stir up dissent among them. In addition, she tried to alienate them from their father, whom she had divorced. After a time and with the help of counseling, the children came to realize the games their mother played and severely limited their contact with her. Still, she continued to cause havoc in their lives, spreading negative stories about them to their own children.

In short, she was a very difficult person; and as she aged her negative behavior became even more intense. Two of her three children began to see her only once or twice a year. Their lives were complicated enough with problems that they attributed to her, and their anger at her made it impossible for them to take responsibility for their own lives.

Eventually, as the woman entered her nineties and became somewhat disabled, the task of caring for her fell on the one daughter who had, with the support of her husband, been able to come to some understanding of why her mother was the way she was. Still, until the day the mother died, she continued to deride this daughter for not doing enough for her.

When the mother died, however, the two absent children experienced great guilt that made their lives even more complicated. But even though caring for her mother had been an onerous task, the caretaker daughter experienced a sense of peace she had not anticipated.

Perhaps the measure she had measured had finally been measured back to her.

MARY G. DURKIN,
from *An Epidemic of Joy*

THE WEDDING DRESS

Once upon a time, not too very long ago, there was a mother who sewed many of her daughters' clothes. This mom had learned the art of sewing from her own mom, who in turn had learned it from her mom.

This mom made holiday dresses, party dresses, and finally prom dresses for her five daughters. When the first of the daughters to marry started looking through bride's magazines, she asked her mom if she might be able to make a wedding dress.

Responding to the challenge, the mom spent many hours over the next five months sewing pearls and sequins on lace that was then attached to the dress. As she sewed, the mom found herself feeling very close to her deceased mother. She remembered the many dresses her mother had made for her over the years, and how proud she always felt in her "originals."

And although her grandmother had died some seventy years before, the mom also began feeling connected to her. Often, as she sat by herself in the evenings, sewing the small beads, she sensed the presence of these two women and experienced a feeling of being loved by both of them.

The woman hoped that her daughter would feel that the love of her mother, her grandmother, and her great-grandmother was sewn into her wedding dress.

And that this memory would help her pass that same love on to the next generation.

MARY G. DURKIN,
from *An Epidemic of Joy*

MOTHERS' ART

Mothers start with stair walls bare, but for a picture
Of two, framed, proportioned, and tacked. Young apprentice of the
Home, her canvas ascends the corridor as children emerge. Each step
labored, painted strokes of pigment turned to flesh. Dabs of color
for each new set of eyes.

Experience and triumph, life's celebrations captured, replace and cover
other walls. Corners splashed with pictures, symbols of our
roots and faith. Office laminate forever goals achieved,
three by five smiles of those who helped, polish the desk. Bedrooms a
continuous hue-like pastels blended, two becoming One in a
limitless spectrum, portraying love's imagery and mystery. Living
room, decorated for guests, felt at home by warm tea and a sad story.
The hearth, solid reminder of our focus, topped with family pigment,
Smiles spread like rainbows.

Mothers are artists of the home and sculptures of Family.
Like the old masters, who covered their works,

reminded of time's need to form a new renaissance.
They employ wisdom to step back and forth,
letting both the potters' wheel and their own fingers
Assist, create and let go, always with an open heart.

DAN DURKIN

BEANNACHT

For Josie, his mother

On the day when
the weight deadens
on your shoulders
and you stumble,
may the clay dance
to balance you.

And when your eyes
freeze behind
the gray window
and the ghost of loss
gets in to you,
may a flock of colors,
indigo, red, green
and azure blue
come to awaken you
a meadow of delight.

When the canvas frays
in the curach of thought
and a stain of ocean
blackens beneath you,

may there come across the waters
a path of yellow moonlight
to bring you safely home.

May the nourishment of the earth be yours,
may the clarity of light be yours,
may the fluency of the ocean be yours,
may the protection of the ancestors be yours.

And so may a slow
wind work these words
of love around you,
an invisible cloak
to mind your life.

JOHN O'DONOHUE

Many religious traditions, recognizing the life-creating and life-sustaining role of mothers, celebrate the sacredness of a mother goddess.

God is Our Father; but even more so God is Our Mother.

POPE JOHN PAUL II

The Mother Moon

And do you know why it is that the Moon has but one eye? It is a short story, but one of the most poetic and beautiful in all the pretty folklore of the Pueblos.

P'ah-hlee-oh, the Moon-Maiden, was the Teewahn Eve—the first and loveliest woman in all the world. She had neither father nor mother, sister nor brother; and in her fair form were the seeds of all humanity—of all life and love and goodness. The Trues, who are the unseen spirits that are above all, made T'hoor-id-deh, the Sun, who was to be the father of all things; and because he was alone, they made for him a companion, the first to be of maids, the first to be a wife. From them began the world and all that is in it; and all their children were strong and good. Very happy were the Father-all and the Mother-all, as they watched their happy brood. He guarded them by day and she by night—only there was no night, for then the Moon had two eyes and saw as clearly as the Sun, and with glance as bright. It was all as one long day of golden light. The birds flew always, the flowers never shut, the young people danced and sang, and none knew how to rest.

But at last the Trues thought better. For the endless light grew heavy to the world's young eyes that knew no tender lids of night. And the Trues said:

"It is not well, for so there is no sleep, and the world is very tired. We must not keep the Sun and Moon seeing alike. Let us put out one of his eyes, that there may be darkness for half the time, and then his children can rest." And they called T'hoor-id-deh and P'ah-hlee-oh before them to say what must be done.

But when she heard that, the Moon-Mother wept for her strong and handsome husband, and cried:

"No! No! take my eyes for my children, but do not blind the Sun! He is the father, the provider—and how shall he watch against harm, or how find us game without his bright eyes? Blind me, and keep him all-seeing."

And the Trues said: "It is well, daughter." And so they took away one of her eyes so that she could never see again so well. Then night came upon the tired earth, and the flowers and birds and people slept their first sleep, and it was very good. But she who first had the love of children, and paid for them with pain as mothers pay, she did not grow ugly by her sacrifice. Nay, she is lovelier than ever, and we all love her to this day. For the Trues are good to her, and gave her in place of the bloom of girlhood the beauty that is only in the faces of mothers.

So mother-pale above us
    She bends, her watch to keep,
Who of her sight dear-bought the night
    To give her children sleep.

from A Collection of Indian Folktales

THE SILENCE & THE SORROW:
A MEDITATION ON THE PIETÀ

Who will come and share my sorrow
Hold my heart 'till wake tomorrow
Is there time that I could borrow
Oh, oh, the silence and the sorrow

When I was young I dreamed of roads not taken
To walk the way so many had forsaken
And I would seek the heart of love's creation
It was found in you.

When love was young I cried with tears of laughter
And deep inside I wondered what came after

How a heart could love without conditions
It was found in you.

When life was young and living seemed forever
I knew somehow you never hid its pleasures
and all my tears uncovered hidden treasures
Love was found in you.

Who will come and share my sorrow . . .

LIAM LAWTON

Fathers are no longer the bystanders in the game of love of children. A father's love is as necessary for the emotional development of a child as a mother's love. The image of the breadwinner father leaving the emotional support of his children to their mother is a caricature of how to raise emotionally healthy children. Sons and daughters need loving fathers involved in their lives. The rewards to these fathers will be the return of love from their children.

TO MY DAUGHTER BETTY, THE GIFT OF GOD

In wiser days, my darling rosebud, blown
To beauty proud as was your mother's prime,
In that desired, delayed, incredible time,
You'll ask why I abandoned you, my own,

And the dear heart that was your baby throne,
To dice with death. And oh! they'll give you rhyme
And reason: some will call the thing sublime,
And some decry it in a knowing tone.
So here, while the mad guns curse overhead,
And tired men sigh with mud for couch and floor,
Know that we fools, now with the foolish dead,
Died not for flag, nor King, nor Emperor—
But for a dream, born in a herdman's shed,
And for the secret Scripture of the poor.

THOMAS M. KETTLE

FATHER AND CHILD

She hears me strike the board and say
That she is under ban
Of all good men and women,
Being mentioned with a man
That has the worst of all bad names;
And thereupon replies
That his hair is beautiful,
Cold as the March wind in his eyes.

W. B. YEATS

SCARLET RIBBONS

A young mother, exhausted after overseeing nine seven-year-old boys at her son's birthday party, decided to take a well-deserved nap. The birthday was in the winter a few days after the end of the holiday season, the second one since her father's death.

When the woman awoke from the nap, she remained in bed, deciding to savor a few more moments of peace and quiet. Suddenly out of nowhere, she heard—quite clearly she says—the music to "Scarlet Ribbons," a song her father used to sing when the family went for a long drive. At the same time, she felt what she describes as "an incredible sense of happiness, the feeling that Dad was telling me that the peace I felt just lying there was how he felt when he died."

The woman had explained to her family at the time of her father's death that it seemed to her his last breath was one of great agony. Though other family members had described the scene as similar to the moment of birth, she had always had a hard time discarding her negative image of that moment.

But now she is convinced that the "Scarlet Ribbons" experience was her father's way of calming her fear and telling her that when he died he had also come to life in a new way.

Like Jesus did to Martha, he came to tell her that we never really die.

MARY G. DURKIN,
from *An Epidemic of Joy*

THE CHILDREN'S HOUR

Between the dark and the daylight,
 When the night is beginning to lower,
Comes a pause in the day's occupations,
 That is known as the Children's Hour.

I hear in the chamber above me
    The patter of little feet,
The sound of a door that is opened,
    And voices soft and sweet.

From my study I see in the lamplight,
    Descending the broad hall stair,
Grave Alice, and laughing Allegra,
    And Edith with golden hair.

A whisper, and then a silence:
    Yet I know by their merry eyes
They are plotting and planning together
    To take me by surprise.

A sudden rush from the stairway,
    A sudden raid from the hall!
By three doors left unguarded
    They enter my castle wall!

They climb up into my turret
    O'er the arms and back of my chair;
If I try to escape, they surround me;
    They seem to be everywhere.

They almost devour me with kisses,
    Their arms about me entwine,
Till I think of the Bishop of Bingen
    In his Mouse-Tower on the Rhine!

Do you think, O blue-eyed banditti,
    Because you have scaled the wall,
Such an old mustache as I am
    Is not a match for you all!

I have you fast in my fortress,
    And will not let you depart,
But put you down into the dungeon
    In the round tower of my heart.

And there will I keep you forever,
   Yes, forever and a day,
Till the walls shall crumble to ruin,
   And moulder in dust away

Henry Wadsworth Longfellow

Fathers and Sons

A Chicago taxi driver, a native of Turkey, told this story, swearing it could be found in the Koran. Once a son, who had assumed the obligation of caring for his elderly father, began to worry about this responsibility. The son, knowing he had barely enough resources to care for himself, his wife, and his family, soon felt the added burden of the father's loss of sight. Having to lead the old man around took time away from what the son felt were more pressing responsibilities.

The son fretted over what he could do. Finally, exasperated by the demands his father placed both on his time and his resources, the son resorted to a drastic solution. He offered to take his father for a walk to the nearby sea. The son led his father up the hill by the seaside. As they approached the edge of the hill, he failed to warn his father of the drop ahead of them. The father died from the fall into the swirling sea waves.

The story goes on to tell how the son's action is repeated through many generations of his family, each son eventually experiencing the fate of his own father. Finally, one day as a son and father begin the journey to the sea, the father turned to the son, and said, "Son, I know where we are going, and I know what you plan for me. It is not necessary for you to take me there. I can find my way to the sea and will do what you want me to do. Go home to your family and do not worry."

The son, ashamed of his proposed deed, asked the father why he would offer to do such a thing. The father responded, "I did the same thing to my father that he had done to his father, and it has been done so for many generations. But if I go on my own, perhaps your son will not know of this solution when you are a burden to him."

The son wept at his father's words and begged his forgiveness. He then brought the father back to his home, where the old man taught his son new ways to increase the family's meager income. His daughter-in-law and grandchildren gained many new insights into the wisdom of the old man, and when his son reached his old age, he and his wife were welcomed into their son's home.

MARY G. DURKIN,
from *An Epidemic of Joy*

KISSING TIME

'Tis when the lark goes soaring
    And the bee is at the bud,
When lightly dancing zephyrs
    Sing over field and flood;
When all sweet things in nature
    Seem joyfully achime—
'Tis then I wake my darling,
    For it is kissing time!

Go, pretty lark, a-soaring,
    And suck your sweets, O bee;
Sing, O ye winds of summer,
    Your songs to mine and me;
For with your song and rapture
    Cometh the moment when

It's half-past kissing time
 And time to kiss again!

So—so the days go fleeting
 Like golden fancies free,
And every day that cometh
 Is full of sweets for me;
And sweetest are those moments
 My darling comes to climb
 Into my lap to mind me
 That it is kissing time.

Sometimes, maybe, he wanders
 A heedless, aimless way—
Sometimes, maybe, he loiters
 In pretty, prattling play;
 But presently bethinks him
 And hastens to me then,
For it's half-past kissing time
 And time to kiss again!

EUGENE FIELD

FOLLOWER

My father worked with a horse-plough,
His shoulders globed like a full sail strung
Between the shafts and the furrow.
The horses strained at his clicking tongue.

An expert. He would set the wing
And fit the bright steel-pointed sock.

The sod rolled over without breaking.
At the headrig, with a single pluck

Of reins, the sweating team turned round
And back into the land. His eye
Narrowed and angled at the ground,
Mapping the furrow exactly.

I stumbled in his hobnailed wake,
Fell sometimes on the polished sod;
Sometimes he rode me on his back
Dipping and rising to his plod.

I wanted to grow up and plough,
To close one eye, stiffen my arm
All I ever did was follow
In his broad shadow round the farm.

I was a nuisance, tripping, falling,
Yapping always. But today
It is my father who keeps stumbling
Behind me, and will not go away.

SEAMUS HEANEY

SOME TIME

Last night, my darling, as you slept,
I thought I heard you sigh,
And to your little crib I crept,
And watched a space thereby;
Then, bending down, I kissed your brow—
For, oh! I love you so—

You are too young to know it now,
But some time you shall know.

Sometime, when, in a darkened place
Where others come to weep
Your eyes shall see a weary face
Calm in eternal sleep;
The speechless lips, the wrinkled brow,
The patient smile may show—
You are too young to know it now,
But some time you shall know.

EUGENE FIELD

THE ICE CREAM PARLOR DAD

Storyteller John Shea tells of a father who brought his four kids to an ice-cream parlor. Only three of them came inside. The teenage girl remained in the car sulking, because she was at that age of life at which teenage girls love to sulk.

Meanwhile the two boys in the group fought over which one of them could choose first, because they both wanted garlic-chocolate-fudge-with-cookie-crumbles—and one could not (of course) order what the other had already ordered. (It was unthinkable!) So the two of them almost came to blows when the older boy did order that ice cream, and the younger one was constrained to settle for orange-ripple-pizza-flavored ice cream.

The little girl of the family (she couldn't have been more than four) wept because all the chocolate-chocolate-chocolate-chip was gone, and nothing would console her—not even a triple scoop of peppermint-fudge-raspberry-mango. She sobbed all through her destruction of the cone.

Finally, the teenager came in and sulked because they didn't have "anything," (though actually there were more than forty flavors). She finally settled on a single scoop of vanilla yogurt "in a dish" as a protest against the injustices of the human condition.

When they got home, however, the father told his wife how much fun he had had on their outing, and he was speaking the truth.

They were his children you see, and he loved them.

And he delighted in feeding them.

ANDREW M. GREELEY,
from *An Epidemic of Joy*

THE BAREFOOT BOY

Blessings on thee, little man,
Barefoot boy, with cheek of tan!
With thy turned-up pantaloons,
And thy merry whistled tunes;
With thy red lip, redder still,
Kissed by strawberries on the hill;
With the sunshine on thy face,
Through thy torn brim's jaunty grace,
From my heart I give thee joy,—
I was once a barefoot boy.
Prince thou art,—the grown-up man
Only is republican,
Let the million-dollared ride!
Barefoot, trudging at his side,
Thou has more than he can buy,
In the reach of ear and eye—
Outward sunshine, inward joy;
Blessings on thee, barefoot boy!

Oh, for boyhood's painless play,
Sleep that wakes in laughing day,

Health that mocks the doctor's rules,
Knowledge never learned of schools,
Of the wild bee's morning chase,
Of the wild-flower's time and place,
Flight of fowl and habitude
Of the tenants of the wood;
How the tortoise bears his shell,
How the woodchuck digs his cell,
And the ground-mole sinks his well;
How the robin feeds her young,
How the oriole's nest is hung,
Where the whitest lilies blow,
Where the freshest berries grow,
Where the ground-nut trails its vine,
Where the wood-grape's clusters shine,
Of the black wasp's cunning way,
Mason of his walls of clay,
And the architectural plans
Of gray hornet artisans!
For, eschewing books and tasks,
Nature answers all he asks,
Hand in hand with her he walks,
Face to face with her he talks,
Part and parcel of her joy,—
Blessings on the barefoot boy!

Oh, for boyhood's time of June,
Crowding years in one brief moon,
When all things I heard or saw,
Me, their master, waited for.
I was rich in flowers and trees,
Humming-birds and honey-bees,
For my sport the squirrel played,
Plied the snouted mole his spade;
For my task the blackberry cone
Purpled over hedge and stone;
Laughed the brook for my delight
Through the day and through the night,
Whispering at the garden wall,

Talked with me from fall to fall;
Mine the sand-rimmed pickerel pond,
Mine the walnut slopes beyond,
Mine, on bending orchard trees,
Apples of Hesperides!
Still, as my horizon grew,
Larger grew my riches too;
All the world I saw or knew
Seemed a complex Chinese toy
Fashioned for a barefoot boy.

Oh, for festal dainties spread,
Like my bowl of milk and bread,
Pewter spoon and bowl of wood,
On the door-stone, gray and rude!
O'er me, like a regal tent,
Cloudy-ribbed, the sunset bent,
Purple-curtained, fringed with gold,
Looped in many a wind-swung fold.
While for music came the play
Of the pied frogs' orchestra,
And, to light the noisy choir,
Lit the fly his lamp of fire.
I was monarch: pomp and joy
Waited on the barefoot boy!

Cheerily, then, my little man,
Live and laugh as boyhood can!
Though the flinty slopes be hard,
Stubble-speared the new-mown sward,
Every morn shall lead thee through
Fresh baptisms of the dew;
Every evening from thy feet
Shall the cool wind kiss the heat;
All too soon these feet must hide
In the prison cells of pride,
Lose the freedom of the sod,
Like a colt's for work be shod,
Made to treat the mills of toil,

Up and down in ceaseless moil;
Happy if their track be found
Never on forbidden ground;
Happy if they sink not in
Quick and treacherous sands of sin,
Ah! that thou couldst known thy joy,
Ere it passes, barefoot boy!

JOHN GREENLEAF WHITTIER

BACK DOOR TO HEAVEN

Once upon a time, well it was really in eternity, Himself went out to make sure that heaven was still a city that works, much like a precinct captain walking his ward or a monsignor walking his parish. Generally he was pleased—all the gold and ivory had been polished, the lawns were neatly cut, the bushes freshly trimmed, the choirs in good tune, and the mall filled with people (Of course there's a mall in heaven!). But as he was ambling through the mall didn't he notice that there were some folk there that didn't belong in the city at all at all. Many of them should have had a long stay in purgatory, others would make it in only the day before the last judgment and weren't some of them not likely to get in save for a last-minute appeal to the Holy Spirit?

So, doesn't he walk out to St. Peter's workstation at the heavenly gates where Peter was fiddling with his fishing rod.

"How come people get inside who don't belong here and yourself with the keys to the kingdom of heaven?"

Peter looked up and sighed. "It wasn't meself that was after letting them in."

"Well who else could have done it?"

"You don't want to know?"

"I do want to know!!"

"Well, after I turn them away, don't they go around to the back door and doesn't your mother let them in!"

ANDREW M. GREELEY

THE GOURMET DAD

Once upon a time, not too long ago, there was a single dad who thought he was a Renaissance man (some daddies are that way, you know). He played golf and basketball, he sang (especially at weddings, even when he wasn't invited), he wrote poetry, he painted, and he was skilled in the mysteries of the Internet. He thought there was nothing he could not do if he set his mind to it.

So one day the dad announced to his five children that he was going to become a gourmet cook. They all laughed at him, politely and lovingly, but they still laughed. So he was even more determined. He went to cooking class every week and practiced on the class and on some of his friends. Finally, one night he announced that on the following Sunday he would cook a feast for his family.

Now, all the kids had something else they would rather do that night, but because they loved their daddy, they came to the meal, suppressing (almost) their giggles.

To their astonishment, the meal was wonderful. So the kids went to their various schools on Monday and bragged that their daddy was the best cook in the world.

And he did it all, they said, because he loves us so much.

ANDREW M. GREELEY,
from *An Epidemic of Joy*

Much is made of sibling rivalry, an almost inevitable situation when a child has to share parents with another child. Despite the inevitability of some youthful rivalry, adult siblings, who are willing to give up a conflict mentality, discover the support and delights of sibling love.

MID-TERM BREAK

I sat all morning in the college sick bay
Counting bells knelling classes to a close.
At two o'clock our neighbours drove me home.

In the porch I met my father crying—
He had always taken funerals in his stride—
And Big Jim Evans saying it was a hard blow.

The baby cooed and laughed and rocked the pram
When I came in, and I was embarrassed
By old men standing up to shake my hand

And tell me they were 'sorry for my trouble.'
Whispers informed strangers I was the eldest,
Away at school, as my mother held my hand

In hers and coughed out angry tearless sighs.
At ten o'clock the ambulance arrived
With the corpse, stanched and bandaged by the nurses.

Next morning I went up into the room. Snowdrops
And candles soothed the bedside; I saw him
For the first time in six weeks. Paler now,

Wearing a poppy bruise on his left temple,
He lay in the four-foot box as in his cot.
No gaudy scars, the bumper knocked him clear.

A four-foot box, a foot for every year.

SEAMUS HEANEY

JUST AN ORDINARY MAN

To say that Tom was from a dysfunctional family would be an under-statement. His father had died early, a victim of alcohol addiction, an addiction Tom's younger brother shared. His older sister was on her third husband. His younger sister was living with a man who refused to work and periodically beat her. His mother was constantly calling him either to help out one or the other of the siblings or to complain about how hard her life was and that no one ever helped her.

That Tom had managed to stay married for more than twenty-five years, was a faithful husband, a good father to his four children, and also a very successful businessman was amazing. In addition, he was always willing to lend a hand with both financial and emotional support when his mother or siblings were in need.

Needless to say, gratitude for this help was never expressed. His family always took it for granted that Tom should help them. (After all he was the "lucky" one.)

So when Tom was named his community's "Man of the Year" and honored at a black-tie dinner, his mother and brother and sisters re-fused to attend. They claimed he was "putting on airs" by inviting them to such a function. Among themselves they agreed that he must have bought the honor. Why else, they said, would anyone find someone so ordinary as Tom to be special?

MARY G. DURKIN,
from *An Epidemic of Joy*

THE GOLDEN BELT

Once upon a day two men who met on the road were walking together toward Salamis, the City of Columns. In mid-afternoon they came to a wide river and there was no bridge to cross it. They must needs swim, or seek another road unknown to them.

And they said to one another, "Let us swim. After all, the river is not so wide." And they threw themselves into the water and swam.

And one of the men who had always known rivers and the ways of rivers, in midstream suddenly began to lose himself, and to be carried away by the rushing waters, while the other who had never swum before crossed the river straightaway and stood upon the farther bank. Then seeing his companion still wrestling with the stream, he threw himself again into the waters and brought him also safely to the shore.

And the man who had been swept away by the current said, "But you told me you could not swim. How then did you cross that river with such assurance?"

And the second man answered, "My friend, do you see this belt which girdles me? It is full of golden coins that I have earned for my wife and my children, a full year's work. It is the weight of this belt of gold that carried me across the river, to my wife and my children. And my wife and my children were upon my shoulders as I swam."

And the two men walked on together toward Salamis.

KAHLIL GIBRAN,
from *The Wanderer*

BROTHER AND SISTER

Long years have left their writing on my brow,
But yet the freshness and the dew-fed beam
Of those young mornings are about me now,
When we two wandered toward the far-off stream

With rod and line. Our basket held a store
Baked for us only, and I thought with joy
That I should have my share, though he had more,
Because he was the elder and a boy.

The firmaments of daisies since to me
Have had those mornings in their opening eyes,
The bunched cowslip's pale transparency
Carries that sunshine of sweet memories,

And wild-rose branches take their finest scent
From those blest hours of infantine content.

GEORGE ELIOT,
No. 11 of the 'Brother
and Sister' sequence

BRAVING THE DARK (IN MEMORY OF HER BROTHER)

Passive, your glove allows me to enter
its five black-soft tunnels

the tips however remain uninhabited,
your fingers having been longer than mine.

The words you typed and left, expecting to return,
file out across their electronic lawn.
I caress them with the cursor, like a medium
stroking the table at a séance.

At your pain on the answerphone tape my voice
sticks, as at the gaps in a linguaphone lesson.
In tears, I sort the wafers of your clothes for friends—
straitjacketed in card you watch, and seem unmoved.

At last, day buckles and, awake in bed, I find you:
the deadweight limbs we turned two-hourly
and powdered to protect your baffled skin
become my own, crook'd flat along the sheet

and from the soft lame triangle that your mouth became
you breathe your childhood out upon my pillow.
Wearing the features of our father,
your frightened face sleeps inside mine.

JANE DRAYCOTT,
from *Prince Rupert's Drop*

SIONNA MARIE

My name is Ed Nolan and I'm almost seventeen. Edmund Burke Nolan, if you want to be supercilious. (Our priest says I like to use big
words, and I get them about ninety percent right.) Everything in my
life is okay except I have this terrible problem with my sister Shannon.

I'm spelling her name the way most people would. She spells it

Sionna ever since the priest told us that's the real Irish way to spell it. It's the name of a river and a goddess. Shanny doesn't think she's a river.

She's really Shannon Marie. Or Sionna Marie. She pronounces her second name the Irish way, "the right way" according to her—Marie pronounced like you have a bad cold which has settled in your sinuses sounds like "Maura."

"Shanny Maura," says the priest. "That sounds like it might be the name of the woman who held the milk can when Mrs. O'Leary's cow kicked over the lantern to start the Chicago fire!"

My sister is quite ineffable. And I looked that word up in the dictionary to make sure I had it right before I typed it into my Apple Macintosh. It's the right word, for sure. Shanny is ineffable. Not infallible (though she thinks she is), but ineffable.

I've always had problems with Shanny. Mostly it was keeping her out of fights. Now . . . well, that's what this story is about and my teacher says I'll ruin it all if I tell you the end now.

Shanny and I are Irish twins, which means I was born eleven months and twenty-nine days after she was. The priest says it wouldn't make any difference if it had been one year and a day, we'd still be Irish twins.

Mostly Shanny and I get along all right, more like real twins than like teenage siblings. That's because she's always been one of the guys, not afraid to climb fences or play basketball or things like that. Now that she's getting ready to go to college next year she says she's given up being a tomboy in public. But she'd still rather hang out with the guys than with the girls her age.

I mean, how many big sisters do you know who come around to watch their little brother practice with the other guys on the wrestling team?

The other guys noticed her, of course. Shanny is the kind you notice.

"Hey, Nolan, is that chick your girl?"

"Nah."

"Then why does she always show up for your matches?"

"She's my sibling?"

"Your *what*?"

"It's nothing dirty. It means brother or sister."

"She's no brother."

"You're putting us on, Nolan, that chick isn't your kid sister."

"You're right, I'm her kid brother."

"No way."

"Really."

"*No way!*"

"Hey, sis, you want to meet the guys?"

She came down the steps of the gym grandstand in two bounds. Sure she wanted to meet the guys. I mean that was a substantial component of why she was there in the first place.

You like that? "Substantial component?"

Well, most girls would have been gross about it and become good friends with one or two of the guys. Not Shanny. She took over the whole team. All of them would come to the house to see her or even up to our place at the lake in the summer. Bother Shanny to be friends with the whole wrestling team?

Not an iota. She loved every second of it.

She sings and dances and acts too. All the guys in the casts think she's cute, though I'm not sure about the kind of guys who go out for drama.

So how come I have to get her out of fights? Guys make passes and that sort of thing?

No way. Shanny can take care of herself in that arena. I mean since she's been lifting weights, she's built, in both connotations of that word. Not muscle-bound or anything like that but strong and tough.

When she water-skis (and she's the best chick on the beach at skiing) she doesn't so much skim the water as attack it.

As you've probably guessed, she is totally bossy. Extremely so. The priest says that Shanny is rarely in error and never in doubt. He asked her once if she ever lost an argument. She thought about it for a moment and then said, "Well, sometimes my dad thinks he wins an argument with me. It's good for his morale."

The priest says that in another age she would have been a pirate queen or a mitred abbess ordaining priests no matter what Rome said, or maybe even an Irish goddess.

"But," he says ruefully (don't bother looking that one up, I got it right), "its the 1980s, and she thinks she's an Irish goddess, regardless."

Tell me about it.

She's also very thoughtful. Well, like my mom goes, more of the time than a lot of teenage girls. Like once last summer up at the lake

I was really bummed out because my current chick's mother had put the quietus on her spending the weekend at our house—like there was enough privacy in our place to do anything wrong even if we wanted to!

Well, Shanny knew I was bummed out and knew why and knew that I might demolish a large complement of six-packs, so she organized a surprise birthday party for me—only five weeks late!

So what about the fights I used to have to get her out of. (I know that's two prepositions at the end of a sentence but you expect me to say, "fights out of which I got her?")

See, you have to know about our little brother Jimmy to understand that. Jimmy was born when Shanny was five and I was four. The poor little guy had just about everything wrong with him. The doctors said he'd only live a couple of months and maybe Mom shouldn't even bring him home from the hospital.

Mom, who is a lot like Shanny, goes, "No way. He's our kid and we love him, no matter what's wrong with him, right?"

I don't remember what he looked like then, though I guess he never changed much. He certainly couldn't see and probably couldn't hear and never learned to walk. In fact, even at twelve years old he is no bigger than a baby. And to be objective about it, the little guy did look kind of different. But he was ours and we loved him, you know?

I guess Mom and Dad were a little nervous when they brought him home, not sure how the rest of us would react. Mom said that Jimmy was sick and probably would never get better, but God loved him and so would we as long as we had him. So there were, according to family mythology, two little kids standing around staring down at this strange-looking baby, wondering what we were supposed to do.

Then Shanny took him in her arms and began to sing a lullaby. I don't remember exactly and I guess I'm superimposing what happened later, but poor little Jimmy would kind of smile whenever Shanny would sing to him.

The doctors said Jimmy wouldn't last a year at the most. We kept him alive for twelve years. They used to bring all of us kids over to the hospital every couple of months to ask us dumb questions. The priest said later that we were probably somewhere in an article in a medical journal about how families can cope.

Don't bother hunting up the article because me and Shanny made up funny answers to their dumb questions. Well Shanny made them up and I regurgitated them.

Mom says that we could have never kept Jimmy with us so long unless all the kids had helped. But all of us know that Shanny was the one who worked the hardest. She told me that she could never remember a time when she didn't get up in the morning and bathe and dress and feed Jimmy. She wasn't complaining (When Shanny complains it's mostly about school being *boring*! And you can hear her all the way to Comiskey Park). She was merely stating a fact.

I guess the doctors who asked the stupid questions were worried about what the effects of having Jimmy around the house would be on the rest of us. Well, as you can tell, I'm a real misfit, right? I mean I'd be okay if the chicks didn't dig me so much I had to fight them off by the dozens. And Shanny sounds deprived, too, doesn't she?

I don't know what would have happened in other families, but Mom doesn't exaggerate when she says that Jimmy brought us all together and made us a family.

The problem was other people—kids, grown-ups, well-meaning friends, and not so well-meaning strangers as the priest said.

That's where the fights come in.

I mean we walk into a restaurant on a trip somewhere and people would take one look at Jimmy and start complaining in whispers which were just loud enough to hear.

"That child is disgusting."

I suppose he did look disgusting. He never did grow much after Mom brought him home. His body was misshapen, his face twisted. After a while we didn't notice. It didn't matter to us. He was ours and we loved him.

"They should put him away."

"Why was he permitted to live?"

"How can we eat with *him* in here?"

My parents would usually try to ignore them. Not Shanny. She would dash over to the table and scream at them, "He's my brother and I love him and you just shut up."

Like, *wow*, huh?

Usually they'd shut up. Occasionally some airhead would go, like, "You poor little thing; you shouldn't have to put up with that monster."

That's when Shanny would start punching and I'd have to pull her off. Mom and Dad would tell her she shouldn't fight that way, but I think they were really proud of her. So was I, but I was always the one who had to drag her away.

See what I mean, Shanny was always a problem.

It was worse with kids. Grown-ups would usually keep their smart-mouth ideas to themselves. When Shanny got a little older and people would complain about Jimmy being down on the beach, she'd chew them out verbally instead of punching them out.

She'd go, "You're so uneducated that you make me sick. Don't you understand that God wants us to love little people like Jimmy?"

For starters.

That would shut them up. Some people would even apologize and ask about Jimmy. Shanny is, like the priest says, nothing if not flexible, so she'd turn on all her "sweet little girl" charm and maybe even make them think a little. She got pretty good at her "canned" lecture after a while.

Kids were harder, especially when, like we were in third and fourth grade, and fifth- and sixth- and seventh-graders—mostly boys but some girls, too—would make fun of Jimmy in the playground or when Shanny would take him out in the stroller.

Well, Shanny didn't put up with it and it didn't make any difference how big the kids were. She'd charge them like she was Richard Dent, right?

And who'd have to pull her off before she killed the big kid?

You got it. Little Eddie Nolan.

I was a little punk then. But quick.

I had to be.

'Course if the big punk caught up with me, Shanny would charge back into the fray. Two against one, we Irish twins were pretty good.

Kind of violent, huh?

Well, you see what the priest meant when he said pirate queen. But you know, it worked. The word went out to leave Jimmy alone and people sure did.

And pretty soon parents were telling their kids what a wonderful girl that sweet little brown-eyed Nolan child is. She loves her handicapped little brother almost as though he were a real child.

Lucky they never said it that way when Shanny was around because Jimmy *was* a real child as far as she was concerned.

And all the rest of us, too.

I found him dead in the bedroom in our house at the lake on Easter Monday morning. The priest goes that no time is a good time to die but Easter is the least bad time. He also goes that we must now think of Jimmy as more alive and more mature than any of us. Why, he's like, he even knows more than Shannon does.

We all laughed, but I'm not sure Shanny thought it was as funny as the rest of us.

It was hard at the wake and funeral because a lot of people would go how fortunate we were to be free of Jimmy. Shanny, acting real grown-up now, would respond that we thought we were fortunate to have him as long as we did.

"I was so mature," she's like to me later, "that I'm disgusted with myself."

"I guess we're growing up, sis."

"Gross!"

The priest told us that we would mourn for about a year just as we would if any member of our family died. I guess some of us did some pretty odd things that year. But we're all right.

Mom and Dad were pretty worried about Shanny, which shows how geeky parents can be.

"Maybe it was too much a burden for such a little kid to carry."

"Ha," the priest goes. "No way Shanny gets points for a deprived childhood. Not with the wrestling team still hanging around."

"But what will happen to her?"

"She'll find some lucky guy at whom to direct all that passionate affection."

And to Shanny he's like, "And the guy better be at least as strong-willed as you are."

"No way I'm going to marry a creep or a wimp."

"That guy you had around last summer . . ."

"Well, I got rid of him, didn't I?"

So how's Shanny a problem to me now?

If you have to ask that question, you don't understand my story. You totally don't understand it.

I'm going to Shanny's college next year, right?

And she has this need to take care of someone, until she finds Mr. Strong Will, right?

So who's she going to take care of and protect from all the six-packs and all the chicks who will throw themselves at his feet?

You got it, folks.

Everyone's favorite Irish twin: poor little Eddie Nolan!

ANDREW M. GREELEY,
from *Angels of September*

ON THE DEATH OF A SISTER

Her disappearance has created a sort of universal wilderness around me; it affects every element of an interior world of which I had gradually made her a partner. The two of us thought together in everything that makes up spiritual activity and the interior life. I shall miss her physical presence terribly; on the other hand I think that her power of inspiring and watching over me has strengthened.

PIERRE TEILHARD DE CHARDIN

SAYADIO IN THE LAND OF THE DEAD

{ *Iroquois* }

Sayadio was a warrior who had a younger sister who died. He grieved for her so much that he resolved to find her and bring her back to life from the land of the spirits. The search took him years, and just when he was about to give up he encountered a wise old man who knew the secrets of the spirit world. This old man gave him a magic gourd in which he might catch the spirit of his sister. Upon further conversation, Sayadio learned that this old man was the guide on the path to the part of the spirit world where his sister now was.

When Sayadio arrived in the land of the spirits, the spirits fled from him in fear. He recognized Tarenyawagon, who had lived on earth as Hiawatha, the great teacher of the Five Nations. Tarenyawagon now was the spirit master of ceremonies, and he was as compassionate as he was when he was on earth. Tarenyawagon told Sayadio that the spirits of the dead were about to have a great dance festival, in which his sister would take part. As soon as the spirits formed the dance line, Sayadio recognized the spirit of his sister. When he went to embrace her, however, she disappeared.

He turned again to Tarenyawagon for advice. The teacher gave him a magic rattle. His sister was so entranced by the dance music and the magic sound of the rattle that Sayadio captured her spirit with ease, placing it in the magic gourd.

Sayadio returned to the village with his sister's spirit in the gourd. Just when the ceremony to reunite the spirit with her body had begun, a foolish curious girl opened the gourd, and the sister's spirit vanished.

from *Parallel Myths*

ON THE ANNIVERSARY OF A BROTHER-IN-LAW'S ORDINATION

Andy's Thirty-Fourth

(May 5, 1988)

It's hard to think of what to say
    that doesn't sound so trite.
The man's a blooming gift from God
    who whets our appetite.

God tells through him that all is grace
    if we just look and think.
We'll see the Lord in every place—
    the sun, a child, a wink.

The collar's there for thirty-four.
    Dear Andy, keep it bright.
We know with you there's more in store,
    and it will be a sight.

Congratulations!

JACK DURKIN

ON THE DEATH OF A BROTHER-IN-LAW

Jack Durkin

(April 14, 1994)

Knight of the Holy Spirit, you made us laugh
Brightened all our lives along the way
Comedy and wit your priceless craft
And a dazzling grin that invited play.

Troubadour of God, herald in a business suit
Funny bard of joy now and yet to come
Graceful tour guide of the absolute,
To show us the way peacefully going home.

ANDREW M. GREELEY

Grandparenthood is a surprise gift adult children present to their maturing parents.

A CHRISTENING POEM FOR SCRUNCH

(March 1989)

Who could look upon one like you
and say that God cannot be here?
You swell our hearts each time you coo.
You captivate us when you're near.

Each move you make, each smile you show
brings wonder to our older eyes.
One look at you, and yes we know
the world is good in spite of lies.

Dear Andrew A., forgive the gush.
We cannot help ourselves, new chum.
You melt us down so much we blush
to think how childlike we've become.

Once more, O Lord, you sent one small.
Another baby leads the way,
reminding us that life's a ball
when we remember how to play.

And you, my first but not my last,
remember on this special fest
while love for Mom and Pop is vast,
a grandpa truly is the best!

JACK DURKIN

FOR KATHRYN ROSE DURKIN ON HER BAPTISM DAY

(October, 1989)

There once was a lass Kathryn Rose.
No one ever knew she had toes
till her baptism day,
when we heard someone say,
"Look, her feet didn't come with those bows."

II.

O Katie dear, now did you hear
the news that's going round?
You're not in limbo anymore;
your Christian roots were found.

So now you wear God's gown of white
that cloaks you with His grace
and makes you such a special one
for all here in this place.

O Kathryn Rose, you know you've friends,
Mom, Pop, and every guest,
but you'll soon learn as Andrew did—
grandparents are the best.

JACK DURKIN

NEIL THOMAS AND KRISTINE MARY'S CHRISTENING TOAST

(February 2, 1992)

Welcome, Neil and Kristine Mary,
    to the faith and your roots so deep.
You're linked to saints legendary
    and angels to watch as you sleep.

The world spins at your feet today,
    and we feel the power of God.
You're Christian now and we must pray,
    while you're off in the land of Nod.

May water and oil smooth your way;
    parents' love show you how to share.
See each day as a holiday;
    know the Lord has made you rare.

God bless you Neil and Kristine.

Sláinte!

JACK DURKIN

NORA GRACE'S CHRISTENING TOAST

(June 13, 1992)

Welcome new Christian, O precious one.
May God's arms enfold you on this day

and spin you out to capture the sun
so your life will be bright all the way.

What support you'll have, O Nora dear—
uncles and aunts, girl cousins and boys,
with parents like yours and angels near,
grandparents to hold you and bring toys.

Our toast to you and your parents, too,
from all who gather to share this fest:
"*Sláinte!*" and "*Prost!*" and "Cheers!" quite a few.
Know in this crowd you're with the best.

JACK DURKIN

BRIGIT CLARE'S CHRISTENING TOAST

(September 25, 1993)

O Brigit Clare, do you know
you've joined our faith today?
The drops you got make you glow.
For your life, all here pray.

You're a lucky little one
with John, Eileen, Nora around,
grandparents to share the fun,
godparents to ensure your holy ground.

The birth miracle captivates us,
enthralls and wows all here.

So if at times for you we fuss,
it's because of your magic air.

To you, dear one,

Prost!
Sláinte!

JACK DURKIN

FAMILY CLASSICS

(December, 1990)

My family tree recycles pulp, paper, the printed page. We read by-product books of fallen trees, then branch out along our own, fed by who reads what, wondering where each synthesis will take us—to bright sun or intertwining brambles. From one-veined parents sprout sisters and brothers, reading into life and one another by our reading.

My father reads mysteries (one a night), thrillers, humor, news-papers, sports. Comic strips he reads out loud across the breakfast table 'til you cannot wait your turn but must get up, go see the gag yourself. He laughs and cries at his own jokes. My dad writes poetry and prayers he reads to us at dinner table eucharists, where we laugh on cue and cry since he is there at all—survival we don't take for granted. Without a peek at printed scores, Dad knows all the words to age-old songs. He never leaves a Hallmark store until he's read the funny cards in every aisle and purchased one for Mom to place on the mantel where all can read, or by her mirror, where we are meant to see not read those times she means to be reminded. His birthday, I buy several cards because it's worth an extra glimpse of reading, laughing, passing 'round addi-tions to his classic stock. Dad savors wit, quick words of wonder, though he has lived and left unsaid, unread, a pain that can't be scripted. At times, he reads like a blank book inscribed with invisible ink. I dream that one day I will find its antidote then through my tears read more than passing paragraphs.

My mother reads at night (mysteries, too) in the morning, at the doctor's, in church, before dinner, against the clock, during lunch, on the beach, and when she finds herself before any refrigerator door. She reads theology, her brother's first drafts, newspapers, novels, sane self-help books, women's magazines, motive, AMA's "bible," the notes on my refrigerator door, and new drafts of anything I write. My mom shares news clips, Dad's writings, the latest family facts by phone, updates on fires near Christmas trees, and books that span her love of life: with Honey Bunch once circus bound, bright Betsy 'neath the city lights, Miss Beverly Grey, college girl, then Cherry Ames a student nurse, while Mr. Blue's a mystery that Heaney's poems unlock with sound. Mom brings me plastic shopping bags of books and tells me if she cried at them or stories I just wrote. We love the essence of books, their bound presence in our hands, the fact of them in stacks that line walls of favorite rooms all theirs once mine. Mom writes theology and wishes more people read love poems by night. From birth, she was my reader first. She taught me to read lines and slip sympathetically between them.

My oldest sister, Laura, reads quite consciously and reacts. Her opinion fires discussions around books. You had better think. Her coffee table artfully displays museum books well stocked. School textbooks, handed down to me with clothes she left at home had names of boys inscribed in hearts of color. She is a mystery fan these days, her early dreams a mystery to me. I cannot picture her curled up with a good book in childhood, although her thoughts were in print, quoted in Uncle's book, before anyone I knew. I gave her *Beverly Grey Goes to College* when she went—still wonder if she saved the book. Today, she reads soft light and shadows locked in a lens. She sets them free—developing art peaceably.

My sister Julie bought a big juicy romance and chocolates the day they learned adoption was the counseled option. Julie read to lose herself until the phone rang heralding joy named Andrew. Her son came home on one sure arm; the other cradled *Doctor Spock*. She reads them both, as once she read the photograph of Wayne to us, interpreting that he would be her husband. While searching for reading along the upstairs hallway shelf, I would peruse her college texts and yearbooks: Northwestern data. She taught me to read ancient dirt, that feature numbers labeling potsherds and bones are free, great finds. She analyzes facts and figures, reports, what's up here in Chicago, and sometimes moods—now hers, now mine. She is my older sister Jules. I've watched her read across genres, then draw from life what she can as she can. She always keeps going.

My brother Sean asked me, when last we met, had I read Alice Walker's recent book. This year, on my birthday, he handed me Murdoch's, unwrapped, and not the annual cassette tape. Does he not know that he is my connection to music and I am MTV-illiterate without him? Sean grew literary reading through the back door of sports trivia, data, crossword puzzles, computer manuals, film, the active life. He now claims to know it all. Yet I'm his elder and remember the nursery rhymes read every night by Mom and Dad to slip him under the covers fast asleep. Of late, with enviable ease, he enters my lifelong world of words, where there is fertile territory and new conversation for us both.

My brother Dan built books for class in grammar, then high school, with help from Mom and Dad. He read more into the homework than most, filling his constructions with fresh poetry and commentary—which they typed. One quiet man he watched for days laid strong poetic foundations. And yet Dan didn't read books, not much, not avidly. They felt discouraged. Come college, he and Sean debunked their beds. One summer, on the small, brown shelf that was his headboard, I found Joyce, Yeats, Thoreau, the Norton volumes, and books I'd not yet read but longed to. These have been my guide to comprehending him, my brother, a fellow English major, plus actor, writer, with a surprising, fraternal love of literature.

My sister Anne once wrote from Rome of beauty and how she wished she had read more poetry, knew more art. A true shopper at heart, she grew up reading labels, catalogues, her friends' telephone numbers. She avoided sitting still at the library but scanned football scores, knew _Glamour_ "do's" and "don't" each month, endured "Great Books" discussion leaders. She figures rows of numbers fast and sums up social scenes with ease. Now, Anne reads novels: sassy, a bit classy, literate as well: Dick Francis, Davies, Lorca's best. She skims my shelf for books to swipe. None faze her. Where in her full life does she make room for them? She is intelligent. We sit close on the beach, our books in hand, and share good stories read and in the making.

Elizabeth, youngest of all, reads from the posture of youth—curled up, comfy, concentrated, lost in the interplay between a reader, writer, words. My sister's reading is a gift to me of having been there at its starting for no sooner did I open her new Golden Books than she breezed through my old. Ahead of time, with open arms, she hailed my fictional friends: Lady Jane, wee woodsy Laura, red-haired Anne. Then college classics that we shared brought joy to me and tables turned—Orlando from her hands to mine. This image of Elizabeth head down in book burrows into a cushion of my heart, sits forever on a sofa there, secure. Yet she quit youth, and I now admire how she opens and closes books, letting each new plot unravel for her on its own.

I climbed this tree to read myself, craving a view of all, not all there is to read but all there is. I cannot help but read my life and spill it with the phonics Mom taught me so that I was reading words, mysteriously, before I learned to, sunk into the couch, hot sand, airplanes, my bed, booking in phases: childhood, Nancy Drew, et al., Great Books, Hercules Poirot, flushed romance, classics, religious, cross disciplines required for class, the popular or not at all. For children-to-be, I've hoarded Honey Bunch in recycled sets. I've been told I'm not critical enough and my response to art too physiological: I happen to forget characters, remember what they felt like, savoring the enviable position of having not yet felt countless classics. People say my family is always reading. With pride, I split off a new branch, sustained by homegrown myths of love.

EILEEN DURKIN

CHAPTER FIVE

Friendship

The bird a nest, the spider a web, man friendship.
WILLIAM BLAKE

Hold a true friend with both your hands.
NIGERIAN PROVERB

Love often enters in the name of friendship.
ROMAN PROVERB

Love and friendship, unlike love and marriage, do not necessarily go together like a horse and carriage. During the course of a lifetime, we develop relationships with a wide variety of people, some of whom we call friends. We have childhood playmates, schoolmates, community acquaintances, neighbors, work associates, recreation partners, and, if we're fortunate, a soul friend.

Many of these relationships are casual and transitory. Others have the potential for friendship. A smaller number might develop into deep and lasting relationships where love and friendship go together, but in a different way than love and marriage. We learn that love has many dimensions.

No hard-and-fast rules govern friendship relationships. No legal requirements make a friendship official. There are no celebrations of commitment to friendship, no offspring provide societal pressure to work out differences that might lead to the breakup of a friendship, no mourning rituals for the end of a friendship. A friend, sometimes consciously while at other times unknowingly, can torpedo a friendship. An opportunity to grow in love is lost.

Many friendships, even long-term deep friendships, end because of misunderstandings. Just as in any love relationship, friends must navigate the ups and downs of their friendship, conscious of the potential for misunderstanding. The motto should be: Never take a friend for granted.

Friendship is like a garden; it must be nurtured. It is never enough to say "I have a friend." We must be a friend. We must be there for a friend in bad times as well as in good times. In that way we discover the love that enters in the name of friendship. The surprise of a friend's love for us and our love for a friend opens us to new dimensions of ourselves.

The stories, sayings, poems, and reflections in this chapter examine various kinds of friendships. The authors invite us to reflect on our own experiences of friendship. When are the times when we have been surprised to discover that someone we have known, often for a long time, is an unacknowledged friend? When have we been involved in a friendship that has carefully prescribed limits that leave us frustrated? When has someone walked the extra mile with us, supporting us when all others seem unconcerned? When have we done these same things with others?

Our selections suggest that if we learn to treasure our friendships, we will be rewarded with a love that releases us from the pangs of loneliness. We experience a special kind of love.

*W*e remember the special moments of our childhood friendships. *Some of these memories delight us. We fondly recall those times when someone surprised us by being a friend. We also remember the times we befriended someone we had not even considered a friend. We sadly recall those times when our actions sabotaged an opportunity for friendship.*

BEST FRIEND

My six-year-old granddaughter, Krissy, came running down the steps to the beach calling "Grandma!"

Suddenly I was four and she was Joycey. In that instant I was back in time and space sitting on the bottom step of the house of the seven-year-old social mistress of the block, a place to which I was banished every day that summer.

All the emotions of that roller-coaster time surfaced. Younger by three years than any other kid on the block and four years younger than my sister, I had no playmates. The older kids didn't want me around, especially when the seven-year-old, an only child, made it clear to all that I was not welcome.

Her house was the center of all kid activity. She had the best toys. Her mother welcomed everyone to the backyard *and* the front porch, a place generally off-limits to kids. Each afternoon anyone hanging around was sure to be invited in for cookies and lemonade or sometimes even black cows. That is, everyone but me.

My tormentor had an uncanny sense of timing. She would hurl the dreaded words, "Go home, crybaby," at me just before her mother would appear with the invitation to have a treat. Of course, I would cry and run home. Four-year-olds are not very good at figuring out cause and effect.

Funny how sixty years later, I still feel the hurt of her rejection. Now I can name the emotions. I was lonely. I was sad. Also with the innocence of a four-year-old, I was foolish. Each day I would traipse behind my sister, thinking I would get a chance to play. I never did.

One day, shortly after I took my assigned place, a car parked in front of the recently sold house two doors away. "Maybe it's the new owners," someone said. Everyone stopped their games and stared openly as a mom, a dad, a boy, and a girl emerged from the car and climbed the steps to the bungalow. All the bigger kids tried to guess the age of the boy. I just stood and stared.

I saw a chubby little girl with long curls grab her mother's hand and trudge up the steep steps of the bungalow. A rag doll dangled from her other hand. I felt a faint glimmer of hope. Could it be that at last someone my age would live on our block? Would I finally have someone who would play with me? Would I have a friend, a word I heard some big kids use when referring to each other?

Three weeks later I had the answer. The mom and daughter, out for a walk around the block, passed by the yard of our corner house. My mom, who was hanging clothes to dry, greeted them. The moms talked. My mom invited our new neighbors into our yard. They talked about how nice it was that their daughters were the same age. We were introduced. I learned her name—Joyce. We were encouraged to play with my dolls while our moms chatted. Soon Joyce became Joycey, and from that day on we became inseparable.

Krissy's "Grandma, Grandma, I'm here. Let's go in the water," brought me out of my regression to age four. For the first time, I noticed how she was almost a carbon copy of my childhood friend. Or at least as I remembered her. As Krissy frolicked on the beach, images from the five happiest years of my childhood flashed across my memory screen.

Joycey at our side door every morning calling me to come out and play. Joycey and I, arms entwined, hurrying past the neighborhood bully's house on our way to the penny candy story. Joycey and I playing with our dolls day after day. Our dancing lessons and the recital with her the Little Dutch Boy and me the Little Dutch Girl having to bump rear ends. I was so embarrassed. The two of us caught in front of the curtain after the final bow at a recital. The first day of first grade with Joycey at our side door a good hour before we had to be at school. Walking to school each day, arm in arm. The day of our First Holy Communion when Joyce called for me and I wasn't even dressed. A girl we played with once in a while angrily accusing us of being worse than the Bobbsey Twins when we shared a secret on the school playground.

August was for me the cruelest month. Joycey's grandparents had a farm in Wisconsin, about a three-hour drive from our house. Every August 1, Joycey would leave for the farm. Her long, thick hair, with its perfect curls was too much work for Grandma, so she would return with a bob cut on August 31. The next morning we would rejoice at being together again. Once her mom mentioned that I might like to visit the farm. I waited and waited for an invitation, but it never came. Maybe two of us would have been too much for Grandma.

Disaster struck near the end of third grade. Joycey's parents bought a new house in another neighborhood. They would be moving the end of the summer. Not only would she be leaving the block. She would be going to another school.

When she moved, I lost my best friend.

For a few years, Joycey and I visited back and forth about four times a year, usually over a weekend. I would take a bus to her house and her dad would drive me home or he would drive her to my house. Still it was never the same. The visiting stopped when we became involved in the many activities of our different high schools.

I did not have a best friend again until, at age seventeen, I met the man I eventually married. I had friends, but we were always a group. During the preteen and early teenage years I read the Maud Lovelace Betsy-Tacy stories. I often imagined how wonderful it would have been to have Joycey to share secrets with as those two did.

At the end of my senior year of high school, I met someone from Joycey's school who told me Joyce, as she called her, was engaged and going to be married the Christmas after graduation. I had a hard time believing it. I, who needed a blind date for the big dance at the beginning of my senior year, couldn't begin to imagine being married. I went to her wedding. She couldn't come to my August wedding three years later. Maybe she still went to the farm. She dropped off a gift. I wasn't home, so I didn't see her.

I never saw her after that. We exchanged Christmas cards for a few years. Then, as often happens, even that contact ended. Years went by when I seldom thought of Joyce. Even when I did think of her, I didn't know where to find her. I had deleted her address from my Christmas card list. Once, while visiting my son who lived in the same area code of Joyce's last address, I checked the phone book for her address and number. They were not listed.

I must have told stories about her to my children. At my sixtieth birthday celebration they noted the year I met Joycey on a time line of my life. Once again, I wondered where she was.

Krissy again interrupted my reverie, begging me to take her to the pool where the water was warmer. Memories of Joyce were put on hold, though I did wonder where she might be.

Later that night, after the beach house quieted down, I remembered the white pages on the Internet. Excitedly, I logged on and searched the address books for phone numbers or e-mail addresses for Joyce and her siblings. Her husband's name was not too common, and I knew her brothers' name. Perhaps her parents were still alive. I thought I had hit on a sure-fire way to find her. Not so. None of them were listed.

I became obsessed with finding her. Every day, I would try a new approach to my Internet search. All my search clues yielded nothing. Then one evening at a committee meeting for a grammar school reunion, I asked if any of the other committee members remembered her. A woman on the committee went to high school with Joyce. She remembered her because she was a very good friend of some of the women the committee member kept in touch with. Joyce and these women had gone to the same grammar school and continued their friendship in high school.

Some of them would be getting together for lunch the next week, and she would ask if they knew where Joyce was. I was thrilled. I looked forward to seeing her and comparing memories from our childhood years. I wondered what her life had been like, how many children and grandchildren she had, if her parents were still alive, what her brothers were doing.

A few weeks later, my committee contact called with information about our reunion. Her voice became somewhat somber as she told me she had met with Joyce's friends and she was sorry to tell me that Joyce had died. They didn't know when or how. All they knew was that six years earlier when they went over the class list for their fortieth reunion, she was listed as deceased.

I still search the Internet, hoping to find a family member who can fill me in on her life since we last met. And, of course, I have Krissy as a reminder of the joy of that very special friendship.

MARY G. DURKIN

And the song, from beginning to end,
I found in the heart of a friend.

HENRY WADSWORTH LONGFELLOW

FRIENDSHIP

And a youth said, Speak to us of Friendship.
And he answered, saying:
Your friend is your needs answered.
He is your field, which you sow with love and reap with thanksgiving.
And he is your board and your fireside.
For you come to him with your hunger, and you seek him for peace.

When your friend speaks his mind you fear
not the "nay" in your own mind, nor do you
withhold the "ay."

And when he is silent your heart ceases not
to listen to his heart;

For without words, in friendship, all thoughts,
all desires, all expectations are born and shared,
with joy that is unacclaimed.

When you part from your friend, you grieve
not;

For that which you love most in him may be
clearer in his absence, as the mountain to the
climber is clearer from the plain.

And let there be no purpose in friendship
save the deepening of the spirit.

For love that seeks aught but the disclosure
of its own mystery is not love but a net cast
forth: and only the unprofitable is caught.

And let your best be for your friend.

If he must know the ebb of your tide, let him
know its flood also.

For what is your friend that you should seek
him with hours to kill?

Seek him always with hours to live.

For it is his to fill your need, but not your
emptiness.

And in the sweetness of friendship let there
be laughter, and sharing of pleasures.

For in the dew of little things the heart finds
its morning and is refreshed.

KAHLIL GIBRAN,
from *The Prophet*

We dasn't stop again at any town for days and days; kept right along down the river. We was down south in the warm weather now, and a mighty long ways from home. We begun to come to trees with Spanish moss on them, hanging down from the limbs like long graying beards. It was the first I ever see it growing, and it made the woods look solemn and dismal. So now the frauds reckoned they was out of danger, and they begun to work the villages again.

First they done a lecture on temperance; but they didn't make enough for them both to get drunk on. Then in another village they started a dancing school; but they didn't know no more how to dance than a kangaroo does; so the first prance they made the general public jumped in and pranced them out of town. Another time they tried to go at yellocution; but they didn't yellocute long till the audience got up and give them a solid good cussing, and made them skip out. They tackled missionarying, and mesmerizing, and doctoring, and telling fortunes, and a little of everything; but they couldn't seem to have no luck. So at last they got just about dead broke, and laid around the raft as she floated along, thinking and thinking, and never saying nothing, by the half a day at a time, and dreadful blue and desperate.

And at last they took a change and begun to lay their heads together in the wigwam and talk low and confidential two or three hours at a time. Jim and me got uneasy. We didn't like the look of it. We judged they was studying up some kind of worse deviltry than ever. We turned it over and over, and at last we made up our minds they was going to break into somebody's house or store, or was going into the counterfeit-money business, or something. So then we was pretty scared, and made up an agreement that we wouldn't have nothing in the world to do with such actions, and if we ever got the least show we would give them the cold shake and clear out and leave them behind. Well, early one morning we hid the raft in a good, safe place about two mile below a little bit of a shabby village named Pikesville, and the king went ashore and told us all to stay hid whilst he went up to town and smelt around to see if anybody had got any wind of the

"Royal Nonesuch" there yet. ("House to rob, you *mean*," says I to myself; "and when you get through robbing it you'll come back here and wonder what has become of me and Jim and the raft—and you'll have to take it out in wondering.") And he said if he warn't back by midday the duke and me would know it was all right, and we was to come along.

So we stayed where we was. The duke he fretted and sweated around, and was in a mighty sour way. He scolded us for everything, and we couldn't seem to do nothing right; he found fault with every little thing. Something was a-brewing, sure. I was good and glad when midday come and no king; we could have a change, anyway—and maybe a chance for *the* chance on top of it. So me and the duke went up to the village, and hunted around there for the king, and by and by we found him in the back room of a little low doggery, very tight, and a lot of loafers bullyragging him for sport, and he a-cussing and a-threatening with all his might, and so tight he couldn't walk, and couldn't do nothing to them. The duke he begun to abuse him for an old fool, and the king begun to sass back, and the minute they was fairly at it I lit out and shook the reefs out of my hind legs, and spun down the river road like a deer, for I see our chance; and I made up my mind that it would be a long day before they ever see me and Jim again. I got down there all out of breath but loaded up with joy, and sung out:

"Set her loose Jim; we're all right now!"

But there warn't no answer, and nobody come out of the wigwam. Jim was gone! I set up a shout—and then another—and then another one; and run this way and that in the woods, whooping and screeching; but it warn't no use—old Jim was gone. Then I set down and cried; I couldn't help it. But I couldn't set still long. Pretty soon I went out on the road, trying to think what I better do, and I run across a boy walking, and asked him if he'd seen a strange nigger dressed so and so, and he says:

"Yes."

"Whereabouts?" says I.

"Down to Silas Phelps's place, two mile below here. He's a runaway nigger, and they've got him. Was you looking for him?"

"You bet I ain't! I run across him in the woods about an hour or two ago, and he said if I hollered he'd cut my livers out—and told me to lay down and stay where I was; and I done it. Been there ever since; afeard to come out."

"Well," he says, "you needn't be afeard no more, becuz they've got him. He run off f'm down South, som'ers."

"It's a good job they got him."

"Well, I *reckon*! There's two hundred dollars' reward on him. It's like picking up money out'n the road."

"Yes, it is—and *I* could 'a' had it if I'd been big enough; I see him *first*. Who nailed him?"

"It was an old fellow—a stranger—and he sold out his chance in him for forty dollars becuz he's got to go up the river and can't wait. Think o' that now! You bet *I'd* wait, if it was seven year."

"That's me, every time," says I. "But maybe his chance ain't worth no more than that, if he'll sell it so cheap. Maybe there's something ain't straight about it."

"But it *is*, though—straight as a string. I see the handbill myself. It tells all about him, to a dot—paints him like a picture, and tells the plantation he's frum, below New*rleans*. No-sirree-*bob*, they ain't no trouble 'bout *that* speculation, you bet you. Say, gimme a chaw tobacker, won't ye?"

I didn't have none, so he left. I went to the raft, and set down in the wigwam to think. But I couldn't come to nothing. I thought till I wore my head sore, but I couldn't see no way out of the trouble. After all this long journey, and after all we'd done for them scoundrels, here it was all come to nothing, everything all busted up and ruined, because they could have the heart to serve Jim such a trick as that, and make him a slave again all his life, and amongst strangers, too, for forty dollars.

Once I said to myself it would be a thousand times better for Jim to be a slave at home where his family was, as long as he'd *got* to be a slave, and so I'd better write a letter to Tom Sawyer and tell him to tell Miss Watson where he was. But I soon give up that notion for two things: she'd be mad and disgusted at his rascality and ungratefulness for leaving her, and so she'd sell him straight down the river again; and if she didn't, everybody naturally despises an ungrateful nigger, and they'd make Jim feel it all the time, and so he'd feel ornery and disgraced. And then think of *me*! It would get all around that Huck Finn helped a nigger to get his freedom; and if I was ever to see anybody from that town again I'd be ready to get down and lick his boots for shame. That's just the way: a person does a low-down thing, and then he don't want to take no consequences of it. Thinks as long as he can hide, it ain't no disgrace. That was my fix exactly. The more I studied about this the more my conscience went to grinding me, and the more wicked and low-down and ornery I got to feeling. And at last, when it hit me all of a sudden that here was the plain hand of Providence slapping me in the face and letting me know my wickedness was being watched all the time whilst from up there in heaven, whilst I was stealing a poor old woman's nigger that hadn't ever done me no harm, and now was showing me there's One that's always on the lookout, and ain't a-going to allow no such miserable doings to go only just so fur and no further, I most dropped in my tracks I was so scared. Well, I tried the best I could to kinder soften it up somehow for myself by saying I was brung up wicked, and so I warn't so much to blame; but something inside of me kept saying: "There was the Sunday-school, you could a gone to it; and if you'd 'a' done it they'd 'a' learnt you there that people that acts as I'd been acting about that nigger goes to everlasting fire."

It made me shiver. And I about made up my mind to pray, and see if I couldn't try to quit being the kind of boy I was and be better. So I kneeled down. But the words wouldn't come. Why wouldn't they? It warn't no use to try and hide it from Him. Nor from *me*, neither. I knowed very well why they wouldn't come. It was because my heart wasn't right; it was because I was playing double. I was letting *on* to give up sin, but away inside of me I was holding on to the biggest one of all. I was trying to make my mouth *say* I would do the right thing and the clean thing, and go and write to that nigger's owner and tell where he was; but deep down in me I knowed it was a lie, and He knowed it. You can't pray a lie—I found that out.

So I was full of trouble, full as I could be; and didn't know what to do. At last I had an idea; and I says, I'll go and write the letter— and *then* see if I can pray. Why, it was astonishing, the way I felt as light as feather right straight off, and my troubles all gone. So I got a piece of paper and a pencil, all glad and excited, and set down and wrote:

Miss Watson, your runaway nigger Jim is down here two mile below Pikesville, and Mr. Phelps has got him and he will give him up for the reward if you send.

Huck Finn.

I felt good and all washed clean of sin for the first time I had ever felt so in my life, and I knowed I could pray now. But I didn't do it straight off but laid the paper down and set there thinking—thinking how good it was all this happened so, and how near I come to being lost and going to hell. And went on thinking. And got to thinking over our trip down the river; and I see Jim before me all the time: in the day and in the nighttime, sometimes moonlight, sometimes storms, and we a-floating along, talking and singing and laughing. But somehow I couldn't seem to strike no places to harden me against him, but only the other kind. I'd see him standing my watch on top of his'n, 'stead of calling me, so I could go on sleeping; and see him how glad he was when I come back out of the fog; and when I come to him again in the swamp, up there where the feud was; and such-like times; and would always call me honey and pet me, and do everything he could think of for me, and how good he always was; and at last I struck the time I saved him by telling the men we had smallpox aboard, and he was so grateful, and said I was the best friend old Jim ever had in the world, and the *only* one he's got now; and then I happened to look around and see that paper.

It was a close place. I took it up, and held it in my hand. I was a-trembling, because I'd got to decide, forever, betwixt two things, and I knowed it. I studied a minute, sort of holding my breath, and then says to myself:

"All right, then, I'll *go* to hell"—and tore it up.

It was awful thoughts and awful words, but they was said. And I let them stay said; and never thought no more about reforming. I shoved the whole thing out of my head, and said I would take up wickedness again, which was in my line, being brung up to it, and the other warn't. And for a starter I would go to work and steal Jim out of slavery again; and if I could think up anything worse, I would do that, too; because as long as I was in, and in for good, I might as well go the whole hog.

Then I set to thinking over how to get at it, and turned over some considerable many ways in my mind; and at last fixed up a plan that suited me. So then I took the bearings of a woody island that was down the river a piece, and as soon as it was fairly dark I crept out with my raft and went for it, and hid it there, and then turned in. I slept the night through, and got up before it was light, and had my breakfast, and put on my store clothes, and tied up some others and cleared for shore. I landed below where I judged was Phelps's place, and hid my bundle in the woods, and then filled up the canoe with water, and loaded rocks into her and sunk her where I could find her again when I wanted her, about a quarter of a mile below a little stream sawmill that was on the bank.

Then I struck up the road, and when I passed the mill I see a sign on it, "Phelps's Sawmill," and when I come to the farm houses, two or three hundred yards further along, I kept my eyes peeled, but didn't see nobody around, though it was good daylight now. But I didn't mind, because I didn't want to see nobody just yet—I only wanted to get the lay of the land. According to my plan, I was going to turn up there from the village, not from below. So I just took a look, and shoved along, straight for town. Well, the very first man I see when I got there was the duke. He was sticking up a bill for the "Royal Nonesuch"—three-night performances—like that other time. *They* had the cheek, them frauds! I was right on him before I could shirk. He looked astonished, and says:

"Hel-lo! Wher'd *you* come from?" then he says, kind of glad and eager, "Where's the raft?—got her in a good place?"

I says:

"Why, that's just what I was going to ask your grace."

Then he didn't look so joyful, and says:

"What was your idea for asking *me*?" he says

"Well," I says, "when I see the king in that doggery yesterday I says to myself, we can't get him home for hours, till he's soberer; so I went a-loafing around town to put in the time and wait. A man up and offered me ten cents to help him pull a skiff over the river and back to fetch a sheep, and so I went along; but when we was dragging him to the boat, and the man left me a-holt of the rope and went behind him to shove him along, he was too strong for me and jerked loose and run, and we after him. We didn't have no dog, and so we had to chase him all over the country till we tired him out. We never got him till dark; then we fetched him over, and I started down for the raft. When I got there and see it was gone, I says to myself, 'They've got into trouble and had to leave; and they've took my nigger, which is the only nigger I've got in the world, and now I'm in a strange country, and ain't got no property no more, nor nothing, and no way to make my living'; so I set down and cried. I slept in the woods all night. But what *did* become of the raft, the?—and Jim—poor Jim!"

"Blamed *if I* know—that is, what's become of the raft. That old fool had made a trade and got forty dollars, and when we found him in the doggery the loafers had matched half dollars with him and got every cent but what he'd spent for whisky; and when I got him home late last night and found the raft gone, we said, 'That little rascal has stole our raft and shook us, and run off down the river.' "

"I wouldn't shake my *nigger*, would I?—the only nigger I had in the world, and the only property."

"We never thought of that. Fact is, I reckon we'd come to consider him *our* nigger; yes, we did consider him so—goodness knows we had trouble enough for him. So when we see the raft was gone and we flat broke, there warn't anything for it but to try the 'Royal Nonesuch' another shake. And I've pegged along ever since, dry as powderhorn. Where's that ten cents? Give it here."

I had considerable money, so I give him ten cents, but begged him to spend it for something to eat, and give me some, because it was all the money I had and I hadn't had nothing to eat since yesterday. He never said nothing. The next minute he whirls on me and says:

"Do you reckon that nigger would blow on us? We'd skin him if he done that!"

"How can he blow? Hain't he run off?"

"No! That old fool sold him, and never divided with me, and the money's gone."

"*Sold* him?" I says, and begun to cry; "why, he was *my* nigger, and that was my money. Where is he?—I want my nigger."

"Well, you can't *get* your nigger, that's all—so dry up your blubbering. Looky here—do you think *you'd* venture to blow on us? Blamed if I think I'd trust you. Why if you *was* to blow on us—"

He stopped, but I never seen the duke look so ugly out of his eyes before. I went on a-whimpering, and says: "I don't want to blow on nobody; and I ain't got no time to blow, no how; I got to turn out and find my nigger."

He looked kinder bothered, and stood there with his bills fluttering on his arm, thinking, and wrinkling up his forehead. At last he says:

"I'll tell you something. We got to be here three days. If you'll promise you won't blow, and won't let the nigger blow, I'll tell you where to find him."

So I promised, and he says:

"A farmer by the name of Silas Ph—" and then stopped. You see, he started to tell me the truth; but when he stopped that way, and begun to study and think again, I reckoned he was changing his mind. And so he was. He wouldn't trust me; he wanted to make sure of having me out of the way the whole three days. So pretty soon he says:

"The man that bought him is named Abram Foster—Abram G. Foster—and he lives forty mile back here in the country, on the road to Lafayette."

"All right," I says, "I can walk it in three days. And I'll start this very afternoon."

"No you won't, you'll start *now*; and don't you lose any time about it, neither, nor do any gabbling by the way. Just keep a tight tongue in your head and move right along, and then you won't get into trouble with *us*, d'ye hear?"

That was the order I wanted, and that was the one I played for. I wanted to be left free to work my plans.

"So clear out," he says; "and you can tell Mr. Foster whatever you want to. Maybe you can get him to believe that Jim *is* your nigger— some idiots don't require documents—leastways I've heard there's such down South here. And when you tell him the handbill and the reward's bogus, maybe he'll believe you when you explain to him what the idea was for getting 'em out. Go 'long now, and tell him anything you want to; but mind you don't work your jaw any *between* here and there."

So I left, and struck for the back country. I didn't look around, but I kinder felt like he was watching me. But I knowed I could tire him out at that. I went straight out in the country as much as a mile before I stopped; then I doubled back through the woods towards Phelps's. I reckoned I better start in on my plan straight off without fooling around, because I wanted to stop Jim's mouth till these fellows could get away. I didn't want no trouble with their kind. I'd seen all I wanted of them, and wanted to get entirely shut of them.

MARK TWAIN,
from *The Adventures of Huckleberry Finn*

Two are better off than one, because together they can work more effectively. If one of them falls down, the other can help him up. But if someone is alone and falls, it's just too bad, because there is no one to help him. If it is cold, two can sleep together and stay warm, but how can you keep warm by yourself? Two people can resist an attack that would defeat one person alone. A rope made of three cords is hard to break.

ECCLESIASTES *4:9–12*

A friend is not a true friend
unless he protects his brother
in three situations:
in his misfortune,
in his absence,
and at his death.

IMAM ALI

THE CONFUSED MARBLE PLAYER

Once upon a time, there was a little boy who loved to play marbles. This young man, whose name was Adelbert, was a very good marbles player. In fact, he was devastating. He won every marbles match during the first month of school and cleaned out all his friends. Pretty soon he was the only kid who had any marbles left.

Then the other boys bought more marbles and came back to take on Adelbert again. He cleaned them out a second time.

Every day Adelbert would take all his marbles from the great bags he stored them in and pour them out on the floor of his family's recreation room just to look at them.

His mother said, "Adie, why are you so obsessed with the marbles?"

"Because they are so beautiful," Adelbert said, his eyes glowing.

The other kids came back with more marbles for a third round, but suddenly Adelbert refused to play anymore. He was too busy admiring the marbles he had won.

"I have all the marbles I need," he told the others. "It's more fun just to look at my big bag of marbles than to waste my time playing with you drips."

Thus did Adelbert confuse the ends with the means.

ANDREW M. GREELEY,
from *An Epidemic of Joy*

The biggest failures are those
who have failed to win friends,
but even bigger failures are those
who lose what friends they have made.

IMAM ALI

he widely held view that women are better than men at friendship is a truism. Some women are very good at friendship. They are open to the concerns of others and available to help in good times and bad. They often are more likely than men to express their commitment to friendship. However, other women are quite circumspect about their friendships. Even after long years of being friends, some women will not make the leap necessary to turn the friendship into love. A fear of intimacy can undermine a chance to experience a supportive love.

EDITH

The hand-addressed letter with a Martinez, California, postmark almost got thrown out with the junk mail. I knew no one in Martinez. Indeed, I had never even heard of Martinez. What made me open the envelope? Once I met the letter writer, I knew she probably willed me to do it. She certainly had that kind of power.

The opening lines caught my eye: *I read your book and want to meet you. Do you ever come to San Francisco? Would you be willing to lecture at our parish forum?* The book was my recently published doctoral dissertation on a theology for suburban women and their changing role in the church.

My spirits were low at that time. Even a published doctoral dissertation on a theology for women had not helped me, a married woman with seven children, secure a position at any of the universities in the Chicago area in the early 1970s. Her words told me someone was reading what I wrote.

By happy coincidence, my husband was going to San Francisco on business, and I had plans to accompany him. I wrote back with this information. Edith scheduled the lecture. Little did I know where this would lead.

We drove out to Martinez for dinner with Edith and her husband, Clarence, a most interesting couple. Edith, a fiery Italian-American. Clarence, a gentle soft-spoken man of Portuguese heritage. Married when she was nineteen and he was twenty, they were self-educated in biblical studies and had written, along with a priest, a Bible studies program. Edith was an only child. Both her parents died when she was in her teens. Their four children, the middle two definite products of the 1960s, joined us for dinner. The conversation was a rapid-fire discussion of ideas with much disagreement on just about every topic. A lot like home.

The lecture was well attended. Used to the academic setting, I prepared the paper I read. The audience seemed attentive and there were some good questions. Later, Edith chastised me for reading the paper. If we were sitting around a living room, wouldn't I just speak my thoughts? That's what I should have done. I never again read a paper except at an academic function. Already this woman was changing me.

Many letters went back and forth between Martinez and my house, each contributing to a deeper appreciation of how much we shared. We were adult pen pals.

I was back in the area a year later. It was spring break time for my daughter. She was flying stand-by from San Francisco to Tokyo. We spent the day before her departure touring San Francisco sights. She flew out the next morning, March 17. I went out to Martinez, where Edith cooked a corned beef and cabbage dinner (her first attempt) for her Irish friend. I made Irish soda bread. We talked until the wee hours of the morning.

The next spring, I gave two papers on religion and ethnicity at an education conference in San Francisco. Edith came into town each day, attended the lectures, gave her stamp of approval, and joined our group for dinner both evenings. Most of my friends at the conference were Italian-American from an ethnicity concerns group. She was in her glory.

Edith phoned after Christmas to tell me her daughter was going to marry in the summer. I was to be sure to keep the date free. She wanted me there. Edith was making the wedding dress and the bridesmaids' dresses. I went out three days before the wedding and helped put the finishing touches on the dresses. Edith said she thought of me as the sister she never had. We were more than pen pals by then.

The following summer my husband and I celebrated the twenty-fifth anniversary of our wedding. Edith and Clarence had talked about making a driving trip around the United States. They planned it so they would be in Chicago for our celebration. Edith joined the pickup choir for the anniversary Mass. By the time the party was over, she had talked to everyone there. They left a few days after the party. That was the last time I saw her.

Two months after our anniversary, my husband was diagnosed with lung cancer. Surgery and radiation and recovery from that kept us close to home for the next year. In a letter at the end of the following summer, Edith described a rather harrowing drive from their cottage in the mountains back to Martinez. She had a bad bout of what she thought was the stomach flu. She wrote that she had never been so sick in her life.

She continued to have bouts of stomach upset. In early January, she phoned from the hospital. She was going to have surgery the following day for a bowel obstruction. Two days later, her daughter phoned to tell me the obstruction turned out to be colon cancer that had spread to her liver. Edith was so run-down from being ill prior to the surgery that the doctors suggested she go home and build herself up before they began radiation and chemotherapy. Her daughters had all the information on diet that would help her prepare for treatment.

Two weeks later, Clarence phoned and put Edith on to talk with me. In a voice so soft I could barely hear her, she told me that she just couldn't follow the doctor's orders for regaining her strength. She tried but it was just all too much. She apologized for causing everyone so much trouble.

I was finishing a book, working under a deadline. I told her I'd be out to see her in two weeks. She died before I made the trip.

I went out to the funeral and helped with the family preparations. Edith had planned her own funeral, in charge even past the end. She was buried in a peaceful site on a hill overlooking a broad expanse of grass and trees. I remember thinking that it was too peaceful for Edith, who was always bustling with energy.

Of course, as I later thought about it, Edith was not there in the ground. The ground could never hold her. Wherever she was, she was busy organizing something. I'm sure that when it's my turn to join her, she will be waiting for me, full of plans for all the things she wants to show me.

MARY G. DURKIN

Friendship is a sheltering tree.

SAMUEL TAYLOR COLERIDGE

FRIENDSHIP

Like a quetzal plume, a fragrant flower,
friendship sparkles
Like heron plums, it weaves itself into finery.
Our song is a bird calling out like a jingle
how beautiful you make it sound!
Here, among flowers that enclose us,
Among flowery boughs you are singing.

AZTEC

I love you just as the Father loves me; remain in my love. If you obey my commands, you will remain in my love, just as I have obeyed my Father's commands and remain in his love. I have told you this so that my joy may be in you and that your joy may be complete. My commandment is this: love one another, just as I love you. The greatest love you can have for your friends is to give your life for them. And you are my friends if you do what I command you. I do not call you servants any longer, because servants do not know what their master is doing. Instead, I call you friends, because I have told you everything I heard from my Father. You did not choose me; I chose you and appointed you to go and bear much fruit, the kind of fruit that endures. And so the Father will give you whatever you ask of him in my name. This, then, is what I command you: love one another.

JOHN *15:9–17*

To Miss Mary A. Sawyer

They say that Friendship's but a name
    A vain and empty sound;

    Has thou ne'er felt its influence,
    A faithful friend ne'er found:

Upon whose breast you might repose
    The burdens of your care;

Whose faithful heart with yours would feel;
    And every trouble share:

And when the tempestuous tide ran high;
    Would love you to the end,

    If not, accept my heart
    In Friendship's strongest Tie;
    And in Friendship let us die.

Accept this dear Mary, as a Tribute of
  Friendship,
  from your friend

S. CAROLINE C. HALSTEAD

TO MY TEACHER ETHELDA COGGAN

Remember me
when gone away
And I the same will do
And when you're with your friends at home
  Then I'll remember you

Forget me ah forget me not
When evenings shades descend
For then my thoughts still turn to thee
  My fondly cherished friend.

August 4th, 1853
From your pupil

ANGELINE HILTON,
from *On Women and Friendship:
A Collection of Victorian Keepsakes and Treasures*

Esther, Liz, and Alix, who in Jane Austen's day would never have met
at all, met in Cambridge in 1952. Just before Christmas, when they
were up for interview from their respective schools. Alix was applying

to read English Literature, Liz to read Natural Sciences (with a view to medicine) and Esther to read Modern Languages. This should have safely prevented any rapport between them, but did not. There were, it is true, many awkwardnesses in their first communications, for none of them was much used to speaking with strangers, but this lack of practice was balanced by a strong desire on the part of all three of them to enter upon a new life in which speaking to strangers was possible. Otherwise, each had separately recognized, the future was circumscribed. Somehow haltingly, over dinner in Hall (chicken, leeks, and tinned spaghetti, a mixture delicious to each after years of post-war whale meat and school meals) they lurched into conversation, having found themselves for not good reason sitting together: Liz and Alix discovered that both came from Yorkshire, and that neither played lacrosse, nor had ever seen it being played, and Esther joined the discussion by volunteering that she herself had managed to avoid playing netball for the past three years on the grounds that she was too small. 'I said I was unfairly handicapped, and they let me do extra Latin instead,' she said. The fact that both Liz and Alix seemed to accept that extra Latin might be preferable to netball indicated that further interchange might be possible, and they continued to talk, through the fruit tart and custard, of nature of intellectual and physical education, of matter and spirit, of Descartes (brought up by Esther), of T. S. Eliot (brought up by Alix) and of schizophrenia (brought up by Liz). The matter was abstract, for none of them knew anything other than abstractions, the tone lofty. It was what they had expected of University, but had not hoped so soon to find.

It would be wrong to give the impression that Liz, Alix and Esther fell into one another's arms with cries of delight when they met again that October, or to suggest that they roved inseparable. But they were, nevertheless, pleased to rediscover one another, and sat up late on their first evening in Esther's room, which had already begun to put out hints to its later decorative eccentricities. They talked of their summer adventures, of their hopes for the future, but mostly of their own provenance. Liz attempted her first sketch of her mother, her first outline for the outside world of the domestic ghost with which she had lived so long: Alix spoke of her relief at escaping from the small boarding school world in which her parents and contemporaries all knew one another far too well: Esther conjured up visions of both deprivation and splendour in her own past. They did not know then, were not to know for many years, were never fully to understand what it was that held them together—a sense of being on the margins of English life, perhaps, a sense of being outsiders, looking in from a cold street through a lighted window into a warm lit room that later might prove to be their own? Removed from the mainstream by a mad mother, a deviant ideology, by refugee status and the war-sickness of Middle Europe? None of this would have meant anything to them, then, as they drank their Nescafe, which in those days came not in granules in jars but in powder tins with brown cream and white labels: tins which cost 2s,6d each. They thought they found one another interesting. And so they became friends.

Liz, Alix, Esther. No, it was not an unbroken friendship, they did not become inseparable; they had distant patches, patches of estrangement that lasted for years at a time, when they met rarely, or distantly. Alix and Esther did not care to see much of Charles, nor he of them, as we have seen, and there were periods when the Liz—Charles' alliance was dominant in Liz's life and excluded other interests. Alix sometimes removed herself in her work, sometimes simply went silent, and answered the telephone forbiddingly. Esther went abroad for months at a time, or took up a new acolyte who absorbed her attention for a while. But by the end of 1977, when this account opens, they had settled down into what looked like being a semi-permanent pattern. They would meet for an evening meal, once a week, once a fortnight, once a month—if a monthly gap occurred, each would feel the need for apology, explanation. They met alone, without their men, as over the years they more often than not had done: a pattern of relationship that was considered mildly eccentric by some, mildly avant-garde by others, but to themselves was natural.

They would eat, drink, talk. They exchanged ideas. Sometimes they exchanged them so successfully that a year later Alix would be putting forward a proposition that she had energetically refuted when Liz had proposed it a year earlier: only to find that Liz, influenced by Alix, had subsequently shifted her ground and herself rejected it. It can only have been through Esther that Liz and Alix began to look at paintings at all, that the Albers' squares hung on the Harley Street stairs. Some of their notions swam, unallocated, in the space between them. The origins of some of their running jokes had been forgotten

Their professional worlds overlapped and, between them their frames of reference was quite wide, although they had been educated at the same college of the same university.

As their professional worlds overlap, so do their diversions—or one, at least, of their diversions. They share, perhaps surprisingly, a love of walking, of the English countryside . . .

Men are not usually invited. Charles is a sporting man, or was once a sporting man, but he is not a walker. Esther's friends have rarely been seen out of doors, even by Esther. Brian has accompanied them once or twice, for Brian loves to walk, but the women tease him about his walking boots. 'How can you lift your feet up, in those great things?' they mockingly wonder. They refuse to let him carry the picnic in his rucksack. So Brian does not often go, although they sometimes invite him. Alix has a photograph, taken by Brian on one of these expeditions; it shows the three of them crouching under a hedge, in the roots of hawthorns, in driving rain, eating a wet sandwich. None of them is looking at the camera: they are looking in different directions, wetly, miserable. Liz has her back to Alix; Esther is sitting some way away staring at the ground. They are very fond of this dismal photograph: the essence of the English landscape, Esther declares. The essence of togetherness.

MARGARET DRABBLE,
from *The Radiant Way*, 1987

LOVE IS LIKE THE WILD ROSE BRIAR

Love Is like the wild rose-briar;
Friendship like the holly-tree.
The holly is dark when the rose-briar blooms,
But which will bloom most constantly?

The wild rose-briar is sweet in spring.
Its summer blossoms scent the air;
Yet wait till winter comes again.
And who will call the wild-briar fair?

Then, scorn the silly rose-wreath now,
And deck thee with the holly's sheen,
That, when December blights thy brow,
He still may leave thy garland green.

EMILY BRONTË

A constant friend is a thing rare and hard to find.

PLUTARCH

In the past, friendship between men and women, especially in adult life, was often limited to casual relationships. A fear of love—spelled sexual attraction—between people who were not married to each other kept men and women from exploring the possibilities of friendship. While there are still some remnants of this misconception, the option for a man and a woman to be good friends, sharing the love of friendship, now exists.

Friendship improves happiness, and abates misery, by doubling our joy, and dividing our grief.

JOSEPH ADDISON

MY LOVELY FRIENDS

My lovely friends
How could I change
towards you
who are so beautiful
I ask you, Sir, to
stand face to face
with me as a friend
would; show me the
favor of your eyes

SAPPHO

Celibacy's pledge does not one sexless make
Nor purge a man from vivid fantasy;
A promise, mystery, for the kingdom's sake—
No harsh puritan but God's free servant,
Vulnerable to imagery and hormone,
Passions harnessed, perhaps, but, yes, still there:
Heart open to hurt and heal, less than stone,
Ready, spongelike, to sop up loving care.

No woman is mine and I belong to none,
Yet I'm shaped, refreshed, and fashioned by their graces,
More than if possessed by only one,
Forced out of myself by their smiling faces—

No complaint, gracious Lord, much less regret;
By You enriched through the women I've met.

ANDREW M. GREELEY,
from *Women I've Met*

*M*en do not hesitate to admit to having men friends. Sadly, many
men would be reluctant to use the word love to describe their feeling for another
man. The love in male bonding reveals dimensions of love that would benefit all
lovers.

GAUTAMA AND THE ELEPHANT

There was once a sage named Gautama who found a motherless baby
elephant and took care of it. He grew to love this elephant and protected it until it became a mighty beast. Indra was watching all this
from heaven, and came to earth in the form of King Dhitarashtra.

In this mortal guise, he tried to take the elephant away from Gautama, but Gautama implored him not to separate him from the elephant, who was indispensable to him as a companion; it carried food
and water. But "Dhitarashtra" replied that such a handsome animal
should be the property of a king, not of some sage living in the forest.

Gautama replied that he did not consider the elephant "property"
or a "possession," but rather his oldest and dearest friend.

"Dhitarashtra" then tried to buy the elephant, offering Gautama
gold, silver, cattle, beautiful maidens, even a palace. Gautama told him,
"Even if you go to the realm of Yama [death] and take me with you,
you will not be able to take my elephant away from me."

Indra, as Dhitarashtra, replied, "Those who go down to the land
of death ruled by Yama are sinful, and slaves of their desires." Gautama

replied, "There is much truth to be found in the land of the dead; there the weak are equal to the powerful and can even overcome them." Then the "king" said, "I am too powerful and too holy to go to the land of Yama." Gautama said, "That may well be, but even if you go up to the highest heaven ruled by Indra, you shall never have my elephant." This persisted until the "king" said, "What if I go to the place of Brahma the Creator and he tells me that the elephant is mine?"

The sage laughed and said, "Brahma the Creator knows all things and loves all things; your power means nothing to him. But the power of love that I feel for my elephant is more powerful than wealth, weapons, or anything else in the universe. I know who you are—you are Indra, who tests the wise."

Indra was so delighted by the faithfulness of Gautama to his elephant that he offered the sage any request. Gautama could have asked for riches or property, but all he asked for was to remain with his elephant. Indra told him, "You need not ask for wisdom; you already have that. As for riches, you are the richest man on earth, he who knows the value of a good friend." Years later, when Gautama was ready to die, Indra took him and the elephant alive together to the highest heaven.

And he who hears this story will be blessed; he who tells it will be twice blessed.

from *Parallel Myths*

FRIENDSHIP

Two sturdy oaks I mean, which side by side
    Withstand the winter's storm
    And spite of wind and tide,
    Grow up the meadow's pride
    For both are strong

Above they barely touch, but undermined
    Down to their deepest source,

Admiring you shall find
Their roots are intertwined
Insep'rably.

HENRY DAVID THOREAU

The making of friends, who are real friends, is the best token we have
of a man's success in life.

EDWARD EVERETT HALE

NO TIME LIKE THE OLD TIME

Fame is the scentless sunflower,
With gaudy crown of gold;
But friendship is the breathing rose,
   with sweets in every fold.

OLIVER WENDELL HOLMES

FRIENDSHIP

Such love I cannot analyse;
It does not rest in lips or eyes,

Neither in kisses nor caress.
Partly, I know, it's gentleness

And understanding in one word
Or in brief letters. It's preserved
By trust and by respect and awe.
These are the words I'm feeling for.

Two people, yes, two lasting friends.
The giving comes, the taking ends.
There is no measure for such things.
For this all Nature slows and sings

ELIZABETH JENNINGS

If you have a friend worth loving, love him.
Yes, and let him know that you love him,
ere life's evening tinge his brow with sunset glow.
Why should good words ne'er be said of a friend—
'til he is dead?

ANONYMOUS

Senior citizens teach us a dimension of love in friendship that we often overlook when we are younger. There is a willingness to admit the importance of friends as we age. We need our friends in the senior years and they need us, especially in a world where younger members of the family often live a great distance from their elders. Also, friends who had been "just friends,"

sometimes for years, often discover how dear their friends are to them. Some will even risk saying "I love you" to a friend. A new appreciation and understanding of love has been embraced.

It is one of the blessings of old friends that you can afford to be stupid with them.

RALPH WALDO EMERSON

You are the people of God; he loved you and chose you for his own. So then, you must clothe yourselves with compassion, kindness, humility, gentleness, and patience. Be tolerant with one another and forgive one another whenever any of you has a complaint against someone else. You must forgive one another just as the Lord has forgiven you. And to all these qualities add love, which binds all things together in perfect unity. The peace that Christ gives is to guide you in the decisions you make; for it is to this peace that God has called you together in the one body. And be thankful. Christ's message in all its richness must live in your hearts. Teach and instruct one another with all wisdom. Sing psalms, hymns, and sacred songs; sing to God with thanksgiving in your hearts. Everything you do or say, then, should be done in the name of the Lord Jesus, as you give thanks through him to God the Father.

COLOSSIANS *3:12–17*

With an increased interest in all forms of spirituality, many people have turned to the practices of monastic life for inspiration. The Anam Cara (soul friend) from the Celtic tradition has spawned interest in this special type of love.

SPEAK TO US OF SOUL FRIENDSHIP

They came to her and said: "Speak to us of soul friends so we may find one for ourselves."

She was quiet for some time.

Then she spoke: "Today many people speak casually of their new-found soul friend or soul mate, with little awareness of what the relationship entails. Soul friendship is serious business. To have a soul friend, you must be a soul friend."

They asked: "What must we do to be a soul friend?"

She replied: "It isn't what you do but what you are that that makes you a soul friend. You will know you are a soul friend when you have allowed someone to weave his or her way into your heart and nestle deep within it, secure in the safety of your friendship."

They protested: "We asked about soul friends not about heart friends."

She sighed and spoke again: "The heart of your body and your soul are one. It is that one heart that keeps the body you see and the soul that is both within and around that body beating in unison. The heart that holds your soul friend will remain with you even after death. Your soul friendship will last forever."

They asked (for they wanted certitude in all things): "How will we know that someone wants to be our soul friend or is our soul friend?"

She paused, reflecting on how to say this so they would understand: "You will know when one day, like the man discovering the oyster with a pearl among a boatload of oysters, you realize that a friend rests in your heart. Perhaps this is a friend you have known for a long time and see often or it might be a fairly new friend. All that really matters is that you now have this special friend and you must tread lightly, but with love, upon his soul."

They asked (for they were still not sure they wanted to commit to a friendship without end): "What happens if a soul friend no longer wants to be a friend? That could happen, couldn't it?"

She agreed it could. Then she continued, "Once someone is imbedded deep in your heart as a soul friend, she cannot be dislodged. If she finds the demands of this friendship a burden and rejects or betrays you, you will still hold her in your heart. You will not feel anger at the soul friend for the lack of his companionship, only great sadness and heartache.

"Your heartache will not destroy your love for your soul friend. It will be a reminder of your promise of never-ending love. The ache will disappear when your soul is finally free of the concerns of this world. Then you will understand, with the peace that surpasses all understanding, why he could no longer be true to the friendship. He remains your friend forever."

After listening to her, they agreed that soul friendship, as she described it, was serious business. Some decided they wanted no part of it. Others still thought they could work around some of the demands her ideas would place on them. A few knew that they had discovered the oyster with the pearl and pledged to treasure what they had found.

MARY G. DURKIN

THE ANAM CARA

In the Celtic tradition, there is a beautiful understanding of love and friendship. One of the fascinating ideas here is the idea of soul love;

the old Gaelic term for this is *anam cara*. *Anam* is the Gaelic word for soul and *cara* is the word for friend. So *anam cara* in the Celtic world was the soul friend. In the early Celtic Church, a person who acted as a teacher, companion or spiritual guide was called an *anam cara*. *Anam cara* was originally someone to whom you confessed, revealing the hidden intimacies of your life. With the *anam cara*, you could share your innermost self, your mind and your heart. This friendship was an act of recognition and belonging. When you had an *anam cara*, your friendship cut across all convention, morality and category. You were joined in an ancient and eternal way with the "friend of your soul." The Celtic understanding did not set limitations of space or time on the soul. There is no cage for the soul. The soul is a divine light that flows into you and into your Other. This art of belonging awakened and fostered a deep and special companionship. In his *Conferences*, John Cassian says this bond between friends is indissoluble: "This, I say, is what is broken by no chances, what no interval of time or space can sever or destroy, and what even death itself cannot part."

In everyone's life, there is great need for an *anam cara*, a soul friend. In this love, you are understood as you are without mask or pretension. The superficial and functional lies and half-truths of acquaintance fall away. You can be as you really are. Love allows understanding to dawn, and understanding is precious. Where you are understood, you are at home. Understanding nourishes belonging. When you really feel understood, you feel free to release your self into the trust and shelter of the other person's soul. This recognition is described in the beautiful line from Pablo Neruda: "You are like nobody since I love you." This art of love discloses the special and sacred identity of the other person. Love is the only light that can truly read the secret signature of the other person's individuality and soul. Love alone is literate in the world of origin; it can decipher identity and destiny.

It is precisely in awakening and exploring this rich and opaque inner landscape that the *anam cara* experience illuminates the mystery and kindness of the divine. The *anam cara* is God's gift. Friendship is the nature of God.

JOHN O'DONOHUE

THE DEATH OF LAZARUS

A man named Lazarus, who lived in Bethany, became sick. Bethany was the town where Mary and her sister Martha lived. (This Mary was the one who poured the perfume on her Lord's feet and wiped them with her hair; it was her brother Lazarus who was sick.) The sisters sent Jesus a message: "Lord, your dear friend is sick."

When Jesus heard it, he said, "The final result of this sickness will not be the death of Lazarus; this has happened in order to bring glory to God, and it will be the means by which the son of God will receive glory."

Jesus loved Martha and her sister and Lazarus. Yet when he received the news that Lazarus was sick, he stayed where he was for two more days. Then he said to the disciples, "Let us go back to Judea."

"Teacher," the disciples answered, "just a short time ago the people there wanted to stone you; and are you planning to go back?"

Jesus said, "A day has twelve hours, doesn't it? So those who walk in broad daylight do not stumble, for they see the light of this world. But if they walk during the night they stumble, because they have no light." Jesus said this and then added, "Our friend Lazarus has fallen asleep, but I will go and wake him up."

The disciples answered, "If he is asleep, Lord, he will get well."

Jesus meant that Lazarus had died, but they thought he meant natural sleep. So Jesus told them plainly, "Lazarus is dead, but for your sake I am glad that I was not with him, so that you will believe. Let us go to him."

Thomas (called the Twin) said to his fellow disciples, "Let us all go along with the Teacher, so that we may die with him!"

When Jesus arrived, he found that Lazarus had been buried four days before. Bethany was less than two miles from Jerusalem, and many Judeans had come to see Martha and Mary to comfort them about their brother's death.

When Martha heard that Jesus was coming, she went out to meet him, but Mary stayed in the house. Martha said to Jesus, "If you had been here, Lord, my brother would not have died! But I know that even now God will give you whatever you ask him for."

"Your brother will rise to life," Jesus told her.

"I know," she replied, "that he will rise to life on the last day."

Jesus said to her, "I am the resurrection and the life. Those who believe in me will live, even though they die; and those who live and believe in me will never die. Do you believe this?"

"Yes, Lord!" she answered. "I do believe that you are the Messiah, the Son of God, who was to come into the world."

After Martha said this, she went back and called her sister Mary privately. "The Teacher is here," she told her, "and is asking for you." When Mary heard this, she got up and hurried out to meet him. (Jesus had not yet arrived in the village, but was still in the place where Martha had met him.) The people who were in the house with Mary comforting her followed her when they saw her get up and hurry out. They thought that she was going to the grave to weep there.

Mary arrived where Jesus was, and as soon as she saw him, she fell at his feet. "Lord," she said, "if you had been here, my brother would not have died!"

Jesus saw her weeping, and he saw how the people with her were weeping also; his heart was touched, and he was deeply moved. "Where have you buried him?" he asked them.

"Come and see, Lord," they answered.

Jesus wept. "See how much he loved him!" the people said.

But some of them said, "He gave sight to the blind man, didn't he? Could he not have kept Lazarus from dying?"

Deeply moved once more, Jesus went to the tomb, which was a cave with a stone placed at the entrance. "Take the stone away!" Jesus ordered.

Martha, the dead man's sister, answered, "There will be a bad smell, Lord. He has been buried four days!"

Jesus said to her, "Didn't I tell you that you would see God's glory if you believed?" They took the stone away. Jesus looked up and said, "I thank you, Father, that you listen to me. I know that you always listen to me, but I say this for the sake of the people here, so that they will believe that you sent me."

After he had said this, he called out in a loud voice, "Lazarus, come out!" He came out, his hands and feet wrapped in grave cloths, and with a cloth around his face. "Untie him," Jesus told them, "and let him go."

JOHN *11:1–44*

The world is so empty if one thinks only of mountains, rivers, and cities; but to know someone who thinks and feels with us, and who, though distant, is close to us in spirit, this makes the earth for us an inhabited garden.

GOETHE

Oh, the comfort, the inexpressible comfort, of feeling safe with a person, having neither to weigh thoughts nor measure words, but to pour them all out as they are, chaff and grain together, knowing that a faithful hand will take and sift them, keep what is worth keeping, and then with a breath of kindness blow the rest away.

GEORGE ELIOT,
from *Middlemarch*

A FRIENDSHIP BLESSING

May you be blessed with good friends.
May you learn to be a good friend to yourself.
May you be able to journey to that place in your soul where
there is great love, warmth, feeling, and forgiveness.
May this change you.
May it transfigure that which is negative, distant, or cold
in you.
May you be brought in to the real passion, kinship, and
affinity of belonging.
May you treasure your friends.
May you be good to them and may you be there for them;
may they bring you all the blessings, challenges, truth,
and light that you need for your journey.
May you never be isolated.
May you always be in the gentle nest of belonging with your
anam cara.

JOHN O'DONOHUE

Of all the things which wisdom provides to make life entirely happy,
much the greatest is the possession of friendship.

EPICURUS,
from *To Menoeceus*

CHAPTER SIX

Everlasting Love

To love in the heart we leave behind is not to die.
THOMAS CAMPBELL

Pray for me as I will for thee
that we may merrily meet in heaven.
ST. THOMAS MORE

We have loved him dearly during life,
let us not abandon him until we have conducted
him by our prayers into the house of the Lord.
ST. AMBROSE

L ove is strong as death"—or so the lover proclaims in *The Song of Songs*. We might add, love is stronger than death. How else can we explain that, in spite of the knowledge that we and those we love will die, we continue to pledge to love another. Though the traditional marriage vow promises "till death do us part," no bride or groom dwells on the possibility of the death of the loved one. We form families, wanting to share our love with our children. We form friendships, making others important to our happiness in this life.

All forms of love present a challenge to the stoic and to the believer.

The stoic agrees that "life [including the possibility of lasting love] is a tale told by an idiot and full of sound and fury, signifying nothing." The believer would claim, along with Teilhard de Chardin that "there is something afoot in the universe." Both stoic and believer fall in love, marry, form friendships, and face the inevitable separations death will bring.

His own impending death or the death of a loved one often leads the stoic to wonder how it is that the love that bound him with another will die. The believer faces death, hopeful that love will survive, but never certain that it will. Both hope that love is stronger than death.

The poets and storytellers in this chapter reflect the universal questions about what happens when we die, focusing on the question about the survival of love. They recognize the mourning that accompanies the death of a love one and the questions that raises for us about our own survival as ones who love. They wonder with us about the cruelty of death as we lose parents, children, lovers, and friends. They explore possible answers to questions of meaning raised when a loved one dies. No one knows with certainty about the survival of our love after death. Most of us live with the hope that love is a sign that we, as well as our love, survive even the ravages of death.

THERE IS A PLACE

There's a time for remembering, a time to recall
The trials and the triumphs, the fears and the falls
There's a time to be grateful, for moments so blest
The jewels of our memory where love is our guest.

There is gold that is gleaming, in a past we once knew
In our tears and our laughter, 'twas love brought us through
There's a road we have travelled where sunlight has kissed
That carries us onwards when loved ones are missed.

    There is treasure in our fields
    There is treasure in our skies
    There is treasure in our dreaming
    From the soul to the eye
    For wherever we gather
    In the light of God's grace
    And for all whom we remember
    There will ever be a place.

There's a promise of God that is written in the stars
For all who may travel, no matter how far
God will be your companion, each journey you make
In the shadow of loved ones, to lighten your way.
    There is treasure in our fields . . .

In the quiet of the evening, at the close of the day
We will rest on the journey, to the Lord we shall pray
May we thank God for blessings for the moments we've shared
As we seek for tomorrow, close by us, you'll stay
    There is treasure in our fields . . .

LIAM LAWTON

They that love beyond the world cannot be separated. Death cannot kill what never dies. Nor can Spirits ever be divided that love and live in the same Divine Principle; the Root and Record of their Friendship. Death is but crossing the world, as Friends do the seas; they live in one another still.

WILLIAM PENN,
from *Fruits of Solitude*

Meditations on the inevitability of our own death often leads us to wonder about its effects on those who love us. Questions about their reactions and advice about how they should respond to our death reveal that we harbor a hope that our influence will continue to be felt by those we love and those who love us. We hope that our goodness will be remembered. These hopes often reflect another hope—that our love will continue to survive. Even without realizing this, we live as if love does survive.

REMEMBER

Remember me when I am gone away,
  Gone far away into the silent land;
When you can no more hold me by the hand
  Nor I half turn to go yet turning stay.
Remember me when no more day by day

You tell me of our future that you planned:
    Only remember me; you understand
    It will be late to counsel then or pray.
    Yet if you should forget me for a while
    And afterwards remember, do not grieve:
    For if the darkness and corruption leave
    A vestige of the thoughts that once I had,
    Better by far you should forget and smile
    Than that you should remember and be sad.

CHRISTINA GEORGINA ROSSETTI

JACOPO DA LENTINI
OF HIS LADY IN HEAVEN

I have in my heart to serve God so
    That into Paradise I shall repair,
    The holy place through the which everywhere
    I have heard say that joy and solace flow.
Without my lady I were loath to go,—
    She who has the bright face and the bright hair;
Because if she were absent, I being there,
    My pleasure would be less than nought, I know.
Look you, I say not this to such intent
    As that I there would deal in sin:
    I only would behold her gracious mien,
And beautiful soft eyes, and lovely face,
    That so it should be my complete content
    To see my lady joyful in her place.

DANTE GABRIEL ROSSETTI

REMEMBER ME

So, as you stand upon a shore, gazing at
    a beautiful sea—
As you look upon a flower, and admire
    its simplicity—
Remember me.
Remember me in your heart, your
Thoughts,
    And your memories of the times
    we loved, the times we fought,
    the times we laughed
For if you always think of me,
    I will never have gone.

ANGELINE HILTON,
from *On Women and Friendship:*
A Collection of Victorian Keepsakes and Treasures

THE LAST ROSE OF SUMMER

'Tis the last rose of summer,
    Left blooming alone;
All her lovely companions
    Are faded and gone;
No flower of her kindred,
    No rose bud is nigh
To reflect back her blushes,
    Or give sigh for sigh!

I'll not leave thee, thou lone one!
    To pine on the stem;
    Since the lovely are sleeping,
    Go, sleep thou with them;

Thus kindly I scatter
   Thy leaves o'er the bed,
Where thy mates of the garden
   Lie scentless and dead.

So soon may I follow,
   When friendships decay,
And from love's shining circle
   Thy gems drop away!
When true hearts lie withered,
   And fond ones are flown,
   Oh! Who would inhabit
   This bleak world alone?

THOMAS MOORE

ONE DAY I WROTE HER NAME

One day I wrote her name upon the strand,
   But came the waves, and washed it away.
   Again I wrote it with a second hand;
   But came the tide, and made my pains his prey.
"Vain man," said she, "that dost in vain assay
   A mortal thing so to immortalize;
   For I myself shall like to this decay,
   And eke my name be wiped out likewise."
"Not so," quoth I; "let baser things devise
   To die in dust, but you shall live by fame:
   My verse your virtues rare shall eternize,
   And in the heavens write your glorious name,
Where, whenas death shall all the world subdue,
   Our love shall live, and later life renew."

EDMUND SPENSER

DEATH IS NOTHING AT ALL

Death is nothing at all. I have only slipped away into the next room. I am I, and you are you. Whatever we were to each other that we still are. Call me by my old familiar name, speak to me in the easy way you always used. Put no difference into your tone, wear no forced air of solemnity or sorrow. Laugh as we always laughed at the little jokes we enjoyed together. Play, smile, think of me. Pray for me. Let my name be the household name it always was. Let it be spoken without the shadow of a ghost in it. Life means all that it ever meant. It is the same as it ever was. What is death but a negligible accident. Why should I be out of your mind because I am out of your sight. All is well, nothing is lost. One brief moment and all will be as it was before.

> HENRY SCOTT HOLLAND,
> from *Fibres of Faith,*
> (Quoted on memorial cards)

As The Vengeance descends from her elevation to do it, the tumbrils begin to discharge their loads. The ministers of Sainte Guillotine are robed and ready. Crash!—A head is held up, and the knitting-women who scarcely lifted their eyes to look at it a moment ago when it could think and speak, count One.

The second tumbril empties and moves on; the third comes up. Crash!—And the knitting-women, never faltering or pausing in their work, count Two.

The supposed Evremonde descends, and the seamstress is lifted out next after him. He has not relinquished her patient hand in getting out, but still holds it as he promised. He gently places her with her back to the crashing engine that constantly whirrs up and falls, and she looks into his face and thanks him.

'But for you, dear stranger, I should not be so composed, for I am naturally a poor little thing, faint of heart; nor should I have been able to raise my thoughts to Him who was put to death, that we might have hope and comfort here to-day. I think you were sent to me by Heaven.'

'Or you to me,' says Sydney Carton. 'Keep your eyes upon me, dear child, and mind no other object.'

'I mind nothing while I hold your hand. I shall mind nothing when I let it go, if they are rapid.'

'They will be rapid. Fear not!'

The two stand in the fast-thinning throng of victims, but they speak as if they were alone. Eye to eye, voice to voice, hand to hand, heart to heart, these two children of the Universal Mother, else so wide apart and differing, have come together on the dark highway, to repair home together, and to rest in her bosom.

'Brave and generous friend, will you let me ask you one last question? I am very ignorant, and it troubles me—just a little.'

'Tell me what it is.'

'I have a cousin, an only relative and an orphan, like myself, whom I love very dearly. She is five years younger than I, and she lives in a farmer's house in the south country. Poverty parted us, and she knows nothing of my fate—for I cannot write—and if I could, how should I tell her! It is better as it is.'

'Yes, yes: better as it is.'

'What I have been thinking as we came along, and what I am still thinking now, as I look into your kind strong face which gives me so much support, is this:—If the Republic really does good to the poor, and they come to be less hungry and in all ways suffer less, she may live a long time: she may even live to be old.'

'What then, my gentle sister?'

'Do you think': the uncomplaining eyes in which there is so much endurance, fill with tears, and the lips part a little more and tremble: 'that it will seem long to me, while I wait for her in the better land where I trust both you and I will be mercifully sheltered?'

'It cannot be, my child; there is no Time there, and no trouble there.'

'You comfort me so much! I am so ignorant. Am I to kiss you now? Is the moment come?'

'Yes.'

She kisses his lips; he kisses hers; they solemnly bless each other. The spare hand does not tremble as he releases it; nothing worse than a sweet, bright constancy is in the patient face. She goes next before him—is gone; the knitting-women count Twenty-Two.

'I am the Resurrection and the Life, saith the Lord: he that believeth in me, though he were dead, yet shall he live: and whosoever liveth and believeth in me shall never die.'

The murmuring of many voices, the upturning of many faces, the pressing on of many footsteps in the outskirts of the crowd, so that it swells forward in a mass, like one great heave of water, all flashed away. Twenty-Three.

They said of him, about the city that night, that it was the peacefullest man's face ever beheld there. Many added that he looked sublime and prophetic.

One of the most remarkable sufferers by the same axe—a woman—had asked at the foot of the same scaffold, not long before, to be allowed to write down the thoughts that were inspiring her. If he had given any utterance to his, and they were prophetic, they would have been these:

'I see Barsad, and Cly, Defarge, The Vengeance, the Juryman, the Judge, long ranks of new oppressors who have risen on the destruction of the old, perishing by this retributive instrument, before it shall cease out of its present use. I see a beautiful city and a brilliant people rising from this abyss, and, in their struggles to be truly free, in their triumphs and defeats, through long long years to come, I see the evil of this time and of the previous time of which this is the natural birth, gradually making expiation for itself and wearing out.

'I see the lives for which I lay down my life, peaceful, useful, prosperous and happy, in that England which I shall see no more. I see Her with a child upon her bosom, who bears my name. I see her father, aged and bent, but otherwise restored, and faithful to all men in his healing office, and at peace. I see the good old man, so long their friend, in ten years' time enriching them with all he has, and passing tranquilly to his reward.

'I see that I hold a sanctuary in their hearts, and in the hearts of their descendants, generations hence. I see her, an old woman, weeping for me on the anniversary of this day. I see her and her husband, their course done, lying side by side in their last earthly bed, and I know that each was not more honoured and held sacred in the other's soul, than I was in the souls of both.

'I see that child who lay upon her bosom and who bore my name, a man winning his way up in that path of life which once was mine. I see him winning it so well, that my name is made illustrious there by the light of his. I see the blots I threw upon it, faded away. I see him, foremost of just judges and honoured men, bringing a boy of my name, with a forehead that I know and golden hair, to this place—then fair to look upon, with not a trace of this day's disfigurement—and I hear him tell the child my story, with a tender and a faltering voice.

'It is a far, far better thing that I do, than I have ever done; it is a far, far better rest that I go to than I have ever known.'

CHARLES DICKENS,
from *A Tale of Two Cities*

We know that by the death of a brother or someone dear to us, the recollection of our coldness and carelessness has sometimes aroused in us a healthy fervor of spirit.

JOHN CASSIAN

The death of a child seems a blasphemy not only to the parents but also to all who grieve with them. "Life is unfair," seems the only proper response. That parents survive and eventually attain some peace despite the pain seems a miracle. The one constant seems to be that the lost child continues to be loved.

Contrary to the general assumption, the first days of grief are not the worst. The immediate reaction is usually shock and numbing disbelief. One has undergone an amputation. After shock comes acute grief. . . . It is as if the intensity of grief fused the distance between you and the dead. Or, perhaps, in reality, part of one dies. Like Orpheus, one tried to follow the dead on the beginning of their journey. But one cannot, like Orpheus, go all the way, and after a long journey one comes back. If one is lucky, one is reborn. Some people die and are reborn many times in their lives. For others the ground is too barren and the time too short for rebirth. Part of the process is the growth of a new relationship with the dead, that "veritable ami mort" Saint Exupéry speaks of. Like all gestation, it is a slow, dark, wordless process. While it is taking place, one is painfully vulnerable. One must guard and protect the new life growing within—like a child.

ANNE LINDBERGH,
from *Hour of Gold, Hour of Lead*

LINES TO THE MEMORY OF AN ONLY CHILD

I ask not even friendship's power
'Tis tears alone that soothe my pain:
That cannot stifle memory's hour,
That cannot give thee back again.

JULIA VAN DUSEN ALBUM,
1829–1861, (Virgina Makis Collection)

THE ARMENIAN MOTHER

I was a mother, and I weep;
 The night is come—the day is sped—
The night of woe profound, for, oh,
 My little golden son is dead!

The pretty rose that bloomed anon
 Upon my mother breast, they stole;
They let the dove I nursed with love
 Fly far away—so sped my soul!

That falcon Death swooped down upon
 My sweet-voiced turtle as he sung;
'Tis hushed and dark where soared the lark,
 And so, and so my heart was wrung!

Before my eyes, they sent the hail
 Upon my green pomegranate-tree—
Upon the bough where only now
 A rosy apple bent to me.

They shook my beauteous almond-tree,
 Beating its glorious bloom to death—
They strewed it round upon the ground,
 And mocked its fragrant dying breath.

I was a mother, and I weep;
 I seek the rose where nestleth none—
No more is heard the singing bird—
 I have no little golden son!

So fall the shadows over me,
  The blighted garden, lonely nest.
Reach down in love, O God above!
  And fold my darling to thy breast.

EUGENE FIELD

SAMUEL

Some boys are very tough. They're afraid of nothing. They are the ones who climb a wall and take a bow at the top. Not only are they brave on the roof, but they make a lot of noise in the darkest part of the cellar where even the super hates to go. They also jiggle and hop on the platform between the locked doors of the subway cars.

Four boys are jiggling on the swaying platform. Their names are Alfred, Calvin, Samuel, and Tom. The men and the women in the cars on either side watch them. They don't like them to jiggle or jump but don't want to interfere. Of course some of the men in the cars were once brave boys like these. One of them had ridden the rail of a speeding truck from New York to Rockaway Beach without getting off, without his sore fingers losing hold. Nothing happened to him then or later. He had made a compact with other boys who preferred to watch: Starting at Eighth Avenue and Fifteenth Street, he would get to some specified place, maybe Twenty-third and the river, by hopping the tops of moving trucks. This was hard to do when one truck turned a corner in the wrong direction and the nearest truck was a couple of feet too high. He made three or four starts before succeeding. He had gotten this idea from a film at school called *The Romance of Logging*. He had finished high school, married a good friend, was in a responsible job and going to night school.

These two men and others looked at the four boys jumping and jiggling on the platform and thought, It must be fun to ride that way, especially since the weather is nice and we're out of the tunnel and way high over the Bronx. Then they thought, These kids do seem to be acting sort of stupid. They *are* little. Then they thought of some of the brave things they had done when they were boys and jiggling didn't seem so risky.

The ladies in the car became very angry when they looked at the four boys. Most of them brought their brows together and hoped the boys could see their extreme disapproval. One of the ladies wanted to get up and say, Be careful you dumb kids, get off that platform or I'll call a cop. But three of the boys were negroes and the fourth was something else she couldn't tell for sure. She was afraid they'd be fresh and laugh at her and embarrass her. She wasn't afraid they'd hit her, but she was afraid of embarrassment. Another lady thought, Their mothers never know where they are. It wasn't true in this particular case. Their mothers all knew that they had gone to see the missile exhibit on Fourteenth Street.

Out on the platform, whenever the train accelerated, the boys would raise their hands and point them up to the sky to act like rockets going off, then they rat-tat-tatted the shatterproof glass pane like machine guns, although no machine guns had been exhibited.

For some reason known only to the motorman, the train began a sudden slowdown. The lady who was afraid of embarrassment saw the boys jerk forward and backward and grab the swinging guard chains. She had her own boy at home. She stood up with determination and went to the door. She slid it open and said, 'You boys will be hurt. You'll be killed. I'm going to call the conductor if you don't just go into the next car and sit down and be quiet.'

Two of the boys said, 'Yes'm', as though they were about to go. Two of them blinked their eyes a couple of times and pressed their lips together. The train resumed its speed. The door slid shut, parting the lady and the boys. She leaned against the side door because she had to get off at the next stop.

The boys opened their eyes wide at each other and laughed. The lady blushed. The boys looked at her and laughed harder. They began to pound each other's back. Samuel laughed the hardest and pounded Alfred's back until Alfred coughed and the tears came. Alfred held tight to the chain hook. Samuel pounded him even harder when he saw the tears. He said, 'Why you bawling? You a baby, huh?' and laughed. One of the men whose boyhood had been more watchful than brave became angry. He stood up straight and looked at the boys for a couple of seconds. Then he walked in a citizenly way to the end of the car, where he pulled the emergency cord. Almost at once, with a terrible hiss, the pressure of air abandoned the brakes and the wheels were caught and held.

People standing in the most secure places fell forward, then backward. Samuel had to let go of his hold on the chain so he could pound Tom as well as Alfred. All the passengers in the cars whipped back and forth, but he pitched only forward and fell head first to be crushed between the cars.

The train had stopped hard, halfway into the station, and the conductor called at once for the trainmen who knew about this kind of death and how to take the body from the wheels and brakes. There was silence except for passengers from other cars who asked, What happened! What happened! The ladies waited around wondering if he might be an only child. The men recalled other afternoons with very bad endings. The little boys stayed close to each other, leaning and touching shoulders and arms and legs.

When the policeman knocked at the door and told her about it, Samuel's mother began to scream. She screamed all day and moaned all night, though the doctors tried to quiet her with pills.

Oh, oh she hopelessly cried. She did not know how she could ever find another boy like that one. However, she was a young woman and she became pregnant. Then for a few months she was hopeful. The child born to her was a boy. They brought him to be seen and nursed. She smiled. But immediately she saw that this baby wasn't Samuel. She and her husband together have had other children, but never again will a boy exactly like Samuel be known.

GRACE PALEY,
from *Enormous Changes
at the Last Minute*

MATERNITY

One wept whose only child was dead,
   New-born ten years ago.
'Weep not; he is in bliss,' they said.
   She answered, 'Even so.

'Ten years ago was born in pain
   A child, not now forlorn.
But oh, ten years ago, in vain,
   A mother, a mother was born.'

ALICE MEYNELL

JOHN

Once upon a time, not too many years ago, John, a young man in his early forties, lay dying, consumed by the last stages of cancer that had spread to his liver. His wife and two young teenage sons, along with his parents, who had come from Ireland, and his siblings from all over the United States were at his bedside, reciting the rosary over and over.

For more than three years, these people and many other friends and relatives of John had stormed the heavens, praying that he would beat the cancer. As John became more and more ill, however, it seemed that those prayers had been in vain. Still, his loved ones never gave up.

When at last John slipped away quite peacefully, his mother observed in her Irish brogue, "Sure now, didn't we pray Johnny into heaven, and wasn't it a good thing for us to be here and see him going home? Now the Good Lord's going to have to help us make it through life without John. And Johnny himself will have to intervene for us."

MARY G. DURKIN,
from *An Epidemic of Joy*

We mourn the loss of parents and siblings, often with an intensity that surprises us. When those who are flesh of our flesh and blood of our blood die, we remember, sometimes with tinges of guilt, the experiences we shared with them. We also confront the inevitability of our own death. We need a time for making peace with the inevitability of death.

LETTING GO

I was shaving my father the last time
when he asked what it was like
on my side of the world.
When I lied, he was out.
And I was left.

Spring had come through the morning,
Brown leaves that held winter
let go swirling in the yard.
Drafts blew through doors the aroma
of baked dishes. The family filled
and emptied the same rooms.

He awoke and played
his side. A thrill ride
on a plane and then a train.
And he said we should all hold on
because it was moving fast.

We tried to remember if this
was some memory, but forgot

when he would grin, point somewhere
through us to passengers,
and wink at the nurses as attendants.
We laughed but knew things
were moving fast as we
lifted him from chair to bed.
As the casting of the face
turned grey we assumed
his reply:

Why fight the drama
of another season when I
can resist the uncertainty of
change by embarking, pleased
with your scent at my feet.

We feared and prayed the breath
would fall. After his poems
were read. Good byes and Slaintés.
Our faith in rhymes. After Ticker stroked
him and whispered for hours the hymn
of the West Side Boys. And then Mom
finally released him, like us at birth,
in bed with blood and soul rising.

DAN DURKIN

BEYOND WINTER'S DEATH

The harbor is filled with winter silence,
barren as a leafless tree.
Boatless and devoid
of the signs of other seasons
the red buoys

bob as signs of hope
anchored to the sea bed.
They pull anchors of the heart
towards the deeper hope
beyond winter's death.
A lonely bird pipes
a stringtime tune
contradicting the mood
of the cold winter eve.

TOMAS CAHALANE,
On the death of his brother

TRUE BIRTH

Called from the helplessness of birth
to the helplessness of death,
called to do what in between?
Master limitless space and time!
Or time and space in absolute limitations?
We move from infancy helplessness
to master walking, talking, knowing and loving.
To enter again
into helplessness.
In birthwatch
there is waiting in hopeful expectation
for the emergence of life.
In death-watch
there is waiting in questioning expectation
for the emergence of silence,
or true birth?

TOMAS CAHALANE,
On the death of his brother

WANDERING AT CHRISTMAS

Release your Christmas mind. Packaged with plans, and
The Pain. Let images warmed by color sounds clink crystal air.
Anticipated expression rewards perfect gifts. Flashlight
Emulsifies the tradition, and the grain of trees.

Leave decorated rooms and wander *sans* borders. Your
Father lies on the native side, nursing earth's elements.
Feel the breath of stories travel on the wave of symbols.
Wit steers souls' wake like a comet tail.

Escape points to places existing without a trace line.
Footprints pull hooves in the desert. Lost labor vanquished
To the dunes. Nighttime travelers rest on a gift of hay.
Experience the birth of new light as a silent question.
Awe mixed with myrrh.

Walk paths of pilgrimage bleached in stone. Rock face
Spirals. Each layer a mineral and a mirror. Peaks cushion
The soles in an altar of heather.
White bulls, clothed in Capes, separate the mist.
Guardians of ancient graves and
Mother queens.

The road is long round the ring. Picks up hedgerow in
A soft rain. Cap tipped so. Nod to the wind with shoulders
Square. Sticks guide and balance the beast. Step through stiles
To emerald pastures. Stone walls shelter our need for food.
Sustenance of the past.

Rest your search in a barn. Cloak hung in stalls where
Country hosts orchestrate the chorus. Refrains when the
Banshees bleat and angels whisper for more.

DAN DURKIN

omen tend to grieve quite openly. In some cultures, at the time of death women are the official keeners expressing the grief of all who mourn. Being able to express grief helps one get through the immediate trauma of a loved one's death. Many women have a harder time with the loneliness that continues after what others consider an appropriate length of mourning.

A REMINISCENCE

Yes, thou art gone! And never more
Thy sunny smile shall gladden me;
But I may pass the old church door,
And pace the floor that covers thee,

May stand upon the cold, damp stone,
And think that, frozen, lies below
The lightest heart that I have known,
The kindest I shall ever know.

Yet, though I cannot see thee more,
'Tis still a comfort to have seen;
And though thy transient life is o'er,
'Tis sweet to think that thou hast been;

To think a soul so near divine,
Within a form, so angel fair,
United to a heart like thine,
Has gladdened once our humble sphere.

ANNE BRONTË

Ode on the Death of Her Husband, King Francis II When He Was Sixteen and She Was Seventeen Years Old, 1560

In my sad, quiet song,
A melancholy air,
I shall look deep and long
At loss beyond compare,
And with bitter tears,
I'll pass my best years.

Have the harsh fates ere
now
Let such a grief be felt,
Has a more cruel blow
Been by Dame Fortune
dealt
Than, O my heart and
eyes!
I see where his bier lies?

In my springtime's
gladness
And flower of my young
heart,
I feel the deepest sadness
Of the most grievous hurt.

Nothing now my heart can
fire
But regret and desire.

He who was my dearest
Already is my plight.
The day that shone the
clearest
For me is darkest night.
There's nothing now so
fine
That I need to make it mine.

Deep in my eyes and heart
A portrait has its place
Which show the world my
hurt
In the pallor of my face,
Pale as when violets fade,
True love's becoming
shade.

In my unwonted pain
I can no more be still,
Rising time and again
To drive away my ill.
All things good and bad
Have lost the taste they
had.

And thus I always stay
Whether in wood or
meadow,
Whether at dawn of day
Or at the evening shadow.
My heart feels ceaselessly
Grief for his loss to me.

Sometimes in such a place
His image comes to me.
The sweet smile on his
face
Up in a cloud I see.

MARY, QUEEN OF SCOTS

PATTERNS

I walk down the garden paths,
And all the daffodils
Are blowing, and the bright blue squills.
I walk down the patterned garden paths
In my stiff, brocaded gown.
With my powdered hair and jewelled fan,
I too am a rare
Pattern. As I wander down
The garden paths.

My dress is richly figured,
And the train
Makes a pink and silver stain
On the gravel, and the thrift
Of the borders.
Just a plate of current fashion,
Tripping by in high-heeled, ribboned shoes.
Not a softness anywhere about me,
Only whalebone and brocade.
And I sink on a seat in the shade
Of a live tree. For my passion
Wars against the stiff brocade.
The daffodils and squills
Flutter in the breeze
As they please.
And I weep;
For the lime tree is in blossom
And one small flower has dropped upon my
bosom.

And the splashing of waterdrops
In the marble fountain

Comes down the garden-paths.
The dripping never stops.
Underneath my stiffened gown
Is the softness of a woman bathing in a
marble basin,
A basin in the midst of hedges grown
So thick, she cannot see her lover hiding,
But she guesses he is near,
And the sliding of the water
Seems the stroking of a dear
Hand upon her.
What is Summer in a fine brocaded gown!
I should like to see it lying in a heap upon
the ground.

I would be the pink and silver as I ran along
the paths,
And he would stumble after,
Bewildered by my laughter.
I should see the sun flashing from his sword-
hilt and the buckles on his shoes.
I would choose
To lead him in a maze along the patterned
paths,
A bright and laughing maze for my heavy-
booted lover,
Till he caught me in the shade,
And the buttons of his waistcoat bruised my
body as he clasped me,
Aching, melting, unafraid.
With the shadows of leaves and the
sundrops,
And the plopping of the waterdrops,
All about us in the open afternoon—
I am very like to swoon
With the weight of this brocade,
For the sun sifts through the shade.

Underneath the fallen blossom
In my bosom,
Is a letter I have hid.
It was brought to me this morning by a rider
from the Duke.
"Madam, we regret to inform you that Lord
Hartwell
Died in action Thursday se'nnight."
As I read it in the white, morning sunlight,
The letters squirmed like snakes.
"Any answer, Madam" said my footman.
"No," I told him.
"See that the messenger takes some
refreshment.
No, no answer."
And I walked into the garden,
Up and down the patterned paths,
In my stiff, correct brocade.
The blue and yellow flowers stood up
proudly in the sun,
Each one.
I stood upright too,
Held rigid to the pattern
By the stiffness of my gown.
Up and down I walked,
Up and down.

In a month he would have been my husband.
In a month, here, underneath this lime,
We would have broke the pattern;
He for me, and I for him,
He as Colonel, I as Lady,
On this shady seat.
He had a whim
That sunlight carried blessing.
And I answered, "It shall be as you have
said."
Now he is dead.

In Summer and in Winter I shall walk
Up and down
The patterned garden-paths
In my stiff, brocaded gown.
The squills and daffodils
Will give place to pillared roses, and to asters,
and to snow.
I shall go
Up and down,
In my gown.
Gorgeously arrayed,
Boned and stayed.
And the softness of my body will be guarded
from embrace
By each button, hook, and lace.
For the man who should loose me is dead,
Fighting with the Duke of Flanders
In a pattern called a war.
Christ! What are patterns for?

AMY LOWELL

THE STORY OF A MARRIAGE

... Now I am setting out into the unknown. It will take me a long
while to work through the grief. There are no shortcuts; It has to be
gone through. ...

A friend calls, reaching out via the phone, and tells me that she
has just come from running an Elderhostel weekend. She had this
group of older men and women go outdoors to try to find a symbol
in nature that would be meaningful for them. One woman came to
her with an empty nutshell, saying, "My husband died a year ago and
I am like this nutshell, empty."

I know that my nutshell is not empty. It is full of memory, memory of all my life, memory of the forty years of Hugh's and my marriage. It is the foundation of this memory which helps me keep on with my work, and that is what Hugh would want me to do. I go to a university campus to give a lecture, and it is hard, because the last two times I was there I was with Hugh, giving readings with him. But this year's students do not know the past. The lecture goes well. I am exhausted, but the step has been taken.

Someone tells me a story of a bishop who lost his wife and child in a tragic accident. And he said to his people, "I have been all the way to the bottom. And it is solid."

Yes.

A couple of years ago a friend called me from her hospital bed demanding, "Madeleine, do you believe everything that you have written in your books?"

I said *yes* then. It is still *yes* today.

But grief still has to be worked through. It is like walking through water. Sometimes there are little waves lapping about my feet. Sometimes there is an enormous breaker that knocks me down. Sometimes there is a sudden and fierce squall. But I know that many waters cannot quench love, neither can the floods drown it.

We are not good about admitting grief, we Americans. It is embarrassing. We turn away, afraid it might happen to us. But it is part of life, and it has to be gone through.

I think of the character Mado (modeled after my great-grandmother Madeleine L'Engle) in *The Other Side of the Sun.* She lost home, husband, children, and she made the journey through the burning flames of the sun. It cannot be gone around; it has to be gone through. But my grief is a clean grief. I loved my husband for forty years. That love has not and does not end, and that is good.

I think again of that evening after I had come home from a speaking trip and said to Hugh, "Wherever I go, you are with me." Surely that is still true.

Does a marriage end with the death of one of the partners? In a way, yes. I made my promises to Hugh "till death us do part," and that has happened. But the marriage contract is not the love that builds up over many years, and which never ends, as the circle of our wedding bands never ends. Hugh will always be part of me wherever I go, and that is good because, despite our faults and flaws and failures, what we gave each other was good. I am who I am because of our years together, freed by his acceptance and love of me. . . .

One evening I sit in my quiet place in my room, to read evening prayer, write in my journal, have some quiet *being* time. The sky over the Hudson is heavy with snow . . . I write in my journal that the more people I love, the more vulnerable I am.

Vulnerable—the moment we are born we are vulnerable, and a human infant is the most vulnerable of all creatures. The very nature of our being leads us to risk.

When I married I opened myself to the possibility of great joy and great pain and I have known both. Hugh's death is like an amputation. But would I be willing to protect myself by having rejected marriage? By having rejected love? No, I wouldn't have missed a minute of it, not any of it.

MADELEINE L'ENGLE,
from *Two-Part Invention*

A HEAVENLY TEA PARTY

My mom and dad were coffee drinkers. From a very early age, I remember lying in bed at night, listening to the murmur of their conversation, the aroma of freshly brewed coffee wafting through the house. My father died when my mom was in her early fifties. Occasionally, a niece or nephew would drop in and join her for a late-night cup. Aside from that she drank her coffee alone. Her three children hated coffee. Milk was our beverage of choice.

When I was seventeen, I began dating a boy who was a tea drinker. During our nearly five-year courtship, he often joined my mom for a nighttime cup of tea. I soon realized that it wasn't the coffee that meant so much to her. It was the companionship. I often wonder if those nighttime cups of tea were responsible for her easy acceptance of my decision to marry immediately after graduation.

Five years later my mother developed "circulation spells." Her symptoms soon resembled what we would now call the late stages of Alzheimer's. She came to live with us and often shared a cup of tea with her son-in-law. She seemed to recognize him. She thought I was the woman they hired to care for her.

A year and a half later, her physical health deteriorated. She was admitted to the hospital in early April and diagnosed with advanced colon cancer. The doctor recommended a nursing home, but said they would keep her in the hospital till after Easter to give us time to find a place. My mother went into a coma on Holy Thursday and died early in the afternoon of Easter Sunday, *April 14, 1963*. The death certificate attributed her death to a pulmonary embolism.

A week after Easter of 1994, we were told that my husband's sixth bout of cancer in twelve and half years was terminal. The doctors said, "Probably six weeks." He came home from the hospital on Friday. We met with Hospice on Tuesday. They made their first visit Wednesday morning.

Shortly after he returned from the hospital, we noticed he would often stare off in the distance as if seeing something. He would then raise his arm and reach out. We wondered among ourselves about this. Finally, on Wednesday, I decided to ask him why he did that.

"What is it, Jack, is something there? Is there something you want?"

After a turn of his head to me and then back to stare ahead and then back to me, he responded, "Yes, there is. And your mother is there."

He lapsed into a coma later that evening and died in the early afternoon of the next day, Thursday, *April 14, 1994*. The death certificate attributed his death to a pulmonary embolism.

I drink tea now. I expect to be part of their tea party someday.

MARY G. DURKIN

REMEMBRANCE

Cold in the earth, and the deep snow piled above thee!
Far, far removed cold in the dreary
Have I forgot, my Only Love, to love thee,
Severed at last by Time's all wearing wave?

Now, when alone, do my thoughts no longer hover
Over the mountains on Angora's shore,
Resting their wings where heath and fern-leaves cover
That noble heart for ever, ever more?

Cold in the earth—and fifteen wild Decembers
From those brown hills have melted into spring—
Faithful indeed is the spirit that remembers
After such years of change and suffering!

Sweet Love of youth, forgive if I forget thee
While the world's tide is bearing me along:
Sterner desires and darker hopes beset me,
Hopes which obscure, but cannot do thee wrong!

No other Sun has lightened up my heaven,
No other Star has ever shone for me;
All my life's bliss from thy dear life was given,
All my life's bliss is in the grave with thee.

But when the days of golden dreams had perished
And even Despair was powerless to destroy,
Then did I learn how existence could be cherished,
Strengthened and fed without the aid of joy.

Then did I check the tears of useless passion,
Weaned my young soul from yearning after thine;
Sternly denied its burning wish to hasten
Down to that tomb already more than mine!

And even yet, I dare not let it languish,
Dare not indulge in Memory's rapturous pain;

Once drinking deep of that divinest anguish,
How could I seek the empty world again?

EMILY BRONTË,
from *R. Alcona to J. Brenzaida*

For the elderly widow and widower, the sadness of their loss is often
intensified by their often-limited ability to escape physically from their aloneness.

HOUSE OF REST

Now all the world she knew is dead
    In this small room she lives her days
The wash-hand stand and single bed
    Screened from the public gaze.

The horse-brass shines, the kettle sings,
    The cup of China tea
Is tasted among cared-for things
    Ranged round for me to see—

Lincoln, by Valentine & Co.,
    Now yellowish brown and stained,
But there some fifty years ago
    Her Harry was ordained;

Outside the Church at Woodhall Spa
    The smiling groom and bride,
And here's his old tobacco jar
    Dried lavender inside.

I do not like to ask if he
    Was "High" or "Low" or "Broad"
Lest such a question seem to be
    A mockery of our Lord.

Her full grey eyes look far beyond
    The little room and me
To village church and village pond
    And ample rectory.

She sees her children each in place
    Eyes downcast as they wait,
She hears her Harry murmur Grace
    Then heaps the porridge plate.

Aroused at seven, to bed by ten,
    They fully lived each day,
Dead sons, so motor-bike-mad then,
    And daughters far away.

Now when the bells for Eucharist
    Sound in the Market Square,
With sunshine struggling through the mist
    And Sunday in the air,

The veil between her and her dead
    Dissolves and shows them clear,
The Consecration Prayer is said
    And all of them are near.

JOHN BETJEMAN,
from *A Few Late Chrysanthemums*

A Marriage, an Elegy

They lived long, and were faithful
to the good in each other.
They suffered as their faith required.
Now their union is consummate
in earth, and the earth
is their communion. They enter
the serene gravity of the rain,
the hill's passage to the sea.
After long striving, perfect ease.

WENDELL BERRY

Most cultures do not allow men the opportunity to display their grief as openly as women do. We should never take for granted that men grieve less intensely.

Requiescat

Tread lightly, she is near
    Under the snow,
Speak gently, she can hear
    The daisies grow.

All her bright golden hair
    Tarnished with rust,
She that was young and fair
    Fallen to dust.

Lily-like, white as snow,
   She hardly knew
She was a woman so
   Sweetly she grew.

Coffin-board, heavy stone,
   Lie on her breast,
I vex my heart alone,
   She is at rest.

Peace, Peace, she cannot hear
   Lyre or sonnet,
All my life's buried here,
   Heap earth upon it.

OSCAR WILDE

SUMMER

O love! Do you remember? country bus
   And England, meadows and blue sky?
The drowsy-sweet lost summer calling us
   To walk there, you and I?

And how you drew my eyes to yours, still gazing
   Till quietly between us two,
Across the bus, our eyes grown soft and praising,
   A summer sweetness grew.

A country stop. A glance. And out we went
   With joy to walk knee-deep in heather,
To drink with summer, holiness: content
   To be in Christ together.

The red bus ambled off. Larks sang. 'Dear one,'
    I murmured. 'On that hill, the tree.'
The moment, underneath that long-gone sun,
    Became eternity.

I woke. It was a dream at dusk, but this—
    A heaven on an English hill,
The sweet surrendering glory of the kiss
    We gave—is with me still.

Yet was it but a dream? Or my dream only?
    Somewhere are you remembering, too?
Or is it only I, remembering, lonely,

    And waiting still for you?

SHELDON VANAUKEN,
from *A Severe Mercy*

SACRAMENT

You, pictured for ever, before me;
I stand in black and wear a white
carnation; you, holding an array
of golden roses, maidenhair, smile up
at me and you are beautiful; your body
washed for me and gently scented;
you, set apart in white, a mystery,
all sacred:
we are holding hands for ever,
dedicated; such are the sighs of a deep
abiding grace.
             Another image

graven on my mind; you lie, again
in white; on your breast a silken
picture of the Virgin; they have washed
your body, closed your eyes, you hold
no flowers; vein-blue traces
of suffering on your skin, your fingers
locked together, away from me.

But it is I who have loved you, known
the deepest secrets of your grace; I take
the golden ring from your finger; I kiss
the bride,

and they close the heavy doors
against me, of that silent, vast cathedral.

JOHN F. DEANE,
from *Irish Love Poems: Danta Gra*

My heart was darkened over with grief, and whatever I looked at was
death. Where I lived was a torment to me; even my own home filled
me with sorrow. Those things which my friend and I used to share
together, now that I was without him, tortured me like the lash of a
whip. My eyes looked for him everywhere and could not find him. All
places were hateful to me, because he was not there. They could not
say to me now, "Look he will soon come," as they used to say when
he was alive and away from me. I had become a great enigma to myself
and asked my soul why it was so sad and why it caused me so much
distress. And my soul did not know what to answer. If I said, "Trust
in God," my soul very rightly did not obey me, because the dearest
friend whom it had lost was more real and better than the fantastic god
in whom it was told to trust. Only tears were my consolation, and tears
had taken the place of my friend in my heart's love.

SAINT AUGUSTINE OF HIPPO,
from *The Confessions*

ove impels us to long to reunite with those we love. If we imagine a life hereafter, we hope that life includes being joined with those we love.

THE BALLAD OF THE OYSTERMAN

It was a tall young oysterman lived by the
    river-side,
His shop was just upon the bank, his boat was
    on the tide;
The daughter of a fisherman, that was so
    straight and slim,
Lived over on the other bank, right opposite
    to him.

It was the pensive oysterman that saw a
    lovely maid,
Upon a moonlight evening, a-sitting in the
    shade;
He saw her wave her handkerchief, as much
    as if to say,
'I'm wide awake, young oysterman, and all
    the folks away.'

Then up arose the oysterman, and to himself
    said he,
'I guess I'll leave the skiff at home, for fear
    that folks should see;
I read it in the story-book, that, for to kiss his
    dear,

Leander swam the Hellespont,—and I will
    swim this here.'

And he has leaped into the waves, and
    crossed the shining stream,
And he has clambered up the bank, all in the
    moonlight gleam;
Oh there were kisses sweet as dew, and
    words as soft as rain,—
But they have heard her father's step, and in
    he leaps again!

Out spoke the ancient fisherman,—'Oh, what
    was that, my daughter?'
' 'Twas nothing but a pebble, sir, I threw into
    the water.'
'And what is that, pray tell me, love, that
    paddles off so fast?'
'It's nothing but a porpoise, sir, that's been
    a-swimming past.'

Out spoke the ancient fisherman,—'Now
    bring me my harpoon!
I'll get into my fishing-boat, and fix the fellow
    soon.'
Down fell that pretty innocent, as falls a
    snow-white lamb,
Her hair drooped round her pallid cheeks,
    like seaweed on a clam.

Alas for those two loving ones! she waked not
    from her swooned,
And he was taken with the cramp, and in the
    waves was drowned;
But Fate has metamorphosed them, in pity of
    their woe,
And now they keep an oyster-shop for
    mermaids down below.

OLIVER WENDELL HOLMES

The Spirit Bride

{ *Algonquin* }

There was once a young warrior whose bride died on the eve of their wedding. Although he had distinguished himself by his bravery and goodness, the death left the young man inconsolable, unable to eat or sleep. Instead of hunting with the others, he just spent time at the grave of his bride, staring into the air.

However, one day he happened to overhear some elders speaking about the path to the spirit world. He listened intently and memorized the directions to the most minute detail. He had heard that the spirit world was far to the south. He immediately set out on his journey. After two weeks, he still saw no change in the landscape to indicate that the spirit world was near.

Then he emerged from the forest and saw the most beautiful plain he had ever seen. In the distance was a small hut where an ancient wise man lived. He asked the wise man for directions.

The old man knew exactly who the warrior was and whom he sought. He told the lad that the bride had passed by only a day before. In order to follow her, the warrior would have to leave his body behind and press on in his spirit. The spirit world itself is an island in a large lake that can be reached only by canoes waiting on this shore. However, the old man warned him not to speak to his bride until they were both safely on the island of the spirits.

Soon the old man recited some magic chants and the warrior felt his spirit leave his body. Now a spirit, he walked along the shore and saw a birchbark canoe. Not a stone's throw away was his bride, entering her own canoe. As he made his way across the water and looked at her, he saw that she duplicated his every stroke. Why didn't they travel together? One can only enter the spirit world alone and be judged only on one's individual merits.

Midway through the journey, a tempest arose. It was more terrible than any he had ever seen. Some of the spirits in canoes were swept away by the storm—these were those who had been evil in life. Since both the warrior and his bride were good, they made it through the tempest without incident and soon the water was as smooth as glass beneath a cloudless sky.

The island of the blessed was a beautiful place where it was always late spring, with blooming flowers and cloudless skies, never too warm or too cold. He met his bride on the shore and took her hand. They had not walked ten steps together when a soft sweet voice spoke to them—it was the Master of Life.

The master told them that the young warrior must return as he came; it wasn't his time yet. He was to carefully trace his steps back to his body, put it on, and return home. He did this and became a great chief, happy in the assurance that he would see his bride once again.

from Parallel Myths

SEVENTY

The poet youth said to the princess, "I love you." And the princess answered, "And I love you too, my child."

"But I am not your child. I am a man and I love you."

And she said, "I am the mother of sons and daughters, and they are fathers and mothers of sons and daughters; and one of the sons of my sons is older than you."

And the poet youth said, "But I love you."

It was not long after that the princess died. But ere her last breath was received again by the greater breath of earth, she said within her soul, "My beloved, mine only son, my youth-poet, it may yet be that some day we shall meet again, and I shall not be seventy."

KAHLIL GIBRAN,
from *The Wanderer*

Some people long to communicate with deceased loved ones. Séances, Ouija boards, and other claims to facilitate this communication attract certain grievers. Dreams about departed loved ones are not uncommon. Periodically, stories are told of reappearance, usually in a time of crisis, of one who has died.

The three eldest Lane children arrived at the same time as the waitress with the tea.

. . . Margaret promptly took charge of arranging and pouring the tea . . .

"Well," Margaret began, pushing aside her hair again. "I suppose you wonder why we're here?"

"I'll admit to some curiosity." He tried his most charming smile with zero effect.

"We want to talk about our mother." Mark had been assigned the first line in the scenario, which his older Irish twin had doubtless planned.

"And your relationship with her." Teri, his one possible ally, sounded miserable.

What was happening? . . .

"It's like Joseph, you know," Teri whispered. "I mean he really didn't like you." . . .

"Now he totally adores you."

"What?"

They all shook their heads. "Totally."

"Why?"

Again the hesitation and exchange of glance.

"WELL—" Margaret took up the baton. "Like last Saturday, Mark and I are upstairs in our rooms studying and Joseph is downstairs playing with his computer. And the doorbell rings. Three times. Like, each time we shout down that Joseph should answer it."

"What's the point in having a little brother if he doesn't answer the doorbell, right?"

They relaxed a little.

"So, you know, he answers it and we don't hear anything for a few minutes, then he runs upstairs to my room crying—no, babbling. I call Mark and we both try to calm him down. But he's so happy that you'd think he was going to explode, you know?

"What was he so happy about?"

"Because of you. He said you had to marry Mom and make her happy and that we'd all be happy and that you'd be a totally excellent father."

They stopped. "Geeks?" Margaret asked ruefully

"Certainly not. But why the change in Joseph?"

"He said that Daddy was the one at the door, in his golf clothes, just like he was coming home from the club, and he bawled Joseph out for not answering the door when we told him to and especially for hating you. And he said that you were a wonderful man and had always loved Mom and would take good care of us and that if it hadn't been for you when a man tried to kill him with a broken bottle he would have never known us and that he's happy and we should should stop worrying about him and that you were the best friend he ever had and that if we loved him even just a little we should love you too."

Neal felt the color drain from his face and his jaws tighten.

"Joseph was upset because of everything," he said tonelessly, "and imagined it all."

"Even the story about the man with the broken bottle?"

"And if Joseph made it up," Mark asked, "why did we hear the doorbell?"

Neal's throat was very dry. When he spoke, his voice sounded hoarse. "I don't know."

"There's only one explanation, Mr. Connors," Mark said, his handsome face wrenched in a concentrated frown. "Dad came back from the dead to tell us to love you."

"There's lots of other explanations."

"Like?"

"Like Joseph wanted to believe that it was all right to like me."

"The story about the man with the broken bottle?"

"Your father told him that once after the two of them had seen me on the tube."

"Dad didn't tell stories like that about himself."

"Maybe he did once."

"We heard the bells," Margaret insisted. "Both of us."

"I understand."

"So you gotta take care of Mom." Teri extended her arms in appeal. "And us, too." ...

He and Mark shook hands firmly. Teri hugged him fiercely. Margaret tentatively pecked at his cheek and then hugged him, too. "Neal, you HAVE to save her."

"I will, Margaret, I really will, but let me judge the best way."

They agreed to that proposal, although he thought their agreement was reluctant.

ANDREW M. GREELEY,
from *Angels of September*

No one has ever returned to tell us the specifics about the death experience or about survival after death or what that might be like. We are curious. We speculate.

When the signs of age begin to mark my body (and still more when they touch my mind); when the ill that is to diminish me or carry me off strikes from without or is born within me; when the painful moment comes in which I suddenly awaken to the fact that I am ill or growing old; and above all at that last moment when I feel I am losing hold of myself and am absolutely passive within the hands of the great unknown forces that have formed me; in all those dark moments, O God, grant that I may understand that it is you (provided only my faith is strong enough) who are painfully parting the fibers of my being in order to penetrate to the very marrow of my substance and bear me away within yourself.

You are the irresistible and vivifying force, O Lord, and because yours is the energy, because, of the two of us, you are infinitely the stronger, it is on you that falls the part of consuming me in the union that should weld us together. Vouchsafe, therefore, something more precious still than the grace for which all the faithful pray. It is not enough that I should die while communicating. Teach me to treat my death as an act of communion.

PIERRE TEILHARD DE CHARDIN,
from *The Divine Milieu*

CHAPTER SEVEN

Love of the Neighbor and the Stranger

If you judge people, you have no time to love them.
MOTHER TERESA

Love makes everything lovely;
Hate concentrates on the thing hated.
GEORGE MCDONALD

The only true gift is a portion of yourself.
RALPH WALDO EMERSON

The first question we have when we are advised to love our neighbor is—Who is our neighbor? The second question is—What does it mean to love him or her?

In this age of mass communication, we encounter, on an almost daily basis, examples both of love of neighbor and of distrust and even hatred of those with whom we need to be neighbors if there is to be peace in our communities, country, and world. When we face the myriad examples of distrust and hatred, we wonder how love is possible. Ethnic- and religious-based wars between and within countries, ethnic- and religious-based political views that often hurt the most vulnerable people in a society, arguments about the limits of political freedom all force us to realize that love of neighbor and stranger does not come naturally to our species. We are free to choose to love or to choose not to love.

When Mother Teresa spoke at an education conference in Chicago in the late 1970s, a man in the audience was quite persistent in wanting her to tell the audience what we Americans could do to help her work among the poor. She referred the questioner back to her earlier remarks thanking the American people for their strong financial support for her mission. Finally she gave him some very pointed advice. "Love those around you. Find the person in your family, on your block, in your neighborhood, in your classroom who most needs love and do what you can to help him or her feel loved."

Her remarks remind us of both the local and the global implications of the command to love our neighbors as ourselves. In the broadest sense of the term, our neighbors are those who share the earth with us. In a more limited sense, our neighbors are the people on our block, in our communities, those we work and play with, those we encounter as we go about the ordinary business of daily living. While we need to love the neighbor and stranger close to us, we cannot ignore the needs of those more distant neighbors.

In a very real sense, love of neighbor stretches us, takes us out of our self-centeredness, invites us to have concern not only for those who will readily return our love but also those for whom we might never have felt any concern. Love of neighbor requires a letting go of stereotypes that make us feel superior and which in turn contribute to a "we versus them" mentality. Stereotypes are the enemy of our desire to acquire the virtue of love of neighbor. There are obstacles, some unconsciously acquired and others chosen, to developing our ability to love the stranger and neighbor.

The selections in this chapter invite us to reflect on love of the stranger and neighbor as both a challenge and a way to a richer life.

The scriptures and stories from many religious traditions emphasize the obligation to love others as well as the rewards that come to those who care for those in need.

BAUCIS AND PHILEMON

{ *Greco-Roman* }

In former days it was common for the gods to venture out among mortals in disguise. This was their best method of "taking the pulse" of the world below. Jupiter [Zeus] and Mercury [Hermes] wanted to find out whether the inhabitants of Phrygia were friendly or not; they had heard complaints about the lack of Phrygian hospitality. Jupiter is the patron of travelers on the road; Hermes is the god of commerce and also a patron of wayfarers. The two gods traveled down in the guise of poor, ragged tramps, going from door to door throughout the length and breadth of Phrygia, among the rich and the poor. Not one door was opened to them.

Finally they came upon the humble little hovel of an elderly couple, Baucis and Philemon. The two old people occupied only one little room and they were very poor indeed. Yet they were the most hospitable people in all Phrygia. They gathered together the few vegetables and scraps of meat they had and offered them to the strangers. Philemon told the guests, "I have a little wine to refresh you," and he poured it out of a crude, cracked clay jar for his guests.

Poor as they were, neither Baucis nor Philemon uttered a single word of complaint. In fact, the gods were deeply moved when the old man told them, "We have very little to offer you, strangers, but what little we have is yours." The gods drank more and more of the wine, and still old Philemon's cracked jar remained full.

A miracle was taking place—not only did the wine jar remain full but, in place of the common table wine originally in the jar, it now held the finest of vintages. Likewise, when the food was brought to the table, still more food appeared out of nowhere. Baucis and Philemon were mystified. Finally, the gods revealed their true identities and the old couple fell to the ground in reverence.

The gods then told the old people how inhospitable the Phrygians had been to them, and how the kindness of Baucis and Philemon had made a deep impression on them both. Jupiter told them that he was aware that the neighbors had been rude and cruel to Baucis and Philemon, despite their kind hearts. As he finished speaking, Jupiter caused the fields around their tiny hut to flood, killing all the neighbors. Despite the wickedness of the Phrygians Baucis and Philemon wept for their countrymen.

While the waters rose, so did the hut of Baucis and Philemon, which remained high and dry. Suddenly it was transformed into a shining temple of marble. Jupiter and Mercury appointed Baucis and Philemon priestess and priest of their temple. They faithfully tended the temple until they were well over one hundred years old.

When the couple became too frail to carry out their duties, a wonderful thing happened. Jupiter remembered that Philemon never wished to be separated from his beloved Baucis. Being a sentimental romantic, Jupiter caused them to grow into a beautiful oak tree with its two trunks entwined. Jupiter had kept his promise: Baucis and Philemon remained together forever.

from *Parallel Myths*

Who being loved is poor?

OSCAR WILDE

THE PROPHET

Then said a rich man, Speak to us of Giving.

And he answered:

You give but little when you give of your possessions.

It is when you give of yourself that you truly give.

For what are your possessions but things you keep and guard for fear you may need them tomorrow?

And tomorrow, what shall tomorrow bring to the overprudent dog burying bones in the trackless sand as he follows the pilgrims to the holy city?

And what is fear of need but need itself?

Is not dread of thirst when your well is full, thirst that is unquenchable?

There are those who give little of the much which they have—and they give it for recognition and their hidden desire makes their gifts unwholesome.

And there are those who have little and give it all.

These are the believers in life and the bounty of life, and their coffer is never empty.

There are those who give with joy, and that joy is their reward.

And there are those who give and know not pain in giving, nor do they seek joy, nor give with mindfulness of virtue;

They give as in yonder valley the myrtle breathes its fragrance into space.

Through the hands of such as these God speaks, and from behind their eyes He smiles upon the earth.

It is well to give when asked, but it is better to give unasked, through understanding;

And to the open-handed the search for one who shall receive is joy greater than giving.

And is there aught you would withhold?

All you have shall some day be given;

Therefore give now, that the season of giving may be yours and not your inheritors'.

You often say, "I would give, but only to the deserving."

The trees in your orchard say not so, nor the flocks in your pasture.

They give that they may live, for to withhold is to perish.

Surely he who is worthy to receive his days and his nights is worthy of all else from you.

And he who has deserved to drink from the ocean of life deserves to fill his cup from your little stream.

And what desert greater shall there be than that which lies in the courage and the confidence, nay the charity, of receiving?

And who are you that men should rend their bosom and unveil their pride, that you may see their worth naked and their pride unabashed?

See first that you yourself deserve to be a giver, and an instrument of giving.

For in truth it is life that gives unto life—while you, who deem yourself a giver, are but a witness.

And you receivers—and you are all receivers—assume no weight of gratitude, lest you lay a yoke upon yourself and upon him who gives.

Rather rise together with the giver on his gifts as on wings;

For to be overmindful of your debt, is to doubt his generosity who has the free-hearted earth for mother, and God for father.

KAHLIL GIBRAN,
from *The Prophet*

Do unto others as you would have them do unto you.

THE GOLDEN RULE

If you put an end to oppression, to every gesture of contempt, and to every evil word; if you give food to the hungry and satisfy those who are in need, then the darkness around you will turn to the brightness of noon. And I will guide you and satisfy you with good things. I will keep you strong and well. You will be like a garden that has plenty of water, like a spring of water that never goes dry.

ISAIAH *58:9b–11*

Rabbi Shelomo said: "If you want to raise a man from mud and filth, do not think it is enough to keep standing on top and reaching down to him a helping hand. You must go all the way down yourself, down into mud and filth. Then take hold of him with strong hands and pull him and yourself out into the light."

CHASSID

In a dream of R. Abbahu, Mr. Pentakaka ("Five sins") appeared, who prayed that rain would come, and it rained. R. Abbahu sent and summoned him. He said to him, "What is your trade?"

He said to him, "Five sins does that man [I] do every day, for I am a pimp: hiring whores, cleaning up the theater, bringing home their garments for washing, dancing, and performing before them."

He said to him, "And what sort of decent thing have you ever done?"

He said to him, "One day that man [I] was cleaning the theater, and a woman came and stood behind a pillar and cried. I said to her,

'What's with you?' And she said to me, 'That woman's [my] husband is in prison, and I wanted to see what I can do to free him, so I sold my bed and cover, and I gave the proceeds to her.' I said to her, 'Here is your money, free your husband, but do not sin.' "

He said to him, "You are worthy of praying and having your prayers answered."

YERUSHALMI TAANIT 1:4.I

One who serves the poor serves Allah.

A SAYING IN ISLAM

GOD IS LOVE

Dear friends, let us love one another, because love comes from God. Whoever loves is a child of God and knows God. Whoever does not love does not know God, for God is love. And God showed his love for us by sending his only Son into the world, so that we might have life through him. This is what love is: it is not that we have loved God, but that he loved us and sent his Son to be the means by which our sins are forgiven.

Dear friends, if this is how God loved us, then we should love one another. No one has ever seen God, but if we love one another, God lives in union with us, and his love is made perfect in us.

. . .

We are sure that we live in union with God and that he lives in
with us, because he has given us his Spirit. And we have seen ar
others that the Father sent his Son to be the Savior of the world. ....
declare that Jesus is the Son of God, we live in union with God and
God lives in union with us. And we ourselves know and believe the
love which God has for us.

God is love, and those who live in love live in union with God and God
lives in union with them. Love is made perfect in us in order that we may
have courage on the Judgment Day; and we will have it because our life
in this world is the same as Christ's. There is no fear in love; perfect love
drives out all fear. So then, love has not been made perfect in anyone
who is afraid, because fear has to do with punishment.

We love because God first loved us. If we say we love God, but hate
others, we are liars. For we cannot love God, whom we have not seen,
if we do not love others, whom we have seen. The command that
Christ has given us is this: whoever loves God must love others also.

1 JOHN *4:7–21*

TEACHING ABOUT REVENGE

"You have heard that it was said, 'An eye for an eye, and a tooth for a
tooth.' But now I tell you: do not take revenge on someone who
wrongs you. If anyone slaps you on the right cheek, let him slap your
left cheek too. And if someone takes you to court to sue you for your
shirt, let him have your coat as well. And if one of the occupation
troops forces you to carry his pack one mile, carry it two miles. When
someone asks you for something, give it to him; when someone wants
to borrow something, lend it to him."

MATTHEW *5:38–42*

LOVE FOR ENEMIES

"You have heard that it was said, 'Love your friends, hate your enemies.' But now I tell you: love your enemies and pray for those who persecute you, so that you may become the children of your Father in heaven. For he makes his sun to shine on bad and good people alike, and gives rain to those who do good and to those who do evil. Why should God reward you if you love only the people who love you? Even the tax collectors do that! And if you speak only to your friends, have you done anything out of the ordinary? Even the pagans do that! You must be perfect—just as your Father in heaven is perfect."

MATTHEW 5:43–48

So great is the love between them and so strong the affection by which they are bound to one another and towards all the brethren that they are an example and wonder to all. If anyone happens to want to live among them, as soon as they are aware of it, each of them offers him his own cell.

RUFINUS,
writing about
the early Christians

St. "Bride"

This is one of the many stories of St. Brigid or "Bride" as she is known in Ireland. Brigid was the daughter of a noble pagan who sold her mother, his Christian concubine, to a druid when he learned of her pregnancy. It is said that once Brigid was of an age to fix her mind on God, all she asked for was granted. And this was no small thing because what she asked for was to satisfy the poor, house the homeless, bring diverse groups together, expel hardship, and spare the miserable.

As a young girl, her chore was to churn the butter for the druid's household. When the druid and his wife came to claim their butter, they discovered that Brigid was giving the butter to the poor and sick. They also discovered that the butter kept multiplying, so there was always enough for them too. This moved the druid to give Brigid and her mother their freedom. He also convinced her noble father to accept the girl.

Once back in her father's house, however, Brigid began giving his things to the poor. She also resolutely refused to marry, a right that the law of her time and place gave her. Fearful that his daughter would give away all he had, the father decided to circumvent the law by selling her back into slavery to the king of Leinster, who had recently converted to Christianity.

While her father negotiated with the king, Brigid was outside giving her father's best sword to the first beggar who came along! She incensed both her father and the king by saying that she did this because the sword was used for war and the beggar would sell it for food. The king declared he wanted no part of Brigid's giving away all his wealth. Suddenly, a great flame appeared behind Brigid as she told him that if she had his wealth, she would give it to the Lord of the Elements and to the people who are the Lord's. The heat of the flame caused the king to break into a sweat that reminded him of the waters of baptism. The king then insisted that her father leave her be, giving Brigid the freedom to commit herself to a life dedicated to God.

MARY G. DURKIN,
from *An Epidemic of Joy*

IF NOT HIGHER

Early every Friday morning, at the time of the Penitential Prayers, the rabbi of Nemirov would vanish.

He was nowhere to be seen—neither in the synagogue nor in the two Houses of Study nor at a *minyan*. And he was certainly not at home. His door stood open; whoever wished could go in and out; no one would steal from the rabbi. But not a living creature was within.

Where could the rabbi be? Where should he be? In heaven, no doubt. A rabbi has plenty of business to take care of just before the Days of Awe. Jews, God bless them, need livelihood, peace, health, and good matches. They want to be pious and good, but our sins are so great, and Satan of the thousand eyes watches the whole earth from one end to the other. What he sees he reports; he denounces, informs. Who can help us if not the rabbi!

That's what the people thought.

But once a Litvak came, and he laughed. You know the Litvaks. They think little of the Holy Books but stuff themselves with Talmud and law. So this Litvak points to a passage in the Gemara—it sticks in your eyes—where it is written that even Moses our Teacher did not ascend to heaven during his lifetime but remained suspended two and a half feet below. Go argue with a Litvak

So where can the rabbi be?

"That's not my business," said the Litvak, shrugging. Yet all the while—what a Litvak can do!—he is scheming to find out.

That same night, right after the evening prayers, the Litvak steals into the rabbi's room, slides under the rabbi's bed, and waits. He'll watch all night and discover where the rabbi vanishes and what he does during the Penitential Prayers.

Someone else might have got drowsy and fallen asleep, but a Litvak is never at a loss; he recites a whole tractate of the Talmud by heart.

At dawn he hears the call to prayers.

The rabbi has already been awake for a long time. The Litvak has heard him groaning for a whole hour.

Whoever has heard the rabbi of Nemirov groan knows how much sorrow for all Israel, how much suffering, lies in each groan. A man's heart might break, hearing it. But a Litvak is made of iron; he listens and remains where he is. The rabbi—long life to him!—lies on the bed, and the Litvak under the bed.

Then the Litvak hears the beds in the house begin to creak; he hears people jumping out of their beds, mumbling a few Jewish words, pouring water on their fingernails, banging doors. Everyone has left. It is again quiet and dark; a bit of light from the moon shines through the shutters.

(Afterward the Litvak admitted that when he found himself alone with the rabbi a great fear took hold of him. Goose pimples spread across his skin, and the roots of his earlocks pricked him like needles. A trifle: to be alone with the rabbi at the time of the Penitential Prayers! But a Litvak is stubborn. So he quivered like a fish in water and remained where he was.)

Finally the rabbi—long life to him!—arises. First he does what befits a Jew. Then he goes to the clothes closet and takes out a bundle of peasant clothes: linen trousers, high boots, a coat, a big felt hat, and a long wide leather belt studded with brass nails. The rabbi gets dressed. From his coat pocket dangles the end of a heavy peasant rope.

The rabbi goes out, and the Litvak follows him.

On the way the rabbi stops in the kitchen, bends down, takes an ax from under the bed, puts it in his belt, and leaves the house. The Litvak trembles but continues to follow.

The hushed dread of the Days of Awe hangs over the dark streets. Every once in a while a cry rises from some *minyan* reciting the Penitential Prayers, or from a sickbed. The rabbi hugs the sides of the streets, keeping to the shade of the houses. He glides from house to house, and the Litvak after him. The Litvak hears the sound of his heartbeats mingling with the sound of the rabbi's heavy steps. But he keeps on going and follows the rabbi to the outskirts of the town.

A small wood stands behind the town.

The rabbi—long life to him!—enters the wood. He takes thirty or forty steps and stops by a small tree. The Litvak, overcome with amazement, watches the rabbit take the ax out of his belt and strike the tree. He hears the tree creak and fall. The rabbi chops the tree into logs and the logs into sticks. Then he makes a bundle of the wood and ties it with the rope in his pocket. He puts the bundle of wood on his back, shoves the ax back into his belt, and returns to the town.

He stops at a back street beside a small broken-down shack and knocks at the window.

"Who is there?" asks a frightened voice. The Litvak recognizes it as the voice of a sick Jewish woman.

"I," answers the rabbi in the accent of a peasant.

"Who is I?"

Again the rabbi answers in Russian. "Vassil."

"Who is Vassil, and what do you want?"

"I have wood to sell, very cheap." And not waiting for the woman's reply, he goes into the house.

The Litvak steals in after him. In the gray light of early morning he sees a poor room with broken, miserable furnishings. A sick woman, wrapped in rags, lies on the bed. She complains bitterly, "Buy? How can I buy? Where will a poor widow get money?"

"I'll lend it to you," answers the supposed Vassil. "It's only six cents."

"And how will I ever pay you back?" asks the poor woman, groaning.

"Foolish one," says the rabbi reproachfully. "See, you are a poor sick Jew, and I am ready to trust you with a little wood. I am sure you'll pay. While you, you have such a great and mighty God and you don't trust him for six cents."

"And who will kindle the fire?" asks the widow. "Have I the strength to get up? My son is at work."

"I'll kindle the fire," answers the rabbi.

As the rabbi put the wood into the oven he recited, in a groan, the first portion of the Penitential Prayers.

As he kindled the fire and the wood burned brightly, he recited a bit more joyously, the second portion of the Penitential Prayers. When the fire was set he recited the third portion, and then he shut the stove.

The Litvak who saw all this became a disciple of the rabbi.

And ever after, when another disciple tells how the rabbi of Nemirov ascends to heaven at the time of the Penitential Prayers, the Litvak does not laugh. He only adds quietly, "if not higher."

I. L. PERETZ (TRANSLATED
BY MARIE SYRKIN)

When you sow love, joy grows.

GERMAN PROVERB

UNDERSTANDING OTHERS

In the mid-1970's, an elderly missionary in Bangladesh told this story to a newly arrived missionary:

. . . One day, as he stood conversing with an educated young Muslim, they both observed a man sprawled in the gutter of the street. Two women wearing identical white garb appeared, approached the man, went down to him and ministered to him. When next the missionary looked at this Muslim acquaintance's face, he was surprised to find him in tears. The sisters' active compassion had touched him. The young Muslim did not thereafter seek to become a Christian. Islam also stresses mercy and compassion toward the afflicted. However, he did understand compassion better, thanks to the example of two Catholic sisters.

BOB MCCAHILL,
from *Dialogue of Life:
A Christian Among Allah's Poor*

A brother in Scete happened to commit a fault, and the elders assembled and sent for Abbot Moses to join them. He, however, did not want to come. The priest sent him a message, saying: "Come, the community of the brethren is waiting for you." So he arose and started off. And taking with him a very old basket full of holes, he filled it with sand, and carried it behind him. The elders came out to meet him, and said: "What is this, Father?" The elder replied: "My sins are running out behind me, and I do not see them, and today I come to judge the sins of another!" They, hearing this, said nothing to the brother but pardoned him.

from *The Desert Fathers*

It is said that soon after his enlightenment, the Buddha passed a man on the road who was struck by the extraordinary radiance and peacefulness of his presence. The man stopped and asked, "My friend, what are you? Are you a celestial being or a god?"

"No," said the Buddha.

"Well, then, are you some kind of magician or wizard?"

Again the Buddha answered, "No."

"Are you a man?"

"No."

"Well, my friend, what then are you?"

The Buddha replied, "I am awake."

BUDDHIST TEACHING

A brother asked one of the elders, saying: "There are two brothers, of whom one remains praying in his cell, fasting six days at a time and doing a great deal of penance. The other one takes care of the sick. Which one's work is more pleasing to God?" The elder replied: "If that brother who fasts six days at a time were to hang himself up by the nose, he could not equal the one who takes care of the sick."

from *The Desert Fathers*

A young village girl told me, when I am about to talk to anyone, I picture to myself Jesus Christ and how gracious and friendly he was to everyone.

JOHN VIANNEY

HOW ST. BRIGID VISITED HEAVEN AND HELL

(A Seanachie's tale told around a peat fire with lots of young'uns listening with their eyes wide)

Once upon a time, long, long ago, there lived in the County of Kildare in Ireland, a very holy Abbess named Brigid. In her monastery there were monks and nuns and scholars and young people and farmers and artisans. She ruled all the lands around the monastery and it was said of her that she was a firm but a fair and gentle ruler. She assigned all the priests to their parishes, and, sure, isn't it said that she even ordained them.

Could she be doing that? Well, I'm in no position to say, but from what we know about the woman, one thing is certain: no one challenged her right to do that. Not twice anyway.

Well she ran a fine monastery. It was always clean and neat and the sacred vessels were polished bright and shiny and the altar linen was always sparkling white and the sacred vestments neat as a pin and the floor of the chapel scrubbed every morning. The monks and the nuns all had warm clothes to wear during the winter and the cottages on her lands were well thatched and whitewashed and she did not tolerate nooks and crannies through which the winds could blow or the rains leak.

Well as the years went on, didn't Brigid spend more of her time in the chapel with her eyes closed? Some said she was meditating, if you take me meaning. Others said that she was sleeping. Still others said it was Ireland after all and why couldn't she be doing both at the same time?

Well one morning, doesn't Michael himself show up, the head of the heavenly armies if you follow me?

"Brigie," he says, tapping herself on the shoulder, "haven't you done a fine job with this monastery now? Isn't it always clean and neat and the sacred vessels polished bright and shiny and the altar linen sparkling white and the sacred vestments neat as a pin and the floor of the chapel scrubbed every morning? Don't the monks and the nuns all have warm clothes to wear during the winter and are not the cottages on your lands well thatched and whitewashed and don't you forbid nooks and crannies through which the winds could blow or the rains leak? And sure, don't you keep the chickens and the cattle outside the monastery except when it's so cold that the poor darlings would starve to death?"

"And if all that be true, what's the point of this blarney and, by the way, who are you?"

"Am I not Michael, the head of the heavenly hosts?"

"Are you now?"

"Haven't I said that I am?"

Well, you know what your angel did? Didn't he turn into a pillar of blazing white light that filled the whole chapel? So Brigid was inclined to believe him.

"Well, then, what do you want with me?"

"Hasn't Himself"—with a nod towards heaven—"sent me down here to tell you that He's noticed your work and is so pleased I am to grant you any request you might make."

Well, as you probably figured without me telling you, Brigid was nobody's fool. So doesn't she give the right answer?

"Ah, well, all I ask for is the salvation of me immortal soul."

"Come on now, woman, you've got that already. Sure, wouldn't there be a lot of trouble in heaven if we tried to take that away? It's kind of a wild card request you can be making."

"Well," says your woman, "then wouldn't I like just a tiny peek inside heaven to sustain me through the rest of me life?"

"We can do that too, but the rules are that you must take a peek inside, ah, the other place too."

"No problem at all, at all. Wouldn't that be good for me soul?"

So as quick as the speed of thought—because your high-class angels move that fast—weren't the two of them on the outskirts of the "other place." And a terrible place it was! It was dark and scary and smelled something awful of sulfur. And smoke and flames were leaping out all over the place and the thick oak walls burned even when you brushed a finger against them. The screams of agony from inside were horrible to hear.

"Open up inside," yells the seraph, " 'tis meself and yuz know better than to argue with me!"

So the huge oak doors swing open with a loud creak and, very gingerly, mind you, doesn't Brigid peek in?

She screams in surprise. Inside she sees ladies and gentlemen dressed in the finest silks. And aren't they gathered around grand banquet tables with Irish linen and Waterford crystal and Belleek china? And isn't there fiddle music playing in the background? And isn't there wonderful food piled upon the tables—Caesar salad, and seven kinds of praties, and the best roast beef in Ireland with your bernaise sauce, and lots of carrots and the best of wines and for dessert flourless chocolate cake with chocolate chip ice cream and raspberries and on top of that chocolate sauce and whipped cream? And themselves screaming in agony.

"What in hell is going on here?" Brig demands.

"Look at their elbows, woman!"

She does and she sees that in hell you can't bend your elbows. Now, yuz colleens and gasoons, let's see if you can eat any of that ice cream you seemed to have found without bending your elbows. No cheating now. Try to put even a spoon of ice cream in your mouth without bending your elbows.

Well, yuz takes me point. The damned can't enjoy any of the good things God has given them, so that's why they're screaming their lungs out.

"Micky," says the holy abbess, "get me out of this damned place!"

"In a twinkling of a thought," says himself.

And aren't they standing in front of the great gold and ivory gates of heaven? And isn't Peter himself sitting at his work station with a Pentium 150 computer and his fishing rod and the tiara, the triple crown of the pope—'cuz he was the first pope, you know—in front of the gate? Well the Mick gives him the sign and he nods real polite-like and presses a control/escape on his computer and the great gold and ivory doors swing open.

As quick as though she were a silly teenager, Brigid runs up to the gate and peers in.

"Well this is a hell of a note!" she says.

What do you think she saw?

Well, I'll be telling you now. Inside she sees ladies and gentlemen dressed in the finest silks. And aren't they gathered around grand banquet tables with Irish linen and Waterford crystal and Belleek china? And isn't there fiddle music playing in the background? And isn't there wonderful food piled up on the tables—Caesar salad, and seven kinds of praties, and the best roast beef in Ireland with your bernaise sauce, and lots of carrots and the best of wines and for dessert flourless chocolate cake with chocolate chip ice cream and raspberries and on top of that chocolate sauce and whipped cream? And themselves laughing and chatting merrily, even though they don't have any elbows here either.

"Heaven is just like hell?" she asks,

"Use the eyes God gave you, woman," the Mick says.

"Ah," she says, real awed-like, "aren't they feeding one another?"

Now you gosoons and colleens, stop whispering and see if you can feed that ice cream to one another without bending your elbows. See, it's easy isn't it?

"Sure," says the Holy Abbess, "I take your meaning now. The only difference between heaven and hell is that the blessed in heaven have learned how to take care of one another!"

And ever after back in monastery at mealtime, wouldn't the Holy Abbess leap out of her throne and help serve the food, beginning with the youngest and lowest of the novices.

"Sure," she'd say, "aren't we closest to heaven here on earth when we're serving one another?"

And I've told my story and I'll tell you no more.

ANDREW M. GREELEY

The Parable of the Good Samaritan is a challenge to all that think they are neighbors. Many people in our midst are present day Good Samaritans. They dare us, by their example, to be the same.

THE PARABLE OF THE GOOD SAMARITAN

A teacher of the Law came up and tried to trap Jesus. "Teacher," he asked, "what must I do to receive eternal life?"

Jesus answered him, "What do the Scriptures say? How do you interpret them?"

The man answered, "Love the Lord your God with all your heart, with all your soul, with all your strength, and with all your mind; and Love your neighbor as you love yourself."

"You are right," Jesus replied; "do this and you will live."

But the teacher of the law wanted to justify himself, so he asked Jesus, "Who is my neighbor?"

Jesus answered, "There was once a man who was going down from Jerusalem to Jericho when robbers attacked him, stripped him, and beat him up, leaving him half dead. It so happened that a priest was going down that road; but when he saw the man, he walked on by on the other side. In the same way a Levite also came there, went over and looked at the man, and then walked on by on the other side. But a Samaritan who was traveling that way came upon the man, and when he saw him, his heart was filled with pity. He went over to him, poured oil and wine on his wounds and bandaged them; then he put the man on his own animal and took him to an inn, where he took care of him. The next day he took out two silver coins and gave them to the inn-keeper. "Take care of him," he told the innkeeper, "and when I come back this way, I will pay you whatever else you spend on him."

And Jesus concluded, "In your opinion, which one of these three acted like a neighbor toward the man attacked by the robbers?"

The teacher of the Law answered, "The one who was kind to him."

Jesus replied, "You go, then, and do the same."

LUKE *10:25–37*

We should learn how to give.

But we should not regard giving as an obligation, but as a desire.

I usually say to our Co-Workers: "I do not need your surplus. I do not want you to give me your leftovers. Our poor do not need your condescending attitude nor your pity. The poor need our love and your kindness."

MOTHER TERESA,
from *No Greater Love*

THE HAPPY PRINCE

High above the city, on a tall column, stood the statue of the Happy Prince. He was gilded all over with thin leaves of fine gold, for eyes he had two bright sapphires, and a large red ruby glowed on his sword-hilt.

He was very much admired indeed. "He is as beautiful as a weather-cock," remarked one of the Town Councillors who wished to gain a reputation for having artistic tastes; "only not quite so useful," he added, fearing lest people should think him unpractical, which he really was not.

"Why can't you be like the Happy Prince?" asked a sensible mother of her little boy who was crying for the moon. "The Happy Prince never dreams of crying for anything."

"I am glad there is someone in the world who is quite happy," muttered a disappointed man as he gazed at the wonderful statue.

"He looks just like an angel," said the Charity Children as they came out of the cathedral in their bright scarlet cloaks and their clean white pinafores.

"How do you know?" said the Mathematical Master, "you have never seen one."

"Ah! but we have, in our dreams," answered the children; and the Mathematical Master frowned and looked very severe, for he did not approve of children dreaming.

One night there flew over the city a little Swallow. His friends had gone away to Egypt six weeks before, but he had stayed behind, for he was in love with the most beautiful Reed. He had met her early in the spring as he was flying down the river after a big yellow moth, and had been so attracted by her slender waist that he had stopped to talk to her.

"Shall I love you?" said the Swallow, who liked to come to the point at once, and the Reed made him a low bow. So he flew round and round her, touching the water with his wings, and making silver ripples. This was his courtship, and it lasted all through the summer.

"It is a ridiculous attachment," twittered the other Swallows; "she has no money, and far too many relations"; and indeed the river was quite full of Reeds. Then, when the autumn came, they all flew away.

After they had gone he felt lonely, and began to tire of his lady-love. "She has no conversation," he said, "and I am afraid that she is a coquette, for she is always flirting with the wind." And certainly, whenever the wind blew, the Reed made the most graceful curtsies. "I admit that she is domestic," he continued, "but I love travelling, and my wife, consequently, should love travelling also."

"Will you come away with me?" he said finally to her, but the Reed shook her head, she was so attached to her home.

"You have been trifling with me," he cried. "I am off to the Pyramids. Good-bye!" and he flew away.

All day long he flew, and at night-time he arrived at the city. "Where shall I put up?" he said; "I hope the town has made preparations."

Then he saw the statue on the tall column. "I will put up there," he cried; "it is a fine position, with plenty of fresh air." So he alighted just between the feet of the Happy Prince.

"I have a golden bedroom," he said softly to himself as he looked round, and he prepared to go to sleep; but just as he was putting his head under his wing a large drop of water fell on him. "What a curious thing!" he cried "there is not a single cloud in the sky, the stars are quite clear and bright, and yet it is raining. The climate in the north of Europe is really dreadful. The Reed used to like the rain, but that was merely her selfishness."

Then another drop fell.

"What is the use of a statue if it cannot keep the rain off?" he said; "I must look for a good chimney-pot," and he determined to fly away.

But before he had opened his wings, a third drop fell, and he looked up, and saw—Ah! what did he see?

The eyes of the Happy Prince were filled with tears, and tears were running down his golden cheeks. His face was so beautiful in the moonlight that the little Swallow was filled with pity.

"Who are you?" he said.

"I am the Happy Prince."

"Why are you weeping then?" asked the Swallow; "you have quite drenched me."

"When I was alive and had a human heart," answered the statue, "I did not know what tears were, for I lived in the Palace of Sans-Souci, where sorrow is not allowed to enter. In the daytime I played with my companions in the garden, and in the evening I led the dance in the Great Hall. Round the garden ran a very lofty wall, but I never cared to ask what lay beyond it, everything about me was so beautiful. My courtiers called me the Happy Prince, and happy indeed I was, if pleasure be happiness. So I lived, and so I died. And now that I am dead they have set me up here so high that I can see all the ugliness and all the misery of my city, and though my heart is made of lead yet I cannot choose but weep."

"What! Is he not solid gold?" said the Swallow to himself. He was too polite to make any personal remarks out loud.

"Far away," continued the statue in a low musical voice, "far away in a little street there is a poor house. One of the windows is open, and through it I can see a woman seated at a table. Her face is thin and worn, and she has coarse, red hands, all pricked by the needle, for she is a seamstress. She is embroidering passion-flowers on a satin gown for the loveliest of the Queen's maids-of-honour to wear at the next Court-ball. In a bed in the corner of the room her little boy is lying ill. He has a fever, and is asking for oranges. His mother has nothing to give him but river water, so he is crying. Swallow, Swallow, little Swallow, will you not bring her the ruby out of my sword-hilt? My feet are fastened to this pedestal and I cannot move."

"I am waited for in Egypt," said the Swallow. "My friends are flying up and down the Nile, and talking to the large lotus-flowers. Soon they will go to sleep in the tomb of the great King. The King is there himself in his painted coffin. He is wrapped in yellow linen, and embalmed with spices. Round his neck is a chain of pale green jade, and his hands are like withered leaves."

"Swallow, Swallow, little Swallow," said the Prince, "will you not stay with me for one night, and be my messenger? The boy is so thirsty, and the mother so sad."

"I don't think I like boys," answered the Swallow. "Last summer, when I was staying on the river, there were two rude boys, the miller's sons, who were always throwing stones at me. They never hit me, of course; we swallows fly far too well for that, and besides, I come of a family famous for its agility; but still, it was a mark of disrespect."

But the Happy Prince looked so sad that the little Swallow was sorry. "It is very cold here," he said; "but I will stay with you for one night, and be your messenger."

"Thank you, little Swallow," said the Prince.

So the Swallow picked out the great ruby from the Prince's sword, and flew away with it in his beak over the roofs of the town.

He passed by the cathedral tower, where the white marble angels were sculptured. He passed by the palace and heard the sound of dancing. A beautiful girl came out on the balcony with her lover. "How wonderful the stars are," he said to her, "and how wonderful is the power of love!"

"I hope my dress will be ready in time for the State-ball," she answered; "I have ordered passion-flowers to be embroidered on it: but the seamstresses are so lazy."

He passed over the river, and saw the lanterns hanging to the masts of the ships. He passed over the Ghetto, and saw the old Jews bargaining with each other, and weighing out money in copper scales. At last he came to the poor house and looked in. The boy was tossing feverishly on his bed, and the mother had fallen asleep, she was so tired. In he hopped, and laid the great ruby on the table beside the woman's thimble. Then he flew gently round the bed, fanning the boy's forehead with his wings. "How cool I feel!" said the boy, "I must be getting better;" and he sank into a delicious slumber.

Then the Swallow flew back to the Happy Prince, and told him what he had done. "It is curious," he remarked, "but I feel quite warm now, although it is so cold."

"That is because you have done a good action," said the Prince. And the little Swallow began to think, and then he fell asleep. Thinking always made him sleepy.

When day broke he flew down to the river and had a bath. "What a remarkable phenomenon!" said the Professor of Orthithology as he was passing over the bridge. "A swallow in winter!" And he wrote a long letter about it to the local newspaper. Everyone quoted it, it was full of so many words that they could not understand.

"Tonight I go to Egypt," said the Swallow, and he was in high spirits at the prospect. He visited all the public monuments, and sat a long time on top of the church steeple. Wherever he went the Sparrows chirruped, and said to each other, "What a distinguished stranger!" so he enjoyed himself very much.

When the moon rose he flew back to the Happy Prince. "Have

you any commissions for Egypt?" he cried "I am just starting."

"Swallow, Swallow, little Swallow," said the Prince, "will you not stay with me one night longer?"

"I am waited for in Egypt," answered the Swallow. "Tomorrow my friends will fly up to the Second Cataract. The river-horse couches there among the bulrushes, and on a great granite throne sits the God Memnon. All night long he watches the stars, and when the morning star shines he utters one cry of joy, and then he is silent. At noon the yellow lions come down to the water's edge to drink. They have eyes like green beryls, and their roar is louder than the roar of the cataract."

"Swallow, Swallow, little Swallow," said the Prince, "far away across the city I see a young man in a garret. He is leaning over a desk covered with papers, and in a tumbler by his side there is a bunch of withered violets. His hair is brown and crisp, and his lips are red as a pomegranate, and he has large and dreamy eyes. He is trying to finish a play for the Director of the Theatre, but he is too cold to write any more. There is no fire in the grate, and hunger has made him faint."

"I will wait with you one night longer," said the Swallow, who really had a good heart. "Shall I take him another ruby?"

"Alas! I have no ruby now," said the Prince: "my eyes are all that I have left. They are made of rare sapphires, which were brought out of India a thousand years ago. Pluck out one of them and take it to him. He will sell it to the jeweller, and buy firewood, and finish his play."

"Dear Prince," said the Swallow, "I cannot do that;" and he began to weep.

"Swallow, Swallow, little Swallow," said the Prince, "do as I command you."

So the Swallow plucked out the Prince's eye, and flew away to the student's garret. It was easy enough to get in, as there was a hole in the roof. Through this he darted, and came into the room. The young man had his head buried in his hands, so he did not hear the flutter of the bird's wings, and when he looked up he found the beautiful sapphire lying on the withered violets.

"I am beginning to be appreciated," he cried; "this is from some great admirer. Now I can finish my play," and he looked quite happy.

The next day the Swallow flew down to the harbour. He sat on the mast of a large vessel and watched the sailors hauling big chests out of the hold with ropes. "Heave a-hoy!" they shouted as each chest came up. "I am going to Egypt!" cried the Swallow, but nobody minded, and when the moon rose he flew back to the Happy Prince.

"I am come to bid you good-bye," he cried.

"Swallow, Swallow, little Swallow," said the Prince, "will you not stay with me one night longer?"

"It is winter," answered the Swallow, "and the chill snow will soon be here. In Egypt the sun is warm on the green palm-trees, and the crocodiles lie in the mud and look lazily about them. My companions are building a nest in the Temple of Baalbec, and the pink and white doves are watching them, and cooing to each other. Dear Prince, I must leave you, but I will never forget you, and next spring I will bring you back two beautiful jewels in place of those you have given away. The ruby shall be redder than a red rose, and the sapphire shall be as blue as the great sea."

"In the quarter below," said the Happy Prince, "there stands a little match-girl. She has let her matches fall in the gutter, and they are all spoiled. Her father will beat her if she does not bring home some money, and she is crying. She has no shoes or stockings, and her little head is bare. Pluck you my other eye, and give it to her, and her father will not beat her."

"I will stay with you one night longer," said the Swallow, "but I cannot pluck out your eye. You would be quite blind then."

"Swallow, Swallow, little Swallow," said the Prince, "do as I command you."

So he plucked out the Prince's other eye, and darted down with it. He swooped past the match-girl, and slipped the jewel into the palm of her hand. "What a lovely bit of glass!" cried the little girl; and she ran home laughing.

Then the Swallow came back to the Prince. "You are blind now," he said, "so I will stay with you always."

"No, little Swallow," said the poor Prince, "you must go away to Egypt."

"I will stay with you always," said the Swallow, and he slept at the Prince's feet.

All the next day he sat on the Prince's shoulder, and told him stories of what he had seen in strange lands. He told him of the red ibises, who stand in long rows on the banks of the Nile, and catch goldfish in their beaks; of the Sphinx, who is as old as the world itself, and lives in the desert, and knows everything; of the merchants, who walk slowly by the side of their camels and carry amber beads in their hands; of the King of the Mountains of the Moon, who is as black as ebony, and worships a large crystal; of the great green snake that sleeps in a palm-tree, and has twenty priests to feed it with honey-cakes; and of the pygmies who wail over a big lake on large flat leaves, and are always at war with the butterflies.

"Dear little Swallow," said the Prince, "you tell me of marvellous things, but more marvellous than anything is the suffering of men and of women. There is no Mystery as great as Misery. Fly over my city, little Swallow, and tell me what you see there."

So the Swallow flew over the great city, and saw the rich making merry in their beautiful houses, while the beggars were sitting at the gates. He flew into dark lanes, and saw the white faces of starving children looking out listlessly at the black streets. Under the archway of a bridge two little boys were lying in one another's arms to try and keep themselves warm. "How hungry we are!" they said. "You must not lie here," shouted the Watchman, and they wandered out into the rain.

Then he flew back and told the Prince what he had seen.

"I am covered with fine gold," said the Prince, "you must take it off, leaf by leaf, and give it to my poor; the living always think that gold can make them happy."

Leaf after leaf of the fine gold the Swallow picked off, till the Happy Prince looked quite dull and grey. Leaf after leaf of the fine gold he brought to the poor, and the children's faces grew rosier, and they laughed and played games in the street. "We have bread now!" they cried.

Then the snow came, and after the snow came the frost. The streets looked as if they were made of silver, they were so bright and glistening; long icicles like crystal daggers hung down from the eaves of the houses, everybody went about in furs, and the little boys wore scarlet caps and skated on the ice.

The poor little Swallow grew colder and colder, but he would not leave the Prince, he loved him too well. He picked up crumbs outside the baker's door when the baker was not looking, and tried to keep himself warm by flapping his wings.

But at last he knew that he was going to die. He had just enough strength to fly up to the Prince's shoulder once more. "Good-bye, dear Prince!" he murmured, "will you let me kiss your hand?"

"I am glad that you are going to Egypt at last, little Swallow," said the Prince, "you have stayed too long here but you must kiss me on the lips, for I love you."

"It is not Egypt that I am going," said the Swallow. "I am going to the House of Death. Death is the brother of Sleep, is he not?"

And he kissed the Happy Prince on the lips, and fell down dead at his feet.

At that moment a curious crack sounded inside the statue, as if something had broken. The fact is that the leaden heart had snapped right in two. It certainly was a dreadfully hard frost.

Early the next morning the Mayor was walking in the square below in company with the Town Councillors. As they passed the column he looked up at the statue: "Dear me! How shabby the Happy Prince looks!" he said.

"How shabby, indeed!" cried the Town Councillors, who always agreed with the Mayor, and they went up to look at it.

"The ruby has fallen out of his sword, his eyes are gone, and he is golden no longer," said the Mayor; "in fact, he is little better than a beggar!"

"Little better than a beggar," said the Town Councillors.

"And here is actually a dead bird at his feet!" continued the Mayor. "We must really issue a proclamation that birds are not to be allowed to die here." And the Town Clerk made a note of the suggestion.

So they pulled down the statue of the Happy Prince. "As he is no longer beautiful he is no longer useful," said the Art Professor at the University.

Then they melted the statue in a furnace, and the Mayor held a meeting of the Corporation to decide what was to be done with the metal. "We must have another statue, of course," he said, "and it shall be a statue of myself."

"Of myself," said each of the Town Councillors, and they quarreled. When I last heard of them they were quarrelling still.

"What a strange thing!" said the overseer of the workmen at the foundry. "This broken lead heart will not melt in the furnace. We must throw it away." So they threw it on a dust-heap where the dead Swallow was also lying.

"Bring me the two most precious things in the city" said God to one of His Angels; and the Angel brought Him the leaden heart and the dead bird.

"You have rightly chosen," said God, "for in my garden of Paradise this little bird shall sing for evermore, and in my city of gold the Happy Prince shall praise me."

OSCAR WILDE

NEIGHBORS

The man that is open of heart to his neighbor.
    And stops to consider his likes and dislikes,
His blood shall be wholesome whatever his labor,
    His luck shall be with him whatever he strikes.
The splendor of Morning shall duly possess him.
    That he may not be sad at the falling of eve.
And, when he has done with mere living—
    God bless him!
And many shall sigh, and one woman will grieve.

But he that is costive of soul towards his fellow,
    Though the ways and the works and woes of this life
Him food shall not fatten, him drink shall not mellow;
    And his innards shall brew him perpetual strife.
His eye shall be blind to God's Glory above him;
    His ear shall be deaf to Earth's Laughter around;
His friends and his Club and his Dog
    Shall not love him;
And his widow shall skip when he goes
    Underground!

RUDYARD KIPLING

Can I see another's woe,
And not be in sorrow too?
Can I see another's grief,
And not seek for kind relief?

WILLIAM BLAKE,
from "On Another's Sorrow"

THE SPIRIT OF CHRISTMAS

Once upon a time, not too long ago, there were four bachelor commodity brokers who spent most of their free time together. Without even thinking twice about it, they took their dates to the most expensive restaurants, smoked the best cigars, wore the trendiest watches, and thoroughly enjoyed the good life. They did these things not to be showy but because they could afford it. And it seemed that everyone they worked with did the same thing.

One Christmas Eve, their workday over early, the quartet of friends did the same thing they did at the end of every workday—they went bar hopping. But things downtown were pretty dead. Eventually they found themselves walking past the cathedral as people were hurrying in to one of the Christmas Eve masses, greeting one another cheerily. This made them uneasy. None of them ever spent much time in church and they certainly had no plans to attend a Christmas service.

When they came to the convenience store just north of the church, one of them decided he wanted some gum. He entered the store to find the owner berating a young woman of about seventeen, who was in tears. He was able to ascertain that she was trying to buy a cheap Christmas toy for her daughter but did not have enough money to pay the tax on the item. The clerk was adamant. She must pay the tax. As she went to leave the store, the broker touched her arm and said, "I think you dropped this money I found just outside the door." He handed her two twenty-dollar bills.

The woman eyed him warily until he said, "I think your daughter will be happy with Santa's gift." He tucked the money into her purse and rapidly left the store without his gum. He told his buddies the story and then said that he thought maybe he'd go back to the cathedral since there wasn't anything else to do.

They all went with him.

MARY G. DURKIN,
from *An Epidemic of Joy*

STRANGERS AND FRIENDS

Once upon a time, not so very long ago, a young mother gave birth to a tiny baby girl who had a heart defect. The doctor at the hospital said the baby would need special medical attention if she were to live.

The mother, a recent immigrant whose husband was unemployed, worried about how they might get help for their beautiful little baby. In addition to being financially strapped, they had an active two-year-old at home and no relatives in the country to help them.

A young girl, a "candy striper" volunteer, overhearing the conversation between the doctor and the new mother, told the story at her family dinner table. Later that evening the girl's mother went to the hospital to see what help the family needed.

The next day the mother organized a group of her friends to help care for the couple's two-year-old and the candy striper and her friends were recruited to baby-sit when their mothers were not available. The women also arranged for their church guild to give the family financial support.

The new parents, the helping women, and the candy striper and her friends all had a grand celebration when a healthy Baby Maria was finally released from the hospital. The baby's parents tell everyone they meet about the kindness of people who were strangers but are now friends.

MARY G. DURKIN,
from *An Epidemic of Joy*

MEG MERRILIES

Old Meg she was a Gipsy
And liv'd upon the Moors:
Her bed it was the brown heath turf,
And her house was out of doors.

Her apples were swart blackberries,
Her currants pods o' broom;
Her wine was dew o' the wild white rose
Her book a churchyard tomb.

Her Brothers were the craggy hills,
Her Sisters larchen trees—
Alone with her great family
She liv'd as she did please.

No breakfast had she many a morn,
No dinner many a noon,
And 'stead of supper she would stare
Full hard against the Moon.

But every morn of woodbine fresh
She made her garlanding,
And every night the dark glen Yew
She wove, and she would sing.

And with her fingers old and brown
She plaited Mats o' Rushes,
And gave them to the Cottagers
She met among the Bushes.

Old Meg was brave as Margaret Queen
And tall as Amazon:
An old red blanket cloak she wore;
A chip hat had she on.
God rest her aged bones somewhere—
She died full long agone!

JOHN KEATS

THE MIRACLE OF THE FLOWERS

Once Father Junipero Serra was riding through the desert on his mule. It was a dark and cold winter night. Though the desert usually was very dry, it was snowing that night. He was worn out from his travels and dead tired. All he wanted to do was find a warm and peaceful place to sleep.

But in the darkness, the priest encountered a young Native American man and his wife trying to find their way through the snow on foot to a place of shelter where the young woman could give birth to her child. Father Junipero put her on his own mule and led the two of them to a hut about which he knew. He lit a fire for them and gave them some of his food and water.

The priest immediately realized how similar their situation was to that of Mary and Joseph. But theirs was a miraculous situation, this

was just a poor couple in trouble. To give them privacy, Father Junipero pitched his tent outside the house and shivered underneath his
blankets for most of the long night, but he was so tired that he did not
get up.

The next morning the sun was shining brightly, the air was warm,
and the mule was grazing happily. Father Junipero remembered what
had happened the night before. He rushed into the house, but the
couple and their child were gone, and the room was filled with flowers.
The priest took as many as he could carry back to his mission, where
they bloomed for many months.

Whenever he told the story, Father Junipero said that he had no
idea whether the couple were anything other than they appeared. What
mattered was that they needed help and he could offer it.

ANDREW M. GREELEY,
from *An Epidemic of Joy*

CHAPTER EIGHT

Senior Love

The wrinkles of the heart are more indelible than those of the brow.
DOROTHÉ DELUZY

True love never becomes old.
AN ITALIAN PROVERB

Senior love—romantic love among people who qualify for membership in AARP—is a myth breaker, shattering two myths about senior citizens. The first myth is that by a certain time in a marriage—thirty-five or more years—romance is long gone. People who stay married to the same partner into their sixties, seventies, and beyond are either in a rut or just used to a particular style of life that is, at best, pretty monotonous. If the partners stay together, it's because of habit and convention, not because of romantic love.

The second myth is that people who meet and fall in love during those years—oftentimes after death or divorce renders them alone—are simply looking for security. Men at that age need someone to care for them, especially if their first wife had always done so. Women are lonely on their own and seeking someone to take care of and also to be their escort.

Even all the ads featuring healthy, physically fit, attractive-looking seniors enjoying a wide range of activities don't dispel that myth. The debunkers of romantic love point to all the bickering seniors they see shopping together or on a cruise ship or at an airport. They see " 'til death do us part" as a life sentence not an opportunity to grow in love. Or they point to the wife who complains when her husband retires and is underfoot all day as a sure sign that romance is long gone by retirement time.

Many seniors also buy into the myth. Some have not grown through repeated cycles of falling in love, settling down, bottoming out, and beginning again. In other words, they have not nurtured romance. As a result they fail to appreciate the chance offered by the time in life when "the mortgage is paid, the kids have moved out, and the dog has died."

Seniors who have nurtured this love through the earlier years of their marriage will continue to find ways to keep romance alive. The couple, who on their thirty-third anniversary bought each other a card with the same verse—"grow old along with me; the best is yet to be"— know something about romance. So does the husband who, seeing a window display of red lingerie in a store near his suburban train depot, stops twice to buy some for his wife of thirty-seven years. The women clerks commented, "We wish we were married to you!"

As for seniors who marry or have relationships in their twilight years, many observers wonder if this is not a sure sign of second childhood. Children worry that one or the other of the partners is after the family fortune—which might not be much of a fortune. Some children—really adults by this time—are angry at what they consider disrespect for the deceased parent. They would condemn the surviving parent to a sheltered life as monument to the memory of the departed spouse. Friends, especially those who have not had romance in their own marriages, worry that the widow or widower is being taken by the new lover.

The storytellers and poets in this chapter invite us to consider how romance in senior years is a reward for a life of openness to the binding power of love.

LOVE'S NOT TIME'S FOOL

Let me not the marriage of true minds
Admit impediments. Love is not love
Which alters when it alterations finds,
Or bend with the remover to remove
Oh, no! It is an ever-fixed mark,
That looks on tempests and is never shaken;
It is the star to every wandering bark,
Whose worth's unknown, although his height be taken.
Love's not time's fool, though rosy lips and cheeks
Within his bending sickle's compass come;
Love alters not with his brief hours and weeks,
But bears it out even to the edge of doom.
If this be error and upon me prove,
I never writ, nor no man ever loved.

WILLIAM SHAKESPEARE

A homilist at a twenty-fifth wedding anniversary mass spoke of how statistics indicate that once a couple reaches the silver anniversary, the probability of the marriage breaking up becomes quite low. Studies also show that the year leading up to the anniversary is one of the make or break times in a relationship.

BELIEVE ME, IF ALL THOSE
ENDEARING YOUNG CHARMS

Believe me, if all those endearing young
    charms,
    Which I gaze on so fondly today,
Were to change by tomorrow, and fleet in my arms
    Like fairy-gifts fading away,
Thou wouldst still be adored, as this moment
    thou art,
    Let thy loveliness fade as it will,
and around the dear ruin each wish of my
    heart
Would entwine itself verdantly still.

It is not while beauty and youth are thine
    own
    And thy cheeks unprofaned by a tear
That the fervor and faith of a soul can be
    known,
    To which time will but make thee more
    dear;
No, the heart that has truly loved never
    forgets
    But as truly loves on to the close,
As the sunflower turns on her god, when he
    sets,
    The same look which she turned when he
    rose.

THOMAS MOORE

Love makes itself felt not in the desire for copulation (a desire that extends to an infinite number of women) but in the desire for a shared sleep (a desire limited to one woman).

MILAN KUNDERA

A happy marriage is a long conversation which always seems too short.

ANDRE MAUROIS

LOVE TRIUMPHANT

With the written declaration that "as surely as the vine
Grew round the stump" she loved me—that old sweet
    heart of mine.

And again I feel the pressure of her slender little hand
As we used to talk together of the future we had planned—
When I should be a poet, and with nothing else to do
But write the tender verses that she set the music to:

When we should live together in a cozy little cot
Hid in a nest of roses, with a fairy garden-spot,
Where the vines were ever fruited, and the weather ever
    fine,
And the birds were ever singing for that old sweetheart
    of mine:

When I should be her lover forever and a day,
And she my faithful sweetheart till the golden hair was
    gray;
And we should be so happy that when either's lips were
    dumb
They would not smile in Heaven till the other's kiss had
    come.

But, ah! My dream is broken by a step upon the stair,
And the door is softly opened, and—my wife is standing there;
Yet with eagerness and rapture all my visions I resign
To greet the living presence of that old sweetheart of mine.

JAMES WHITCOMB RILEY

TO JUICE ON AUGUST 11, 1981

Marriage is impossible.
    Consider the odds:
two unique minds,
    two different bods,

attracted to union,
    affected by history,
an ongoing challenge
    to understand mystery.

Grasping its meaning
    an impossible task;
so in its sweet wine,
    let's drink from the cask.

Where we began?
    A simple blind date.
The matchmaker's hand,
    was it our fate?

God sent me presents,
    a few clinkers, too.
He honored me, though,
    with someone like you.

We've laughed and we've cried,
    altered our roles,
reveled in ecstasy,
    created new souls.

Twenty-five have passed,
    some needed suture,
yet mended we are,
    creating our future.

But scary it is,
    this intimate life;
it pulls and its pushes
    a husband and wife—

Two steps ahead
    and sometimes one back.
We're blessed, though, you know,
    when we're on the track.

Go back for a moment
    to our wedding day
when two naive dreamers
    viewed the world as play.

We've changed and we've not;
    that may be a clue
to seeking the answer
    about me and you.

We've grown, that's for sure,
    in more ways than one,
but still we're convinced
    that life should be fun.

Look how we celebrate
    this milestone we've passed.
We gather the folks
    to have a big blast.

And somehow in that
    we think there's a story
that marriage holds promise
    of God's greatest glory.

Twenty-five more ones,
    a marvelous view—
what more can I say:
I'll always love you.

JACK DURKIN

1956–1981

Young we were my dear, on that warm August day.
Filled with dreams of Eden's delights,
We planted our troth, proclaimed our love, and
went forth gaily in the dark. We would conquer all.

Surprised we've been, my love, nine thousand days and more.
Children, hybrids blossoming, rare Irish specimens.
The selves we pledged unfolding unexpected mixtures of
spouse, parent, worker, student, lover. We were conquering all.

Dismayed we've been, my friend, on dark and dismal days,
weeds of isolation blocking out the sun and sucking up
the waters of our troth. We forget our dreams and
wait for death to come. Can we conquer all?

Renewed we've been, my friend, days and nights alike,
watered by God, by kids, by family, by friends.
Our drooping branches stretch across abyss and together
reach upwards for the sun. We can hope to conquer all.

Young we are, again, my beloved, on this fair August day,
our garden rich with fruit, our gardening skills refined.
So, giddy with celebration of silver-tinged love,
we journey forth believing: Love will conquer all.

MARY G. DURKIN

Crosswicks is not a perfect house. It has suffered from wear and tear and years of neglect. The walls and floors are crooked. There is no way to weatherproof it so that in winter moles and field mice do not seek and find entrance. So throughout the years we have had cats, varying in number, because it is in the nature of cats to keep rodents out of their house. Some of the rooms need a second wallpapering, some a third. About a quarter of a century ago we reupholstered the living room furniture—I think of it as new. Babies and animals have stained the rugs. But Crosswicks is comfortable, warm, welcoming. Friends coming in for the first time have frequently remarked, "What a lovely house!"

And so, I hope, are Hugh and I, in our own human and fallible way. We were not a latter-day Héloïse and Abelard, Pelléas and Mélisande when we married. For one thing the Héloïses and Abelards, Pelléases and Mélisandes, do not get married and stay married for forty years. A love which depends solely on romance, on the combustion of two attracting chemistries, tends to fizzle out. The famous lovers usually end up dead. A long-term marriage has to move beyond chemistry to compatibility, to friendship, to companionship. It is certainly not that the passion disappears, but that it is conjoined with other ways of love.

We have both, throughout the forty years of our marriage, continued to respond with excitement to the same beauty—for instance, to certain pieces of music. . . . On a cold and dank day we walked along a beach in southern Portugal, arm in arm, gazing with awe at the great eyes painted on the prows of the fishermen's boat. One night we stood by the railing of a freighter and were dazzled by the glory of the Southern Cross against the blackness of an unpolluted sky. If this kind of simultaneous wonder diminishes, it is a sign of trouble. Thank God it has been a constant for us.

Love of music, of sunsets and sea; a liking for the same kind of people; political opinions that are not radically divergent; a similar stance as we look at the stars and think of the marvelous strangeness of this universe—these are what build a marriage. And it is never to be taken for granted.

Periodically during my life I have needed times of assessment, of stepping back from my life, our life, and contemplating. When I was twenty-nine I wrote in my journal that I did not expect to die soon, but if I did, at least I would know that I had lived.

That was at twenty-nine, when I had been married for two years. It is far more true today when thirty-eight more years of marriage have been added. This is a summer for reviewing and reassessing. My husband is ill and I do not know how it is all going to end.

Of course we never do.

MADELEINE L'ENGLE,
from *Two-Part Invention*

ilver-tinged love often means dealing with the heartaches of ill health and impending death.

TO MARY

The twentieth year is well-nigh past,
Since first our sky was overcast;
Ah would that this might be the last!
       My Mary!

Thy spirits have a fainter flow.
I see thee daily weaker grow—
'Twas my distress that brought thee low
       My Mary!

Thy needles, once a shining store,
For my sake restless heretofore,
Now rust disus'd, and shine no more.
       My Mary!

For though thou gladly wouldst fulfill
The same kind office for me still,
Thy sight now seconds not thy will.
       My Mary!

But well thou play'dst the housewife's part,
And all the threads with magic art
Have wound themselves about this heart,
       My Mary!

My indistinct expressions seem
Like language utter'd in a dream;
Yet me they charm, whate'er the theme
    My Mary!

Thy silver locks, once auburn bright,
Are still more lovely in my sight
Than golden beams of orient light,
    My Mary!

For could I view nor them nor thee,
What sight worth seeing could I see?
The sun would rise in vain for me,
    My Mary!

Partakers of thy sad decline,
Thy hands their little force resign;
Yet, gently pressed, press gently mine,
    My Mary!

And then I feel that still I hold
A richer store ten thousandfold
Than misers fancy in their gold,
    My Mary!

Such feebleness of limbs thou prov'st
That now at every step thou mov'st,
Upheld by two; yet still thou lov'st,
    My Mary!

And still to love, though prest with ill,
In wintry age to feel no chill,
With me is to be lovely still,
    My Mary!

But ah! By constant heed I know,
How oft the sadness that I show
Transforms thy smiles to looks of woe,
    My Mary!

And should my future lot be cast
With much resemblance of the past,
Thy worn-out heart will break at last,
  My Mary!

William Cowper

A Toast on the Fortieth Anniversary of a Blind Date

(Given on October 27 at Durkinfest '91, a celebration of thirty-five years
of marriage, delayed because of his chemotherapy)

Jack,

Forty years, 14,610—give or take a day or two—days ago, the trick or treat bag of my heart was empty. The treat you dropped into my heart that long ago night didn't seem all that exceptional; and yet it definitely was a bit of magic.

For that surprise treat expanded until it filled not only my heart but also my life with wonders I could never have imagined. And the most impressive of all the wonders is you, my love. A boy who grew out of the charming cocoon of late adolescence into a man of Irish charm, wit, courage, strong faith, and hopefulness, into a gracious friend, a caring father, a special grandfather, a dedicated worker, a party lover, and most of all, an ideal lover, into a man with the appeal of a most enchanting butterfly, in other words, into a man with class! And so, my love, I propose a toast to you:

May your Irish charm rain a fine mist of good moods into the lives of those who know you.

May your wit, and your tears of laughter at your own jokes, continue to shine.

May your courage, oh, yes, your wonderful courage that inspires us all, never desert you.

May you be surrounded by true friends and loving family members who remind you that the God of your faith cares for you.
May your hopefulness sustain your love of good times, even when times are less than great.
May you delight in the admiration we feel for your classiness.
May you, my love, be mine and I be thine not only as we grow old together but forever.

And, finally, when you make the journey into heaven may St. Brigit and the three Marys, and all the heavenly hosts welcome you and invite you to sit with them by the lake of beer so you may sing and dance and add your cheer to God's Eternalfest! *Sláinte*, My love!

MARY G. DURKIN

Falling in love at fifty, sixty, seventy, and eighty often comes as an unexpected surprise, a gift that takes us out of the grief of loss—of a spouse or a friend or a job. The discovery that someone can love us when most of the world views us as ready for the retirement center gives us a new lease on life.

BROKEN DREAMS

There is grey in you hair.
Young men no longer suddenly catch their breath
When you are passing;
But maybe some old gaffer mutters a blessing
Because it was your prayer
Recovered him upon the bed of death.
For your sole sake—that all heart's ache have known,

And given to others all heart's ache,
From meager girlhood's putting on
Burdensome beauty—for your sole sake
Heaven has put away the stroke of her doom,
So great her portion in that peace you make
By merely walking in a room.

Your beauty can but leave among us
Vague memories, nothing but memories.
A young man when the old men are done talking
Will say to an old man, 'Tell me of that lady
The poet stubborn with his passion sang us
When age might well have chilled his blood.'

Vague memories, nothing but memories,
But in the grave all, shall be renewed.
The certainty that I shall see that lady
Leaning or standing or walking
In the first loveliness of womanhood,
And with the fervour of my youthful eyes,
Has set me muttering like a fool.

You are more beautiful than any one,
And yet your body had a flaw:
Your small hands were not beautiful,
And I am afraid that you will run
And paddle to the wrist
In the mysterious, always brimming lake
Where those that have obeyed the holy law
Paddle and are perfect. Leave unchanged
The hands that I have kissed,
For old sake's sake.

The last stroke of midnight dies.
All day in the one chair
From dream to dream and rhyme to rhyme I have ranged
In rambling talk with an image of air:
Vague memories, nothing but memories.

W. B. YEATS

Friendships are dear to us in our senior years. When the mortgage is paid, etc., we have time to reconnect with old friends and open ourselves to meeting new friends. They become great supports for us.

LOVE AT SECOND SIGHT

Once upon a time, there were two young people who fell in love at a resort in the middle of summer. They were convinced that this affection was the love of their lives. They promised that they would love each other forever. They would write after they went back to college, they would attend each other's homecoming dances in the fall, they would see each other at Thanksgiving and Christmas. Their hunger for each other would always exist.

Alas, as the cynical Brazilian proverb puts it, "Love is forever, but it does not last."

By Christmas, the couple's eternal love was forgotten. Eventually they each married other lovers and forgot about each other . . . almost. There was always a little part of their memories in which the other remained. It was foolish summer love, they realized, but it had been too sweet to forget completely.

Many, many years later, when both their families were raised and they were widow and widower, they met and fell in love again. Or perhaps they merely rediscovered that corner of their memories where their love had always persisted.

And so, although they were now much older, the two of them married and lived happily ever after.

Some love, you see, does last. The hunger for it just takes a while to be filled.

Andrew M. Greeley,
from *An Epidemic of Joy*

It is great to have friends when one is young, but indeed it is still more so when you are getting old. When we are young, friends are, like everything else, a matter of course. In the old days we know what it means to have them.

Edvard Grieg

GILBERTE

When fact, he reflected, begins to model itself after fiction, it should stick to the script.

"Aren't the Bears wonderful this year?" she said, a line that he would never write.

She wasn't supposed to be an enthusiast for the Chicago Bears. Neither in the treasured memory of his adolescent admiration nor in the paradigm of the woman who flitted through his stories in various shapes and guises was there any room for the Mighty Monsters of the Midway (whose headquarters were in Lake Forest, about as far from the Midway as you could get and still vote in Cook County). He was the Bears expert; he remembered Clyde "Bulldog" Turner and George "One Play" McAfee; he knew that the 1942 Bears had been unbeaten until the playoff game, the only unbeaten team before the Miami Dolphins of 1972.

Yet the handsome upper-middle-class grandmother, marked by age indeed but hardly ravaged by it, who sat across the table from him in the slightly baroque splendor of the Arts Club—a wall of windows, polished black floors, infinitely polite waiters—could match him story for story. She knew that Jim McMahon was the best quarterback since Sid Luckman and that Ray "Scooter" McLean had once drop-kicked a point after a touchdown in 1940.

"Who would have thought," she continued, "that Mike Ditka could handle the Refrigerator story with such grace? Remember when he was tight end? He sort of invented the role, didn't he?"

What bothered him about this story in which he was one of the two principals (the less important, in all candor) was that he couldn't quite figure out what metaphor the Storyteller had in mind.

"He and John Mackey."

"Of the Colts, wasn't he? Before they moved to Indianapolis?"

Fair enough. Despite endless autumn Sunday-afternoon agony in front of the TV screen, he'd been to one Bears game in thirty years. She seemed hardly to have missed one.

At first he had felt like he was in a Hindu myth, an author caught up inside one of his own tales in which he and another person recite lines that he has already written, all part of the dream of some medium-caste god. Three, maybe four videotapes, playing at the same time.

The Hindu myths, however, stick to their scenarios. Mike Ditka does not intrude, Refrigerator in tow, to disconcert and unhinge.

"I knew you would reappear in our lives." She eased her fruit salad to one side. "I wasn't surprised at all when you wrote at the time of Tim's death."

"Really?" In his stories he would ask why. Love never dies, even distant and unspoken love, even when the loved person becomes a myth and invades your stories.

Still, in the myth in his head, as distinct from the myth in his stories, the fascination was supposed to be one way.

"I phoned your sister's house a few years ago. Did you get the message?" she asked.

"They said you'd call back."

"You've changed. You were so quiet we hardly knew you."

He was talking to three different women, a past, a present, and a dream, the last of which had become a myth. The boundaries separating the three faded and then reappeared. She was a story become real, perhaps so that she might become a story again.

"You've changed, too."

"Not as much. But what happened to make you change?"

He tried to explain that when you find yourself a pariah in the Church because there is a new administration, you discover that freedom has been thrust on you whether you want it or not. Since you have no intention of leaving, you use that freedom, first gingerly, then with increasingly reckless leprechaun flair. The quiet rule-keeper had been an unperceived mask all along.

"I kept all the rules till I was thirty."

"My daughters"—she laughs at herself—"say that I never broke a rule in all my life."

He sensed that he had explained poorly, but she nods quickly, seeming to understand. In all the versions, her intelligence was decisively quick.

The young waiter carefully offered the plate of roast lamb from which they were to help themselves. The Arts Club was like home— you ate what was put before you.

"You've had an interesting priesthood, haven't you? Exciting even?"

"Not what I'd expected. Things changed." The male in his stories had much better lines. "The excitement I could often do without."

"I suppose so." She nods again, once more seeming to understand his cryptic responses. "Any regrets?"

As she nibbles at her roast lamb she is exploring the boundaries, making sure she understands the geography.

"No. I'd do it all again." This is the time to define the boundaries sharply. "I wouldn't even leave if they tried to throw me out. Stay and bother them."

She laughs for the first time in the conversation. "As in marriage, I'm sure faithfulness has something to do with it."

"I had a hard time understanding those who left until I was forced to put myself inside the soul of one of them in a story. It's not my path."

The waiter clears away the dishes. Outside, traffic is already backed up on the crowded street which feeds the hungry Kennedy Expressway.

"Blueberry cobbler? With ice cream? I'd love it. I've always had a sweet tooth. And weight isn't my problem. Just the opposite. My daughters are always on my case because I'm too thin."

The woman in the story had a sweet tooth, too. He did not know the past woman well enough to have learned her tastes. So quickly had she been transformed from a beautiful girl to a lingering myth. Now reality was imitating the myth again. Or maybe he'd made a good guess.

Before lunch, he had tried characteristically to order his thoughts and emotions for the drama with models of Marcel Proust's Gilberte and Jim Farrell's Lucy Scanlan. Why not start with two of the most shimmering young loves in all of storytelling?

Neither one of whom is as beautiful as she was.

Unlike Marcel Proust he had recognized his Gilberte at a dinner party after forty years. Instantly.

Proust's metaphor was Gilberte's daughter. The daughter of his "Gilberte" was dazzling, too. But "Gilberte" was the metaphor. Whatever the metaphor was.

"You stared all evening," his companion said.

"Can you blame me?"

"Not the first time."

Did Jim Farrell ever think of the real-life counterpart of Lucy Scanlan as anything more than an object for Studs's doomed dreams?

Very young love is an illusion; intense, preoccupying, unbearably sweet, but finally shallow, transient, and deceptive. Right?

Maybe not.

An author who tried to peddle the plot of *A la recherche* today would be laughed out of the offices of any self-respecting New York publishing company. Similarly a writer who suggested that young love might be revelatory, sacramental, a hint of what life is finally about, would find himself dismissed as an incurable romantic.

Which doesn't mean necessarily that he is wrong.

It all depends on your Gilberte, doesn't it? Or your Lucy Scanlan? Or the god, possibly Hindu, in whose dreams you live?

What if you were lucky? Or had enormously good taste?

Even in first grade?

Okay, lucky. Either in your Beatrice or in the god into whose dreams you have managed to intrude.

"It's hard to express in words," she begins, her eyes always the sparkling blue of a pretty Wisconsin lake stirred by light summer breezes, smiling even if her face is serious. "Or it is for me anyway, how I feel when I read a book by someone I knew long ago."

"It must be."

"It's not that I don't like them"—she hastens to dispel any thought of criticism—"and I'm astonished by your memory. You don't forget anything, do you?"

"The images and memories come back"—he knows that he must have written this exchange in one of his books—"when the story requires them. Nothing happens in the stories quite the way it did in life—not even that spelling bee between two people, both of whom we might think we know." His face becomes warm. "And no one in the stories is drawn from life exactly either. It's all what didn't happen but might have happened."

"Or should have happened?"

"Not necessarily."

"I've read them all. I think we all have. Looking for ourselves"—a quick, shy blush—"shocked if we recognize ourselves and disappointed if we don't."

He had wondered when his stories became popular whether those whom he hadn't seen in four decades would read them. He had assumed that they would not. Then it turned out that they did indeed read them—as quickly as they could grab them off the stands. How come, my own people in my own country?

"They're not exactly autobiographical. I mean, a storyteller—this one anyway—rewrites it all to make the story. It's not a video replay. Even the great autobiographical novelists, Proust and Joyce, retold their lives to fit the story."

Lit 101. She probably hadn't read either *Portrait* or *A la recherche*, not that it mattered. She should read Studs, however. It was about their own kind, the incorrigible Chicago Irish.

"Are you the narrator in the first book?"

"My sister says twenty percent of the time and I'd like to have been forty percent of the time."

"No Ellen?"

"That's what the cardinal asked me once. No, no Ellen."

"That's too bad, in a way."

"He thought so, too."

"But you know a lot about women."

"I'm a male member of the human race, with all the hormones that accompany that."

"That doesn't always make much difference."

"Thank you for the compliment. I'm still trying—in the process of learning."

Why do you fall in love with a little girl when you're both in first grade, worship her from a distance for eight years, see her once or twice after graduation, and hold her in a place of honor in your memory ever after? So much so that your childhood and adolescent images of her survive for four decades and explode in your stories, almost every one of them?

Because you are an incurable romantic, that's why.

All right, but even for a romantic she must have been someone special.

She was pretty, she was smart, she was good, she was self-possessed, she was a resilient academic rival. Are those not enough good reasons?

Still pretty, still smart, still resilient—tense and nervous as she fought off pain and grief and adjusted to life alone, yet determined to survive and survive well, a burden to no one. No, not all that different. From a distance, and not much of a distance, in skirt and sweater, she made it 1942 again.

But what's the metaphor here? What does this mean in the dream of a god who loves surprises? No Hindu god, that.

"The stories bring back a lot of memories for me, too. You were so smart. I think I was probably envious of that."

His temptation is to say that to her alone envy is permitted. Instead he tells the truth: "You had reason to be angry. You were a girl, you were too pretty, and you weren't going to a seminary. No way you could win."

She laughs, not convinced. "I never thought I'd become as much of a feminist as I have in the last five years." She folds her glasses and puts them in her purse. "There really is terrible discrimination against women."

"Women priests?"

"I don't know."

"There's only one reason to exclude them. If they're inferior human beings."

"They're *not* inferior." The feisty rival once more. "But I do think of God as a mother. I mean, if you've had a mother and been a mother and loved and been loved both ways, how could you not?"

He hadn't written that line. But unlike talk about Mike Ditka and Jim McMahon and the Fridge, he wished he had.

Certainly no medium-caste Hindu god was writing this story. It was Yahweh, Good Old. And Lady Wisdom, God's self-disclosure in the order and charm of the cosmos. Lady Wisdom, whom he'd once told a reporter was an Irish comedienne.

"If God is a mother as well as a father, why not women priests?"

"I suppose." She was thoughtful again, slipping up to a big question perhaps. "None of us thought you would be a novelist."

"I didn't either and I'm not sure I am."

"I am the girl in this book?" She held it in front of her, like a shield, or maybe a prayer book. "Kind of?"

"Bits and pieces." He swallowed much too large a piece of blueberry cobbler.

"My daughters didn't recognize me. So I didn't tell them. They all say it's their favorite." The same magic smile from first grade. Special indeed. "I know you much better after reading these books than you know me." She opens the book tentatively. "Yet you know a lot about me that you couldn't possibly know."

The God in whose dreams he lived, perhaps not at all the God who dreamed Proust and Farrell, is a God who enjoys surprises, twists and turns, kinks and ironies, and happy endings. Ultimately anyway.

Nonetheless, it was excessive of Her to write him into the kind of story into which he had written his own characters.

"A lot of the girl in the book is based on my imagination of what you might have become. Some of it was pretty thin. . . ."

"And some pretty accurate, too. I can't understand how you did it."

"All the people are composites. I dream up the story line and then the characters come rushing out of my imagination, fully grown." He omits any reference in this writer's workshop lecture to Venus from the sea. "Only afterward do I realize that bits and pieces of people I've known through the years have been incorporated."

"Am I in the other women?"

"Most of them, I guess."

"That's nice. . . ." She reaches for her glasses again, as though to reread the book. "I like the books. And I like the women, too."

"I was half-afraid that you might read this one especially, recognize yourself, and be angry."

Another quick blush. "Certainly not angry. Surprised. Maybe flattered. Anyway"—pointing at the girl on the cover—"*she* wouldn't be angry, would she?"

"*She* would love it. Maybe I should have trusted my imagination."

Neither of them says what they both know. To have so influenced stories after forty years, she must have occupied an enormous place in his imagination.

A new Cadillac is becalmed outside the window beneath their table. Not at all like the startling Studebakers of 1946. He imagines a study on the street and thinks that Proust, genius that he was, erred. Time is neither lost nor found, but given.

"You wrote that poem, the rivals one, about me, too? The one that ends, 'We shall be young again, we shall laugh again'?"

"Who else fits it?"

"Thank you for that, too."

As someone else remarked when she heard about this tête-à-tête at the Arts Club, no one is anything but pleased to discover that they've been loved for fifty years.

Or, for that matter, to say that one has loved for fifty years and is fully prepared to love for fifty more.

Which is certainly true, though it doesn't help much in the search for a metaphor. He ought to be depressed. No one could live up to his residual adolescent fantasies. Only somehow she went beyond them, not as a two-dimensional fantasy, but as a three-dimensional person.

Is the Author trying to tell him something?

"Do you think the Bears will go to the Super Bowl?" She nods at the waiter for more coffee.

Is that what the Author had in mind? He thinks this story is being changed into a comedy.

"No doubt." He crosses his fingers and together they laugh with the hollow cheer of the dogged Chicago sports fan.

"None at all. Will you watch it at our house?"

Forty years—the span of a woman's adult life: falling in love, courtship, marriage, the difficult early days of parenthood, struggle against initial economic problems, life for a while in a strange city, marvelous but contentious kids (in the nature of the creature), sorrows, disappointments, failures, difficult decisions, intense if all too transient joys, unexpected surprises, pride of accomplishment, interludes of contentment that slip through your fingers, tragedy, the somber realization that most of the joys are in the past and were not embraced as fervently as they might have been, grim awareness that the end is now much closer than the beginning. Life too quickly almost done before it has even begun.

By all odds and according to all conventional wisdom, he ought to be disappointed with the impact of such a life on her, either with a sense of lost opportunity like Studs or painful disillusionment like Marcel.

In fact, she delights him, as much as in first grade if for different reasons. Better ones, come to think of it.

There's a metaphor there someplace if he could only find it.

"I should begin the drive home before the rush hour."

"I'll walk you to the parking lot."

"Thanks for lunch . . . and thanks for the books." She gestures with one of them. "And thanks for coming back into our lives."

"The gratitude should be the other way around."

If he had walked a different path in his life, there would never have been romance between them. They were not star-crossed lovers. Whatever metaphor the Author had in mind, it did not involve sadness over what might have been, nor joy over what might yet be. They will continue to walk different paths in the years ahead, though not nearly so far apart. The metaphor is not about that sort of issue.

It was somehow more subtle or maybe more simple—like our dreams are never grand enough. No, that wasn't it either. Close perhaps, but with metaphors, close didn't help.

It's all right, fella, the Author seemed to be saying, for you to use those images in your story. I play a different game, because I'm not only into surprises, but offbeat surprises. You yourself called me a comedienne, right?

Right.

He kissed her good-bye at the parking lot and promised indeed that on January 26 he would watch the Super Bowl with her family.

Go Fridge!

A wind off the lake had swept the clouds away from the Michigan Avenue skyline. As he walked east the tall buildings, framed in deep blue, shone silver and gold in the late-afternoon winter sunlight.

Life goes on, not in Gilberte but her daughter. Lucy Scanlan is the lost angel of light for one whose life does not go on.

Come on, guys, don't try to give me those clichés!

His Author, a Hindu god turned Jewish and then turned Celtic, had a much better metaphor, not in a woman who had lost her vitality but in one who had kept it. Nor in a woman who was less than imagined but, in intricate complexity, more.

It was surely an excellent metaphor, but he didn't quite know how to interpret it.

He might have to write another story.

ANDREW M. GREELEY,
from *Women I've Met*

CHAPTER NINE

Lost Love

*To love someone who loves you not
is a curse on one begot.*
A SPANISH PROVERB

*Love is a springtime plant that perfumes everything with its hope,
Even the ruins to which it clings.*
FLAUBERT

To love and lose might be better than never to have loved;
But most of us, when we lose a love—not through death
but through love's demise—would be hard-pressed to
find this oft-repeated Tennyson quote very consoling.
Love is risky business. Yet when we fall in love, only the
most calculated and cautious individuals project ahead to the end of
the relationship. Even when the love is one-sided, most lovers hope
their love will be reciprocated. They dream—and daydream—of the
time when this will happen.

When love is one-sided from the beginning, the one who loves,
caught up in the attraction of love, fails to read the signals from the
other and creates a scenario that is bound to lead to disappointment.
Teenage crushes are examples of this. Most people look back at these
with bittersweet memories: How could I have been so dumb? Still it

was wonderful and I learned from it. Didn't I? Did I?

Real love, love that will last through the good times and the bad, is scary. Love makes demands, love needs to be nurtured, love disappoints, love is not constant. When people settle down in a love relationship, they tend to start taking each other for granted.

Even though both partners make a commitment to love, each brings different expectations about what loving another means.

When we reflect on lost love, and what might be the cause of the heartbreak, we have two options. We can say that what leads us to fall in love is proof that life is a tale told by an idiot. Or we can say there is something afoot in the universe and each of us plays a part in making that something come alive for others and for ourselves. We are not passive recipients of love's ups and downs. We play a role in how life happens to us.

The stories and poetry and sayings in this chapter tell of the heartbreak of love's endings. Though in each instance we are privy to only one side of the tale, it is not hard to imagine that another tale is telling the other side. Still, as long as we have recorded tales, we know that people fall in love, that love sometimes disappoints, and yet each new set of lovers—even when one or both partners have been through a loss of love—feeds the perfume of love's hopefulness.

At times love is one-sided from the beginning or never expressed so the loved one is unaware of the other's attraction to him or her. At other times, the person loved has no interest in being the object of the other person's affection.

They bore a love for each other
Which neither had spoken of;
Each had cold looks for the other
While being consumed with love.

They parted at last and since then
Only in dreams still met;
They had died the Lord knows when,
But were not aware of it yet.

HEINRICH HEINE,
from *Songs of Love and Grief*

Heart-whole, I started to beseech
That she would be my lady sweet.
I swore to her with heartfelt heat
My steadfast duty firm and true,
And love that would be always new.
To guard her honour evermore,

And serve no other, then I swore
To do my best. I promised this:
"For yours is all that ever there is,
My sweetheart. Barring dreams untrue,
I never shall be false to you,
As sure as God's intents prevail!"

And when I thus had told my tale,
God knows, my love and pain and awe
She seemed to think not worth a straw.
To tell it briefly as it is,
Her answer was most truly this:
I cannot perfectly convey
Exactly what she had to say:
The gist of it was simply "No"
And nothing more.

GEOFFREY CHAUCER,
from *The Book of Duchess*

THE DIVINE COMEDY: CANTO 5

When I replied, my words began: "Alas,
how many gentle thoughts, how deep a longing,
had led them to this agonizing pass!"
Then I addressed my speech again to them,
and I began: "Francesca, your affliction
moves me to tears of sorrow and of pity.
But tell me, in the time of gentle sighs,
with what and in what way did Love allow you
to recognize your still uncertain longings?"
And she to me: "There is no greater sorrow

than thinking back upon a happy time
in misery, and this your teacher knows.
Yet if you long so much to understand
The first root of our love, then I shall tell
my tale to you as one who weeps and speaks.

DANTE ALIGHIERI

SONG OF DAWN

Chattering parrots, nightingales,
What songs you sing to greet the dawn!
Bring me news of my love's travails,
As I wait silent and forlorn.

The midnight hour has past 'er long
But still no sign of thee.
Tell me if another's blithe song
Keeps him away from me.

from *Treasury of Spanish Love*

The rejected or neglected lover often carries silent wounds, sometimes consciously and at other times unacknowledged. The deepest wounds come from the beloved's seeming lack of concern at the pain they have inflicted.

A BROKEN APPOINTMENT

You did not come,
And marching Time drew on, and wore me
    numb.
Yet less for loss of your dear presence there
Than that I thus found lacking in your make
That high compassion which can overbear
Reluctance for pure loving kindness' sake
Grieved I, when, as the hope-hour stroked its
    sum
    You did not come.

You love not me,
And love alone can lend you loyalty;
—I know and knew it. But, unto the store
O human deeds divine in all but name,
Was it not worth a little hour or more
To add yet this: Once you, a woman, came
To soothe a time-torn man; even though it be
    You love not me?

THOMAS HARDY

TO MY INCONSTANT MISTRESS

When thou, poor excommunicate
    From all the joys of love, shall see
The full reward and glorious fate
    Which my strong faith shall purchase me,
    Then curse thine own inconstancy.

A fairer hand than thine shall cure
That heart, which thy false oaths did wound;
And to my soul a soul more pure
    Than thine shall by Love's hand be bound.
    And both with equal glory crown'd.

Thou shall now weep, entreat, complain,
    To Love, as I did once to thee;
When all thy tears shall be as vain
    As mine were then, for thou shalt be
    Damn'd for thy false apostacy.

THOMAS CAREW

GREENSLEEVES

Chorus:
Greensleeves was all my joy,
Greensleeves was my delight;
Greensleeves was my heart of gold,
And who but Lady Greensleeves.

Alas, my love! Ye do me wrong
To cast me off discourteously;
And I have loved you so long,
Delighting in your company.

I have been ready at your hand,
To grant whatever you would crave:
I have both wagered life and land,
Your love and goodwill for to have.

I bought thee kerchers to thy head,
That were wrought fine and gallantly;
I kept thee both at board and bed,
Which cost my purse well favouredly.

I bought thee petticoats of the best,
The cloth so fine as fine might be;
I gave thee jewels for thy chest,
And all this cost I spent on thee.

Thy purse and thy gay gilt knives,
Thy pincase gallant to the eye;
No better wore the burgess wives,
And yet thou wouldst not love me.

Thy gown was of grassy green,
Thy sleeves of satin hanging by,
Which made thee be our harvest queen,
And yet thou wouldst not love me.

My gayest gelding I thee gave,
To ride wherever liked thee;
No lady ever was so brave,
And yet thou wouldst not love me.

My men were clothed all in green,
And they did ever wait on thee;
All this was gallant to be seen,
And yet thou wouldst not love me.

For every morning when thou rose,
I sent thee dainties orderly,
To cheer thy stomach from all woes,
And yet thou wouldst not love me.

Well, I will pray to God on high,
That thou my constancy mayst see,
And that yet once before I die,
Thou wilt vouchsafe to love me.

Greensleeves, now farewell! Adieu!
God I pray to prosper thee;
For I am still thy lover true.
Come once again and love me.

Greensleeves was all my joy,
Greensleeves was my delight;
Greensleeves was my heart of gold,
And who but Lady Greensleeves.

ANONYMOUS

*Rejected lovers bemoan their fate, often claiming love is cruel. Even
many years later, when they have long accepted the impossibility of a particular
love being returned, there is a sting when they think of the rejection. Sometimes
they are even surprised at their own bitterness.*

WILD WATER

Insidious cruelty is this
that will allow the heart
a scent of wild water
in the arid land—
that holds out the cup
but to withdraw the hand.

Then says to the heart: Be glad
that you have beheld the font

where lies requitement,
and identified your thirst.
Now, heart, take up your desert;
this spring is cursed.

MAY SWENSON

A LONG-AGO AFFAIR

Hubert Marsland, the landscape painter, returning from a day's sketching on the river in the summer of 1921, had occasion to stay the progress of his two-seater about ten miles from London for a minor repair, and while his car was being seen to, strolled away from the garage to have a look at a house where he had often spent his holidays as a boy. Walking through a gateway and passing a large grave-pit on his left, he was soon opposite the house, which stood back a little in its grounds, Very much changed! More pretentious, not so homely as when his Uncle and Aunt lived there, and he used to play cricket on this warren opposite, where the cricket ground, it seemed, had been turned into a golf course. It was late—the dinner-hour, nobody playing, and passing on to the links he stood digesting the geography. Here must have been where the old pavilion was. And there—still turfed—where he had made that particularly nice stroke to leg, when he went in last and carried his bat for thirteen. Thirty-nine years ago—his sixteenth birthday. How vividly he remembered his new pads! A. P. Lucas had played against them and only made thirty-two—one founded one's style on A. P. Lucas in those days—feet in front of the bat, and pointed a little forward, elegant; you never saw it now, and a good thing too—one could sacrifice too much for style! Still, the tendency was all the other way; style was too much 'off,' perhaps!

He stepped back into the sun and sat down on the grass. Peaceful—very still! The haze of the distant downs was visible between his Uncle's old house and the next; and there was the clump of elms on the far side behind which the sun would be going down just as it used to then. He pressed the palms of his hands to the turf. A glorious summer—something like that summer of long ago. And warmth from the turf, or perhaps from the past, crept into his heart and made it ache a little. Just here he must have sat, after his innings, at Mrs. Monteith's feet peeping out of a flounced dress. Lord! The fools boys were! How headlong and uncalculating their devotions! A softness in voice and eyes, a smile, a touch or two—and they were slaves! Young fools, but good fools. And standing behind her chair—he could see him now—that other idol Captain MacKay, with his face of browned ivory—just the colour of that elephant's tusk his Uncle had, which had gone so yellow—and his perfect black moustache, his white tie, check suit, carnation, spats, Malacca cane—all so fascinating! Mrs. Monteith, 'the grass widow' they had called her! He remembered the look in people's eyes, the tone in their voices. Such a pretty woman! He had 'fallen for her' at first sight, as the Yanks put it—her special scent, her daintiness, her voice! And that day on the river, when she made much of him, and Captain MacKay attended Evelyn Curtiss so assiduously that he was expected to propose. Quaint period! They used the word courting then, wore full skirts, high stays: and himself a blue elastic belt around his white-flannelled waist. And in the evening afterwards, his Aunt had said with an arch smile: 'Good night, *silly* boy!" Silly boy indeed, with a flower the grass widow had dropped pressed by his cheek into his pillow! What folly! And that next Sunday—looking forward to Church—passionately brushing his top hat; all through the service spying at her creamy profile, two pews in front on the left, between goat-bearded old Hallgrave her Uncle, and her pink, broad, white-haired Aunt; scheming to get near her when she came out, lingering, lurking, getting just a smile and the rustle of her flounces. Ah, ha! A little went a long way then! And the last day of his holidays and it's night with the first introduction to reality. Who said the Victorian Age was innocent! Marsland put his palm up to his cheek No! The dew was not yet falling. And his mind lightly turned and tossed his memories of women, as a man turns and tosses hay to air it; but nothing remembered gave him quite the feeling of that first experience.

His Aunt's dance! His first white waistcoat, bought *ad hoc*, from the local tailor, his tie laboriously imitating the hero—Captain MacKay's.

All came back with such freshness in the quiet of the warren—the expectancy, the humble shy excitement, the breathless asking for a dance, the writing 'Mrs Monteith' twice on his little gilt-edged program with its tiny tasseled white pencil; her slow-moving fan, her smile. And the first dance when it came; what infinite care not to tread on her white satin toes; what a thrill when her arm pressed his in the crush— such holy rapture, about all the first part of the evening, with yet an- other dance to come! If only he could have twirled her and 'reversed' like his pattern, Captain MacKay! Then delirium growing as the second dance came near, making him cut his partner—the cool grass-scented air out on the dark terrace, with the chafers booming by, and in the starshine the poplars wondrously tall; the careful adjustment of his tie and waistcoat, the careful polishing of his hot face! A long breath then, and into the house to find her! Ballroom, supper-room, stairs, library, billiard-room, all drawn bland—'Estudiantina' going on and on, and he a wandering, white-waistcoated young ghost. Ah! The conserva- tory—and the hurrying there! And then the moment which has always been, was even now, such a blurred confused impression. Smothered voices from between a clump of flowers: 'I saw her' 'Who was the man?' A glimpse, gone past in a flash, of an ivory face, a black mous- tache! And then her voice: 'Hubert'; and her hot hand clasping his, drawing him to her; her scent, her face smiling, very set! A rustling behind the flowers, those people spying; and suddenly her lips on his cheek, the kiss sounding in his ears, her voice saying very softly: 'Hub- ert, dear boy!' The rustle receded, ceased. What a long silent minute, then among the ferns and blossoms in the dusk with her face close to his, pale, perturbed, before she led him out into the light, while he was slowly realizing she had made use of him to shelter her. A boy—not old enough to be her lover, but old enough to save her name and that of Captain MacKay! Her kiss—the last of many—but not upon *his* lips, *his* cheeks! Hard work realizing that! A boy—of no account—a boy, who in a day would be at school again, kissed that *he* and *she* might renew their intrigue unsuspected!

How had he behaved the rest of that evening of romance bedrab- bled? He hardly knew. Betrayed with a kiss! Two idols in the dust! And did they care what he was feeling? Not they! All they cared for was to cover up their tracks with him! But somehow—somehow—he had never shown her that he knew. Only, when their dance was over, and someone came and took her for her next, he escaped up to his little room, tore off his gloves, his waistcoat; lay on his bed, thought bitter thoughts. A boy! There he had stayed with the thrum of the music in his ears, till it died away for good and the carriages were gone, and the night was quiet.

Squatting on the warren grass, still warm and dewless, Marsland rubbed his knees. Nothing like boys for generosity! And, with a little smile, he thought of his Aunt next morning, half-arch and half concerned: 'It isn't nice, dear, to sit out in dark corners, and—well, perhaps, it wasn't your fault, but still, it isn't nice—not—quite—' and of how suddenly she had stopped, looking in his face, where his lips were curling in his first ironic laugh. She had never forgiven him that laugh—thinking him a cynical young Lothario? And Marsland thought: 'Live and learn! Wonder what became of those two? Victorian Age! Hatches were battened down in those days! But, innocent—my hat!'

Ah! The sun was off, dew falling! He got up, rubbing his knees to take the stiffness out of them. Pigeons in the wood beyond were calling. A window in his Uncle's old home blazed like a jewel in the sun's last rays between the poplar trees. Heh! dear—a little long-ago affair!

JOHN GALSWORTHY

P arting decreed by others (family, cultural norms, religious traditions) is the theme of some of the great tragedies of literature. Perhaps some of the pain of parting is lessened by the thought that the beloved was not untrue. The lovers' bitterness can be aimed at the cruelty of life in general, where love is not honored as sufficient motive for a relationship. Still, the loss devastates.

CASHEL OF MUNSTER

I'd wed you without herds, without money or rich array,
And I'd wed you on a dewy morn at day-dawn gray;
My bitter woe it is, love, that we are not far away
In Cashel town tho' the bare deal board were our marriage-bed
  this day!

O fair maid, remember the green hill-side,
Remember how I hunted about the valleys wide;
Time now has worn me, my locks are turn'd to gray;
The year is scarce and I am poor—but send me not, love, away!

O deem not my blood is of base strain, my girl;
O think not my birth was as the birth of a churl;
Marry me and prove me, and say soon, you will
That noble blood is written on my right side still.

My purse holds no red gold, no coin of the silver white;
No herds are mine to drive through the long twilight;
But the pretty girl that would take me, all bare tho' I be and 'lone,
O, I'd take her with me kindly to the County Tyrone!

O my girl, I can see 'tis your people's reproach you bear!
—I am a girl in trouble for his sake with whom I fly,
And, O, may no other maiden know such reproach as I.

SIR SAMUEL FERGUSON,
from *Irish Love Poems: Danta Gra*

HÉLOÏSE TO ABELARD

Mid-twelfth Century

You know, beloved, as the whole world knows, how much I have lost in you, how at one wretched stroke of fortune that supreme act of flagrant treachery robbed me of my very self in robbing me of you; and how my sorrow for my loss is nothing compared with what I feel for the manner in which I lost you. You are the sole cause of my sorrow, and you alone can grant me the grace of consolation. You alone have the power to make me sad, to bring me happiness or comfort. God knows I never sought anything in you except yourself; I wanted simply you, nothing of yours.

I looked for no marriage-bond, no marriage portion, and it was not my own pleasures and wishes I sought to gratify, as you well know, but yours. The name of wife may seem more sacred or more binding, but sweeter to me will always be the word mistress, or, if you will permit me, that of concubine or whore.

Remember, I implore you, what I have done, and think how much you owe me. While I enjoyed with you the pleasures of the flesh, many were uncertain whether I was prompted by love or lust; but no the end is proof of the beginning. I have finally denied myself every pleasure in obedience to your will, kept nothing of myself except to prove that now, even more, I am yours.

And so, in the name of God to whom you have dedicated yourself, I beg you to restore your presence to me in the way you can—by writing me some word of comfort, so that in this at least I may find increased strength and readiness to serve God. I beg you, think what you owe me, give ear to my pleas, and I will finish a long letter with a brief ending;

farewell, my only love.

ISOLATION

To Marguerite

We were apart; yet, day by day,
I bade my heart more constant be.
I bade it keep the world away,
And grow a home for only thee;
Nor feared but thy love likewise grew,
Like mine, each day, more tried, more true.

The fault was grave! I might have known,
What far too soon, alas! I learned—
The heart can bind itself alone,
And faith may oft be unreturned.
Self-swayed our feelings ebb and swell—
Thou lov'st no more;—Farewell! Farewell!

Farewell!—and thou, lonely heart,
Which never yet without remorse
Even for a moment didst depart
From thy remote and spherèd course
To haunt the place where passions reign—
Back to thy solitude again!

Back! With the conscious thrill of shame
Which Luna felt, that summer-night,
Flash through her pure immortal frame,
When she forsook the starry height
To hang over Endymion's sleep
Upon the pine-grown Latmian steep.

Yet she, chaste queen, had never proved
How vain a thing is mortal love
Wandering in Heaven, far removed.
But thou hast long had place to prove
This truth—to prove, and make thine own
"Thou has been, shalt be, art, alone."

Or if not quite alone, yet they
Which touch thee are unmating things—
Oceans and clouds and night and day;
Lorn autumns and triumphant springs;
And life, and others' joy and pain,
And love, if love, of happier men.

Or happier men—for they, at least,
Have dreamed two human hearts might blend
In one, and were through faith released
From isolation without end
Prolonged; nor knew, although not less
Alone than thou, their loneliness.

MATTHEW ARNOLD

PARTING

If parting be decreed for the two of us,
Stand yet a moment while I gaze upon thy face. . . .
By the life of love, remember the days of thy longing
As I remember the night of thy delight.
As thine image passeth in my dreams,
So let me pass, I entreat thee, into thy dreams.
Between me and thee roar the waves of a sea of tears
But O, if thy steps should draw nigh to cross—
Then would its waters be divided at the touch of thy
        foot,
Would that after my death unto mine ears should
        come
The sound of the golden bells upon thy skirts!
Or should thou be asking how farest thy beloved, I
        from the depths of the tomb

Would ask of thy love and thy welfare
Verily, to the shedding of mine heart's blood
There be witnesses, thy cheeks and thy lips.
How sayeth thou it is not true, since these by my
    witnesses
For my blood, and that thine hands have shed it?
Why desirest thou my death, whilst I but desire
To add years unto years of thy life?
Thou, thou does rob my slumber in the night of my
    longing,
Would I not give the sleep of mine eyes unto thy
    eyelids? . . .
Yea, between the bitter and the sweet standeth my
    heart—
The gall of parting, and the honey of thy kisses.
After the words have pounded my heart into thin
    plates,
Thine hands have cut it into shreds.
It is the likeness of rubies over pearls
What time I behold thy lips over thy teeth.
The sun is on thy face and thou spreadest out the night
Over his radiance with the clouds of thy locks.
Fine silk and broidered work are the covering of thy
    Body,
But grace and beauty are the covering of thine eyes.
The adornment of maidens is the work of human
    hands,
But thou—majesty and sweetness are thine
    adornment . . .
In the field of the daughters of delight, the sheaves of
    love
Make obeisance unto thy sheaf . . .
I cannot hear thy voice, but I hear
Upon the secret places of my heart, the sound of thy
    steps
On the day when thou wilt revive
The victims whom love for thee hath slain—on the
    day when thy dead shall live anew

Then turn again to my soul to restore it to my body;
    for on the day
Of thy departure, when thou wentest forth, it went out after thee.

JUDAH HALEVI,
from *Treasury of Jewish Love*

The end of a marriage is high on any stress factor scale even for the one who initiates the breakup. Promises made have not been kept, which might be the reason the marriage ends. Children, in-laws, friends all feel the effects. Time might heal the wounds; but not all of them, especially for the rejected partner. Life goes on; but it is never the same. In those cases where the breakup was caused by constant discord life often turns out to be better—at least for one of the partners.

CLEARING THE PATH

My husband gave up shoveling snow
at forty-five because, he claimed,
that's when heart attacks begin.

Since it snowed regardless, I,
mere forty, took the shovel, dug.
now fifty, still it falls to me

to clean the walk. He's gone on
to warmer climes and younger loves
who will, I guess, keep shoveling for him.

In other seasons here, I sweep
plum petals or magnolia cones
to clear the way for heartier loves.

ELISAVIETTA RITCHIE

There are very few people who are not ashamed of having been in love
when they no longer love each other.

LA ROCHEFOUCAULD,
Maxim 71

*P*oetry *best expresses the depth of sadness, and sometimes of the rage
and bitterness, rejected lovers undergo. They question their own worth as lovable
persons. They wonder: Will love ever come again? Over time, most move on to
other loves but with a caution not previously experienced.*

'TIS BETTER TO HAVE
LOVED AND LOST

I envy not in any moods
The captive void of noble rage,
The linnet born within the cage,
That never knew the summer woods.

I envy not the beast that takes
His license in the field of time,
Unfetter'd by the sense of crime,
To whom a conscience never wakes;

Nor, what may count itself as blest,
The heart that never plighted troth
But stagnates in the weeds of sloth;
Nor any want-begotten rest.

I hold it true, whate'er befall;
I feel it, when I sorrow most;
'Tis better to have loved and lost
Than never to have loved at all.

ALFRED, LORD TENNYSON

LAST NIGHT

I sat with one I love last night,
She sang to me an olden strain;
In former times it woke delight,
Last night—but pain.

Last night we saw the stars arise,
But clouds soon dimmed the ether blue;
And when we sought each other's eyes
Tears dimmed them too!

We paced along our favorite walk,
But paced in silence broken-hearted;
Of old we used to smile and talk;
Last night—we parted

GEORGE DARLEY

LOVE'S SECRET

Never seek to tell thy love,
Love that never told can be;
For the gentle wind doth move
Silently, invisibly.

I told my love, I told my love,
I told her all my heart,
Trembling, cold, in ghastly fears.
Ah! she did depart!

Soon as she was gone from me,
A traveller came by,
Silently, invisibly:
He took her with a sigh.

WILLIAM BLAKE

THE SOOTE SEASON

The soote season, that bud and bloom forth brings,
　　With green hath clad the hill and eke the vale;
The nightingale with feathers new she sings,
　　The turtle to her make hath told her tale.
Summer is come, for every spray now springs;
　　The hart hath hung his old head on the pale,
The buck in brake his winter coat he flings,
　　The fishes float with new repaired scale,

The adder all her slough away she slings.
    The swift swallow pursueth the flies small,
The busy bee her honey now she mings.
    Winter is worn that was the flowers' bale.
And thus I see among these pleasant things
Each care decays; and yet my sorrow springs.

HENRY HOWARD,
EARL OF SURREY

The idea that it is better to have loved and lost than never to have loved is in no way apparent to a grieving lover. The person who has lost love remains leery of entering into a new relationship. They wonder, "How can I trust another or even myself? Might I not make the same mistake again?" Will their broken wings ever again carry them to heights of love? What might help them regain their sense of self-worth?

A SHATTERED LUTE

Touched the heart that loved me as a player
Touches a lyre. Content with my poor skill,
No touch save mine knew my beloved (and still
I thought at times; Is there no sweet lost air.

Old loves could wake in him, I cannot share?)
O he alone, alone could so fulfill
My thoughts in sound to the measure of my will.
He is gone, and silence takes me unaware.

The songs I knew not he resumes, set free
From my constraining love, alas for me!
His part in our tune goes with him; my part

Is locked in me for ever; I stand as mute
As one with full strong music in his heart
Whose fingers stray upon a shattered lute.

ALICE MEYNELL

SONG

A place in thy memory, dearest,
Is all that I claim,
To pause and look back when thou hearest
The sound of my name.
Another may woo thee nearer,
Another may win and wear;
I care not, though he be dearer,
If I am remembered there.

Could I be thy true lover, dearest,
Couldst thou smile on me,
I would be the fondest and nearest
That ever loved thee.
But a cloud o'er my pathway is glooming
Which never must break upon thine,
And Heaven, which made thee all blooming,
Ne'er made thee to wither on mine.

Remember me not as a lover
Whose fond hopes are crossed,
Whose bosom can never recover

The light it has lost;
As the young bride remembers the mother,
She loves, yet never may see,
As a sister remembers a brother,
Oh, dearest, remember me.

GERALD GRIFFIN

O let the solid ground
Not fail beneath my feet
Before my life has found
What some have found so sweet;
Then let come what come may
What matter if I go mad,
I shall have had my day.

Let the sweet heavens endure,
Not close and darken above me
Before I am quite quite sure
That there is one to love me;
Then let come what come may
To a life that has been so sad,
I shall have had my day.

ALFRED, LORD TENNYSON,
from *Maud: A Monodrama*, XI

CHAPTER TEN

Love: The Divine/Human Encounter

All that we do
is touched with ocean, yet we remain
on the shore of what we know.
FOR DUDLEY IN *WALKING TO SLEEP*

There is a secular world and a holy world . . . These worlds contradict
one another. . . . In our limited perception we cannot reconcile the
sacred and the secular. . . . Yet at the pinnacle of the universe they are
reconciled, at the site of the holy of holies.
THE ESSENTIAL KABBALAH

Man has two eyes
One only sees what moves in fleeting time
The other
What is eternal and divine.
THE BOOK OF ANGELUS SILESIUS

e humans like to know the meaning of things, at least those things that are important to us at particular times. Why doesn't something work the way we planned it would; why didn't we get the promotion; why doesn't a person return our love; and other questions are common examples of questions asked by meaning-seeking people. The list of whys we face on a daily basis is endless and would drive us mad if we didn't, at some level, have some sense that their was an ocean full of answers somewhere.

At times, we find ourselves wondering about deeper questions of meaning. What is the real, deep-down meaning of things? Why do some people suffer and others have it so good? How did life—our own, others', the world, the universe—get its start? What sustains all life? Why is there good and evil? What happens to me when I die?

These latter questions move us into the ocean. Once we enter the ocean, we need the eye that sees the eternal and divine. There we seek to discover what is the ultimate meaning of life. And we find new questions.

Do we find graciousness or disinterest? Is there no such thing as ultimate meaning or only what happens to us in the here and now? If there is no meaning, what is the sense of being good or doing good?

The way we answer these questions is determined, to some degree, by what we believe is the ultimate answer: whether, that is, there is meaning or there is no meaning. We need to find some meaning, even if the meaning is that there is no meaning. We need some principle to guide us as we encounter the ups and downs, the why and wherefore of life. We might not live with an ever-present consciousness of that meaning. Short-term goals, individual and group interests lead us out of the ocean. Even though we have a hint of goodness, we fall back into practices that often reflect "man's inhumanity to man."

Religions point the way to answers to our ultimate meaning questions. They promote a way of life, a way of relating to our fellow human beings that reflects the answers found through religious beliefs. They encourage their members to a life of love flowing from the understanding of the divine found in their belief system.

If we and our religious leaders only give lip service to religious answers or if we try to avoid their ultimate challenges, we find ourselves back seeing with only one eye. We only need consider all the inhumanities committed in the name of a religious belief. Wars, both in the past and in many places in our world today, often have their roots in earlier animosities between religious faiths. Believers, committed to converting heretics, often wind up killing the people they claimed they wanted to convert. Branches of the Christian faith fight over who has the right to control sacred sites in the Holy Land. Conquerors try to force their beliefs on those they defeat either by forcing a new religion on them or by systematically destroying every vestige of the religion they practiced. All in the name of love of the Divine.

Stories from religious traditions, the wisdom of mystics, the reflections of poets and songwriters, folktales, and novels invite us to take a deeper look at the possibilities of finding love as the ultimate meaning of life, love that is as deep as the ocean and as high as the sky. Love that invites response. Love that requires us to use both eyes and our hearts.

FINDING GOD

Two men were walking in the valley, and one man pointed with his finger toward the mountain side, and said, "See you that hermitage? There lives a man who has long divorced the world. He seeks but after God, and naught else upon this earth."

And the other man said, "He shall not find God until he leaves his hermitage, and the aloneness of his hermitage, and returns to our world, to share our joy and pain, to dance with our dancers at the wedding feast, and to weep with those who weep around the coffins of our dead."

And the other man was convinced in his heart, though in spite of his conviction he answered, "I agree with all that you say, yet I believe the hermit is a good man. And may it not well be that one good man by his absence does better than the seeming goodness of these many men?"

KAHLIL GIBRAN,
from *The Wanderer*

*S*tories, *legends, and myths of creation from various religions and cultures tell of the relationship between the human and the divine. People found divine love when they considered the wonders of their particular lives. A recurring theme is: this love wants response.*

FIRST TALE

A Legend of the Hopi Indians, retold by G. M. Mullett
(Hopi cosmology does not provide a clear-cut creation legend. This turn-of-the-century version is said, by some, to be closer to the Zuni conception of creation.)

In the Beginning there were only two: Tawa, the Sun God, and Spider Woman, the Earth Goddess. All the mysteries and power in the Above belonged to Tawa, while Spider Woman controlled the magic of the Below. In the Underworld, abode of the gods, they dwelt and they were All. There was neither man nor woman, bird nor beast, no living thing until these Two willed it to be.

In time it came to them that there should be other gods to share their labors. So Tawa divided himself and there came Muiyinwhu, God of All Life Germs; Spider Woman also divided herself so that there was Huzruiwuhiti, Woman of the Hard Substances, the goddess of all hard ornaments of wealth such as coral, turquoise, silver, and shell. Huzruiwuhti became the always-bride of Tawa. They were the First Lovers and of their union came into being those marvelous ones the Magic Twins—Puukonhoya, the Youth, and Palunhoys, the Echo. As time unrolled there followed Hicanavaiya, Ancient of Six (The Four World Quarters, The Above, and the Below), Man-Eagle, The Great Plumed Serpent, and many others. But Masauwuh, The Death God, did not come of these Two but was bad magic who appeared only after the making of creatures.

And then it came about that these Two had one Thought and it was a mighty Thought—that they would make the Earth to be between the Above and the Below where now lay shimmering only the Endless Waters. So they sat them side by side, swaying their beautiful bronze bodies to the pulsing music of their own great voices, making the First Magic Song, a song of rushing winds and flowing waters, a song of light and sound and life.

"I am Tawa," sang the Sun God, "I am Light. I am Life. I am the Father of all that shall ever come."

"I am Kokyanwuhti," the Spider Woman crooned in softer note. "I receive Light and nourish life. I am Mother of all that shall ever come."

"Many strange thoughts are forming in my mind—beautiful forms of birds to float in the Above, of beasts to move upon the Earth and fish to swim in the Waters," intoned Tawa.

"Now let these things that move in the Thought of my lord appear," chanted Spider Woman, the while her slender finger caught up clay from beside her and made the Thoughts of Tawa take form. One by one she shaped them and laid them aside—but they breathed not nor moved.

"We must do something about this," said Tawa. "It is not good that they lie thus still and quiet. Each thing that has a form must also have a spirit. So now, my beloved, we must make a mighty Magic."

They laid a white blanket over the many figures, a cunningly woven woolen blanket, fleecy as a cloud, and made a mighty incantation over it, and soon the figures stirred and breathed.

"Now, let us make ones like unto you and me, so that they may rule over and enjoy these lesser creatures," sang Tawa, and Spider Woman shaped the Thoughts of her lord into man figures and woman figures like unto their own. But after the blanket magic had been made the figures still stayed inert. So Spider Woman gathered them all in her arms and cradled them in her warm young bosom, while Tawa bent his glowing eyes upon them. The two now sang the Magic Song of Life over them, and at last each man figure and woman figure breathed and lived.

"Now that was a good thing and a mighty thing," quoth Tawa. "So now all this is finished, and there shall be no new things made by us. Those things we have made shall multiply, each one after his own kind. I will make a journey across the Above each day to shed my blazing shield upon the Endless Waters, so that the Dry Land may appear. And this day will be the first day upon the Earth."

"Now I shall lead all these created things to the land that you shall cause to appear above the Waters," said Spider Woman.

Then Tawa took down his burnished shield from the turquoise wall of the kiva and swiftly mounted his glorious way to the Above. After Spider Woman had bent her wise, all-seeing eyes upon the thronging creatures about her, she wound her way among them, separating them into groups.

"Thus and thus shall you be and thus shall you remain, each one in his own tribe forever. You are Zunis, you are Kohoninos, you are Pah-Utes—" The Hopis, and all people were named by Kokyanwuhti then.

Placing her Magic Twin beside her, Spider Woman called all the people to follow where she led. Through all the Four Great Caverns of the Underworld she led them, until they finally came to an opening, a sipapu, which led above. This came out at the lowest depth of the Pisisbaiya (the Colorado River) and was the place where the people were to come to gather salt. So lately had the Endless Waters gone down that the Turkey, Koyona, pushing eagerly ahead, dragged his tail feathers in the black mud where the dark bands were to remain forever.

Mourning Dove flew overhead, calling to some to follow, and those who followed where his sharp eyes had spied out springs and build beside them were called "Huwinyame" after him. So Spider Woman chose a creature to lead each clan to a place to build their house.

The Puma, the Snake, the Antelope, the Deer, and the other Horn creatures, each led a clan to a place to build their house. Each clan henceforth bore the name of the creature who had led them.

Then Spider Woman spoke to them thus: "The woman of the clan shall build the house, and the family name shall descend through her. She shall be housebuilder and homemaker. She shall mold the jars for the storing of food and water. She shall grind the grain for food and tenderly rear the young. The man of the clan shall build kivas of stone under the ground where he shall pay homage to his gods. In these kivas the man shall make sand pictures which will be his altars. Of colored sand shall he make them and they shall be called 'ponya.' After council I shall whisper to him; he shall make prayer sticks or paho to place upon the ponya to bear his prayers. There shall be the Wupo Paho, the Great Paho, which is mine. There shall be the four paho of blue, The Cawka Paho—one for the great Tawa, one for Muiyinwuh, one for the Woman of the Hard Substances and one for the Ancient of Six. Each of these paho must be cunningly and secretly wrought with prayer and song. The man, too, shall weave the clan blankets with their proper symbols. The Snake clan shall have its symbol and the Antelope clan its symbol; thus it shall be for each clan. Man shall fashion himself weapons and furnish his family with game."

Stooping down, she gathered some sand in her hand, letting it run out in a thin, continuous stream. "See the movement of the sand. That is the life that will cause all things therein to grow. The Great Plumed Serpent, Lightning, will rear and strike the earth to fertilize it. Rain

Cloud will pour down waters and Tawa will smile upon it so that green things will spring up to feed my children."

Her eyes now sought Above where Tawa was descending toward his western kiva in all the glory of red and gold. "I go now, but have no fear, we Two will be watching over you. Look upon me now, my children, ere I leave. Obey the words I have given you and all will be well, and if you are in need of help, call upon me and I will send my sons to your aid."

The people gazed wide-eyed upon her shining beauty. Her woven upper garments of soft white wool hung tunic-wise over a blue skirt. On its left side was woven a band bearing the woman's symbols, the Butterfly and the Squash Blossom, in designs of red and yellow and green with bands of black appearing between. Her beautiful neck was hung with heavy necklaces of turquoise, shell and coral, and pendants of the same hung from her ears. Her face was fair, with warm eyes and tender red lips, and her form most graceful. Upon her small feet were skin boots of gleaming white, and they now turned toward where the sand spun about in whirlpool fashion. She held up her right hand and smiled upon them, then stepped upon the whirling sand. Wonder of Wonders, before their eyes the sands seemed to suck her swiftly down until she disappeared entirely from their sight.

from *Spider Woman Stories*

THE GOLDEN APPLE

One day Connla, Son of Caomh Céadchathach the reigning High King, was standing on the great hill of Uisneach in County Westmeath, the very heart of Ireland. Suddenly, there appeared before him a beautiful woman dressed in rich garments and golden jewelry. She recited a poem in which she explained that she had come from *Tir na nÓg*—the Land of Eternal Youth—where there was no aging or decay or death. She had fallen in love with him from afar, she said, and had come to take him with her to this land of perpetual summer.

Connla fell completely in love with the girl as she spoke the poem and with all his heart he wanted to go with her to *Tir na nÓg*. But then he remembered that all his people were here in this world, that his home was here, and that he would be King when his father died. And so, he told the girl sadly, he could not accompany her to *Tir na nÓg*. As she left, she handed Connla an apple, the sacred food of *Tir na nÓg*, for *Tir na nÓg* was the Land of Apples.

For a whole month, Connla ate the apple, but though he continued to eat it, it never diminished. He found that it was having an effect on him: his attachment to this world was decreasing and his mentality was changing. Matters of immense importance became less so—the world receded in his mind.

A month passed, and once again Connla stood on the hill of Uisneach. Suddenly the girl appeared. This time there was no hesitation. He jumped into her crystal boat, and while his people watched as far as the eye could see, they sailed over the horizon to *Tir na nÓg* and were never seen again. . . .

A retelling of an Irish Legend

The Great Spirit Says That He Loves You

Now is the time when he hears us,
He hears us all,
The One who made the Medewiwin
Now listen to me,
to what I am about to say to you.
If you take heed of what I say to you,
You shall continue your life always.
Today I make known to you the Great Spirit,
and what He says.

This is what the Great Spirit says;
It is that he loves you.

That which the Great Spirit says,
I impart to you.
My child,
that knowledge shall give you life.

Algonquin oral tradition

GRANDMOTHER SPIDER

A Native American tale about Grandmother Spider reminds us of Pope John Paul I's words: "God is Father, but, especially, Mother."

A long time ago when all the Spirits lived in the sky and all the creatures lived below on the earth, the creatures were secure because they felt protected by the sky above them. However, one day they noticed that the sky was moving away from them, and they became very frightened. How could they continue to exist if the Spirits were to abandon them?

So after many days of worrying, the creatures gathered around the campfire and wondered what they might do. Bear came forward and said, "I am the strongest of all creatures. I will grab the sky and hold it in place and then we will be safe." But with even the Bear holding on with all his strength, the sky was still able to continue its slow movement away from earth.

Next Coyote stepped forward. "I am the best trickster," he said. "I can trick anything. I will trick the sky into staying with us." But all of Coyote's tricks did not succeed in keeping sky where it belonged above the earth.

Finally, those around the campfire heard a meek little voice say, "I will try to keep sky joined to us." Everyone laughed when they saw Grandmother Spider crawl out of the tall grass. How could a lowly spider (and especially a woman spider) hope to do what had been impossible for mighty Bear and Coyote?

But Grandmother Spider paid no attention to their jeers. She just began spinning away until she had a very long string, which she aimed at the sky. On her third try, when she was almost completely exhausted, her string reached the sky and she climbed up to the sky, rested for a short time and then began spinning again. All day she spun her web, going down and then back up between sky and earth. Finally, at the end of the day, sky and earth were firmly connected once again.

RETOLD BY MARY G. DURKIN,
from *An Epidemic of Joy*

The Religions of the Book—Judaism, Christianity, and Islam—tell of a Creator God, who remains in an ongoing relationship with the world, especially with the people of that world. The Hebrew Scriptures recount the wonders and the demands involved in that relationship. Divine love for humans is the central theme of the Christian Scripture, with its account of Christ's life and death and its effect on those who followed him. The dervishes of Islam tell of how their encounter with God reveals divine love.

THE GREAT COMMANDMENT

"Israel, remember this! The Lord and the Lord alone is our God. Love the Lord your God with all your heart, with all your soul, and with all your strength. Never forget these commands that I am giving you today.

Teach them to your children. Repeat them when you are at home and when you are away, when you are resting and when you are working. Tie them on your arms and wear them on your foreheads as a reminder. Write them on the doorposts of your houses and on your gates.

DEUTERONOMY 6:4–9

THE RESTORATION OF JERUSALEM

The Lord says to his people,
    "When the time comes to save you, I will show you favor and answer your cries for help.
    I will guard and protect you and through you make a covenant with all peoples.
    I will let you settle once again in your land that is now laid waste.
I will say to the prisoners, 'Go free!'
and to those who are in darkness, 'Come out to the light!'
They will be like sheep that graze on the hills;
    they will never be hungry or thirsty.
Sun and desert heat will not hurt them, for they will be led by one who loves them.
    He will lead them to springs of water.

"I will make a highway across the mountains
    and prepare a road for my people to travel.
My people will come from far away,
from the north and the west, and from Aswan in the south."

"Sing, heavens! Shout for joy, earth!
    Let the mountains burst into song!
    The Lord will comfort his people; he will have pity on his suffering people."

But the people of Jerusalem said,
    "The Lord has abandoned us!
    He has forgotten us."
So the Lord answers,
    "Can a woman forget her own baby and not love the child she
bore?
    Even if a mother should forget her child, I will never forget you.
Jerusalem, I can never forget you!
    I have written your name on the palms of my hands.
"Those who will rebuild you are coming soon,
and those who destroyed you will leave.
Look around and see what is happening!
    Your people are assembling they are coming home!
As surely as I am the living God, you will be proud of your people,
    as proud as a bride is of her jewels.

"Your country was ruined and desolate but now it will be too small
    for those who are coming to live there.
And those who left you in ruins will be far removed from you.
Your people who were born in exile will one day say to you,
'This land is too small we need more room to live in!'
Then you will say to yourself, Who bore all these children for me?
I lost my children and could have no more.
I was exiled and driven away who brought these children up?
I was left all alone where did these children come from?"

The Sovereign Lord says to his people:
    "I will signal to the nations, and they will bring your children
home.
Kings will be like fathers to you; queens will be like mothers.
They will bow low before you and honor you;
    They will humbly show their respect for you.
Then you will know that I am the Lord;
no one who waits for my help will be disappointed."

Can you take away a soldier's loot?
    Can you rescue the prisoners of a tyrant?
The Lord replies,

"That is just what is going to happen.
The soldier's prisoners will be taken away,
and the tyrant's loot will be seized.
I will fight against whoever fights you, and I will rescue your children.
I will make your oppressors kill each other;
 they will be drunk with murder and rage.
Then all people will know that I am the Lord, the one who saves you
and sets you free.
They will know that I am Israel's powerful God."

ISAIAH *49:8–26*

THE LORD OUR SHEPHERD

The Lord is my shepherd; I have everything I need.
He lets me rest in fields of green grass and leads me to quiet pools of
fresh water.
He gives me new strength.
He guides me in the right paths, as he has promised.
Even if I go through the deepest darkness, I will not be afraid, Lord,
for you are with me.
Your shepherd's rod and staff protect me.

You prepare a banquet for me, where all my enemies can see me;
you welcome me as an honored guest and fill my cup to the brim.
I know that your goodness and love will be with me all my life;
and your house will be my home as long as I live.

PSALMS *23:1–6*

IN PRAISE, OF THE LORD'S GOODNESS

Praise the Lord!

You servants of the Lord, praise his name!
May his name be praised, now and forever.
From the east to the west praise the name of the Lord!
The Lord rules over all nations; his glory is above the heavens.

PSALMS *113:1–3*

GOD'S COMPLETE KNOWLEDGE AND CARE

Lord, you have examined me and you know me.
You know everything I do; from far away you understand all my thoughts.
You see me, whether I am working or resting; you know all my actions.
Even before I speak, you already know what I will say.
You are all around me on every side; you protect me with your power.
Your knowledge of me is too deep; it is beyond my understanding.

Where could I go to escape from you? Where could I get away from your presence?
If I went up to heaven, you would be there;
      if I lay down in the world of the dead, you would be there.
If I flew away beyond the east or lived in the farthest place in the west,
you would be there to lead me, you would be there to help me.

I could ask the darkness to hide me or the light around me to turn into night,
but even darkness is not dark for you, and the night is as bright as the day.

    Darkness and light are the same to you.

You created every part of me; you put me together in my mother's womb.
I praise you because you are to be feared; all you do is strange and wonderful.

    I know it with my heart.
When my bones were being formed, carefully put together in my mother's womb,

    when I was growing there in secret, you knew that I was there; you saw me

    before I was born.
The days allotted to me had all been recorded in your book, before any of them ever began.
O God, how difficult I find your thoughts; how many of them there are!
If I counted them, they would be more than the grains of sand.

    When I awake, I am still with you.

PSALMS *139:1–18*

The Christian Bible includes the stories of God from the Hebrew tradition and adds many examples of the breath of Divine Love. The followers of Jesus hear from him about the Father's love for them and how they are to share this love with others.

THE LOST SHEEP

One day when many tax collectors and other outcasts came to listen to Jesus, the Pharisees and the teachers of the Law started grumbling, "This man welcomes outcasts and even eats with them!" So Jesus told them this parable:

"Suppose one of you has a hundred sheep and loses one of them, what do you do? You leave the other ninety-nine sheep in the pasture and go looking for the one that got lost until you find it. When you find it, you are so happy that you put it on your shoulders and carry it back home. Then you call your friends and neighbors together and say to them, I am so happy I found my lost sheep. Let us celebrate! In the same way, I tell you, there will be more joy in heaven over one sinner who repents than over ninety-nine respectable people who do not need to repent."

MATTHEW *18:12–14*

THE LOST SON

Jesus went on to say, "There was once a man who had two sons. The younger one said to him, 'Father, give me my share of the property now.' So the man divided his property between his two sons. After a few days the younger son sold his part of the property and left home with the money. He went to a country far away, where he wasted his money in reckless living. He spent everything he had. Then a severe famine spread over that country, and he was left without a thing. So he went to work for one of the citizens of that country, who sent him out to his farm to take care of the pigs. He wished he could fill himself with the bean pods the pigs ate, but no one gave him anything to eat. At last he came to his senses and said, 'All my father's hired workers have more than they can eat, and here I am about to starve!' I will get up and go to my father and say, 'Father, I have sinned against God and against you. I am no longer fit to be called your son; treat me as one of your hired workers.' So he got up and started back to his father.

"He was still a long way from home when his father saw him; his heart was filled with pity, and he ran, threw his arms around his son, and kissed him. 'Father,' the son said, 'I have sinned against God and against you. I am no longer fit to be called your son.' But the father called to his servants. 'Hurry!' he said. 'Bring the best robe and put it on him. Put a ring on his finger and shoes on his feet. Then go and get the prize calf and kill it, and let us celebrate with a feast! For this son of mine was dead, but now he is alive; he was lost, but now he has been found.' And so the feasting began.

"In the meantime the older son was out in the field. On his way back, when he came close to the house, he heard the music and dancing. So he called one of the servants and asked him, 'What's going on?' 'Your brother has come back home,' the servant answered, 'and your father has killed the prize calf, because he got him back safe and sound.' The older brother was so angry that he would not go into the house; so his father came out and begged him to come in. But he spoke back to his father, 'Look, all these years I have worked for you like a slave, and I have never disobeyed your orders. What have you given me? Not even a goat for me to have a feast with my friend! But this son of yours wasted all your property on prostitutes, and when he comes back home, you kill the prize calf for him!' 'My son,' the father answered, 'you are always here with me, and everything I have is yours. But we had to celebrate and be happy, because your brother was dead, but now is alive; he was lost, but now he has been found.' "

LUKE *15:11–32*

TEACHING ABOUT PRAYER

"When you pray, do not use a lot of meaningless words, as the pagans do, who think that their gods will hear them because their prayers are long. Do not be like them. Your Father already knows what you need before you ask him. This, then, is how you should pray:

"Our Father in heaven:
May your holy name be honored;
may your Kingdom come;
may your will be done on earth as it is in heaven.
Give us today the food we need.
Forgive us the wrongs we have done,
    as we forgive the wrongs that others have done to us.
Do not bring us to hard testing, but keep us safe from the Evil One."

"If you forgive others the wrongs they have done to you, your Father in heaven will also forgive you. But if you do not forgive others, then your Father will not forgive the wrongs you have done."

MATTHEW 6:7–14

THE WORKERS IN THE VINEYARD

"The Kingdom of heaven is like this. Once there was a man who went out early in the morning to hire some men to work in his vineyard. He agreed to pay them the regular wage, a silver coin a day, and sent them to work in his vineyard. He went out again to the marketplace at nine o'clock and saw some men standing there doing nothing, so he told them, 'You also go and work in the vineyard, and I will pay you a fair wage.' So they went. Then at twelve o'clock and again at three o'clock he did the same thing. It was nearly five o'clock when he went to the marketplace and saw some other men still standing there. 'Why are you wasting the whole day here doing nothing?' he asked them. 'No one hired us,' they answered. 'Well, then, you go and work in the vineyard,' he told them.

· · ·

"When evening came, the owner told his foreman, 'Call the workers and pay them their wages, starting with those who were hired last and ending with those who were hired first.' The men who had begun to work at five o'clock were paid a silver coin each. So when the men who were the first to be hired came to be paid, they thought they would get more; but they too were given a silver coin each. They took their money and started grumbling against the employer. 'These men who were hired last worked only one hour,' they said, 'while we put up with a whole day's work in the hot sun yet you paid them the same as you paid us!' 'Listen, friend,' the owner answered one of them, 'I have not cheated you. After all, you agreed to do a day's work for one silver coin. Now take your pay and go home. I want to give this man who was hired last as much as I gave you. Don't I have the right to do as I wish with my own money? Or are you jealous because I am generous?' "

And Jesus concluded, "So those who are last will be first, and those who are first will be last."

MATTHEW *20:1–16*

COME TO ME AND REST

At that time Jesus said, "Father, Lord of heaven and earth! I thank you because you have shown to the unlearned what you have hidden from the wise and learned. Yes, Father, this was how you were pleased to have it happen.

"My Father has given me all things. No one knows the Son except the Father, and no one knows the Father except the Son and those to whom the Son chooses to reveal him.

"Come to me, all of you who are tired from carrying heavy loads, and I will give you rest. Take my yoke and put it on you, and learn from me, because I am gentle and humble in spirit; and you will find rest. For the yoke I will give you is easy, and the load I will put on you is light."

MATTHEW *11:25–30*

GOD'S LOVE IN CHRIST JESUS

In view of all this, what can we say? If God is for us, who can be against us? Certainly not God, who did not even keep back his own Son, but offered him for us all! He gave us his Son will he not also freely give us all things? Who will accuse God's chosen people? God himself declares them not guilty! Who, then, will condemn them? Not Christ Jesus, who died, or rather, who was raised to life and is at the right side of God, pleading with him for us! Who, then, can separate us from the love of Christ? Can trouble do it, or hardship or persecution or hunger or poverty or danger or death?

No, in all these things we have complete victory through him who loved us! For I am certain that nothing can separate us from his love; neither death nor life, neither angels nor other heavenly rulers or powers, neither the present nor the future, neither the world above nor the world below there is nothing in all creation that will ever be able to separate us from the love of God which is ours through Christ Jesus our Lord.

ROMANS *8:31–35, 37–39*

THE PARABLE OF THE HIDDEN TREASURE

"The Kingdom of heaven is like this. A man happens to find a treasure hidden in a field. He covers it up again, and is so happy that he goes and sells everything he has, and then goes back and buys that field."

MATTHEW *13:44*

THE PARABLE OF THE PEARL

"Also, the Kingdom of heaven is like this. A man is looking for fine pearls, and when he finds one that is unusually fine, he goes and sells everything he has, and buys that pearl."

MATTHEW *13:45*

PIED BEAUTY

Glory be to God for dappled things—
For skies of couple-colour as a brinded cow;
For rose-moles all in stipple upon trout that swim;

Fresh-firecoal chestnut-falls; finches' wings;
Landscape plotted and pieced, fold, fallow, and plough;
And all trades, their gear and tackle and trim.

All things counter, original, spare, strange;
Whatever is fickle, freckled (who knows how?)
With swift, slow; sweet, sour; adazzle, dim;
He fathers-forth whose beauty is past change:
Praise him.

GERARD MANLEY HOPKINS

A direct, mystical experience of the divine, as recounted by many mystics, reinforces the image of a loving power eager to share that love with all.

Thither my own wings could not carry me,
But that a flash my understanding clove,
Whence its desire came to it suddenly.
High phantasy lost power and here broke off;
Yet a wheel moves smoothly, free from jars,
My will and my desire were turned by love.
The love that moves the sun and the other stars.

DANTE ALIGHIERI,
from *Paradiso*

ollowing the rules and regulations of a religious tradition does not guarantee anyone a loving relationship with the divine. In their appeal to our imagination, poets and composers invite us to open our souls to the wonder of divine love and its longing for union with us. They invite us to consider how we might respond to this love.

GOD THE TEENAGER

That God exists the world is not a proof
But a metaphor for who She really is,
An unrestrained adolescent, showing off,
An excessive, exuberant, playful whiz,
Determined gamester with the quantum odds,
An ingenious expert in higher math,
This frolicsome and comic dancing God
Is charming and just a little daft.

Will God grow up? Will She become mature?
In the creation game announce a lull,
Her befuddled suppliants assure
A cosmos that is quiet, safe, and dull?
Can God be innocent of romance?
No WAY! On with the multicosmic dance!

ANDREW M. GREELEY

GOD THE STORYTELLER

The pure, anguished notes of a Mahler postilhorn
As they tumble round a mountaintop
Gossamer rainbow wings on fragile breezes born,
A hasty kiss I pray will never stop.
With a cleansing gust of wind the front arrives
The hull tilts, sails flap, I duck the swinging boom
The soggy gray clouds gone, my soul revives
Ballooning spinnakers briskly tug for home.

A melody, changing wind, a quick embrace
Metaphoric gifts that need not be but are
Mystery, wonder, marvel, amazing grace
Seducing comic hints sent from afar
Of eternal surprise a tempting race
For my dark night journey a newborn star.

ANDREW M. GREELEY

THE KINGDOM OF GOD

"The Kingdom of God is at hand!"

Not heaven's city of God, ivory and gold,
Nor a spired Byzantium here on earth,
A theocracy biblical and old,
Benignly ruled by goodly king and pious pope.

But a raging torrent, smashing through the ice
To rush in lethal flood madly towards the sea,
A firestorm that consumes and devastates,
A blood red furnace spilling molten steel.

A dangerous demanding dynamism,
Yet somehow winsome the famished divine
Desire unleashed, that is the kingdom of God!
The Creator's lustful fervor arisen,
A tumultuous, delicate hurricane
The rapacious love of God falls upon the world!

ANDREW M. GREELEY

GOD THE ROMANTIC LOVER

"Love is forever but it does not last."
Brazilian parable.

Paralyzed in a fragrant languid bog,
Hostage to an incurable obsession,
Enveloped in a gentle rosy fog
A willing victim of sweet infection
I become a clown, a shameless naked slave,
Bounced between ecstasy and dejection
A lunatic on a roller-coaster wave,
A fool, innocent of all discretion.

"God is love" this is what it really means?
Is God so heedless of my imperfection?
Captivated by daffy romantic dreams?
God, brokenhearted by my rejection?

Like a lovesick and disappointed teen,
Does God hope love's death ends in resurrection?

ANDREW M. GREELEY

THE PATHOS OF GOD

(After Rabbi Abraham Joshua Heschel)

Like a geranium wilting in a drought
Or a weeping child lost in crowded store
A lovely woman, alone, frightened, hurt,
My sensitive and tender care implores.
I wipe away her tears and beg a smile;
I want to heal, to cherish, to ease her pain,
To gently say that in a little while
She'll laugh and love and begin her life again.

Is her pathos a sacrament of God
Who, some say, weeps each time a baby cries?
Is the desire she stirs in me the barest hint
Of her ultimate, astonishing surprise?
Can it be, O truly dazzling wonderment,
That God requires my most delicate abandonment?

ANDREW M. GREELEY

THE GOD OF THE PARABLES

An indulgence no parent could defend
Warm welcome to a fawning, worthless son;
A day's pay for those mumbling at the end
From a silly farmer when day's work is done;
A woman whose sins all right minds offend,
Her forgiveness from the judge quickly won;
A man whom no one will befriend
Finds himself redeemed by a Samaritan.

O God of Jesus, you're quite round the bend,
By human folly not to be outdone.
What sort of crazy message do You intend?
By what madness do You propose to stun?
"The big surprise you cannot comprehend?
The triumph of My Love has just begun!"

ANDREW M. GREELEY

IRISH PARENT GOD

After watching Irish parents play with their children at a small amusement
park on the strand at Bray on a Sunday afternoon.

Sweeping the laughing boy up with his arm,
Grinning and mounting the stairs of a giant slide,
He squeezes a tiny hand to bless from harm:
Father and son begin the gallant ride,
As mother and sister in spasms of giggles wait,
Munching on rich vanilla ice-cream cones.
All four shout, ecstatically defying fate,
As two heroes plunge bravely to the ground.

You too are a doting parent who enjoys
The celebrations of your girls and boys,
Who frolics with us at our play and toys
And protects us from what may destroy
Our innocent happiness and childish nose,
An Irish parent God who lives for our joy.

Andrew M. Greeley

The Clouds' Veil

Refrain

Even though the rain hides the stars, even though the mist swirls the
hills,
even when the dark clouds veil the sky, You are by my side.
Even when the sun shall fall in sleep, even when at dawn the sky
shall weep,
even in the night when storms shall rise, you are by my side, you are
by my side.

Verses

Bright the stars at night that mirror heaven's way to you.
Bright the stars in light where dwell the saints in love and truth.

Deep the feast of life where saints shall gather in deep peace,
Deep in heaven's light where sorrows pass beyond death's sleep.

Blest are they who sing the fellowship of saints in light.
Blest is heaven's King. All saints adore the Lord, Most high.

Liam Lawton

THE GIFT OF PEACE

Far above the earth he soars,
circling the clear sky,
flying over forests dim,
peering in shadows,
seeking far and wide his children,
to give them peace.

NANCY VAN LAAN,
from *In a Circle Long Ago*

CHAPTER ELEVEN

Love of Nature

Everything that lives is holy.
WILLIAM BLAKE

L ove of nature is different than our other loves. It widens our circle of love beyond love for other human beings. At the same time, love of nature could be considered a form of narcissism. After all, we are part of nature.

Moreover, when we speak of the things of nature that we love—plants, animals, the sea, the sky, the land—the love is one-sided. We are not loved back save perhaps in some limited way by domesticated animals.

Despite the difference between this love and other forms of love, our love for the things of nature is an integral component of an analysis of human love. We are immersed in nature, surrounded by it at all times. Nature is both mysterious and terrifying and as such confronts us with questions of meaning. We often turn to nature for solace in times of stress, for rejuvenation, and for inspiration.

Nature affects our moods. Cold, dark winter days when snow impedes our progress often contribute to depression. Blizzards, hurricanes, tornadoes, and earthquakes cause misery for those caught in their paths. Bright sunny comfortably cool days can lift our spirits.

A man began his journey toward death from cancer in the ending days of summer. A rainy autumn and near-blizzard winter conditions reflected his downward spiral. Finally, early in April, on a surprisingly warm bright sunny day, his daughter opened the sliding door to the deck off his room.

As warm air and the song of the birds nestled in the budding tree in the yard wafted through the room, his family and friends came to say their last good-byes. In the early afternoon, with his family gathered around his bed, he drew his last breath.

Four days later on an equally beautiful day, the mourners gathered around his newly dug grave, beneath a recently planted fruit tree. Family members placed pink roses on the casket and those gathered sang and prayed. Nature provided a softening touch to their grief.

While nature doesn't return our love, it provides us with opportunities to ask the right questions as we search for meaning and seek to love.

To look on nature, not as in the hour
Of thoughtless youth, but hearing oftentimes
The still, sad music of humanity,
Nor harsh or grating, though of ample power
To chasten and subdue. And I have felt
A presence that disturbs me with the joy
Of elevated thoughts; a sense sublime
Of something far more deeply interfused,
Whose dwelling is the light of setting suns,
And the round ocean, and the living air,
And the blue sky, and in the mind of man;
A motion and a spirit that impels
All thinking things, all objects of all thought,
And rolls through all things. Therefore am I still
A lover of the meadows and the woods,
And mountains; and of all that we behold
From this green earth; of all the mighty world
Of eye and ear, both what they half-create,
And what perceive; well pleased to recognize
In nature and the language of the sense
The anchor of my purest thoughts, the nurse,
The guide, the guardian of my heart, and soul
Of all my moral being . . .

WILLIAM WORDSWORTH,
from "Lines Composed Above Tintern Abbey"

What They Mean

A Robin Red breast in a Cage
Puts all Heaven in a Rage.
A dove house filled with doves & Pigeons
Shudders Hell thro' all its regions.
A dog starved at his Master's Gate
Predicts the ruin of the State.
A Horse misused upon the Road
Calls to Heaven for Human blood.
Each outcry of the hunted Hare
A fibre from the Brain does tear.
A Skylark wounded in the wing,
A Cherubim does cease to sing.
The Game Cock clipped & armed for fight
Does the Rising Sun affright.
Every Wolf's & Lion's howl
Raises from Hell a Human Soul.
The wild deer wandering here & there,
Keeps the Human Soul from Care.
The Lamb misused breeds Public strife
And yet forgives the Butcher's Knife.
The Bat that flits at close of Eve
Has left the Brain that won't Believe.
The Owl that calls upon the Night
Speaks the Unbeliever's fright
He who shall hurt the little Wren
Shall never be beloved by Men
He who the Ox to wrath has moved
Shall never be by Woman loved.
The wanton Boy that kills the Fly
Shall feel the Spider's enmity.
He who torments the Chafer's sprite
Weaves a Bower in endless Night.
The Caterpillar on the Leaf
Repeats to thee thy Mother's grief.
Kill not the Moth nor Butterfly,
For the Last Judgment draweth nigh.
He who shall train the Horse to War

Shall never pass the Polar Bar.
The Begger's Dog & Widow's Cat,
Feed them & thou wilt grow fat.
The Gnat that sings his Summer's song
Poison gets from Slander's tongue.
The poison of the Snake & Newt
Is the sweat of Envy's Foot.
The poison of the Honey Bee
Is the Artist's jealousy. . . .

WILLIAM BLAKE,
from "Auguries of Innocence"

NOT IN VAIN

If I can stop one heart from breaking,
I shall not live in vain:
If I can ease one life the aching,
Or cool one pain,
Or help one fainting robin
Unto his nest again,
I shall not live in vain.

EMILY DICKINSON

WHEN I SEE THE LARK

When I see the lark
moving its wings in joy
   against the light
until at last it forgets
   and lets itself fall
by reason of the sweetness
   that fills its heart,
oh, such envy comes to me
of those whose happiness I see
   that I marvel that
my heart does not melt away
   at once with desire!

BERNARD DE VENTADOUR

THE KING OF THE BIRDS

When I was five I had an experience that marked me for life. Pathé News sent a photographer from New York to Savannah to take a picture of a chicken of mine. This chicken, a buff Cochin Bantam, had the distinction of being able to walk either forward or backward. Her fame had spread through the press, and by the time she reached the attention of Pathé News I suppose there was nowhere left for her to go forward or backward. Shortly after that she died as now seems fitting.

If I put this information in the beginning of an article on peacocks, it is because I am always being asked why I raise them, and I have no short or reasonable answer.

From that day with the Pathé man I began to collect chickens. What had been only a mild interest became a passion, a quest. I had to have more and more chickens. I favor those with one green eye and one orange or with overlong necks and crooked combs. I wanted one with three legs or three wings but nothing in that line turned up. I pondered over the picture in Robert Ripley's book, *Believe It or Not*, of a rooster that had survived for thirty days without his head; but I did not have a scientific temperament. I could sew in a fashion and I began to make clothes for chickens. A gray bantam named Colonel Eggbert wore a white piqué coat with a lace collar and two buttons on the back. Apparently Pathé News never heard of any of these other chickens of mine; it never sent another photographer.

My quest, whatever it was actually for, ended with peacocks. Instinct, not knowledge, led me to them. I had never seen or heard one. Although I had a pen of pheasants and a pen of quail, a flock of turkeys, seventeen geese, a tribe of mallard ducks, three Japanese silky bantams, two Polish Crested ones, and several chickens of a cross between these last and the Rhode Island red, I felt a lack. I knew that the peacock had been the bird of Hera, the wife of Zeus, but since that time it had probably come down in the world—the Florida *Market Bulletin* advertised three-year-old peafowl at sixty-five dollars a pair. I had been quietly reading these ads for some years when one day, seized, I circled an ad in the *Bulletin* and passed it to my mother. The ad was for a peacock and hen with four seven-week-old peabiddies. "I'm going to order me those," I said.

My mother read the ad. "Don't those things eat flowers?" she asked.

"They'll eat Startena like the rest of them," I said.

The peafowl arrived by Railway Express from Eustis, Florida, on a mild day in October. When my mother and I arrived at the station the crate was on the platform and from one end of it protruded a long royal-blue neck and crested head. A white line above and below each eye gave the investigating head an expression of alert composure. I wondered if this bird, accustomed to parade about in a Florida orange grove, would readily adjust himself to a Georgia dairy farm. I jumped out of the car and bounded forward. The head withdrew.

At home we uncrated the party in a pen with a top on it. The man who sold me the birds had written that I should keep them penned up for a week or ten days and then let them out at dusk at the spot where I wanted them to roost; thereafter they would return every night to the same roosting place. He had also warned me that the cock would not have his full complement of tail feathers when he arrived; the peacock sheds his tail in late summer and does not regain it fully until after Christmas.

As soon as the birds were out of the crate, I sat down on it and began to look at them. I have been looking at them ever since, from one station or another, and always with the same awe as on the first occasion; though I have always, I feel, been able to keep a balanced view and an impartial attitude. The peacock I had bought had nothing whatsoever in the way of a tail, but he carried himself as if he not only had a train behind him but a retinue to attend it. On that first occasion, my problem was so greatly what to look at first that my gaze moved constantly from the cock to the hen to the four young peachickens, while they, except that they gave me as wide a berth as possible, did nothing to indicate they knew I was in the pen.

Over the years their attitude toward me has not grown more generous. If I appear with food they condescend, when no other way can be found, to eat it from my hand; if I appear without food, I am just another object. If I refer to them as "my" peafowl, the pronoun is legal, nothing more. I am the menial, at the beck and squawk of any feathered worthy who wants service. When I first uncrated these birds, in my frenzy I said, "I want too many of them that every time I go out the door, I'll run into one." Now every time I go out the door, four or five run into me—and give me only the faintest recognition. Nine years have passed since my first peafowl arrived. I have forty beaks to feed. Necessity is the mother of several other things besides invention.

For a chicken that grows up to have such exceptional good looks the peacock starts life with an inauspicious appearance. The peabiddy is the color of those large objectionable moths that futter about light bulbs on summer nights. Its only distinguished features are its eyes, a luminous gray, and a brown crest which begins to sprout from the back of its head when it is ten days old. This looks at first like a bug's antennae and later like the head feathers of an Indian. In six weeks green flecks appear in its neck, and in a few more weeks a cock can be distinguished from a hen by the speckles on his back. The hen's back gradually fades to an even gray and her appearance becomes shortly what it will always be. I have never thought the peahen unattractive, even though she lacks a long tail and any significant decoration. I have even once or twice thought her more attractive than the cock, more subtle and refined; but these moments of boldness pass.

The cock's plumage requires two years to attain its pattern, and for the rest of his life this chicken will act as though he designed it himself. For his first two years he might have been put together out of a rag bag by an unimaginative hand. During his first year he has a buff breast, a speckled back, a green neck like his mother's, and a short gray tail. During his second year he has a black breast, his sire's blue neck, a back which is slowly turning the green and gold it will remain; but still no long tail. In his third year he reaches his majority and acquires his tail. For the rest of his life—and a peachicken may live to be thirty-five—he will have nothing better to do than manicure it, furl and unfurl it, dance forward *and backward* with it spread, scream when it is stepped upon, and arch it carefully when he steps through a puddle.

Not every part of the peacock is striking to look at, even when he is full-grown. His upper wing feathers are a striated black and white and might have been borrowed from a Barred Rock fryer; his end wing feathers are the color of clay; his legs are long, thin, and iron-colored; his feet are big; and he appears to be wearing the short pants now so much in favor with playboys in the summer. These extend downward, buff-colored and sleek, from what might be a blue-black waistcoat. One would not be disturbed to find a watch chain hanging from this, but none does. Analyzing the appearance of the peacock as he stands with his tail folded, I find the parts incommensurate with the whole. The fact is that with his tail folded, nothing but his bearing saves this bird from being a laughingstock. With his tail spread he inspires a range of emotions, but I have yet to hear laughter.

The usual reaction is silence at least for a time. The cock opens his tail by shaking himself violently until it is gradually lifted in an arch around him. Then, before anyone has had a chance to see it, he swings around so that his back faces the spectator. This has been taken by some to be insult and by others to be whimsy. I suggest it means only that the peacock is equally well satisfied with either view of himself. Since I have been keeping peafowl, I have been visited at least once a year by first-grade schoolchildren, who learn by living. I am used to hearing this group chorus as the peacock swings around, "Oh, look at his underwear!" This "underwear" is a stiff gray tail, raised to support the larger one, and beneath it a puff of black feathers that would be suitable for some really regal woman—a Cleopatra or a Clytemnestra— to use to powder her nose.

When the peacock has presented his back, the spectator will usually begin to walk around him to get a front view; but the peacock will continue to turn so that no front view is possible. The thing to do then is to stand still and wait until it pleases him to turn. When it suits him the peacock will face you. Then you will see in a green-bronze arch around him a galaxy of gazing, haloed suns. This is the moment when most people are silent.

"Amen! Amen!" an old negro woman once cried when this happened, and I have heard many similar remarks at this moment that show the inadequacy of human speech. Some people whistle; a few, for once, are silent. A truck driver who was driving up with a load of hay and found a peacock turning before him in the middle of the road shouted, "Get a load of that bastard!" and braked his truck to a shattering halt. I have never known a strutting peacock to budge a fraction of an inch for truck or tractor or automobile. It is up to the vehicle to get out of the way. No peafowl of mine has ever been run over, though one year one of them lost a foot in the mowing machine.

Many people, I have found, are congenitally unable to appreciate the sight of a peacock. Once or twice I have been asked what the peacock is "good for"—a question which gets no answer from me because it deserves none. The telephone company sent a lineman out one day to repair our telephone. After the job was finished, the man, a large fellow with a suspicious expression half hidden by a yellow helmet, continued to idle about trying to coax a cock that had been watching him to strut. He wished to add this experience to a large number of others he had apparently had. "Come on now, bud," he said, "get the show on the road, upsy-daisy, come on now, snap it up, snap it up."

The peacock, of course, paid no attention to this.

"What ails him?" the man asked.

"Nothing ails him," I said. "He'll put it up tereckly. All you have to do is wait."

The man trailed about after the cock for another fifteen minutes or so; then, in disgust he got back in his truck and started off. The bird shook himself and his tail rose around him.

"He's doing it!" I screamed. "Hey, wait! He's doing it!"

The man swerved the truck back around again just as the cock turned and faced him with the spread tail. The display was perfect. The bird turned lightly to the right and the little planets above him hung in bronze then he turned slightly to the left and they were hung in green. I went up to the truck to see how the man was affected by the sight.

He was staring at the peacock with rigid concentration, as if he were trying to read fine print at a distance. In a second the cock lowered his tail and stalked off.

"Well, what did you think of that?" I asked.

"Never saw such long ugly legs," the man said. "I bet that rascal could outrun a bus."

Some people are genuinely affected by the sight of a peacock, even with his tail lowered but do not care to admit it; others appear to be incensed by it. Perhaps they have the suspicion that the bird has formed some unfavorable opinion of them. The peacock himself is a careful and dignified investigator. Visitors to our place instead of being barked at by dogs rushing from under the porch, are squalled at by peacocks whose blue necks and crested heads pop up from behind tufts of grass, peer out of bushes, and crane downward from the roof of the house, where the bird has flown, perhaps for the view. One of mine stepped from under the shrubbery one day and came forward to inspect a carful of people who had driven up to buy a calf. An old man and five or six white-haired, bare-footed children were piling out the back of the automobile as the bird approached. Catching sight of him, they stopped in their tracks and stared, plainly hacked to find this superior figure blocking their path. There was silence as the bird regarded them with his head drawn back at its most majestic angle, his folded train glittering behind him in the sunlight.

"Whus is thet thang?" one of the small boys asked finally in a sullen voice.

The old man had got out of the car and was gazing at the peacock with an astounded look of recognition. "I ain't seen one of them since my grandaddy's day," he said, respectfully removing his hat. "Folks used to have 'em, but they don't no more."

"Whut is it?" the child asked again in the same tone he had used before.

"Churren," the old man said, "that's the king of the birds!"

The children received this information in silence. After a minute they climbed back into the car and continued from there to stare at the peacock, their expressions annoyed, as if they disliked catching the old man in the truth.

The peacock does most of his serious strutting in the spring and summer when he has a full tail to do it with. Usually he begins shortly after breakfast, struts for several hours, desists in the heat of the day, and begins again in the late afternoon. Each cock has a favorite station where he performs every day in the hope of attracting some passing hen; but if I have found anyone indifferent to the peacock's display, besides the telephone lineman, it is the peahen. She seldom casts an eye at it. The cock, his tail raised in a shimmering arch around him, will turn this way and that, and with his clay-colored wing feathers touching the ground, will dance forward and backward his neck curved, his beak parted, his eyes glittering. Meanwhile the hen goes about her business, diligently searching the ground as if any bug in the grass were of more importance than the unfurled map of the universe which floats nearby.

Some people have the notion that only the peacock spreads his tail and that he does it only when the hen is present. This is not so. A peafowl only a few hours hatched will raise what tail he has—it will be about the size of a thumbnail—and will strut and turn and back and bow exactly as if he were three years old and had some reason to be doing it. The hens will raise their tails when they see an object on the ground which alarms them, or sometimes when they have nothing better to do and the air is brisk. Brisk air goes at once to the peafowl's head and inclines him to be sportive. A group of birds will dance together or four or five will chase one another around a bush or tree. Sometimes one will chase himself, end his frenzy with a spirited leap into the air, and then stalk off as if he had never been involved in the spectacle.

Frequently the cock combines the lifting of his tail with the raising of his voice. He appears to receive through his feet some shock from the center of the earth, which travels upward through him and is released: *Eee-ooo-ii Eee-ooo-ii!* To the melancholy this sound is melancholy and to the hysterical it is hysterical. To me it has always sounded like a cheer for an invisible parade.

The hen is not given to these outbursts. She makes a noise like a mule's bray—*heehaw, heehaw, aa-aawww*—and makes it only when necessary. In the fall and winter, peafowl are usually silent unless some racket disturbs them; but in the spring and summer, at short intervals during the day and night, the cock, lowering his neck and throwing back his head will give out with seven or eight screams in succession as if this message were the one on earth which need most urgently to be heard.

At night these calls take on a minor key and the air for miles around is charged with them. It has been a long time since I let my first peafowl out at dusk to roost in the cedar trees behind the house. Now fifteen or twenty still roost there; but the original old cock from Eustis, Florida, stations himself on top of the barn, the bird who lost his foot in the mowing machine sits on a flat shed near the horse stall, there are others in the trees by the pond, several in the oaks at the side of the house, and one that cannot be dissuaded from roosting on the water tower. From all these stations calls and answers echo through the night. The peacock perhaps has violent dreams. Often he wakes and screams "Help! Help!" and then from the pond and the barn and the trees around the house a chorus of adjuration begins:

Lee-yon lee-yon,
Mee-yon mee-yon!
Eee-e-yoy eee-e-yoy!
Eee-e-yoy eee-e-yoy!

The restless sleeper may wonder if he wakes or dreams.

It is hard to tell the truth about this bird. The habits of any pea-chicken left to himself would hardly be noticeable, but multiplied by forty, they become a situation. I was correct that my peachickens would all eat Startena; they also eat everything else. Particularly they eat flowers. My mother's fears were all borne out. Peacocks not only eat flowers, they eat them systematically, beginning at the head of a row and going down it. If they are not hungry, they will pick the flower anyway, if it is attractive, and let it drop. For general eating they prefer chrysanthemums and roses. When they are not eating flowers, they enjoy sitting on top of them, and where the peacock sits he will eventually fashion a dusting hole. Any chicken's dusting hole is out of place in a flower bed, but the peafowl's hole, being the size of a small crater, is more so. When he dusts he all but obliterates the sight of himself with sand. Usually when someone arrives at full gallop with the leveled broom, he can see nothing through the cloud of dirt and flying flowers but a few green feathers and a beady, pleasure-taking eye.

From the beginning, relations between these birds and my mother were strained. She was forced at first to get up early in the morning and go out with her clippers to reach the Lady Bankshire and the Herbert Hoover roses before some peafowl had breakfasted upon them; now she has halfway solved her problem by erecting hundreds of feet of twenty-four-inch-high wire to fence the flower beds. She contends that peachickens do not have enough sense to jump over a low fence. "If it were a high wire," she says, "they would jump onto it and over but they don't have sense enough to jump over a low wire."

It is useless to argue with her on this matter. "It's not a challenge," I say to her; but she has made up her mind.

In addition to eating flowers, peafowl also eat fruit, a habit which has created a lack of cordiality toward them on the part of my uncle, who had the fig trees planted about the place because he has an appetite for figs himself. "Get that scoundrel out of that fig bush!" he will roar, rising from his chair at the sound of a limb breaking, and someone will have to be dispatched with a broom to the fig trees.

Peafowl also enjoy flying into barn lofts and eating peanuts off peanut hay. This has not endeared them to our dairyman. And as they have a taste for fresh garden vegetables, they have often run afoul of the dairyman's wife.

The peacock likes to sit on gates or fence posts and allow his tail to hang down. A peacock on a fence post is a superb sight. Six or seven peacocks on a gate are beyond description; but it is not very good for the gate. Our fence posts tend to lean in one direction or another and all our gates open diagonally.

In short, I am the only person on the place who is willing to underwrite with something more than tolerance, the presence of pea-fowl. In return, I am blessed with their rapid multiplication. The population figure I give out is forty, but for some time now I have not felt it wise to take a census. I had been told before I bought my birds that peafowl are difficult to raise. It is not so, alas. In May the peahen finds a nest in some fence corner and lays five or six large buff-colored eggs. Once a day, thereafter she gives an abrupt *hee-haa-awww!* and shoots like a rocket from her nest. Then for half an hour her neck ruffled and stretched forward she parades around the premises, announcing what she is about. I listen with mixed emotions.

In twenty-eight days the hen comes off with five or six mothlike, murmuring peachicks. The cock ignores these unless one gets under his feet (then he pecks it over the head until it gets elsewhere), but the hen is a watchful mother and every year a good many of the young survive. Those that withstand illnesses and predators (the hawk, the fox, and the opossum) over the winter seem impossible to destroy, except by violence.

A man selling fence posts tarried at our place one day and told me that he had once had eighty peafowl on his farm. He cast a nervous eye at two of mine standing nearby. "In the spring, we couldn't hear ourselves think," he said. "As soon as you lifted your voice, they lifted their'n, if not before. All our fence posts wobbled. In the summer they ate all the tomatoes off the vines. Scuppernongs went the same way. My wife said she raised her flowers for herself and she was not going to have them eat up by a chicken no matter how long his tail was. And in the fall they shed the feathers all over the place anyway and it was a job to clean up. My old grandmother was living with us then and she was eighty-five. She said, 'Either they go, or I go.'"

"Who went?" I asked.

"We still got twenty of them in the freezer," he said.

"And how," I asked, looking significantly at the two standing nearby, "did they taste?"

"No better than any other chicken," he said, "but I'd a heap rather eat them than hear them."

I have tried imagining that the single peacock I see before me is the only one I have, but then one comes to join him; another flies off the roof, four or five crash out of the crepe-myrtle hedge; from the pond one screams and from the barn I hear the dairyman denouncing another that has got into the cowfeed. My kin are given to such phrases as "Let's face it."

I do not like to let my thoughts linger in morbid channels but there are times when such facts as the price of wire fencing and the price of Startena and the yearly gain in peafowl all run uncontrolled through my head. Lately I have had a recurrent dream: I am five years old and a peacock. A photographer has been sent from New York and a long table is laid in celebration. The meal is to be an exceptional one: myself. I scream, "Help! Help!" and awaken. Then from the pond and the barn and the trees around the house, I hear that chorus of jubilation begin:

Lee-yon lee-yon,
Mee-yon mee-yon!
Eee-e-yoy eee-e-yoy!
Eee-e-yoy eee-e-yoy!

I intend to stand firm and let the peacocks multiply, for I am sure that, in the end, the last word will be theirs.

FLANNERY O'CONNOR,
from *Mystery and Manners*

ODE TO A NIGHTINGALE

My heart aches and a drowsy numbness pains
My sense, as though of hemlock I had drunk,
Or emptied some dull opiate to the drains
One minute past, and Lethe-wards had sunk:
'Tis not through envy of thy happy lot,
But being too happy on thine happiness,—
That thou, light-wingèd Dryad of the trees,
In some melodious plot
Of beechen green, and shadows numberless,
Singest of summer in full-throated ease.

O, for a draught of vintage! that hath been
Cooled a long age in the deep-delved earth,
Tasting of Flora and the country green,
Dance, and Provençal song, and sunburnt mirth!
O, for a beaker full of the warm South!
Full of the true, the blushful Hippocrene,
With beaded bubbles winking at the brim,
And purple-stained mouth;
That I might drink, and leave the world unseen,
And with thee fade away into the forest dim:

Fade far away, dissolve, and quite forget
What thou among the leaves hast never known,
The weariness, the fever, and the fret
Here, where men sit and hear each other groan;
Where palsy shakes a few, sad last gray hairs,
Where youth grows pale, and spectre-thin and dies;
Where but to think is to be full of sorrow
And leaden-eyed despairs;
Where Beauty cannot keep her lustrous eyes,
Or new Love pine at them beyond to-morrow.

Away! away! for I will fly to thee,
Not charioted by Bacchus and his pards,
But on the viewless wings of Poesy,
Though the dull brain perplexes and retards:
Already with thee! tender is the night,
And haply the Queen-Moon is on her throne,
Clustered around by all her starry Fays;
But here there is no light,
Save what from heaven is with the breezes blown
Through verdurous glooms and winding mossy ways.

I cannot see what flowers are at my feet,
Nor what soft incense hangs upon the boughs,
But, in embalmed darkness, guess each sweet
Wherewith the seasonable month endows
The grass the thicket, and the fruit-tree wild;
White hawthorn, and the pastoral eglantine;
Fast fading violets covered up in leaves:
And mid-May's eldest child,
The coming musk-rose, full of dewy wine,
The murmurous haunt of flies on summer eves.

Darkling I listen; and for many a time
I have been half in love with easeful Death,
Called him soft names in many a mused rhyme,
To take into the air my quiet breath;

Now more than ever seems it rich to die,
To cease upon the midnight with no pain,
While thou art pouring forth thy soul abroad
In such an ecstasy!
Still wouldst thou sing and I have ears in vain—
To thy high requiem become a sod.

Thou wast not born for death, immortal Bird!
No hungry generations tread thee down;
The voice I hear this passing night was heard
In ancient days by emperor and clown:
Perhaps the self-same song that found a path
Through the sad heart of Ruth, when, sick for home,
She stood in tears amid the alien corn;
The same that oft-times hath
Charm'd magic casements, opening on the foam
Of perilous seas, in faery lands forlorn.

Forlorn! the very word is like a bell
To toll me back from thee to my sole self!
Adieu! the fancy cannot cheat so well
As she is fam'd to do, deceiving elf.
Adieu! adieu! thy plaintive anthem fades
Past the near meadows, over the still stream,
Up the hill-side; and now 'tis buried deep
In the next valley-glades:
Was it a vision or a waking dream?
Fled is that music:—Do I wake or sleep?

JOHN KEATS

THE DARKLING THRUSH

I leant upon a coppice gate
　　When Frost was spectre-gray,
And Winter's dregs made desolate
　　The weakening eye of day.
The tangled bine-stems scored the sky
　　Like strings of broken lyres,
And all mankind that haunted nigh
　　Had sought their household fires.

The land's sharp features seemed to be
　　The Century's corpse outleant,
His crypt the cloudy canopy,
　　The wind his death-lament.
The ancient pulse of germ and birth
　　Was shrunken hard and dry,
And every spirit upon earth
　　Seemed fervourless as I.

At once a voice arose among
　　The bleak twigs overhead
In a full-hearted evensong
　　Of joy illimited;
An aged thrush, frail, gaunt, and small,
　　In blast-beruffled plume,
Had chosen thus to fling his soul
　　Upon the growing gloom.

So little cause for carolings
　　Of such ecstatic sound
Was written on terrestrial things
　　Afar or nigh around,
That I could think there trembled through
　　His happy good-night air
Some blessed Hope, whereof he knew
　　And I was unaware.

THOMAS HARDY

THE SKY AND THE CROW

A Crow once flew into the sky
with a piece of meat in its beak.
Twenty crows set out in pursuit
of it and attacked it viciously.
The crow finally let the piece of
meat drop. Its pursuers then
left it alone and flew shrieking
after the morsel.
Said the crow, "I've lost the meat and
gained this peaceful sky."

from the *Bhagavata Purana*

The tiniest bug, the fiercest tiger, and all forms of busy life in between belong to the mysterious rhythms of life. When we are attentive to their experiences, we often gain insight into the meaning of our lives.

KISSING THE TOAD

Somewhere this dusk
a little girl puckers her mouth,
considers kissing
the toad her little brother has just plucked
from the cornland, hands
her in both hands, rough and lichenous
but for that immense ivory belly, like bellies
of all entrepreneurs one sees
sunning themselves at Mediterranean resorts
with popped eyes
it watches the girl who just might kiss it,
quakes, pisses
unable to widen its smile
to love on, oh yes to love on.

GALWAY KINNELL

BUILDERS OF THE BRIDGE

In Antioch where the river Assi goes to meet the sea, a bridge was built
to bring one half of the city nearer to the other half. It was built of
large stones carried down from among the hills on the backs of the
mules of Antioch.

When the bridge was finished, upon a pillar thereof was engraven in
Greek and in Aramaic, "This bridge was builded by King Antiochus
II."

And all the people walked across the good bridge over the goodly
river Assi.

And upon an evening, a youth, deemed by some a little mad, de-
scended to the pillar where the words were engraven, and he covered

over the graving with charcoal, and above it wrote, "The stones of this bridge were brought down from the hills by the mules. In passing to and fro over it you are riding upon the backs of the mules of Antioch, builders of this bridge."

KAHLIL GIBRAN,
from *The Wanderer*

TEARS AND LAUGHTER

Upon the bank of the Nile at eventide a hyena met a crocodile and they stopped and greeted one another.

The hyena spoke and said, "How goes the day with you, Sir?"

And the crocodile answered saying, "It goes badly with me. Sometimes in my pain and sorrow I weep, and then the creatures always say, 'they are but crocodile tears.' And this wounds me beyond all telling."

Then the hyena said, "You speak of your pain and your sorrow, but think of me also, for a moment. I gaze at the beauty of the world, its wonders and its miracles, and out of sheer joy I laugh even as the day laughs. And then the people of the jungle say, 'It is but the laughter of a hyena.' "

KAHLIL GIBRAN,
from *The Wanderer*

THE TIGER

Tiger! Tiger! burning bright
In the forests of the night,
What immortal hand or eye
Could frame thy fearful symmetry?

In what distant deeps or skies
Burnt the fire of thine eyes?
On what wings dare he aspire?
What the hand dare seize the fire?

And what shoulder and what art
Could twist the sinews of thy heart?
And, when thy heart began to beat,
What dread hand? and what dread feet?

What the hammer? What the chain?
In what furnace was thy brain?
What the anvil? What dread grasp
Dare its deadly terrors clasp?

When the stars threw down their spears,
And water'd heaven with their tears,
Did he smile his work to see?
Did he who made the lamb make thee?

Tiger, tiger, burning bright
In the forests of the night,
What immortal hand or eye
Dare frame thy fearful symmetry?

WILLIAM BLAKE

THE DONKEY

When fishes flew and forests walked
    And figs grew upon thorn,
Some moment when the moon was blood
    Then surely I was born.

With monstrous head and sickening cry
    And ears like errant wings,
The devil's walking parody
    On all four-footed things.

The tattered outlaw of the earth,
    Of ancient crooked will;
Starve, scourge, deride me: I am dumb,
    I keep my secret still.

Fools! For I also had my hour;
    One far fierce hour and sweet:
There was a shout about my ears,
    And palms before my feet.

G. K. CHESTERTON

ANIMALS ENJOYING LIFE

The heart is hard in nature, and unfit
For human fellowship, as being void
Of sympathy, and therefore dead alike
To love and friendship both, that is not pleased
With sight of animals enjoying life,
Nor feels their happiness augment his own.
The bounding fawn, that darts across the glade
When none pursues, through mere delight of heart,

And spirits buoyant with excess of glee;
The horse as wanton, and almost as fleet,
That skims the spacious meadow at full speed,
Then stops and snorts, and throwing high his heels,
Starts to the voluntary race again;
The very kine that gambol at high noon,
The total herd receiving first from one
That leads the dance a summons to be gay,
Though wild their strange vagaries, and uncouth
Their efforts, yet resolved with one consent
To give such act and utterance as they may
To ecstasy too big to be suppressed;
These, and a thousand images of bliss,
With which kind nature graces every scene,
Where cruel man defeats not her design,
Impart to the benevolent, who wish
All that are capable of pleasure pleased.
A far superior happiness to theirs,
The comfort of a reasonable joy.

WILLIAM COWPER,
from *The Task, VI*

Things that grow—grass, flowers, trees, even weeds—firmly rooted in the earth and yet with a beauty visible above the earth speak to us of our rootedness and our connections. Their cycles, like ours, speak of birth, life, death, and rebirth.

THE RED EARTH

Said a tree to a man, "My roots are in the deep red earth, and I shall give you of my fruit."

And the man said to the tree, "How alike we are. My roots are also deep in the red earth. And the red earth gives you power to bestow upon me of your fruit, and the red earth teaches me to receive from you with thanksgiving."

KAHLIL GIBRAN,
from *The Wanderer*

PLANT A TREE

He who plants a tree
    Plants a hope.
    Rootlets up through fibres blindly grope;
Leaves unfold into horizons free.
    So man's life must climb
    From the clods of time
    Unto heavens sublime.
Canst thou prophesy, thou little tree,
What the glory of thy boughs shall be?

He who plants a tree
    Plants a joy;
    Plants a comfort that will never cloy;
Every day a fresh reality,
    Beautiful and strong,
    To whose shelter throng
    Creatures blithe with song.
If thou couldst but know, thou happy tree,
Of the bliss that shall inhabit thee!

He who plants a tree
 He plants peace.
 Under its green curtains jargons cease
Leaf and zephyr murmur soothingly;
 Shadows soft with sleep
 Down tired eyelids creep,
 Balm of slumber deep.
Never hast thou dreamed, thou blessed tree,
Of the benediction thou shalt be.

He who plants a tree,
He plants youth;
 Vigor won for centuries in sooth;
Life of time, that hints eternity!
 Boughs their strength uprear:
 New shoots, every year,
 On old growths appear;
Thou shalt teach the ages sturdy tree,
Youth of soul is immortality.

He who plants a tree,
 He plants love,
 Tents of coolness spreading out above
Wayfarer she may not live to see.
 Gifts that grow are best;
 Hands that bless are blest;
 Plant! life does the rest!
Heaven and earth help him who plants a tree,
And his work its own reward shall be.

LUCY LARCOM

THE SHADOW

Upon a June day the grass said to the shadow of an elm tree, "You move to right and left over-often, and you disturb my peace."

And the shadow answered and said, "Not I, not I. Look skyward. There is a tree that moves in the wind to the east and to the west between the sun and the earth."

And the grass looked up, and for the first time beheld the tree. And it said in its heart, "Why, behold, there is a larger grass than myself."

And the grass was silent.

KAHLIL GIBRAN,
from *The Wanderer*

Mulla Nasrudin decided to start a flower garden. He prepared the soil and planted the seeds of many beautiful flowers. But when they came up, his garden was filled not just with his chosen flowers but also overrun by dandelions. He sought out advice from gardeners all over and tried every method known to get rid of them but to no avail. Finally he walked all the way to the capital to speak to the royal gardener at the sheik's palace. The wise old man had counseled many gardeners before and suggested a variety of remedies to expel the dandelions but Mulla had tried them all. They sat together in silence for some time and finally the gardener looked at Nasrudin and said, "Well, then I suggest you learn to love them."

SUFI

BEHIND A WALL

I own a solace shut within my heart,
A garden full of quaint delight
And warm with drowsy, poppied sunshine: bright.
Flaming with lilies out of whose cups dart
Shining things
With powdered wings.

Here terrace sinks to terrace, arbors close
The ends of dreaming paths: a wanton wind
Jostles the half-ripe pears and then, unkind,
Tumbles a-slumber in a pillar rose,
With content
Grown indolent.

By night my garden is o'erhung with gems
Fixed in an onyx setting. Fireflies
Flicker their lanterns in my dazzled eyes.
In serried rows I guess the straight, stiff stems
Of hollyhocks
Against the rocks.

So far and still it is that, listening.
I hear the flowers talking in the dawn;
And where a sunken basin cuts the lawn,
Cinctured with iris, pale and glistening,
The sudden swish
Of a waking fish.

AMY LOWELL

There is a language in each flower
    that opens to the eye,
A voiceless but a magic power,
    Doth in earth's blossoms lie.

CATHARINE H. WATERMAN

THE DAFFODILS

I wandered lonely as a cloud
That floats on high o'er vales and hills
When all at once I saw a crowd,
A host, of golden daffodils:
Beside the lake, beneath the trees,
Fluttering and dancing in the breeze.

Continuous as the stars that shine
And twinkle on the milky way,
They stretched in never-ending line
Along the margin of a bay:
Ten thousand saw I at a glance,
Tossing their heads in sprightly dance.

The waves beside them danced; but they
Outdid the sparkling waves in glee:
A poet could not but be gay,
In such a jocund company:
I gazed and gazed but little thought
What wealth the show to me had brought:

For oft, when on my couch I lie
In vacant or in pensive mood,
They flash upon that inward eye

Which is the bliss of solitude;
And then my heart with pleasure fills,
And dances with the daffodils.

WILLIAM WORDSWORTH

The cycles of four seasons remind us of the continuing process of birth, growth, aging, death, and rebirth. Even in areas were the seasons are not distinct, nature goes through changes, sometimes daily, that imitate the process. Our experiences are in tune with this rhythm. They, too, are part of a natural process.

STOPPING BY WOODS ON
A SNOWY EVENING

Whose woods these are I think I know.
His house is in the village though;
He will not see me stopping here
To watch his woods fill up with snow.

My little horse must think it queer
To stop without a farmhouse near
Between the woods and frozen lake
The darkest evening of the year.

He gives his harness bells a shake
To ask if there is some mistake.
The only other sound's the sweep
Of easy wind and downy flake.

The woods are lovely, dark and deep.
But I have promises to keep,
And miles to go before I sleep,
And miles to go before I sleep.

ROBERT FROST

FALLOWNESS

All Nature seems at work.
Slugs leave their lair—
The Bees are stirring—birds are on the wing—
And Winter, slumbering in the open air,
Wears on his smiling face a dream of Spring!
And I, the while, the sole unbusy thing,
Nor honey make, nor pair, nor build, nor sing.

SAMUEL TAYLOR COLERIDGE,
from *Work Without Hope*

SUMMER DREAM

(For John and Ann Marie)

Summers were hotter then, it seems to me.
Courting couples walked arm-linked down my street,
Sure that the Depression would always be.
Stockyard smell at night . . . How I loved the heat!
I dreamed often of a house by the lake

And caressing waters in the sunset glow.
Then cruel, wrenching waves through the windows break,
Clutching dragging all happiness below.

And I still yearn for humid summer days
And revel in each thick and steamy night,
In dreams still see the harsh, shattering wave
Crashing towards the house, blotting out the light.
I'm not sure why but things have oddly changed:
Now the waves fall back and the house remains.

ANDREW M. GREELEY

SIGNS OF SUMMER

Minutes into Michigan, just off Route 12, immediately over the railroad line, stands the white arch welcoming people into the village of summer homes by the lake. The arch has been there for as long as most can remember, always freshly painted, with the sign swinging from the top identifying the community. The village heralds itself in big, black letters, with no excuses, as "Grand Beach." It proclaimed itself thus even during the years when Lake Michigan's encroaching waters kept the beach from being grand either in size or majesty—kept it, in fact, practically nonexistent.

But now there is beach. And it is grand again—or still.

There were years in my childhood when the signage was not as consistent. Some years, the crew in our Rambler wagon would say "Good-bye!" to Indiana and "Hello!" to Michigan; cross the tracks; slip under the arch; and wind past the golf course, tennis courts, and old playground without ever being officially alerted to the grandeur ahead. The swaying sign simply wouldn't be there. Other years, it would appear, mysteriously, at night, just before the Fourth of July. One of us would spot it during the daily trip back over the tracks and across Route

12 to the neon-signed "Beer-Wine-To-Go" store, which stocked un-advertised milk and candy for the summer set.

The summer that my cousins came to stay for a week, the Grand Beach sign was not up. Not yet. My aunts and uncles came with my cousins. We slept, nine of us girls, ages three to eleven, in the corner room upstairs, with an old-fashioned washstand and a real vanity table all to ourselves. Two pull-out-and-up trundle beds and one twin were pushed against each other and against the row of windows overlooking the dune and the lake. It was impossible to tell where one bed began, one cover ended, and which arm or leg resembled which side of the family. The floorboards creaked, the windows rattled, and the vanity mirrors threatened to shatter when we jumped, almost simultaneously, onto the wide bed. We pressed our faces against the screens to watch fireflies we'd been chasing minutes earlier. We listened to the waves and let the mild breeze of summer caress our sticky, sunburned noses and peeling shoulders. We smelled, even after a shower, of quintessential Midwest summer: Coppertone, Bactine, Off.

We were exhausted after the long days of somersaulting through water, rearranging sand dunes, and steering inflatable rafts over the bounding Lake Michigan main. Still, it took us forever to fall asleep. Someone always had sand between her toes, which made its way onto the cotton sheets. Organized drills to clear everyone off the big bed and shove the sand onto the floor were rarely successful. I feared getting seasick from all the tossing and turning and scratching of mosquito bites on board. An occasional spider would make us scream—first in fright and then because it sounded great—until an aunt or uncle or parent would come in to kill it and threaten us. We'd manage a minute at most of angelic silence until someone would open for discussion the issue of whether it was really right to eat the charred skin of a baked potato. We'd observed one branch of the family doing so calmly at dinner.

"How come you don't throw up?"

"Well, how come you guys put the sugar on the cornflakes before the milk?"

"Our dad says."

It was our first introduction to different organizational systems: Cultural Anthropology 101.

One night, the cousins had finally, miraculously, settled down to sleep—all except me and many crickets. I had determined, after endless experimentation, that if I lay perfectly still on my sunburned stomach and pulled up my legs so that I would not be kicked as often, I might fall asleep. I drew my legs under me slowly, but moving one set of limbs set off machinery down the line. My neighbor turned over, hers stole the covers, and hers awoke startled from a dream about ladybugs flying away home. The questionable spring on the middle trundle bed gave out loudly, like metal folding chairs collapsing on tile. The mattress and its occupants plummeted to floor level, while the cousins wedged into cracks to the right and left rolled over into the valley of the baby doll pajamas.

After a chorus of shrieks, we were all awake enough to determine that some had, in fact, only fallen a few feet onto a mattress and each other. The rest of us crawled over to the edge of the rift and, with condolences and openmouthed, wide-eyed surprise, helped relive the exhilaration of the moment. The noise, the shock, the timing, the fear, and the happy ending made the drama worth savoring. But just as my sister warned, "They're coming!" the rest of the household, big and small and the boy cousins, burst into the room.

Thank God for the littlest cousins of both sexes, who, overcome, turned on tears just in time. The aunts, uncles, and parents who'd rushed down the hall rehearsing alternate reactions of fear and anger ("I told you so!"), left the room minutes later. They bestowed on us one of childhood's greatest gifts: it was "no one's fault."

With that blessing, sleep could wait. We discovered that at least nine of us and our pillows could squeeze into the now-hidden valley. Once again, there were endless schemes to talk about, to plan for. Though most of us had chattered together all day (some had pouted alone all afternoon), the dark cover of night protected secrets that we longed to create and share. We had countless mysteries to explore with those whose blood we'd trusted before we were born. That night, there was the enigma of missing names . . . of Grand Beach.

Just where was that sign that had been included in the directions my parents had given to the aunts and uncles? Two branches of the family had gotten lost because they couldn't see it anywhere. Maybe this place had no name. My sisters and I insisted: we were all in Grand Beach. There really was a sign over the arch. Or ought to be.

"Someone just took it."

"Maybe someone took it to change the name. Someone in that

haunted house"—a dilapidated, Sears-catalogue special—"could be thinking up a terrifying new name."

"Nobody would ever come here again."

"Only witches would look in the mirrors, and the vanity would burst into flames!"

It couldn't be true. But to protect Grand Beach, vacations in general, and our future in particular, we made up a code name for Grand Beach as we knew it. Each of us blurted out different inspired choices, laughing more at ourselves than at the strange combinations and then hurriedly muffling our hysteria with pillows. Gasping for air, we finally agreed on the perfect name: Blisterfield Sandgilly. We agreed because the cousin who dreamt it up kept repeating it over and over until it spun through the sound waves and the night air with a life of its own, meaning not only this place and this week of our childhood but the giggles that couldn't be quieted each time she said it. We swore to secrecy and hoped that by morning, my three-year-old sister would remember what a secret was or at least forget the new Grand Beach code name.

She neither remembered nor forgot, but she couldn't pronounce the magical name. Each time she tried to utter the delicious sounds, the boy cousins looked at her strangely or told her to go away. The aunts and uncles worried that maybe she had, after all, gotten a concussion the night before. Her girl cousins and sisters, however, blew bubbles of laughter under the water, splashed ferociously any who looked about to burst with the secret, and ran down the dune with her in tow, crying into the rushing wind, "Blisterfield Sandgilly!"

My cousins left under the arch two days later, joining the Sunday-evening caravan back to the city. We separated the beds and had the vanity and rafts to ourselves. The next week, the Grand Beach sign was hoisted to its glory, as July began the summer season in earnest. I made a mental note during a trip to Beer-Wine-To-Go that "Blisterfield Sandgilly" would never fit on that sign.

Blisterfield Sandgilly didn't really fit anywhere outside of the magical circle and cherished place that inspired it. Later that summer, back home, my cousins came to visit. With their permission, we shared the secret of Blisterfield Sandgilly with neighbor friends down the block, all of us jumping to its rhythms on the hot August sidewalk. It still sounded glorious to let the words roll loudly and deliciously off our tongues. We were zealous, generous missionaries, eager to share family secrets with friends.

The next day, though, my sisters and I suffered as the kids across the street taunted us with the name we'd created as sign and symbol. The neighbors who usually played with us had crossed sides with whimsy and betrayed our code to bullies. My three-year-old sister cried at the grating pitch the uninitiated gave to the sounds we loved.

So we went inside to quench righteous indignation with Kool-Aid and to wonder when we might see our friends from school again. The seasons, at least, would not fail us, would wind around eventually to June and Grand Beach. The world, as it had been doing so far, would get bigger for us before it got smaller. Even in our sorrow, we sensed that, along the way, we might pick up new friends, new confidantes. There had to be people outside our family who understood about whispering in darkness, about stringing sounds together so that words could swing from arches and reverberate with joy.

EILEEN DURKIN

ODE TO AUTUMN

Season of mists and mellow fruitfulness!
    Close bosom-friend of the maturing sun;
Conspiring with him how to load and bless
    With fruit the vines that round the thatch-eaves run;
To bend with apples the mossed cottage-trees,
    And fill all fruit with ripeness to the core;
        To swell the gourd, and plump the hazel shells
With a sweet kernel; to set budding more,
    And still more, later flowers for the bees,
    Until they think warm days will never cease,
        For summer has o'er-brimmed their clammy cells.

Who hath not seen thee oft amid thy store?
  Sometimes whoever seeks abroad may find
Thee sitting careless on a granary floor,
  Thy hair soft-lifted by the winnowing wind;
Or on a half-reaped furrow sound asleep,
  Drowsed with the fume of poppies, while thy hook
    Spares the next swath and all its twined flowers:
And sometimes like a gleaner thou dost keep
  Steady thy laden head across a brook;
  Or by a cider-press, with patient look,
    Thou watchest the last oozings hours by hours.

Where are the songs of spring? Ay, where are they?
  Think not of them, thou has thy music, too,—
While barred clouds bloom the soft-dying day,
  And touch the stubble-plains with rosy hue;
Then in a wailful choir the small gnats mourn
  Among the river sallows, borne aloft
    Or sinking as the light wind lives or dies;
And full-grown lambs loud bleat from hilly bourn;
  Hedge-crickets sing; and now with treble soft
The redbreast whistles from a garden croft;
  And gathering swallow twitter in the skies.

JOHN KEATS

The sky and the sea—air, water, the rain, the clouds—are ever-present reminders that growth in all things, including love, must be nurtured.

A WINDY DAY

My soul is awakened, my spirit is soaring
And carried aloft on the wings of the breeze;
For above and around me the wild wind is roaring,
Arousing to rapture the earth and the seas.

The long withered grass in the sunshine is glancing.
The bare trees are tossing their branches on high;
The dead leaves beneath them, are merrily dancing.
The white clouds are scudding across the blue sky.

I wish I could see how the ocean is lashing
The foam of its billows to whirlwinds of spray;
I wish I could see how its proud waves are dashing,
And hear the wild roar of their thunder to-day!

ANNE BRONTË

THE CLOUD

I bring fresh showers for the thirsting flowers
    From the seas and the streams;
I bear light shade for the leaves when laid
    In their noonday dreams.
From my wings are shaken the dews that waken
    The sweet buds every one,
When rocked to rest on their mother's breast,
    As she dances about the sun.
I wield the flail of the lashing hail,
    And whiten the green plains under,
And then again I dissolve it in rain,
    And laugh as I pass in thunder.

I sift the snow on the mountains below,
    And their great pines groan aghast;
And all the night 'tis my pillow white,
    While I sleep in the arms of the blast.
Sublime on the towers of my skiey bowers,
    Lightning my pilot sits;
In a cavern under is fettered the thunder,
    It struggles and howls at fits;
Over earth and ocean, with gentle motion,
    This pilot is guiding me,
Lured by the love of the genii that move
    In the depths of the purple sea;
Over the rills, and the crags, and the hills,
    Over the lakes and the plains,
Wherever he dream, under mountain or stream,
    The Spirit he loves remains;
And I all the while bask in Heaven's blue smile,
    Whilst he is dissolving in rains.

The sanguine Sunrise, with his meteor eyes,
    And his burning plumes outspread,
Leaps on the back of my sailing rack,
    When the morning star shines dead;
As on the jag of a mountain crag,
    Which an earthquake rocks and swings,
An eagle alit one moment may sit
    In the light of its golden wings.
And when Sunset may breathe, from the lit sea beneath,
    Its ardours of rest and of love,
And the crimson pall of eve may fall
    From the depth of Heaven above,
With wings folded I rest, on mine aëry nest,
    As still as a brooding dove.

That orbèd maiden with white fire laden,
    Whom mortals call the Moon,
Glides glimmering o'er my fleece-like floor,
    By the midnight breezes strewn;

And wherever the beat of her unseen feet,
    Which only the angels hear,
May have broken the woof of my tent's thin roof,
    The stars peep behind her and peer;
And I laugh to see them whirl and flee,
    Like a swarm of golden bees,
When I widen the rent in my wind-built tent,
    Till the calm rivers, lakes, and seas,
Like strips of the sky fallen through me on high,
    Are each paved with the moon and these.

I bind the Sun's throne with a burning zone,
    And the Moon's with a girdle of pearl;
The volcanoes are dim, and the stars reel and swim,
    When the whirlwinds my banner unfurl.
From cape to cape, with a bridge-like shape,
    Over a torrent sea,
Sunbeam-proof, I hang like a roof,
    The mountains its columns be.
The triumphal arch through which I march
    With hurricane, fire, and snow,
When the Powers of the air are chained to my chair,
    In the million-colored bow;
The sphere-fire above it soft colours wove,
    While the moist Earth was laughing below.

I am the daughter of Earth and Water,
    And the nursling of the Sky;
I pass through the pores of the ocean and shores;
    I change, but I cannot die.
For after the rain when with never a stain
    The pavilion of Heaven is bare,
And the winds and sunbeams with their convex gleams
    Build up the blue dome of air,
I silently laugh at my own cenotaph,
    And out of the caverns of rain,
Like a child from the womb, like a ghost from the tomb,
    I arise and unbuild it again.

PERCY BYSSHE SHELLEY

IT IS A BEAUTEOUS EVENING, CALM AND FREE

It is a beauteous evening, calm and free,
The holy time is quiet as a Nun
Breathless with adoration; the broad sun
Is sinking down in its tranquility;
The gentleness of heaven broods o'er the Sea;
Listen! the mighty Being is awake,
And doth with his eternal motion make
A sound like thunder everlastingly.
Dear Child! dear Girl! that walkest with me here,
If thou appear untouched by solemn thought.
Thy nature is not therefore less divine:
Thou liest in Abraham's bosom all the year;
And worshipp'st at the Temple's inner shrine,
God being with thee when we know it not.

WILLIAM WORDSWORTH

UPON THE SAND

Said one man to another, "At the high tide of the sea, long ago, with
the point of my staff I wrote a line upon the sand; and the people still
pause to read it, and they are careful that naught shall erase it."

. . .

And the other man said, "And I too wrote a line upon the sand, but it was at low tide, and the waves of the vast sea washed it away. But tell me, what did you write?"

And the first man answered and said, "I wrote this: 'I am he who is.' But what did you write?"

And the other man said, "This I wrote: 'I am but a drop of this great ocean.' "

KAHLIL GIBRAN,
from *The Wanderer*

We are part of nature and when we reflect on what we share with the rest of the natural world, we ask questions. How did this all come to be? Where is it going? What does it all mean, if indeed it has any meaning? Throughout human history people have tried to answer those questions.

HIAWATHA'S CHILDHOOD

By the shores of Gitche Gumee,
By the shining Big-Sea-Water,
Stood the wigwam of Nokomis,
Daughter of the Moon, Nokomis.
Dark behind it rose the forest,
Rose the black and gloomy pine-trees,

Rose the first with cones upon them;
Bright before it beat the water,
Beat the clear and sunny water,
Beat the shining Big-Sea-Water,
    There the wrinkled old Nokomis
Nursed the little Hiawatha,
Rocked him in his linden cradle,
Bedded soft in moss and rushes,
Safely bound with reindeer sinews;
Stilled his fretful wail by saying,
"Hush! the Naked Bear will hear thee!"
Lulled him into slumber, singing,
"Ewa-yea! my little owlet!
Who is this, that lights the wigwam?
With his great eyes lights the wigwam?
Ewa-yea! My little owlet!"
    Many things Nokomis taught him
Of the stars that shine in heaven;
Showed him Ishkoodah, the comet,
Ishkoodah, with fiery tresses;
Showed the Death-Dance of the spirits,
Warriors with their plumes and war-clubs,
Flaring far away to northward
In the frosty nights of winter;
Showed the broad white road in heaven,
Pathway of the ghosts, the shadows,
Running straight across the heavens,
Crowded with the ghosts, the shadows.
    At the door on summer evenings,
Sat the little Hiawatha;
Heard the whispering of the pine-trees,
Heard the lapping of the waters,
Sounds of music, words of wonder;
"Minne-wawa!" said the pine-trees,
"Mudway-aushka!" said the water.
    Saw the fire-fly Wah-wah-taysee,
Flitting through the dusk of evening,
With the twinkle of its candle
Lighting up the brakes and bushes,

And he sang the song of children
Sang the song Nokomis taught him:
"Wah-wah-taysee, little fire-fly,
Little flitting, white-fire insect,
Little, dancing, white-fire creature,
Light me with your little candle,
Ere upon my bed I lay me,
Ere in sleep I close my eyelids!"
　　Saw the moon rise from the water,
Rippling, rounding from the water,
Saw the flecks and shadows on it,
Whispered, "What is that, Nokomis?"
And the good Nokomis answered:
"Once a warrior, very angry,
Seized his grandmother, and threw her
Up into the sky at midnight;
Right against the moon he threw her;
'Tis her body that you see there."
　　Saw the rainbow in the heaven,
In the eastern sky the rainbow,
Whispered, "What is that, Nokomis?"
And the good Nokomis answered:
" 'Tis the heaven of flowers you see there;
All the wild-flowers of the forest,
All the lilies of the prairie,
When on earth they fade and perish,
Blossom in that heaven above us."
　　When he heard the owls at midnight,
Hooting, laughing in the forest,
"What is that?" he cried in terror;
"What is that," he said, "Nokomis?"
And the good Nokomis answered:
"That is but the owl and owlet,
Talking in their native language,
Talking, scolding at each other."
　　Then the little Hiawatha
Learned of every bird its language,
Learned their names and all their secrets,
How they built their nests in summer,

Where they hid themselves in winter,
Talked with them whene'er he met them,
Called them "Hiawatha's Chickens."
Of all beasts he learned the language,
Learned their names and all their secrets,
How the beavers built their lodges,
Where the squirrels hid their acorns,
How the reindeer ran so swiftly,
Why the rabbit was so timid,
Talked with them whene'er he met them,
Called them "Hiawatha's Brothers."

HENRY WADSWORTH LONGFELLOW

ODE: INTIMATIONS OF IMMORTALITY FROM RECOLLECTIONS OF EARLY CHILDHOOD

'The Child is father of the Man;
And I could wish my days to be
Bound each to each by natural piety.'

There was a time when meadow, grove, and stream,
    The earth, and every common sight,
    To me did seem
    Apparelled in celestial light,
    The glory and the freshness of a dream.
    It is not now as it hath been of yore;—
      Turn whereso'er I may,
      By night or day,
The things which I have seen I now can see no more.

    The Rainbow comes and goes,
    And lovely is the Rose,

The Moon doth with delight
Look round her when the heavens are bare,
Waters on a starry night
Are beautiful and fair;
The sunshine is a glorious birth;
But yet I know, wher'er I go,
That there hath past away a glory from the earth.

Now, while the birds thus sing a joyous song,
And while the young lambs bound
As to the tabor's sound,
To me alone there came a thought of grief:
A timely utterance gave that thought relief,
And I again am strong:
The cataracts blow their trumpets from the steep;
No more shall grief of mine the season wrong;
I hear the Echoes through the mountains throng,
The Winds come to me from the fields of sleep,
And all the earth is gay;
Land and sea
Give themselves up to jollity,
And with the heart of May
Doth every Beast keep holiday;—
Thou Child of Joy,
Shout round me, let me hear thy shouts, thou happy Shepherd-boy!

Ye blessed Creatures, I have heard the call
Ye to each other make; I see
The heavens laugh with you in your jubilee;
My heart is at your festival,
My head hath its coronal,
The fullness of your bliss, I feel—I feel it all.
Oh evil day! if I were sullen
While Earth herself is adorning
This sweet May-morning,
And the Children are culling
On every side,
In a thousand valleys far and wide,
Fresh flowers; while the sun shines warm,

And the Babe leaps up on his Mother's arm:—
    I hear, I hear, with joy I hear!
    —But there's a tree, of many, one,
    A single Field which I have looked upon,
Both of them speak of something that is gone:
    The Pansy at my feet
    Doth the same tale repeat:
    Whither is fled the visionary gleam?
Where is it now, the glory and the dream?

    Our birth is but a sleep and a forgetting:
The Soul that rises with us, our life's Star,
    Hath had elsewhere its setting,
    And cometh from afar:
    Not in entire forgetfulness,
And not in utter nakedness,
But trailing clouds of glory do we come
    From God, who is our home:
    Heaven lies about us in our infancy!
    Shades of the prison-house begin to close
    Upon the growing Boy,
But He beholds the light, and whence it flows,
    He sees it in his joy;
The youth, who daily farther from the east
    Must travel, still is Nature's Priest,
    And by the vision splendid
    Is on his way attended;
At length the Man perceives it die away,
And fade into the light of common day.

Earth fills her lap with pleasures of her own;
    Yearnings she hath in her own natural kind,
And, even with something of a Mother's mind,
    And no unworthy aim,
    The homely Nurse doth all she can
To make her Foster-child, her Inmate Man,
    Forget the glories he hath known,
And the imperial palace whence he came.

Behold the Child among his new-born blisses,
　　A six years' Darling of a pigmy size!
See, where 'mid work of his own hand he lies,
　　Fretted by sallies of his mother's kisses,
With light upon him from his father's eyes!
　　See at his feet some little plan or chart,
Some fragment from his dream of human life,
　　Shaped by himself with newly-learned art;
　　A wedding or a festival,
　　A mourning or a funeral;
　　And this hath now his heart,
　　And unto this he frames his song:
　　Then will he fit his tongue
To dialogues of business, love, or strife;
　　But it will not be long
　　Ere this be thrown aside,
　　And with new joy and pride
　　The little Actor cons another part;
Filling from time to time his "humorous stage"
　　With all the Persons, down to palsied Age,
　　That Life brings with her in her equipage;
　　As if his whole vocation
　　Were endless imitation.

Thou, whose exterior semblance doth belie
　　Thy Soul's immensity;
Thou best Philosopher, who yet dost keep
　　Thy heritage, thou Eye among the blind,
That, deaf and silent, read'st the eternal deep,
　　Haunted forever by the eternal mind,—
　　Mighty Prophet! Seer blest!
　　On whom those truths do rest,
Which we are toiling all our lives to find,
In darkness lost, the darkness of the grave;
　　Thou, over whom thy Immortality
Broods like the Day, a master o'er a Slave,
　　A Presence which is not to be put by;
Thou little Child yet glorious in the might
Of heaven-born freedom on thy being's height,

Why with such earnest pains dost thou provoke
        The years to bring the inevitable yoke,
        Thus blindly with thy blessedness at strife?
Full soon thy Soul shall have her earthly freight,
        And custom lie upon thee with a weight,
        Heavy as frost, and deep almost as life!

        O joy! that in our embers
        Is something that doth live,
        That nature yet remembers
        What was so fugitive!
The thought of our past years in me doth breed
        Perpetual benediction: not indeed
For that which is most worthy to be blest;
        Delight and liberty, the simple creed
        Of Childhood, whether busy or at rest,
With new-fledged hope still fluttering in his breast:—
        Not for these I raise
        The song of thanks and praise;
But for those obstinate questionings
        Of sense and outward things,
        Fallings from us, vanishings;
        Blank misgivings of a Creature
        Moving about in worlds not realised,
High instincts before which our mortal Nature
Did tremble like a guilty Thing surprised:
        But for those first affections,
        Those shadowy recollections,
        Which, be they what they may,
Are yet the fountain-light of all our day,
Are yet a master-light of all our seeing;
Uphold us, cherish, and have power to make
Our noisy years seem moments in the being
        Of the eternal Silence: truths that wake,
        To perish never:
Which neither listlessness, nor mad endeavour,
        Nor Man nor Boy,
Nor all that is at enmity with joy,
        Can utterly abolish or destroy!

Hence in a season of calm weather
    Though inland far we be,
Our Souls have sight of that immortal sea
    Which brought us hither,
Can in a moment travel thither,
    And see the Children sport upon the shore,
And hear the mighty waters rolling evermore.

Then sing, ye Birds, sing, sing a joyous song!
    And let the young Lambs bound
    As to the tabor's sound!
We in thought will join your throng,
    Ye that pipe and ye that play,
Ye that through your hearts to-day
    Feel the gladness of the May!
What though the radiance which was once so bright
    Be now for ever taken from my sight,
    Though nothing can bring back the hour
Of splendour in the grass, of glory in the flower;
    We will grieve not, rather find
    Strength in what remains behind;
    In the primal sympathy
    Which having been must ever be;
In the soothing thoughts that spring
    Out of human suffering;
In the faith that looks through death,
In years that bring the philosophic mind.

And O, ye Fountains, Meadows, Hills, and Groves,
    Forbode not any severing of our loves!
Yet in my heart of hearts I feel your might;
I only have relinquished one delight
To live beneath your more habitual sway.
I love the Brooks which down their channels fret,
    Even more than when I tripped lightly as they;
The innocent brightness of a new-born Day
    Is lovely yet;
The Clouds that gather round the setting sun
    Do take a sober colouring from an eye

That hath kept watch o'er man's mortality;
Another race hath been, and other palms are won.
Thanks to the human heart by which we live,
Thanks to its tenderness, its joys, and fears,
To me the meanest flower that blows can give
Thoughts that do often lie too deep for tears.

WILLIAM WORDSWORTH

SOME KEEP THE SABBATH
GOING TO CHURCH

Some keep the Sabbath going to church;
I keep it staying at home,
With a bobolink for a chorister,
And an orchard for a dome.

Some keep the Sabbath in surplice;
I just wear my wings,
And instead of tolling the bell for church,
Our little sexton sings.

God preaches,—a noted clergyman,—
And the sermon is never long;
So instead of getting to heaven at last,
I'm going all along!

EMILY DICKINSON

My heart leaps up when I behold
A rainbow in the sky;
So was it when my life began;
So is it now I am a man;
So be it when I shall grow old,
Or let me die!

WILLIAM WORDSWORTH,
from "My Heart Leaps Up When I Behold"

Chapter Twelve

A Place to Belong

I know not what course others may take; but as for me
Give me liberty or give me death.
PATRICK HENRY

When I shall be dead, tell the kingdom of the earth
That I loved it much more than I ever dared say.
BERNANOS

We live in a variety of places—a dwelling, a community (city, suburb, or rural), a nation, a world, a universe. We belong to places—a school, a religious community, a club. Of some of these we would say, "I love this." Of others, we give at most a passing interest to its significance for our lives. Often it is only when a threat to the place becomes evident that we realize we love it.

In either case, our love for the places in our lives is both similar and different than our love for the people in our lives. When we love a place, that love, like all loves, takes us outside our self-centered desires, out of ourselves. The place becomes important to our sense of happiness. We think about it. We remember how it became important.

We care what happens to it. We will do all in our power to protect it from harm. We might even sing its praises to others. We will make sacrifices, even, in some cases, of our lives, to ensure its survival.

While we have a love for special places, places do not return that love. They do not do anything to make themselves more lovable. They provide shelter and protection from those who might wish to harm us. They offer us a place of rest, a place to enjoy. They are there for us to love or ignore. Often, without even realizing it, we form a special relationship with a place.

At times, as in a love affair, we can't explain to others why we love a particular place. They might look at our neighborhood or our city or our vacation spot or our country and find nothing lovable about it.

At other times, just like a lover, we are irrational in our love of place. We see others, who become outsiders to our minds, wanting to rob us of our place. Protection of our space or expansion of our space has been the motive for wars throughout human history. The wars of the twentieth century, as well as the many ethnic and religious wars of the present century, have their roots in what is considered infringement on space that has taken on a sacred character, often to both sides in the battle.

Certain places are like neglected lovers. Without the land, the air, the lakes and sea, the universe, we could not survive. As we begin the twenty-first century with all its technological marvels, we are more aware that our place is not just our house, neighborhood, community, city, or country. We are citizens of a world and a universe.

We often are inattentive lovers of the community of our world. The starving child in the Sudan or Bangladesh and a mistreated child in our local community are a blot on the dream that humans will ever be able to build a world community. The pollution of lakes and streams affect more than just the people who live near them. Wars with the intent to totally destroy an enemy, even when they are in far-off places, undermine our hopes for world peace.

Human have always looked upon the universe with a sense of awe. Remains from ancient sites reveal that the sun, the moon, the stars, and the elements all played a role in human culture quite early on. The great leaps in understanding this universe, especially with the work of astrophysicists and the voyages of astronauts, along with the imaginations that produce *Star Wars* and *Star Trek* increase the awe. We live in a very, very ancient universe.

The stories, poems, and selections in this chapter take us to the variety of places in which humans dwell. They reveal a side of a unique love affair open to everyone.

A dwelling place, whether it be a palace or a hut or a stone cave or a Bedouin tent in the middle of nowhere gives, at a minimum, the shelter we need to protect ourselves from the elements of nature. As humans became more domesticated and lived longer, the dwelling became a place for families to congregate, where traditions are passed on, where the gods are acknowledged, where love begins to grow.

Our love of our country, of our native land and our sorrows when we are separated from it, tell of a love that, even after many years, and sometimes down through generations, continues to hold sway on us.

O beautiful for spacious skies for amber waves of grain
For purple mountain majesties above the fruited plain
America! America! God shed his grace on thee
And crown thy good with brotherhood from sea to shining sea.

KATHARINE LEE BATES,
from "America the Beautiful"

This land is your land, this land is my land
From California, to the New York Island
From the redwood forest, to the Gulf Stream waters
This land was made for you and me.

WOODY GUTHRIE,
from "This Land Is Your Land"

THE LAY OF THE LAST MINSTREL

Breathes there the man with soul so dead
Who never to himself hath said:
    "This is my own, my native land"?
Whose heart hath ne'er within him burned
As home his footsteps he hath turned,
    From wandering on a foreign strand?
If such there breathe, go mark him well;
For him no minstrel raptures swell;
High though his titles, proud his name,
Boundless his wealth as wish can claim;
Despite those titles, power and pelf,
The wretch concentrated all in self,
Living, shall forfeit renown
And, doubly, dying shall go down
To the vile dust from whence he sprung,
Unwept, unhonored, and unsung.

SIR WALTER SCOTT

O Son of God, it would be sweet, a lovely journey,
To cross the wave, the fount in flood, and visit Ireland:
    to Eolarg Plain, by Foibne Hill, across Loch Febail,
    and listen there to the matching music of the swans.

Flocks of gulls would fill with pleasure as we sailed swiftly
    Into the welcome of Port na Ferg in our 'Red with Dew.'
I am full of sorrow that I left Ireland when I had my strength
    and then grew tearful and full of sadness in a foreign land.

ATTRIBUTED TO
ST. COLUM CILLE

During times of oppression, the Irish often wrote poetry and songs referring to their country as a woman. A modern poet (a Yank on a visit) celebrates the womanliness of Dublin.

DARK ROSALEEN

O my dark Rosaleen,
Do not sigh, do not weep!
The priests are on the ocean green,

They march along the deep.
There's wine from the royal Pope,
Upon the ocean green;
And Spanish ale shall give you hope,
My dark Rosaleen!
My own Rosaleen!
Shall glad your heart, shall give you hope,
Shall give you health and help, and hope,
My Dark Rosaleen.

Over hills, and through dales,
Have I roamed for your sake;
All yesterday I sailed with sails
On river and on lake.
The Erne, at its highest flood,
I dashed across unseen,
For there was lightning in my blood,
My dark Rosaleen!
My own Rosaleen!
Oh! There was lightning in my blood,
Red lightning, lightened through my blood,
My Dark Rosaleen!

All day long in unrest,
To and fro do I move,
The very soul within my breast
Is wasted for you, love!
The heart in my bosom faints
To think of you, my Queen,
My life of life, my saint of saints,
My dark Rosaleen!
My own Rosaleen!
To hear your sweet and sad complaints,
My life, my love, my saint of saints,
My Dark Rosaleen!

Woe and pain, pain and woe,
Are my lot, night and noon,
To see your bright face clouded so,

Like to the mournful moon.
But yet will I rear your throne
Again in golden sheen;
'Tis you shall reign, shall reign alone,
My dark Rosaleen!
My own Rosaleen!
'Tis you shall have the golden throne,
'Tis you shall reign, shall reign alone,
My Dark Rosaleen!

Over dews, over sands,
Will I fly for your weal:
Your holy, delicate white hands
Shall girdle me with steel.
At home in your emerald bowers,
From morning's dawn to e'en,
You'll pray for me, my flower of flowers,
My dark Rosaleen!
My fond Rosaleen!
You'll think of me your daylight's hours,
My virgin flower, my flower of flowers,
My Dark Rosaleen!

I could scale the blue air,
I could plow the high hills,
Oh, I could kneel all night in prayer,
To heal your many ills!
And one beamy smile from you
Would float like light between
My toils and me, my own, my true,
My dark Rosaleen!
My fond Rosaleen!
Would give me life and soul anew,
A second life, a soul anew,
My Dark Rosaleen!

O! The Erne shall run red
With redundance of blood,
The earth shall rock beneath our tread,

And flames wrap hill and wood,
And gun-peal, and slogan cry
Wake many a glen serene,
Ere you shall fade, ere you shall die,
My dark Rosaleen!
My own Rosaleen!
The Judgment Hour must first be nigh
Ere you can fade, ere you can die,
My Dark Rosaleen!

James Clarence Mangan

Dublin

Some cities are male: my own,
Commodity broker not hog butcher of the world,
Still has broad Slavic shoulders
Beneath his carefully tailored jacket.

But Dublin surely is a woman,
Voluptuous matron in her middle years,
Demanding, attractive, repellent—
This city is Molly Bloom,

Wanton, faithful, prudish, enticing,
Weary, unlaced, experienced,
Quick to reject you, turn you off
And then cradle you in her arms.

Fitzwilliam prim, Ringsend raw,
Sandycove cold, Anna Livia dark
Gandon solemn, Grafton gypsy, Mountjoy mean,
Born in the Liberties, degree from T.C.D.

Asleep when you want to play,
Eager for frolic when you need rest,
Milanese fashions if it suits her whim—
Old clothes when you show her off.

In succession she is all her women:
Gore-Booth, Brigid of Kildare, Seanad,
Maude Gonne, Molly Malone, Delvacheem,
Kathleen Ni Houlihan, and always Mrs. Bloom.

ANDREW M. GREELEY

The American Indians, driven, by governmental decree, from their homelands in the eastern part of the continent to the barren land of the West, cry out in sadness at the loss of their land and the failure of their oppressors to realize the rich heritage they are destroying.

Brother: When you were young, we were strong; we fought by your side; but our arms are now broken. You have grown large; my people have become small. My voice is weak; you can scarcely hear me; it is not the shout of a warrior but the wail of an infant. I have lost it in mourning over the misfortunes of my people. These are their graves, and in those aged pines you hear the ghosts of the departed. Their ashes are here and we have been left to protect them. . . . Here are our dead. Shall we go, and give their bones to the wolves?

CHIEF COBB, CHOCTAW

The vitality of our race still persists. We have not lived for naught. We are the original discoverers of this continent, and the conquerors of it from the animal kingdom, and on it first taught the arts of peace and war and first planted the institutions of virtue, truth, and liberty. The European nations found us here and were made aware that it was possible for man to exist and subsist here. We have given to the European people on this continent our thought forces—the best blood of our ancestors having intermingled with their best statesmen and leading citizens. We have made ourselves an indestructible element in their national history. We have shown that what they believed were arid and desert places were habitable and capable of sustaining millions of people. We have led the vanguard of civilization in our conflicts with them for tribal existence from ocean to ocean. The race that had rendered this service to the other nations of mankind cannot utterly perish.

PLEASANT PORTER

Cities have their own special magic. Memories and stories of these human made places, hint at the powerful hold they have on our imaginations.

When everything else has gone from my brain—the President's name, the state capital, the neighborhoods where I lived, and then my own name and what it was on earth I sought, and then at length the faces of my friends, and finally the faces of my family—when all this has dissolved, what will be left, I believe is topology: the dreaming memory of land as it lay this way and that.

I will see the city poured rolling down the mountain alley like slag, and see the city lights sprinkled and curved around the hills' curves, rows of bonfires winding. At sunset a red light like housefires shines from the narrow hillside windows; the house's bricks burn like glowing coals . . .

In 1753, young George Washington surveyed for the English this point of land where rivers met. To see the forest-blurred lay of the land, he rode his horse to a ridgetop and climbed a tree. He judged it would make a good spot for a fort. And an English fort it became, and a depot for Indian traders to the Ohio Country, and later a French fort and way station to New Orleans.

But it would be another ten years before any settlers lived there on that land where the rivers met, lived to draw in the flowery scent of June rhododendrons with every breath. It would be another ten years before, for the first time on earth, tall men and women lay exhausted in their cabins, sleeping in the sweetness, worn out from planting corn.

ANNIE DILLARD,
from *An American Childhood*

FOR THE SYMBOLICAL CEREMONY OF THE WEDDING OF VENICE AND THE SEA

She was a maiden city, bright and free,
No guile seduced, no force could violate,
And when she took unto herself a mate
She must espouse the everlasting sea

Quoted in *Medieval People*

FOR MY NEIGHBORS — MAGGIE, RICH NORA, PATRICK, LALLY

A city set on a mountain top cannot be hidden.
MATTHEW *5:14*

In Chicago our God lurks everywhere—
In the elevated train's husky roar,
Beside the blinking lights of intensive care,
In the clamor of the soybean trading floor,
With those who suffer poverty and fright,
In the humid mist of summer by the lake,
On the Ryan through an icy winter night,
With a young widow weeping at a wake.

A city of beauty, hilarity, and pain,
Boundless energy and permanent unrest.
A terrifying, troubled, hopeful place—
Its challenges intricate and arcane,

Its opportunity . . . ah, the very best:
To be an unclouded light of love and grace!

ANDREW M. GREELEY

Hangchow and Sugui
Shang yeu t'ang,
Hia yeu Su Hang
(There's Paradise above, 'tis true
But here below we've Hang and Su.)

Quoted in *Medieval People*

S*pecial places of childhood and of family gatherings are never forgotten.*

TWIN LAKES

A sad bell clangs that suppertime is near
And the fat man with his dizzy jokes
Feet still dangling from the dark wooden pier
A castle hidden among the giant oaks
Enchanted wonder, great endless silver sheets
Smooth waters sliced by darting speedboat wakes

Gravel path and joyous sands beneath my feet
Faces of lost friends—summertime at Twin Lakes
Wonder, surprise, joy, magic do not last;
Weep little boy for Youth and What Might Have Been.
Search not for sad sweet relics of the past
It's too late, you can't go home again
Old friends, dark castle, and magic silver lake
Oft found in dreams but lost when I awake

ANDREW M. GREELEY

THE LAKE

Oh I should have known you'd be
    showing off.
Your bag of tricks never seems wanting
    and today you outdid yourself.
Thirty years ago, charm, mystery, placid
    episodes and passionate tantrums
    resided within your majestic body
    and were singularly displayed
    according to your whim.
I envied the manner in which you
    commanded attention then.
Even today, the youthful beauty and
    energy which surged within my
    being in bygone days, is ebbing toward
    unknown shores, while you bold
    beauty and playfulness show no
    reluctance, no shame.
I envy you Lake, and thank you.

NANCY WEST

THE CAMELOTS OF OUR LIVES

The word *prairie* was brought by the French to describe the broad grassy tracts of land settlers discovered on the frontiers of the Midwest. As children growing up in Midwestern cities of the thirties and forties, we used that word to describe what adults simply labeled *empty* lots. But I'm here to say that neither the settlers nor the adults ever knew the magic that we found season after season in those little untended Camelots!

In my case—raised on the West Side of Chicago during the Depression—there was little of today's organized fun for children. Ah, but those prairies. To the untrained eye, nothing more than empty plots neither bank nor owner could afford to develop. To us, however, living fantasylands which changed faces throughout the year.

Each January the cycle began in the same way. My friends and I would happily drag the discarded Christmas tree to the prairie. Within days the pile grew to about twenty feet of browning boughs that had served their noble purpose. On the appointed night the local fire department would light this postsolstice pyre. To them it was solving a refuse problem. To those of us who knew better, it was the annual ritual by which the gloom that followed the holidays was mystically dispelled in the great fire's glow.

And the ritual continued, because within the next few days the firemen used their hoses to flood the cleared prairie. Suddenly an ice-skating rink as grand and glorious as any Olympic Hall. Well, not to the firefighters who did it just to keep us out of trouble, but again, we knew better and savored those frosty days and nights together for weeks to come.

Winter's frozen grip on our young lives inevitably loosened about March, and then, as if according to some unwritten tribal calendar, the prairie took on a new role. Kiting. Local candy stores and drugstores featured the latest kites and we felt instinctively obligated to buy and boast the best our nickels and dimes could afford. Why on the prairie?

Because where else could you find the proper takeoff and fly-time space on March's windy days.

March quickly gave way to April when all over America the crack of bats proclaimed the new baseball season. At our age and skill level, the sixteen-inch softball games were the next best thing and, yes, the prairie was the appointed place. With genetically encoded precision, we paced off the baselines, wedged in mounds and markers, then launched a schedule of after-school and Saturday games that continued through about June. This season of the prairie was mostly a boys' domain back in those more sexist times, although there were always girls to impress or be impressed along the grassy sidelines.

As June and July grew, so did the height of the prairie grass. Usually that meant baseball games gave way to those that thrive best in hidden terrain. And so the hot summer months on our prairies tended to feature cowboys-and-Indians or war games. As I look back it still amazes me how unspoken tradition passed on the rules of these unpatented games. Somehow everyone just knew what they were.

All too quickly, the lazy hazy days of summer surrendered to the new school year. My friends and I unlocked yet another facet to this childhood fantasyland. Now, with the grass thinning and browning, it suddenly became a football field. And, oh, how we rushed home from school to get in all four quarters of the contests before the shortening days left our wondrous gridiron in unplayable shadows.

Halloween was the next major transition point in the prairie's twelve-month life cycle. On this most eerie of nights, boys and girls alike made it our disembarkation point. That meant hurrying through dinner, putting on the oldest oddest clothes we could call a costume, then dashing to the prairie where we could engage in the ancient custom of selecting neighborhood targets for our prankish imaginations.

Halloween's end pretty much meant the end of the prairie for the next few months. With days too short and weather too unpredictable, there was a collective pause among our ranks as we looked ahead to the excitement of Thanksgiving and the wonder of Christmas. Once those seasonal passages had been completed, the prairie's barrenness once more gave way to its annual post-Christmas aura. . . .

JACK B. SPATAFORA,
from *Empty Lots*

FRONT PORCH

Quiet were the streets, peaceful summer nights
On tottering chairs youthful experts all
We solved for the world many ancient fights
Precisely which ones I cannot quite recall
With root beer we sipped, unread, Marx and Freud
We nibbled on law and love and God
And potato chips, our Catholic passions buoyed
We charge ahead youthful energy unawed
So easy 'tween two wars our youthful dreams
For those days, coming alive, memory sighs
Gone, driven on the wind, only nightmare screams
Noisy are the crickets under humid skies
The picture fades, I watch time's curtain fall
Who were they? Odd, I cannot quite recall

ANDREW M. GREELEY

SURVIVOR'S GRACE

Out the cottage window we gaze in wonder at the expanse,
Gorse bush, Clew Bay, and Achill Island.
We are voyeurs of West Mayo,
Sensing mystery between the elements.
The wind speaks, rushed, between Croagh Patrick,
Round Old Heard, and the sea.

Dew reveals images, momentarily framed between the dawn and the
day.
You feel the setting sun's colors streak upon the clouds,
Spread like wings between the stars and the fields.
Elemental experiences transform fragments of time, place, into history,
Catalyst of the mind, they awaken us to our stories.

"I am a survivor," you say.
Restless, city bred child, uprooted,
Fosters instincts on a train to the east,
By boat to The West. Roots embraced
The rocky fields of Cullonaughton, as Tir na nÓg.
"I would have farmed this land," you said.
Fingers grown thick, and arms muscled.
Under this western sky you would wrestle the earth,
Then rest upon a wall, and wonder
About tomorrow. But circumstances displaced the dream,
And you returned. A spade blade wedged under a rock
Remains there, as a symbol.

Heart and mind became your tools to survive. Education,
Work ethic, forgotten memories, and a wit dry and slick.
You devised and built, without plans, a model.
You envisioned, without experience, a foundation of strength,
And created influences, as father, lover, poet, and friend.
Unbending faith survived unending tests of sickness,
Forgiveness, and hope.

On a hill in Kilsalagh, in a nave in Old St. Patrick's, we celebrate
A survivor's grace. Manifest in creative ancestral wisdom,
Nurtured in the effort of self-improvement, and spiritual growth.
Revealed in the microcosm of family and friends, as love.

DAN DURKIN

The many places where we belong and that fill us with awe and wonder and a love, often rooted in our unbreakable attachment to them, confront us with questions about the ultimate meaning of life. Neither religion nor sciences supply ultimate, rational explanations. Each invites us to continue our search so we may find answers. Stories cause us to consider our own attitudes and behaviors.

There is a secular world and a holy world, secular worlds and holy worlds. These words contradict one another. The contradiction, of course, is subjective. In our limited perceptions we cannot reconcile the sacred and the secular, we cannot harmonize their contradictions. Yet at the pinnacle of the universe they are reconciled, at the site of the holy of holies

from *The Essential Kabbalah*

If I could, I'd give every child a terrestrial globe. . . .
    If possible, even a globe that would light up,
In the hope of opening those young eyes
    As wide as they will go. . . .

DOM HELDER CAMARA

A STORY

Once upon a time, long, long ago, there was a great king in the Kingdom of Kerry in the West of Ireland named Fergus MacDiarmud UiDonal (McDermot O'Donnell, if you wish). He was a great and good and wise and brave king and he ruled his people justly and wisely. There was peace and prosperity in the whole Kingdom of Kerry during the half century he ruled and his people called him Fergus the Good.

But at last he grew old as we all must and his health failed and he knew he was going to die. So he summoned his councilors and his warriors and his poets and his priests and ordered his servants to carry him out to the meadow in front of his ring fort. There he said a tearful goodbye to his wife of fifty years and his children and his grandchildren and even his little great-grandaugther, a blond-haired toddler about three years old.

Then as life was slipping away he looked up at the green hills and the blue sky and the golden fields and the silver lakes of the Kingdom of Kerry and loved all the kingdom and all its people. Finally, just as he commended his soul to God, he scooped up in his right hand a clump of thick, rich Kerry turf.

Well, the next thing he knew he was at the gates of a big city with great ivory walls and a big gold-and-silver gate. In front of the gate was a man, dressed in white robes and wearing a triple crown, sitting at an IBM PC AT computer, with a fishing rod next to it.

"And who would you be," says your man Simon Peter, alias Pope Peter I, "and what would you be wanting from us?"

"Well," says the king, respectful, but not afraid, "I'm Fergus MacDiarmud UiDonal, king of Kerry, and if it's all the same to you, I wouldn't mind if you let me into that city."

"UiDonal, is it? Well, now, let me see." Your man called up his Lotus 1-2-3 and punched in an entry. He made a mistake—infallibility does not apply to operating a PC—corrected it, and touched the

ENTER key. "Ah, yes, your majesty, we have a long record on you here in our data base. And most of it's good, very good indeed. A few wild moments when you were young, but, sure, Himself forgave them long before you did. To tell you the truth, me bucko, there's no purgatory at all, at all for you."

"Well, I'm grateful to you for that, God knows," King Fergus said with a great west of Ireland sigh.

The Pope punched in an escape sequence and, pretty as you please, the great silver-and-gold gates began to swing open.

"Ah, just a minute now, your majesty," your man says as King Fergus slipped by him. "What's that you're holding in your hand?"

" 'Tis nothing at all."

" 'Tis too." Peter punched a Control C and the gate stopped swinging. "What have you got there?"

"Sure, 'tis nothing but a wee bit of Kerry turf, to remind me of home, if you take my meaning."

"I take your meaning, all right, but you can't have it. Against the rules. No one enters the kingdom of heaven save with empty hands."

"Well, your reverence, if that's the lay of the land"—King Fergus was not the kind of man you'd want to fool with when his back was up—"I'd just as soon not go in, if I can't bring me piece of Kerry turf with me."

"Rules is rules," your man insists.

"Then I'll just wait out here."

The Pope put in a hurry-up call, murmured discreetly into the phone, listened, said "Aye," and hung up.

A minute later the big silver-and-gold gates swung open and out strode the Lord God Himself. He's ten feet tall and has long blond hair and looks like a linebacker for the Chicago Bears. He embraced the king, slapped him on the back, and boomed out in a rich baritone voice, "Faith, its good to see you, Fergus me boy; we've been waiting up for a long time for you. Come on right in, we'll have a wee talk about how difficult it is to be king. Just toss aside that little bit of Kerry turf and come on in. There'll be the singing and dancing and the telling of tales all night long."

Your man Fergus MacDiarmud UiDonal was moved by this warm greeting, but not moved enough. Like I say, when he got his back up, he could be a difficult man.

"Saving your reverence," the king says, "I'll not be coming in unless I can bring me little handful of Kerry turf. Sure it won't do any harm at all, at all."

Well, the Lord God seemed greatly disappointed, "Faith, we can't let you do that, Fergus me friend. Rules is rules. You can't come into the kingdom of heaven save with empty hands. I don't make the rules, you know. Well, actually I do, but that's one we just can't change, if you take my meaning."

And the great silver-and-gold gates clanked shut.

"You might go around to the back and see if Herself will let you in," says your man Simon Peter. "Sure, She gets a lot of folks in that way, and Herself having a lot of Clout. But that's one rule even She won't bend."

"If it's all the same to you," he said, still real stubborn, "I'll wait here in the rain." . . .

The Lord God is devious and will stop at nothing to get us into the heavenly city. So He disguised Himself as an Irish countryman— you know, the gray suit which hasn't been cleaned or pressed for forty years, the old brown sweater, the dirty tie, the big galoshes, the cap pulled down over his head—and put a big Havana cigar in his mouth. Then He slipped out of the gates and stood next to King Fergus MacDiarmud UiDonal, watching in silence as the mists rose up over the bogs.

"Have one," says the Lord God, offering a cigar to the king. "They don't hurt you up here."

"Aye, don't mind if I do," says King Fergus.

" 'Tis a bad night."

" 'Tis."

" 'Tis warm and comfy inside."

"Is it now?"

" 'Tis." They both sighed together.

"We have some fine Jameson's and the best Guinness in the cosmos inside. They won't hurt you up here either."

"Is that true?"

" 'Tis."

They sighed again.

"You could come in and have a drop of Jameson's by the fire, if only you will get rid of that handful of dirt you've got there."

"I know who you are," Fergus explodes. "You're no countryman, you're the Lord God. And You ought to be ashamed of Yourself with all them tricks. I'll not come in without me Kerry turf."

"Ah, but we can't allow that, don't you see. Sure, no one comes into the kingdom of heaven . . ."

"Save with empty hands," the king finishes for him.

So the Lord God, dejected-like, walked back into the heavenly city. And the big silver-and-gold gates clanked shut.

The next trick the Lord God pulled was to disguise Himself as a wee blond colleen, with a few freckles on her nose, looking just like the king's great-granddaughter. . . .

And the colleen who was really the Lord God slipped up to King Fergus MacDiarmud UiDonal, and says to him, "O King Fergus, they're having a wonderful party inside for all the little kids, but I can't go unless I can find a grown-up to take me. Would you ever think of being me grown-up?"

Well, the king was moved, let me tell you. "You can't find another grown-up?"

"Not at all, at all."

"Well . . ."

"Just put down that silly old turf and we can both go to the party."

"I'll not be taken in by your tricks," the king shouted. "I know who You are. You're not a wee lass. You're the Lord God in disguise. And I won't come in without me Kerry turf and don't repeat the rules, I know them by heart . . ."

So King Fergus and the Lord God and your man Simon Peter all said together, "No one enters the kingdom of heaven save with empty hands."

And with tears in her eyes, the little blond colleen with the freckles on her nose went back into the heavenly city.

And the big silver-and-gold doors clanked shut.

Well, the night got darker and the rain colder and the Kerry turf more crumbly. And King Fergus began to think about it.

Sure, Fergus, he says to himself, a prize amadon you are. This isn't Kerry, it's the kingdom of heaven. They make their own laws here and they're not going to change them for you, even if you wait till all eternity. You've been counting on sneaking through those gates since you were a wee lad. Isn't it time you'd be after coming to your senses?

So with the loudest sigh all day, doesn't he stroll over to St. Peter's desk and toss the turf on the ground.

"Begging your reverence's pardon, but there's no sense in fighting the Lord God, is there now?"

"Not at all, at all," says your man Simon Peter happily. He punched in the escape code, making no mistake this time. The big silver-and-gold gates of heaven clanked open. "There's no one goes through those gates save with empty hands."

"Aye," says the king, feeling like he was pretty much the fool, if you take my meaning, but still mourning for his lost Kerry turf.

And so he walked through the big silver-and-gold gates. And do you know what he found inside?

Do you?

Ah, you don't.

Sure, you do.

Well, I'll tell you. Inside waiting for King Fergus MacDiarmud UiDonal was . . . what?

The green hills and the blue skies and the golden fields and the silver lakes and the whole Kingdom of Kerry.

ANDREW M. GREELEY

AFTERWORD

...

Love After Love

Love is eternal, says the Brazilian proverb, but it doesn't last. On the record God claims not to be that way. Thus he insists that his love is implacable. It does not vary from season to season nor from age to age. It never goes away, though sometimes perhaps it appears to us that it does. On our side of the bargain, we have to reconcile with God constantly. She doesn't seem to mind. Indeed She seems to enjoy taking us back.

Other loves we know are not invariant. Love can grow weary, it can become tired, it can be BORING!, it can die. It can, most terribly, be killed. Parents reading selections in this book hopefully will be inspired by so much beauty gathered between two covers. They will want their children to read passages which are especially pertinent. They will say, see, how wonderful, how beautiful, how attractive love is. Perhaps they will think to themselves on occasion, I don't want the kids to know how many disillusions can spoil the path of true love.

The clergy person who presides over many marriages can easily become cynical. The radiant young lovers who are plighting their troth until death do they part may well not stay together. The average duration of a marriage which ends in divorce is six years. What happens to the exalted love which seemingly illumined their wedding day? The cleric is especially disillusioned when marriages, which he thought as durable as the rising of the sun, fall apart.

Love is killed by brutality, by indifference, by the pressures of time and obligation, by inability to talk about problems, by drink, by disagreement over child-rearing, by impatience, by money, by insensitivity, by prudery, by emotional disturbance, by the realization that you may have made a horrible mistake, by a desire to return to the carefree single life in which one has few serious responsibilities.

Love may be a torrent as we claimed in the forward, but it is a torrent which, like the tide, ebbs and flows. Love has its seasons, its cycles, its rhythms. Lovers who are determined to love must learn to adjust to these seasons, as do the lovers in the two strawberry stories in this volume. Such adjustments are necessary in all the love relationships which we have portrayed in this volume, not merely that between husband and wife. Children, parents, friends, neighbors, must all tend to relationships they wish to change, adjusting to the rhythms of change in the others and to the rhythms in themselves. The path of true love never runs straight. It always gets sidetracked. The litany of love which St. Paul celebrated for the Corinthians is simply a recipe for the care of a healthy love affair. Is there someone out there waiting for you in the strawberry patch? Or should you slow down and wait for someone who is trying to catch up?

The name of love after love is reconciliation.

How many reconciliations? As Professor Teresa Sullivan of the University of Texas once remarked, marriages which do not end in divorce (still substantially more than half of them) a hundred years ago lasted on the average for twelve years. Now they last on the average for forty-eight years. That means, Professor Sullivan noted, a lot more than four times as many reconciliations.

And, she might have added, four times as many apologies. Reconciliation is difficult in prospect and normally delightful in the event. So too an apology is daunting until you have uttered it, and then immensely satisfying. Apologies, alas, can be rebuffed. Reconciliation can be rejected. Love can be killed.

Yet there is no other way to return to the path of true love than by saying, I'm sorry. Let's try again. Time after time. There are few stories in this book about such reconciliation because literature does not yet recognize its possibility, its necessity. Perhaps the reason is that literature has yet to adjust to the enormous increase in our span of years in this century. Yet in truth one is never too old to fall in love again with the same persons—whether that person be a spouse or a child or a parent or an old friend.

No one ever said it's easy.

Sometimes reconciliation is impossible. Violence, drunkenness, flagrant and repeated adultery deal fatal blows to the trust which is necessary to try to reconcile. No one should accept violence as part of the promise to love till death do us part. Moreover, for reasons of selfishness or immaturity or hardness of heart or neurosis, efforts at reconciliation can fail. "You can see a counselor if you want, but I don't need it."

Perhaps marriage only becomes a sacrament that reveals God's implacable love for us only after the reconciliation which terminates the first truly major crisis in a marriage. Do some unions fail to become sufficiently mature for such a sacramental reconciliation? It would certainly seem so, especially marriages in which both spouses are incapable of saying, "I'm sorry," and meaning it.

The same paradigm applies to our other love relationships. Sometimes too much has happened between parents and children for them ever to renew the love which (perhaps) once existed. Similarly with friends. One can be "too generous" to friends in time of need and earn lifelong resentment. Nor can love subsist in a relationship where one partner tries to dominate completely the life of another.

Yet the promise of love is not destroyed even if statistically it is often blighted by the weakness, the ignorance, the immaturity, the pressures of human life. It is always possible to ask for forgiveness.

Forgiveness is not one of the stoic virtues which are exalted in various books about virtue. This too is strange given the conservative (and indeed Catholic) orientation of some of these books. The key passage in the Lord's Prayer, the central message of the revelation of God's love in the life and death of Jesus is that we are to forgive as we are forgiven. We do not earn God's forgiveness by forgiving others. God's forgiveness, is a given, as implacable as Her love. Rather our forgiveness reflects God's love to those around us. Finally, the secret of love after love is forgiveness, a difficult activity until we've done it and find how much it renews love.

MGD

AMG

Grand Beach

Summer 2001

COPYRIGHT
ACKNOWLEDGMENTS